Paddling Eastern North Carolina

PADDLING
EASTERN
NORTH
CAROLINA

Paul Ferguson

Raleigh, North Carolina

Pocosin Press
4916 Grinnell Drive
Raleigh, NC 27612
www.PocosinPress.com

www.PaddlingEasternNC.com

Printed in the United States of America

09 08 07 06 05 04 03 02   5 4 3 2 1

Cover design by Les Fry

All photographs by the author

Back cover photo: Dan Benson on Great Coharie Creek

Library of Congress Cataloging-in-Publication Data

Ferguson, Paul, 1943-
  Paddling eastern North Carolina / Paul Ferguson.
      p. cm.
Includes index.
  ISBN 0-9720268-0-0 (pbk. : alk. paper)
  1. Canoes and canoeing--North Carolina--Guidebooks. 2. North
Carolina--Guidebooks. I. Title.
  GV776.N74 F47 2002
  796.1'22'09756--dc21
                              2002009683

Contents

Preface

The reason for a new guidebook to paddling eastern North Carolina is not only because of many changes made to access areas, gauges, and dams since the first one was written but also to expand the coverage, especially toward the coast.

I also wanted to see many rivers I had ignored in my paddling career. There always seemed to be a pull to go back to a familiar river. To create this book, I could no longer stay with old favorites. I found that paddling each new river section was always worthwhile. Sometimes the going was tough because of a tree-choked section, a difficult access, or low water, but it was always a memorable trip.

Some of these runs were done solo with a bicycle for a shuttle, but mostly I had the fine companionship of many friends. There were too many to name, but special thanks goes to two paddlers who did many hundreds of miles with me.

Elmer Eddy was always happy to be paddling a river. His great enthusiasm provided excellent company. He found wonder in every deer track and jumping fish. On one trip, he told me his secret, "What I have always wanted in my life was to paddle rivers, and here I am, at age 80, paddling more than I ever have."

Pete (*Swamp Man*) Peterson and I canoe-camped many rivers and explored some of the seldom-run river sections. Sometimes we took a wrong turn, spent the night unexpectedly in a swamp, or found the take-out with assistance from a flashlight. He was always undaunted and would say, "It was an adventure—where do we go next?"

Many provided comments on working drafts. Les Fry was especially helpful with key input in the early stages, and he used his graphic skills to supply the front cover design.

Melinda Van Gieson contributed valuable suggestions and used her sharp eyes and editing skills on the final draft.

I thank the many paddlers who helped by answering questions about their home rivers, and thanks to Bob Benner and Tom McCloud for inspiring me with their 1987 guidebook to paddling eastern North Carolina.

■

You can't step twice into the same river.
—Heraclitus of Ephesus (540–480 B.C.)

Introduction

This guidebook is written for both the beginning and experienced paddler. Its purpose is to help select and prepare for trips on many of the rivers of eastern North Carolina.

Learning how to paddle is beyond the scope of this book. There are companies and paddling clubs offering paddling courses. Books on paddling techniques are noted in the appendices. It is possible to learn without formal instruction, but avoid getting in over your head. Practice on a lake to learn flatwater paddling strokes. In the beginning stages, choose river sections that are rated within your skill level, moderate distances, low to medium water levels, and favorable weather.

The beginning paddler should read all of the introductory chapters (pages 1–37). The appendices contain information on paddling clubs and conservation organizations to assist in finding others interested in rivers.

The experienced paddler should read the chapter on River Descriptions (page 31) to learn how rivers are described in this guidebook.

When trying to decide where to take a paddling trip, the over 2,600 miles of rivers included give many choices. River Selection (page 27) is a set of tables to help narrow your search to a particular river. For each river, the tables give river difficulty, suitability for camping, and general water conditions. After finding a river of interest, turn to the pages describing the river to choose one or more sections for a trip.

The goal was to make this guidebook as accurate as possible, but some errors are inevitable. There will also be changes wrought by storms, floods, development, or maintenance. The scope of this book does not allow for disclosure of all the potential hazards and risks. For a safer and more enjoyable experience, learn as much as possible about paddling, prepare for the unexpected, and be cautious.

Comments and corrections are appreciated for use in possible future editions. Send them to: mail@PaddlingEasternNC.com or Pocosin Press, 4916 Grinnell Drive, Raleigh, NC 27612.

As time permits, corrections and changes to this guidebook will be posted at: http://PaddlingEasternNC.com/

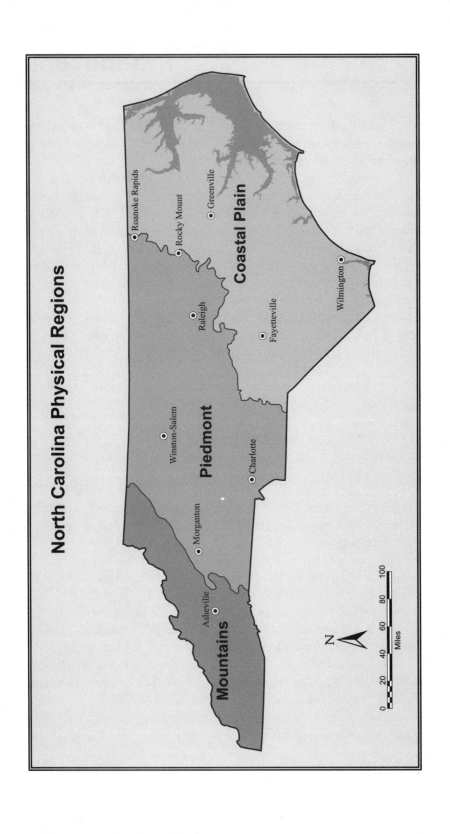

North Carolina Physical Regions

North Carolina

North Carolina is rich in its resources of beautiful land and water. From west to east, rugged mountains, foothills, coast, and barrier islands reveal the great variety. The water changes as dramatically. Steep, clear-water rivers come off the Blue Ridge Mountains. Brown-water rivers of the foothills head for the coast. Blackwater rivers meander through bottomland forests and swampland. Estuaries and sounds lead to barrier islands, where the Atlantic Ocean constantly changes the eastern shores.

North Carolina can be divided into three primary physical regions: Mountains, Piedmont, and Coastal Plain. The rivers of each region have their own characteristics.

A few billion years ago, this land we call North Carolina was under a sea. Shifting plates caused landmasses to rise in western North America. Rivers eroded the land, carrying sediment and building the eastern part of the continent. As plates continued to clash, they raised a great mountain range running through western North Carolina. Erosion took down this range and raised land to the east.

The plates of present-day North American and Euro-African continents pulled apart to form an ocean. Later they came together to clash and raise the great Appalachian Mountain range. Peaks thought to be as high as 30,000 feet stood in part of what is now eastern North Carolina. As the mountains were being eroded, the continental plates separated, and sediments were deposited to form the base of our Coastal Plain.

Streams eroded the Appalachian range, leaving our present-day Blue Ridge Mountains and rolling hills of the Piedmont. At the eastern part of the Piedmont, streams falling into the lower Coastal Plain created a band of rapids and steep-sided valleys. This area at the Piedmont and Coastal Plain boundary is known as the Fall Line. Many of our cities were built near the Fall Line to harness the waterpower, and because the rapids formed the upstream limit of navigation.

Sea level changed many times because of global climate changes. As the sea rose to different levels and retreated from the Coastal Plain, escarpments and terraces were left behind.

The rising sea also surrounded ridges of land, creating islands. Currents swept sand along the direction of the current, extending the islands, and dunes formed to raise the profile. These barrier islands run along most of the present coastline.

Paddling the waters of North Carolina offers an excellent opportunity to view the results of geologic evolution. The story is written in the rapids running over rocks, clay layers, and fossils exposed on banks, sand ridges, and peat layers of swamps. For more details of the geologic history, refer to *North Carolina: The Years Before Man* by Fred Beyer.

The Mountains region has very steep land with underlying hard rock mainly of granite and metamorphic (quartz) rocks. The streams have a high gradient with waterfalls and frequent rapids. Flow characteristics are highly variable. Rain typically runs off rapidly, and many of these rivers can only be paddled after rain. The western part of the Piedmont region borders the Mountains region, and these Piedmont streams have much in common with streams of the Mountains.

The Piedmont has rolling hills with broad ridges, sharply indented stream valleys, and low gradient streams composed of a series of sluggish pools separated by riffles and occasional small rapids. The floodplains are relatively narrow and mostly forested. There are no natural lakes in the region. Highly erodible clay soils are typical. Underneath the soils are fractured rock formations with limited water storage capacity, limiting the supply of groundwater. Streams in the Piedmont tend to have low summer flows and are often too low to paddle in dry times.

The Coastal Plain is relatively flat with blackwater streams and low-lying swamplands and estuaries. Streams are much more meandering than streams of other regions. They are slow moving, with low banks, and are often lined by extensive swamps, bottomland hardwood forests or marshes. Swamps and marshes are more typical in the lower eastern half of this region, sometimes called the outer Coastal Plain. Streams flowing through swampland areas are naturally discolored by tannic acid from decomposing plant material and become tea-colored, giving them the name blackwater. The soil has deep sand deposits and contains much groundwater. Many of the streams of the Coastal Plain can be paddled during very dry times.

River Basins

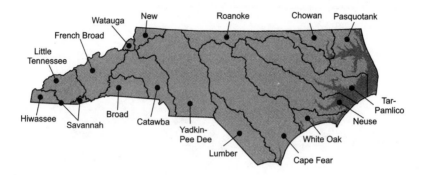

What is a River Basin? A map of river basins available from the Office of Environmental Education in the North Carolina Department of Environment and Natural Resources states it this way:

A river basin encompasses all land surface drained by many finger-like streams and creeks flowing downhill into one another and eventually into one river, which forms its artery and backbone. As a bathtub catches all the water that falls within its sides and directs the water out its drain, a river basin sends all the water falling within its surrounding ridges into its system of creeks and streams to gurgle and splash downhill into its river and out to the ocean.

The shape of the river basin comes from the collective and opposing forces of mountain building and weathering. Geological forces pushed mountains up into the sky, and weathering from rain and wind wears mountainsides into hillsides and valleys and plains. A jigsaw puzzle of river basins reflects in three dimensions the outcome of these combined forces molding the landscape.

As an artery connects the parts of a body to one another, so a river threads together the creeks and streams, and valleys and hills, springs and lakes that share a common assembly of water. What happens to the surface or underground water in one part of the river basin will find its way to other parts. If water is diverted out of its usual course in one part of the river basin, other parts will know its absence. A river basin comes closer than any other defined area of land, with the exception of an isolated island, to meeting the definition of an ecosystem in which all things are connected and interdependent.

North Carolina contains seventeen river basins. Only the Cape Fear, Neuse, Tar-Pamlico and White Oak Basins are contained solely within North Carolina. The other basins collect water from bordering states or flow into them.

This guidebook contains selected rivers from the Yadkin-Pee Dee Basin and all basins to the east:

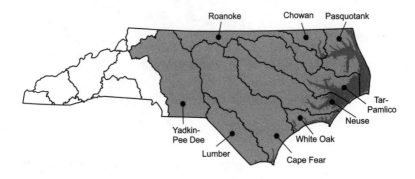

A typical river basin is composed of tributary streams joining a main stem as the main stem flows to the sea. The Neuse River Basin fits this typical view, but for some other basins the view has to be altered slightly.

Some North Carolina basins appear to contain rivers that are not connected. In the Lumber Basin, the Lumber and Waccamaw Rivers are part of the basin, but they do not join within North Carolina. If the view is expanded to include South Carolina, one sees that the Lumber and Waccamaw Rivers join the Pee Dee and Great Pee Dee Rivers in South Carolina. If state boundaries are not considered when defining river basins, the Lumber Basin is part of the Pee Dee Basin.

There are also basins containing rivers that do not join before reaching a sound or ocean. An example in the Lumber Basin is Lockwoods Folly River, which empties into the Atlantic Ocean. The river is relatively small, and rather than define a separate basin for it, the Lumber Basin boundary was drawn to include some of the coastal waters. Similar cases exist in other basins. The White Oak Basin includes coastal waters that receive flow from the New, Newport, North, and White Oak Rivers.

In defining river basins, considering state boundaries and coastal regions leaves room for differing definitions. There are some differences in basin boundaries defined by North Carolina and basin boundaries as defined by the United States Geological Survey (USGS). The USGS considers the New River near Jacksonville to be part of the New River Basin, but the state considers it to be part of the White Oak Basin. Another example is that the state places the Lumber River as part of the Lumber Basin, but the USGS assigns it to the Yadkin-Pee Dee Basin. In this guidebook, the state basin boundaries are used. Keep in mind that there are basin differences when viewing USGS information.

Raven Rock State Park
Cape Fear River, Section 2

Paddling Safety

As with any outdoor activity, there is a risk of discomfort, injury, or death posed by hazards encountered while paddling. The risk can be reduced to a minimum by understanding the hazards and taking precautions.

There are many books devoted to paddling safety and river rescue. The information provided here is only an introduction. See Appendix C for paddling safety and river rescue books. For additional whitewater rules, including hand and paddle signals, see the American Whitewater safety code at: http://americanwhitewater.org/

Taking courses on first aid, wilderness medicine, paddling safety, and river rescue is an excellent way to learn how to treat injuries and prevent or mitigate accidents on the river. These courses may be offered through organizations such as larger outfitters and paddling clubs.

Skill and Knowledge

Choosing to paddle a river within one's ability is the first line of defense in paddling safely. News of deaths or river rescues following high water or floods is too common. The problem begins when people without the necessary skills for the conditions decide to paddle. They see smooth water flowing under a bridge. Anticipating a fun time and a fast trip, they put in to find the current overpowering as turbulence kicks up waves around the bend. After capsizing the paddlers end up on an island, where a helicopter makes a rescue.

Without the knowledge of existing hazards, experience to evaluate river conditions, and knowledge of one's paddling ability, the "accident" is almost assured. The only question is how serious will it be?

To reduce the risk, be conservative when new to paddling. Learn to paddle on flatwater before paddling whitewater. Choose short trips. Join a club and paddle with others. Read about hazards and paddling techniques. Evaluate what has been learned and what needs work. Consider instruction, safety, rescue, and first-aid courses. Skill and knowledge will build slowly but surely, allowing enjoyment of paddling without subjecting you or others to unnecessary risk.

High Water

Rivers change dramatically when water rises far above normal levels. Eddies disappear and calm water near the bank picks up speed. As water continues rising, obstructions that were above water, such as downed trees and large rocks, become submerged, and powerful waves and currents are formed. Water rises above the first level of banks. Large debris that was beached is swept downstream. The river flows over islands and through trees.

The increased water speed means paddling decisions must be made quickly. The current makes some maneuvers harder to execute. If a paddler turns over and is separated from the boat, recovery is difficult. There is little time to avoid hazards downstream.

Paddling rivers at high water is only for paddlers who have attained a high degree of skill and knowledge. Paddling safely requires knowing the river at normal levels. Moving to higher water levels should be done incrementally and with experienced groups as paddling skill develops.

Wind

Wind on small streams usually only hinders or helps progress, depending on its direction. Strong wind on wide rivers, lakes, and sounds can whip up whitecaps and become dangerous. Open canoes are especially vulnerable to swamping because of waves breaking over them. Closed-boats, such as kayaks, are more suitable to paddling in large waves. The skills needed to paddle in whitecaps are similar to those needed to paddle in difficult whitewater. Aggressive paddling, bracing, and rolling can allow it to be done safely.

Consider wind before paddling on any large body of water. Check weather reports before going. Be prepared for unexpected wind, and if it becomes too strong, go to the bank and wait for it to subside.

Dams and Hydraulics

Many old milldams have been broken in places and now provide rapids through the breaks. Scout these routes carefully because they can contain metal debris. Metal may not be visible because it is underwater, but it can be an extreme hazard to a boat or swimmer.

Intact dams should be portaged. The flow over a dam usually drops onto rocks or into a powerful recirculating current. Some dams have water flowing over them, but others have water running into a sluice or through a gate, keeping water from flowing over the dam. Where water flows over the dam, there is usually a horizon line across the river. Extra caution should be used at high water because faster current gives little time for a paddler to recognize the danger and get to the bank.

A *low-head* dam is a dam having a small vertical drop, usually only one to a few feet, with water flowing over it. Low-head dams are especially dangerous because their small drop seems easy to paddle over, but there is a powerful recirculating current (often called a *hydraulic*) at their base that will trap anything that floats. Paddlers have drowned when running low-head dams after becoming trapped in the recirculating current. A paddler might run a low-head dam with sufficient speed and balance to make it look easy, but a small mistake can be deadly.

Abrupt drops can also result from natural ledges in a river. They should be scouted and portaged if there are hydraulics.

Strainers

A strainer is an obstacle that lets water pass through, but blocks (strains out) objects. The most common strainer is formed by a downed tree in a river. The current will carry a swimmer beneath the tree and into underwater limbs. The force of the current prevents the swimmer from returning upstream, and the limbs prevent going downstream. With the swimmer's head underwater, drowning is swift.

If a person is in the dangerous position of swimming in water approaching a downed tree, getting carried under the tree should be prevented by swimming aggressively toward the bank. If the bank cannot be reached, the last resort is to swim headfirst toward the strainer and pull or throw oneself over the tree as soon as it is within reach. The top of a tree trunk and any above water limbs can be used for leverage. It is extremely important to do this quickly because there will be only seconds between being able to grab the strainer and being swept under it.

A paddler can become a swimmer before reaching a strainer, but becoming a swimmer at a strainer is likely. If a boat hits a downed tree, the boat will usually swing broadside to the current, be forced against the tree, and taken under. The split second after hitting the tree is the last opportunity to get on top of or over the strainer.

Strainers must be recognized as far in advance as possible and portaged. Blind turns in current must be approached with caution and scouted when necessary.

Foot Entrapment

Paddlers who become swimmers have drowned when their foot has entered a rock crevice on the riverbed in fast water. The current pushes them downstream, making it impossible to free the foot. The crevice is often formed by a rock slanting upstream, but debris can also create a place where a foot can become lodged.

Foot entrapment can happen anytime that one attempts to walk in fast current. To avoid foot entrapment when being swept down the river, the swimmer should keep feet near the surface and swim to shallow water. If the current is too great to swim against, the swimmer should float face up with feet kept up and used to fend off rocks above water.

Broaching

When kayaks or canoes fill with water, they ride low in the water and are susceptible to turning broadside to the current. As the current pushes the boat downstream, it will be stopped by any unmovable obstacle, such as a boulder, tree, or bridge pier. The force on the boat in only a mild current can total several thousand pounds. Anything trapped between the boat and the obstacle will be crushed.

When a boat is swamped with water and the paddler becomes a swimmer, it is important to quickly get upstream of the boat so there is no chance of becoming trapped between the boat and an obstacle.

Whitewater paddlers usually have airbags strapped into their boats to provide extra flotation. The airbags prevent the space they occupy from filling with water, and the boat rides higher in the water when swamped, lessening the chance it will broach and wrap around an obstacle.

Hypothermia

Our bodies lose heat rapidly when immersed in water. Water conducts body heat away up to twenty-six times faster than air of the same temperature. A person in 50° F water can survive only up to several hours. Hypothermia results when the body temperature drops. Symptoms include uncontrollable shivering, slurred speech, memory lapses, stumbling, and exhaustion. When out of water, wet clothes and wind continue to rob heat. Preventing further heat loss and rewarming is necessary for recovery. Extreme hypothermia results in death.

The risk from cold water is obvious during winter, but during spring the air temperature can be fairly warm while the water is still cold.

Paddlers can prevent hypothermia by dressing for the possibility of getting wet. Wetsuits or drysuits can be worn to prevent rapid heat loss. Clothing layers, such as synthetic fleece, that do not retain much water should be used. Having additional layers to add or subtract will help to adjust to changing conditions. Wearing clothes that hold much water, such as cotton, will hasten heat loss through evaporation. Taking a change of clothes is better than not having one, but much heat will be lost before changing.

Heat

In hot weather our bodies regulate temperature by sweating. If we do not drink enough to replace the water lost, we can become dehydrated, resulting in muscle cramping. Heat exhaustion is more serious. Symptoms can be nonspecific but may include fatigue, nausea and vomiting, headache, dizziness, muscle cramps, and irritability.

Heat stroke is the most serious form of heat illness. The body temperature soars to 106° F or higher. The person may be delirious, unconscious, or having seizures. Their temperature must be reduced quickly.

Paddlers should prevent heat-related illnesses by drinking plenty of water to stay well-hydrated.

Slippery Banks and Rocks

Paddlers can be injured by slips and falls when out of their boats. The put-ins, take-outs, rest stops, portages, and scouting paths are often in rough terrain. Large rocks in or near the river can have a thin coating of soil or algae. The coating may appear to be part of the rock, but it can be extremely slippery when wet. Use extra care when walking on river rocks.

Poisonous Plants and Animals

Poison ivy, oak, and sumac cause allergic reactions in most people. Poison ivy is common on the riverbanks and trees in eastern North Carolina. Learn to recognize the plants and avoid contact with them. Flush skin with water as soon as possible after contact.

Hornets and wasps sometimes build their nests in tree limbs over water. An unwary paddler can disturb a nest by brushing against a limb containing a nest. Low limbs should be inspected before going under them.

Most snakes encountered by paddlers are non-poisonous, and snakebites are rare. The water moccasin (cottonmouth) is the only venomous water snake in North Carolina, but other poisonous snakes are found near rivers. Snakes typically avoid human contact. They are sometimes found in tree branches hanging over water. If a snake senses the movement of a boat going under a limb, the snake may drop to the water but end up in the boat. Low limbs should be inspected before going under them.

Lightning

If thunderstorms develop while paddling in open water, get off the water as quickly as possible. Lightning seeks the easiest path to ground, which means the highest object in the vicinity. A boat in open water becomes the highest object.

The shelter of the tallest trees should be avoided because tall trees are also lightning targets. Objects projecting above the surrounding landscape should be avoided. In a forest, the safer shelters are in low spots under a thick growth of small trees. In open areas, low places are safer.

If you feel a tingling sensation or your hair stands on end, lightning may be about to strike. Immediately crouch down and cover your ears. Do not lie down or place your hands on the ground.

Getting Lost

It may seem difficult to get lost on a river, but with a group it can be easy to lose track of a paddler. If someone is missing, the group may not know if the missing paddler is ahead or behind. Assistance may be required quickly, so it is important to know the direction to search.

A common safety practice in a paddling group is to appoint a lead boat and a sweep boat. Other boats should not pass the lead boat, and each boat except the sweep boat should keep sight of a boat behind. If sight of the boat behind is lost, wait or search for the missing boat.

Getting lost in swamps is quite easy. There is often no current to follow, and downed trees may prevent paddling a straight path. If trying to return on the same route as used going in, the view can be different. A compass and topo maps can be useful, and a Global Positioning System (GPS) device can make retracing a route simple.

Paddling upstream on a river can be confusing where tributaries enter. The direction of current is of no help. A careful study of maps can assist in making the correct choices.

Equipment

At least a minimum amount of safety equipment should be in every boat. A well-fitting personal flotation device (PFD) should be worn when on the water. Helmets are standard for kayakers and are recommended for canoeists in rapids above Class II (see River Rating Systems, page 13). A throw-rope can help rescue a paddler or boat as well as assist in lowering and raising boats on steep banks. In a group of paddlers, at least one first-aid kit should be taken on the trip. Carrying a first-aid kit in each boat is a good idea.

Canoe broached on the Haw River, Section 8

River Rating Systems

Smooth Water

The smooth water (often called flatwater) rating system depends on the speed of the flowing water.

Class A   Standing and slow-flowing water. The current does not exceed 2 miles per hour.

Class B   Flowing water moving between 2 and 4 miles per hour. A boater can typically back paddle and hold a position in this flow.

Class C   Flowing water moving greater than 4 miles per hour. A boater cannot remain in position by back paddling. Simple obstacles, such as sandbars, bridge abutments, and shore construction, can create eddies, requiring a greater degree of boat control.

Whitewater

The whitewater rating system is a summary of the American version of the international scale of river difficulty. For the complete version, see: http://americanwhitewater.org/

Class I   Fast moving water with riffles and small waves. Few obstructions, all obvious and easily missed with little training. Risk to swimmers is slight; self-rescue is easy.

Class II   Straightforward rapids with wide, clear channels which are evident without scouting. Occasional maneuvering may be required, but rocks and medium-sized waves are easily missed by trained paddlers. Swimmers are seldom injured and group assistance, while helpful, is seldom needed.

Class III   Rapids with moderate, irregular waves which may be difficult to avoid and which can swamp an open canoe. Complex maneuvers in fast current and good boat control in tight passages or around ledges are often required; large waves or strainers may be present but are easily avoided. Strong eddies and powerful current effects can be found, particularly on large-volume rivers. Scouting is advisable for inexperienced parties. Injuries while swimming are rare; self-rescue is usually easy but group assistance may be required to avoid long swims.

Class IV   Intense, powerful but predictable rapids requiring precise boat handling in turbulent water. Depending on the character of the river, it may feature large, unavoidable waves and holes or constricted passages demanding fast maneuvers under pressure. A fast, reliable eddy turn may be needed to initiate maneuvers, scout rapids, or rest. Rapids may require "must" moves above dangerous hazards. Scouting may be necessary. Risk of injury to swimmers is moderate to high, and water conditions may make self-rescue difficult. Group assistance for rescue is often essential but requires practiced skills. A strong Eskimo roll is highly recommended.

Class V   Extremely long, obstructed, or very violent rapids which expose a paddler to added risk. Drops may contain large, unavoidable waves and holes or steep, congested chutes with complex, demanding routes. Rapids may continue for long distances between pools, demanding a high level of fitness. What eddies exist may be small, turbulent, or difficult to reach. At the high end of the scale, several of these factors may be combined. Scouting is recommended but may be difficult. Swims are dangerous, and rescue is often difficult even for experts. A very reliable Eskimo roll, proper equipment, extensive experience, and practiced rescue skills are essential.

Class VI   These runs have almost never been attempted and often exemplify the extremes of difficulty, unpredictability and danger. The consequences of errors are very severe and rescue may be impossible.

■

Eventually, all things merge into one, and a river runs through it. The river was cut by the world's great flood and runs over rocks from the basement of time. On some of the rocks are timeless raindrops. Under the rocks are the words, and some of the words are theirs. I am haunted by waters.
—Norman Maclean, *A River Runs Through It* (1976)

Paddlers' Rights

Rights to Paddle Streams

For the large rivers that have traditionally supported trade and commerce, it is clear in federal law they are navigable. For smaller streams, state laws usually govern public rights.

The surface and ground waters in North Carolina are legally waters of the state and are held in public trust by the state.

Rulings of the North Carolina Supreme Court have stated that citizens have the right to travel by small craft used for pleasure, including canoes and kayaks, on waters that are, in their natural condition, capable of such use. The owner of land adjoining a watercourse has no right to control or interfere with public travel by boat on streams that are navigable in fact.

This does not permit the right to trespass on the shore. Paddlers have no right to land upon and use the bank at a place other than a public landing without the consent of the owner. The banks of most navigable streams are private property.

In an early case, the court said that it was not prepared to say how far up a stream public rights may extend. At some point, navigability ceases and public trust rights give way to those of private property. A landowner may be able to put a water gate across a creek even though someone could pole a canoe up the creek.

The state may also properly exercise its police power to regulate the use of navigable waters to protect the public health, safety, or welfare.

Access to Streams

There is no public right to cross private property to reach streams, lakes, tidal areas or other waters that the public has a right to use. Some landowners permit paddlers to cross their land. The chances of gaining access are improved when permission is requested politely before crossing private land. Paddlers should be polite and understanding even if permission is refused. People who leave trash and cross private property without asking permission cause landowners to deny access to all. If paddlers cultivate good relationships with landowners, they can often gain access.

Many convenient access points are where public roads cross streams. Paddlers park on road shoulders and get to the water using land at the side of bridges. Typically the state owns a narrow strip of land on either side of bridges, and paddlers have traditionally used the land for access. In some cases, the state does not own land on a bridge side, but has only a right-of-way lease. Whether the public can use a leased right-of-way has not been tested in the courts.

What should you do when a landowner says you are on private property, but you believe it is public property? Confronting the land-owner is the wrong approach. It is likely the landowner has had unpleasant encounters with people considered trespassers. Your best option is to avoid arguing, be as polite as possible, and be on your way. Work to solve the problem later by working with the assistance of government agencies, paddling clubs, and national paddling organizations. It may take persistent effort to clarify access rights, but it is work that benefits all paddlers.

Respect private property
Sign on the Neuse River bank

Paddling Courtesy

Most land near the river is private property, and permission to cross it should be requested. It is rare to be turned down when asking politely. It is almost certain to cause problems when treating private land as public land.

River access points are the places where paddlers are most often seen by the public and impressions are formed. Paddlers should avoid public nudity when changing into or out of river gear, raucous behavior, or display of alcoholic drinks. Vehicles should be parked so that access to any road, driveway, or mailbox is not obstructed. Driving courteously is important, especially in small communities.

Paddlers share rivers with fishermen, hikers, picnickers, and sometimes power boaters who may have come to enjoy their solitude and not a loud or extended conversation. A simple wave will test their mood. Fishing lines are often difficult to see. The fishing area and fishing lines should be given a wide berth.

Hikers have long recommended a policy of "pack it in, pack it out" and "leave only footprints." Paddlers can do even better on their trails except for hulls scraping rocks and leaving marks, but their impact is felt mostly at put-ins, take-outs, and lunch stops. Bank erosion can be minimized by not dragging boats or equipment over well-used areas.

Litter detracts from the beauty of the river. Paddling groups sometimes schedule river cleanups. Participate in these whenever possible, but the rivers and banks can be improved by carrying and filling a trash bag on each river trip. Little by little, we can make a significant contribution.

Overnight campsites require special consideration. The remains of fires on the ground are unsightly and scar the area. Whenever possible, a fire-pan should be used to keep the fire off the ground. Smoldering coals can start a fire and should not be left. Ashes should be put in water or buried.

Human waste and toilet paper should be buried at least 4 inches deep. In areas where the campsite gets high usage or there is little ground suitable for burial, waste should be packed out.

Before leaving, campsites should be inspected carefully for the small bits of trash that can go unnoticed in the first cleanup so that no traces of usage remain.

River Camping

Many enjoy extending their paddling trips by camping overnight on rivers. The feeling of self-sufficiency, cooking outdoors, sleeping under the stars, and listening to the night sounds of insects, owls, and beavers are experiences to be savored. River camping also offers more time on the river and less time driving because there is no shuttle to run each day.

Selecting a river for a camping trip is a bit different from selecting one for a day trip. The boat will weigh more because of the additional food and camping gear carried. The water level may be adequate for a day trip, but not adequate for a camping trip. A boat loaded with equipment is also less maneuverable than an almost-empty boat. It can mean that a trip one would normally consider through rapids or fast water on a day trip would be too difficult in a loaded boat.

The first requirement for an adequate campsite is dry ground that will not be flooded by the river rising during the night from rain or a dam water release. Next comes ground with enough flat, cleared area for tents or tarps. Beyond this, it is a matter of personal preferences in pursuit of the perfect campsite. With a campsite well above any expected rising water, boats should be moved to higher ground and tied to a tree if possible. Having a boat drift away at night can ruin a trip.

Finding a campsite where there is explicit permission to camp is often difficult. There are some public paddle-in campsites on riverbanks, and they are noted in the descriptions of rivers covered by this guidebook. Some of these sites are managed by parks or conservation groups. They have a designated area for camping, and may have picnic tables and a fire-ring for campfires.

There are some public lands where camping is allowed even though there are no designated campsites. Camping is allowed anywhere on national forest land except in designated wildlife fields, in trail parking lots, or where signs specifically prohibit camping. When camping along riverbanks within a national forest, check a detailed map available from the national forest offices to identify forest-owned land on riverbanks. Non-forest maps often show only the outside forest borders (*proclamation boundaries*), but there are usually many privately-owned tracts of land within these borders. National forest land on riverbanks can often be identified by small signs posted on trees.

Public and private lands in North Carolina managed by the Wildlife Resources Commission for public hunting, trapping, and fishing are designated collectively as *Game Lands*. Use of Game Lands for purposes other than hunting, trapping, and fishing is subject to the control of the landowners. It is unlawful to camp on Game Lands except in an area designated by the landowner for camping.

Sometimes paddlers must search for a campsite where there is no landowner nearby to ask permission. What happens in practice is paddlers select a site that is not posted and is well away from signs of civilization, accepting the chance that they could be asked to leave. North Carolina Statutes require properly posted land to have signs conspicuously posted and no more than 200 yards apart. Camping on islands and high sandbars reduces the chances of problems from landowners.

The land should be left as it was before camping. Plants or trees should not be cut. A campfire should be avoided because it can attract attention and cause concern of it spreading. If a campfire is to be built, it should be small and contained in a fire-pan so it does not scar the ground.

The search for a campsite can be filled with questions. A site is found, but is it too early to stop? Is there a better site downstream? If the terrain changes, making fewer dry sites, will darkness come before finding camp? In a group, it is rare that everyone agrees a particular site is the best choice. Some experienced river campers help the decision process by setting a time when the group will start looking for a campsite and a time by which they must make camp. They might pick 4 P.M. to start looking and 5 P.M. as the latest time to camp. Having a set window of time helps limit the questions that can keep a group paddling until dark.

Unless arrangements are made to be met at the end of a camping trip, vehicles are usually left parked at the put-in and take-out. Vandalism and theft are always a risk, but the risk can be reduced by not leaving valuables inside.

A vehicle left overnight at a bridge or access area can attract the attention of the local sheriff or police, causing them to investigate a possible problem or consider having the car towed. This can be prevented by notifying the local authorities in advance of the license numbers and locations of vehicles to be left.

River Gauges

The amount of water flowing in a river greatly influences paddling conditions. More water added to a river channel increases both the depth of the water and its velocity. As more and more water is added, the primary channel overflows its banks, and the river reaches flood stage.

Paddlers consider the amount of water in a stream by *height* or *flow*. Height is a measure of the water surface above some reference point. Flow is a measure of the volume of water moving downstream each second.

Paddling Gauges

The height of a water surface can be measured simply by observing markings on something fixed to the river bottom, such as a bridge pier. Height is typically expressed in feet. Paddlers usually refer to the height of the water as a *level*, and the markings are called a *gauge*. Paddlers have painted these gauges, mainly on bridge piers, where they want to be able to read the water level.

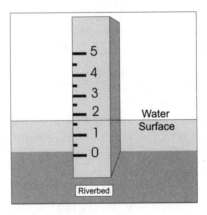

Paddling Gauge

For a gauge to be useful to paddlers, information is needed relating the gauge readings to paddling conditions. Randy Carter was a pioneer whitewater paddler in the 1960s. He painted gauges so that the zero-foot mark was at the point he estimated was the minimum water level for solo canoeing. Not everyone painted gauges using this convention. Some gauges use 6 inches below the zero-foot mark as a minimum, and others have arbitrary starting points. To know the meaning of a gauge reading, one needs experience paddling the river, or information from other paddlers or guidebooks.

Paddlers sometimes say the level is "zero" when they mean the gauge is at the minimum level they would consider paddling the stream. This leads to confusion when someone takes this to mean water is at the zero-foot mark on the gauge. It is better to say "minimum" or the actual gauge reading than use "zero" as a generic term for minimum.

USGS Gauges

The United States Geological Survey (USGS) has a widespread stream gauging system. USGS uses the alternative-spelling *gage*. Their gauges often have a metal ruler, called a *staff gage*, fixed to a concrete base in the riverbed, and equipment housed on the bank to record the water height and transmit it back to the USGS. Water height is expressed in feet and hundredths of a foot (such as 5.34 feet). The gauge has its zero reading below the riverbed, preventing negative height readings.

Some gauging stations do not have staff gages that can be viewed, but the USGS places readings from most of their gauges on the Internet, providing paddlers with accurate gauge readings for rivers without having to drive to the river. Previous gauge readings are also available and can be used to forecast changes.

The height of the river at a USGS gauging station is similar to a paddling gauge reading—it is useful if you have other information relating it to paddling conditions.

Water flow measures the volume of water in cubic feet per second (cfs) moving past a cross-section of the river. Flow is usually not measured directly by most gauging stations. Tables are used to correlate height to flow readings. The tables are developed by measuring speed of the water at many points across a stream and at different depths. The result is an estimate of flow for a given height. The process is repeated for various heights to produce a height versus flow table. For most USGS gauge readings on the Internet, both height and flow are reported (such as 5.34 feet, 2050 cfs).

Changes in a stream channel near a gauge can affect the height versus flow table, especially at low flows. The changes are often caused by debris in the channel, bank erosion, or movement on the streambed. The USGS evaluates gauges and modifies the height versus flow tables when required.

For paddlers, there are advantages to using flow readings rather than height readings. If a river is paddled at a gauge reading of 1.5 feet (225 cfs) and paddled months or years later at 1.5 feet (160 cfs), it will not be in the same water conditions as the first trip. The height versus flow correlation has changed.

Flow can also be used for comparisons of different rivers. If two river gauges each have a height of 5.0 feet, it is unlikely their flows are equal because the gauges start at different points relative to the riverbed, and the river channels have different sizes and shapes. A flow reading of 2,000 cfs at two different gauges means exactly the same amount of water is flowing in each river at the gauge locations. Knowing the relative size of the river channel, previous experience can be used to estimate what the flow might mean for paddling water conditions.

USGS Internet Data

The USGS offers water data on the Internet at: http://water.usgs.gov/ The format may change, but the current procedure on this page is to select *Real-Time* under the *Water Data* heading, then select the state containing the gauges of interest.

Gauges are identified by a *Station Number* and *Station Name*. Data for each gauge are *Date/time* of the last reading, *Gage height* (in feet), *Stream-flow* (in cfs), and *Long-term median flow* for this day of the year in all previous years of record.

Clicking on a *Station Number* shows recent previous readings from the gauge. Graphs show changes over time and are useful for forecasting.

Appendix B has a list of the USGS gauges referred to in this guidebook. The location of each gauge is given along with the total area drained in the watershed upstream of the gauge.

Tides

The affect of tides can be seen at some of the USGS gauges near the coast. The tidal influence is generally small in Albemarle and Pamlico Sounds but much greater in rivers having a direct outlet to the ocean, such as the Cape Fear River. At high stream-flow, tidal influence diminishes. Tide tables are available from many sources on the Internet such as:

http://co-ops.nos.noaa.gov/tp4days.html
http://tideworld.com/us/nc/

Frank Held portaging the dam near US 1
Deep River, Section 11

Water Quality

Increased development in our river basins has caused water quality problems in many streams. Pollutants from human activities go into streams and directly affect water quality. Pollutants come from point sources and nonpoint sources.

Point sources are discharges from pipes out of municipal wastewater treatment plants, industrial facilities, and large urban and industrial stormwater systems. Pollutants from point sources are regulated by permits issued by the state.

Nonpoint sources are sediment, nutrients, fecal coliform, heavy metals, oil and grease, and any substance that can be washed off the ground or deposited from the atmosphere into surface waters.

Classification

North Carolina has a water quality classification and standards program consistent with the Federal Clean Water Act. Surface waters are assigned a primary classification based on the *best use* of the water. An example is *Water Supply 1*, where the number indicates the level of protection required. For each classification, there is a set of standards establishing the level of water quality that must be maintained.

Some waters also receive a supplemental classification to provide special protection for sensitive or highly-valued resource waters. *High Quality Waters* is for surface water having excellent water quality. *Outstanding Resource Waters* is for surface waters having excellent water quality and an associated outstanding resource designation as one of the following: outstanding fisheries; high level of water-based recreation; National Wild and Scenic River; National Wildlife Refuge; within a state park, national park, or national forest; special ecological or scientific significance.

The requirements for Outstanding Resource Waters are more stringent than those for High Quality Waters, and special protection measures apply. Few streams have sections designated as Outstanding Resource Waters. Those included in this guidebook are Alligator River, Black River, Elk Creek, Milltail Creek, Mitchell River, Six Runs Creek, and South River. Additional information on classification can be found at: http://h2o.enr.state.nc.us/csu/

Monitoring

The Department of Water Quality collects a variety of biological, chemical, and physical data over time to monitor water quality. Examples are pH, fish tissue sampling, conductivity, fecal coliform counts, and dissolved oxygen. Another important tool is monitoring of aquatic insect larvae living in and on the bottom of rivers. They are sensitive to subtle changes in water quality, and their variety and increase or decrease is an important indicator.

Impaired Waters

If the results of water quality monitoring show a stream does not meet the standards for its classification, it is considered to be *impaired waters*. A goal of the Department of Water Quality is to restore impaired waters. Often the task is complicated because nonpoint sources of pollution are involved. Identifying these sources and developing a plan for correction takes much effort. The Federal Clean Water Act requires states to develop a management strategy for all impaired waters. North Carolina has about 2,400 miles of impaired waters. For more information and a complete list, see: http://h2o.enr.state.nc.us/tmdl/General_303d.htm

Basinwide Water Quality Plans

An excellent source of information is in Basinwide Water Quality Plans. A plan is prepared every five years for each of North Carolina's seventeen major river basins. Basinwide management allows the state to examine each river basin in detail and to determine the interaction between upstream and downstream point and nonpoint pollution sources. Basinwide Water Quality Plans are available at: http://h2o.enr.state.nc.us/basinwide

Paddlers' Assistance

Paddlers can help improve water quality in several ways. The place to start is in our own backyards. Water quality should be kept in mind when making decisions affecting areas we control. This includes decisions about stream buffers, paving, lawn fertilizing, car maintenance, and disposal of waste.

Many groups are dedicated to protecting and improving our streams. Some of the groups have their own water quality monitoring projects. Joining one or more of these groups is a way to contribute to better water quality.

Paddlers can adopt a section of a stream through the state's Stream Watch program. All that is required is energy and commitment. A Stream Watcher is encouraged to become the local expert on their stream and act on behalf of its best interests. The program is administered through Water Resources within the Department of Environment and Natural Resources. For more information, see: http://www.dwr.ehnr.state.nc.us/wrps/swhome.htm

While paddling rivers, we often have the opportunity to observe areas few people see. Pollution seen on paddling trips should be reported to the Water Quality regional office. For a listing of regions and contacts, see: http://www.enr.state.nc.us/files/regnoffs.htm

The sedimentation of streams and lakes is a major pollution problem. Sedimentation occurs from the erosion or depositing of soil and other materials into waters, principally from construction sites and road maintenance. Problems with sedimentation pollution can be reported through a statewide toll-free hotline: 866-StopMud (866-786-7683). For additional information, see: http://www.dlr.enr.state.nc.us

■

When we try to pick out something by itself, we find it hitched to everything else in the universe.

—John Muir (1891)

River Selection

When planning a paddling trip, there are many rivers from which to choose. Some considerations are the group's skill, water levels, and suitability for camping.

Reading all the detailed descriptions of rivers in this guidebook is a way to pick the river and section, but the following tables are designed to assist in narrowing the search.

The tables are grouped by river basin and summarize the flatwater or whitewater class, when the river has water, and suitability for camping. Information is provided for the entire river, not for individual sections. For example, where the difficulty changes across different sections of a river, all of the classes covered are listed. Refer to the river descriptions to choose a particular river section.

Class   The smooth water (A, B, C) or whitewater (I–VI) rating. To review these definitions, see River Rating Systems (page 13).

Water   When the river sections have enough water to be paddled:

✓   Always above minimum level. River can be paddled in all seasons except when too high or during long droughts.

✳   Rain dependent. Water level is sometimes or often below minimum paddling level.

❙   Dam controlled. Water is controlled by release from a dam, and the minimum release may be below minimum paddling level.

Camping   Identifies rivers suitable for multi-day trips where camping overnight is feasible. Some rivers have areas where public camping is allowed, but most potential campsites are on private property. Posted land should be avoided (see River Camping, page 18):

✓ 2   Suitable for camping, and the number indicates how many public camping areas are available (2 in this example).

✗   Not generally suitable for camping because river is short, lacks dry ground, or is in a highly developed area.

Cape Fear Basin

Name	Class	Water	Camping
Black River	A	✓ ❄	✓ 2
Cape Fear River	A, I, II	✓ ∎ ❄	✓ 1
Deep River	I, II, III	✓ ❄	✓ 0
Great Coharie Creek	A	❄	✓ 0
Haw River	II, III	❄	✓ 0
Holly Shelter Creek	A	✓ ❄	✗
Little Coharie Creek	A	❄	✓ 0
Lower Little River	B, I	❄	✓ 1
Moores Creek	A	✓	✗
New Hope Creek	III	❄	✗
Northeast Cape Fear River	A	✓ ❄	✓ 1
Rockfish Creek	II	❄	✗
Rocky River	II, III	❄	✗
Six Runs Creek	A	❄	✓ 0
South River	A	✓ ❄	✓ 0
Town Creek	A	✓	✗
Upper Little River	II	❄	✗

Chowan Basin

Name	Class	Water	Camping
Bennetts Creek	A	✓	✗
Chowan River	A	✓	✓ 0
Dillard Creek	A	✓	✗
Meherrin River	A	✓	✓ 0
Merchants Millpond	A	✓	✓ 1
Potecasi Creek	A	❄	✗
Warwick & Catherine Creeks	A	✓	✗
Wiccacon River	A	✓	✓ 0

Lumber Basin

Name	Class	Water	Camping
Big Swamp	A	✳	X
Drowning Creek	B	✳	X
Lockwoods Folly River	A	✓	X
Lumber River	A, B	✓ ✳	✓ 8
Waccamaw River	A	✓ ✳	✓ 2

Neuse Basin

Name	Class	Water	Camping
Brice Creek	A	✓	X
Contentnea Creek	A, I, II	✓ ✳	✓ 0
Crabtree Creek	A, I, II	✳	X
Eno River	I, II, III	✳	X
Flat River	II, III	✳	X
Little River (near Durham)	II, III	✳	X
Little River (near Goldsboro)	A, I	✓ ✳	✓ 0
Neuse River	A, I, II	✓ ■	✓ 2
Trent River	A	✓ ✳	✓ 0

Pasquotank Basin

Name	Class	Water	Camping
Alligator River	A	✓	X
Jean Guite Creek	A	✓	X
Little River	A	✓	X
Milltail Creek	A	✓	X
Perquimans River	A	✓	X
Scuppernong River	A	✓	X

Roanoke Basin

Name	Class	Water	Camping
Cashie River	A	✓	✗
Dan River	I, II, III	✓ ✳ ▮	✓ 0
Gardner Creek	A	✓	✓ 2
Mayo River	I, II, III	✳	✗
Roanoke River	A, B, C, III	✓	✓ 8
Sweetwater Creek & Devil's Gut	A	✓	✓ 2

Tar-Pamlico Basin

Name	Class	Water	Camping
Chicod Creek	A	✳	✗
Fishing Creek	A, II	✳	✓ 0
Little Fishing Creek	A	✳	✗
Pungo River	A	✓	✗
Tar River	A, I, II, III	✓ ✳	✓ 0
Tranters Creek	A	✓	✗

White Oak Basin

Name	Class	Water	Camping
New River	A, I	✓ ✳	✗
Newport River	A	✓	✗
White Oak River	A	✓ ✳	✓ 5

Yadkin-Pee Dee Basin

Name	Class	Water	Camping
Ararat River	I, II	✳	✗
Buffalo Creek	III	✳	✗
Elk Creek	III	✳	✗
Fisher River	II	✳	✗
Mitchell River	II	✳	✗
Rocky River	I, II	✓ ✳	✓ 0
South Yadkin River	A, I, II	✓ ✳	✓ 0
Uwharrie River	I, II	✳	✓ 6
Yadkin River	A, I, II	✓ ✳	✓ 7

River Descriptions

The rivers basins covered by this guidebook are included in alphabetic order. Rivers are in alphabetic order within their basin.

Basins

A basin is introduced with a map showing selected rivers in the basin and major cities. All of the rivers described in this guidebook are shown on the map, and additional rivers may be shown to give a better view of the basin.

The page opposite the basin map gives a brief overview of the basin. The pages following the basin overview describe the basin's rivers.

Rivers

A river description begins with names of counties and topographical (topo) maps. The maps are listed in order as one paddles downstream on the sections described. The topo maps listed are the quadrangle names of the 7.5 minute (1:24,000 scale) series.

After the list of maps, there is a brief introduction for the entire river.

River Sections

Following the river introduction, each section of the river is described. Section "1" is the most upstream section included. In dividing a river into sections, distance and access points have been considered. Where there are additional access points within a section, they are mentioned to allow making a shorter trip. Multiple sections can also be combined for longer trips.

Section Tables

Each river section begins with a table in this format:

Location of put-in bridge or access to location of take-out bridge or access		
Difficulty I–II	**Width** 50–85 ft	
Distance 8.3 mi	**Gradient** 3.8 ft/mi	
Scenery A (50%), B (25%), C (25%)	**Map** page 40	

 The section number of the portion of the river described.

Location   Defines where the section put-in and take-out are by naming the road or other facilities nearest to start and end of the section. The put-ins and take-outs are also shown on the maps.

Where parking is on the road shoulder, and the path to the river uses a bridge right-of-way, the location includes *bridge*. Where a road ends near the river, *end* is used. If access to the river is provided by a public or private facility, *access* is used.

Where required, more information about a put-in or take-out is provided under **Notes**.

Difficulty   The rating is given as **A**, **B**, or **C** for smooth (flat) water or I–VI for whitewater. For explanation of the ratings, see River Rating Systems (page 13).

A section can include multiple ratings. For example, if a section contains long sections of slow flatwater and some Class I and II rapids, the difficulty would be noted as A–I–II.

To distinguish a rapid as being on the low or high side of a rating, a + or – is attached to the Class. A low Class II rapid would be II⁻, and a high Class III would be Class III⁺.

The rating for the river is given for low to medium water levels. The difficulty can be very different at high and flood levels.

Distance   The distance from the put-in to the take-out measured along the course of the river.

Scenery   A rating of how much evidence of human habitation and development is seen while paddling the section. Letter grades are assigned for scenery:

A   Little to no development is evident from the stream. Except for a rare bridge or house, the stream appears to be in a remote area.

B   Occasional development is evident from the stream, but it is more intermittent than constant.

C   Frequent development is evident from the stream, often including many houses, or factories and commercial buildings.

Often there is a variation in the amount of development seen while paddling an entire river section. Each section was evaluated by observing the amount of development every two miles and assigning a letter grade. If there were different grades assigned across the 2-mile segments in a section, the range of grades is shown along with the percentage of the section receiving each grade. For example, an 8-mile section having two segments rated **A**, one segment rated **B**, and one segment rated **C**, would receive the following scenery rating: **A** (50%), **B** (25%), **C** (25%).

Comments about natural scenic features of particular interest are given under Notes.

Width   Distance across the river channel from the smallest to largest width observed (such as 50–85 feet). Where the river divides into channels around islands, the width of the channel paddled is used rather than the entire width of the river.

Width can be useful in choosing a section to paddle. Wind causes more problems on wide rivers, but downed trees are more likely to be a problem on narrow rivers (less than about 100 feet) where a single downed tree can span the channel.

Gradient   The total drop divided by the section distance, where drop is the elevation (height above sea level) of the river at the start of the section minus the elevation of the river at the end of the section. Usually more gradient indicates more difficult whitewater, but gradient is only an average. The drop is usually not uniformly distributed in a river section. All of the drop may occur at a dam or in only a few rapids.

Map   The page number of the map showing this section.

Gauge

Following the section table, the location or name of the nearest gauge is given. If a USGS gauge is named, its exact location can be found in Appendix B.

A gauge recommendation is usually given in both flow in cubic feet per second (cfs) and height in feet. The correlation between flow and height can vary over time. If there is a difference between a flow and height figure in this guidebook and the latest USGS gauge data, use the book's flow figure and disregard height. For general information on using gauges, see River Gauges (page 20).

Always above minimum is used to describe sections where there is sufficient water to paddle even in dry weather; however there are cases during extreme drought when all but the largest rivers can be too dry to paddle.

For sections known to fall below the minimum water needed for paddling, a minimum gauge reading is recommended. The term *estimated minimum* is used if the stream was not paddled close enough to minimum to be able to be as accurate as other recommendations.

The minimum water required can be subjective. Some paddlers refer to it as the minimum level they consider to be fun, requiring waves for surfing and no scraping of their boat hull. The minimum water level used in this guidebook is the lowest level needed to paddle the section solo in a 15-foot open canoe without having to get out and drag. It often requires reading the water carefully, and choosing the best route. This minimum figure should be raised for a short boat requiring more water, paddling tandem, loaded with equipment, or to avoid scraping the hull.

Tidal influence is noted where applicable. For tide table references, see Tides (page 23).

Notes

This follows gauge information and includes information on a river section.

For access areas, the managing organization is named if known. An area noted as *Wildlife boating access* is operated by the North Carolina Wildlife Resources Commission. Where necessary, details are given to assist in locating the put-in or take-out.

Other access points, bridges, and special points of interest are mentioned. Mileage given is the distance from the section put-in to the feature being described, unless otherwise noted.

For put-ins and take-outs on Secondary Routes (SR), the road name is usually given in addition to the SR number. Secondary Routes are sometimes referred to as *county roads*. Road names are easier to recognize on signs and are used by residents, but road names can be changed by local governments. Use the road number when the road name given in this guidebook does not match the name on the signpost. Also note that many rivers are county borders, and an SR road number and road name usually change as a road crosses into a different county.

Known hazards and rapids are noted. Left and right are always referenced to traveling downstream, unless otherwise noted.

Estimated time required to paddle a section is not given because it will vary with current, wind, paddling effort, solo or tandem, boat design, and scouting or portages required. Typical paddling speed without current and wind is 2–3 miles per hour. If in doubt, estimate 2 miles per hour when actually paddling. Add additional time for stops, portages, and the unexpected.

The river sections have not been rated for water quality because it varies over time and requires test equipment. Any obvious water quality problems seen and known to be persistent, such as odors or odd colors, are mentioned. See Water Quality (page 24) for more information and where to report water quality problems. Any stream designated Outstanding Resource Waters is mentioned.

Maps

For each river, maps of the sections follow the last section description. Each map shows one or more river sections, roads leading to the area, and roads along the river that can be used to travel to put-ins or take-outs.

A circle containing the section number points to the put-in. The take-out for the section is the put-in for the next section, unless the next symbol downstream is a hexagon (stop-sign) containing *End* or if the next symbol is a circle containing a U-turn arrow to indicate the turnaround point for a round-trip section.

A map scale and compass pointer are shown on each map. The scale and pointer vary from map to map so that complete sections can be shown on a single page.

Dams requiring portage are shown on the maps. Broken dams that are often run are usually not shown on the maps.

To make the maps easier to read, not all roads in the area depicted are shown, and roads may extend farther than shown. A road shown ending at an intersection with another road may actually cross the road. To view all roads and possible shortcuts, it is useful to have additional maps. For getting to the river and setting a shuttle, a state road map and county road maps are helpful. County road maps show all of the Secondary Route (SR) roads. Secondary Routes have 4-digit road numbers (3 digits in Virginia, 2–3 digits in South Carolina) and road names. Both the numbers and names are usually shown on road signs, but road names are not used on county road maps.

The *North Carolina Atlas & Gazetteer* shows both topographical features and roads at a scale of 1:150,000 (1 inch = 2.4 miles). It uses mainly county road names rather than SR numbers, but often these names do not match the road signs. The SR numbers on county road maps are usually dependable because they rarely change.

For navigation on swampy rivers and exploring off the main channel, USGS topographical maps at a scale of 1:24,000 (1 inch = 0.4 miles) are available.

For map resources, see Appendix C.

■

The face of the water, in time, became a wonderful book—a book ... which told its mind to me without reserve, delivering its most cherished secrets as clearly as if it uttered them with a voice. And it was not a book to be read once and thrown aside, for it had a new story to tell every day. Throughout the long twelve hundred miles there was never a page that was void of interest, never one that you could leave unread without loss, never one that you would want to skip, thinking you could find higher enjoyment in some other thing. There never was so wonderful a book written by man; never one whose interest was so absorbing, so unflagging, so sparklingly renewed with every re-perusal.

—Mark Twain, *Life on the Mississippi* (1883)

Multilane Divided Road Access Controlled		Put-In for section 2, take-out for section 1	
Interstate Route (95)		Section take-out if next section put-in is not the take-out (End)	
US Route (52)		Return point for a round-trip section (J)	
State Route (87)		North pointer (N)	
Secondary Route (county road) 1234		City (over 10,000)	
Forest Route 121		City/town (2,000 to 10,000)	
County boundary			
State boundary		Town (under 2,000)	
River channel			
Dam		Map scale 0 1 2 3 4 5 Miles	

Legend for maps of river sections

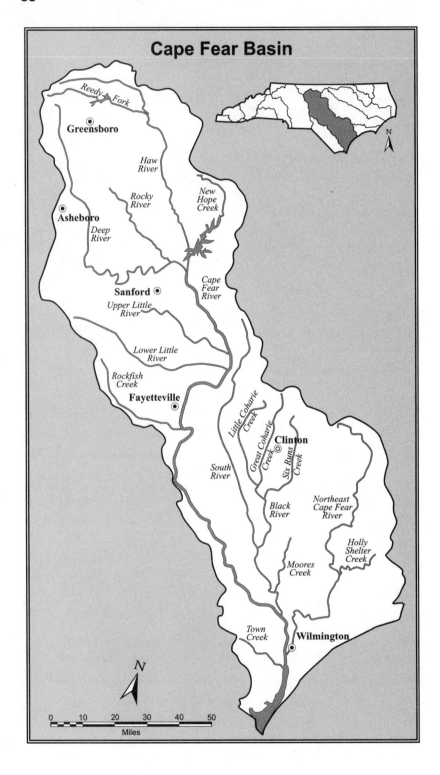

Cape Fear Basin

Reedy Fork

Greensboro

Haw River

Rocky River

New Hope Creek

Asheboro

Deep River

Cape Fear River

Sanford

Upper Little River

Lower Little River

Rockfish Creek

Fayetteville

Little Coharie Creek

Great Coharie Creek

Clinton

Six Runs Creek

South River

Northeast Cape Fear River

Black River

Holly Shelter Creek

Moores Creek

Town Creek

Wilmington

N

0 10 20 30 40 50
Miles

Cape Fear Basin

The Cape Fear Basin is North Carolina's largest river basin, draining 9,322 square miles. Its watershed is completely contained within the state's boundaries.

Water originates from twenty-six of the state's one hundred counties, and more than one-quarter of the state's population live within the basin. The most populated regions of the basin are in and near the Greensboro-Burlington-High Point, Durham-Chapel Hill, and Fayetteville areas.

Large freshwater rivers, blackwater swamps, and estuaries are found in the basin as the terrain changes from the Piedmont to the Coastal Plain.

The headwaters are in the Piedmont above Greensboro, Burlington, High Point, Chapel Hill, and part of Durham. The uppermost reaches in Forsyth County begin near 1,000 feet above sea level.

Major tributaries are the Haw and Deep Rivers, which meet 10 miles northeast of Sanford to form the Cape Fear River in the backwater of Buckhorn Dam, 6 miles downstream.

The Cape Fear River passes Lillington and enters the Coastal Plain near Fayetteville. Between Fayetteville and Wilmington there are three locks and dams, operated by the Corps of Engineers, to make the river navigable by large boats all the way to Fayetteville. The locks were built in the early 1900s for commercial traffic, but there has been none in many years.

Below the last lock and dam, the Black River, a major blackwater tributary, joins the tidal portion of the Cape Fear River.

At Wilmington, the Cape Fear River is joined by the Northeast Cape Fear River, another major blackwater tributary. The port city of Wilmington is 26 miles from the open sea with a 38-foot deep channel in the river for large ships.

Below Wilmington, the Cape Fear River is wide and adds a few coastal rivers, such as Town Creek, as it flows to the Atlantic Ocean at Southport and Bald Head Island.

Black River

Counties   Sampson, Bladen, Pender

Topos   Ingold, Tomahawk, Harrells, Rowan, Atkinson, Point Caswell, Currie, Leland

The Black River is formed by the confluence of Great Coharie and Six Runs Creeks, 15 miles south of Clinton. It picks up the South River and flows into the Cape Fear River above Wilmington.

The Black River is a popular paddling destination because it has sufficient water even in droughts and runs through land that is largely undisturbed forest. Its blackwater swamps contain the oldest known living trees in eastern North America. Camping is also popular, but most sites are on private land.

The Black River has been known for excellent water quality and was designated Outstanding Resource Waters in 1994. The high concentration of hog farms near its tributaries has caused concern. Great Coharie and Six Runs Creeks have shown decreased water quality in recent years.

---

1 NC 903 bridge over Great Coharie Creek to NC 411 bridge at Clear Run

Difficulty A	**Width**	30–85 ft
Distance 6.7 mi	**Gradient**	1.5 ft/mi
Scenery A (70%), B (30%)	**Map**	page 47

Gauge USGS *Black River near Tomahawk*. Estimated minimum is 125 cfs (2.3 ft).

Notes NC 903 at the put-in is also called Lisbon Bridge Road (Sampson Co. 1134).

At the NC 411 bridge, upstream right, there is a private, gated-road to the bank. Obtain permission or use the steeper banks from the bridge.

A sign near the NC 411 bridge notes "Naval stores and lumber were primary cargo for vessels navigating the Black River (1875–1914). Remains of the steamer, A J Johnson, 60 yards south." The bow can be seen embedded in the bank when water is low.

Great Coharie Creek has many trees shading the run and sandy banks over 10 feet high. Sandbars are exposed at low water and require searching for the deeper channels.

Six Runs Creek (mi 1.2) joins to form the beginning of the Black River. The channel becomes wider and more open. Cypress trees are near the water, and banks are up to 20 feet high.

2 NC 411 bridge at Clear Run to NC 41 bridge

Difficulty A	**Width** 50–75 ft
Distance 6.5 mi	**Gradient** 0.5 ft/mi
Scenery A (60%), C (40%)	**Map** page 47

Gauge USGS *Black River near Tomahawk*. Estimated minimum is 75 cfs (1.8 ft).

Notes See the previous section about putting in at NC 411 and the sign noting the old steamboat bow embedded in the bank near the bridge.

The banks are sandy with cypress and pine trees. An unusual high bank (mi 2.7) of 50 feet rises on the right and is covered in evergreen trees and mountain laurel.

The last mile of this section is heavily developed with trailers and cabins along the right bank.

3 NC 41 bridge to Wildcat Road (Sampson Co. 1007) bridge

Difficulty A	**Width** 55–95 ft
Distance 6.0 mi	**Gradient** 0.3 ft/mi
Scenery A	**Map** page 47

Gauge See Section 2.

Notes When water is low, many sandbars stand out. The white sand is especially noticeable contrasted against the blackwater.

The banks range up to 20 feet high, and there are few houses along this section.

---

4 Wildcat Road (Sampson Co. 1007) bridge to Ivanhoe Road
(Sampson Co. 1100) access, south of Ivanhoe

Difficulty A		**Width** 65–100 ft	
Distance 9.0 mi		**Gradient** 0.9 ft/mi	
Scenery A (90%), B (10%)		**Map** page 47	

Gauge See Section 2.

Notes A Wildlife boating access is 0.5 miles south of Ivanhoe, off Ivanhoe Road.

Bloody Bluff (mi 3.6) rises 30 feet on the right at a sharp left turn, where the river comes within a few hundred yards of Dr. Kerr Road (Sampson Co. 1105).

After passing under Dr. Kerr Road (mi 7.9) near Ivanhoe, land on the right bank is part of a conservation easement the Coastal Land Trust purchased from International Paper Company with a grant from the Clean Water Management Trust Fund. The easement protects a narrow buffer of 271 acres, running 5 miles to the confluence with the South River and extending 2 miles up the left bank of the South River.

---

5 Ivanhoe Road (Sampson Co. 1100) access, south of Ivanhoe, to Beattys Bridge Road (Bladen Co. 1550) bridge

Difficulty A		**Width** 40–125 ft	
Distance 7.6 mi		**Gradient** 0.9 ft/mi	
Scenery A (75%), B (25%)		**Map** page 47	

Gauge See Section 2.

Notes See the previous section about the Ivanhoe Road access.

The conservation easement from the previous section continues on the right bank.

The first bluff on the right bank (mi 1.9) is in a left bend and rises about 15 feet.

At a sharp 180-degree left bend (mi 3.1), another bluff begins on the right bank and continues to the next left bend (mi 3.4), where it is 20 feet above the river. Through an agreement with International Paper Company, Cape Fear River Watch manages a primitive campsite on this bluff. Reservations can be made by calling 800-380-3485. The best landing for campsite access is on the downstream right, where the high ground ends.

The South River (mi 3.9) enters from the right, where the Black River makes a left turn.

A turn to the left must be made to stay in the main channel (mi 4.4). Going straight leads into a curving dead-end channel.

At a bluff (mi 6.5) over 40 feet high, a turn must be made to the left or right. Take the right turn because the left leads into a long cove.

The house upstream left of the take-out bridge was where much of the movie *Rambling Rose* was filmed in 1991.

6	Beattys Bridge Road (Bladen Co. 1550) bridge to Hunts Bluff Road access off Longview Road (Bladen Co. 1547)		
Difficulty A		**Width** 15–200 ft	
Distance 12.9 mi		**Gradient** 0.4 ft/mi	
Scenery A (80%), B (20%)		**Map** page 48	

Gauge USGS *Black River near Tomahawk.* Always above minimum, except for the Three Sisters (area of the Narrows) in the middle of this section. At 225 cfs (2.9 ft), this area required walking a quarter-mile. At 600 cfs (5.4 ft), there was plenty of water to paddle through. An estimated minimum for no walking is 400 cfs (4.3 ft).

Notes A Wildlife boating access is at the end of Hunts Bluff Road. From the NC 53 bridge, downstream right, take Longview Road 1.2 miles to Hunts Bluff Road on the left.

An option to the put-in at Beattys Bridge is Henry's Landing, a private access charging $2 per boat to launch, $5 per car for overnight parking. It eliminates paddling the first 1.5 miles where the river is wide, straight, and developed. From Beattys Bridge Road, take NC 210 south and go 1.3 miles. Turn left at the sign to Henry's Landing. The NC 53 bridge can be used as a take-out, making the trip 1.7 miles shorter. Putting in at Henry's Landing and taking out at NC 53 makes a 9.7-mile trip.

Henry's Landing also has camping spaces, canoe rental, and shuttle service. For reservations, call 910-669-2783.

This is a popular section because of the ancient cypress trees and dramatic changes in width. Almost all high ground is posted, making camping difficult.

The river takes a left bend (mi 1.5) where Henry's Landing is in the cove to the right just before the turn. Downstream, the river is more narrow and winding, with many coves and few houses.

At a sweeping right bend, Squalling Bluff (mi 3.9) rises 20 feet on the left. It is part of Cone's Folly, a private 8,000-acre wildlife and timber preserve, extending from near the put-in to NC 53. Camping is possible with permission, but it is rarely granted. People trespassing have caused access to be more restricted. A resident manager patrols the area and can be reached at 910-283-5512.

Water leaves the main channel (mi 6.1) and flows past trees into many smaller channels. This swampy area is known as the Three Sisters or Narrows. Water continues to be lost to small side channels, and the main channel (mi 6.3) is reduced to only 20 feet wide. At low water, only a few inches of water or less flow over the sand bottom, but there is usually enough to float an empty boat. It is time to get out and wade for about a quarter-mile until the small channels rejoin to return enough water to resume paddling.

Three Sisters contains the oldest living trees known in eastern North America. In 1986 researchers took core samples from bald cypress trees to reconstruct climate changes in North Carolina using tree rings. From a sample taken 15 feet above ground, one tree was found to have rings dating to 372 A.D. They estimated this tree was at least 1,700 years old when growth below the core sample was considered. They also believed there were 2,000-year-old trees in the area, but many of the very old trees have heart-rot, preventing accurate tree-ring dating.

The river (mi 7.3) widens to 100 feet, and there is a house straight ahead on 50-foot high Haw Bluff. To the right is a cove containing more old cypress trees. Paddle into the cove to get a close look at the ancient ones.

There are a few houses downstream of the NC 53 bridge (mi 11.2), and the river is up to 100–200 feet wide.

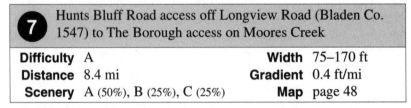

7 Hunts Bluff Road access off Longview Road (Bladen Co. 1547) to The Borough access on Moores Creek		
Difficulty A	**Width** 75–170 ft	
Distance 8.4 mi	**Gradient** 0.4 ft/mi	
Scenery A (50%), B (25%), C (25%)	**Map** page 48	

Gauge USGS *Black River near Tomahawk.* Always above minimum. Tides affect this section and range about 1.5 feet at the take-out and lag Wilmington tides by about 3 hours. Wind affects paddling progress more than tide does.

Notes See the previous section about Hunts Bluff Road access.

See Moores Creek (page 111) about The Borough access. An alternative to using this private access is to paddle up Moores Creek to NC 210, adding 3.8 miles to the trip.

There are many coves, some with mouths as large as the main channel. When there is little or no downstream flow, the route may be confusing.

Red Star Camp (mi 2.3) has many homes on the left bank. Just past them, there are two channels (mi 2.8). Take the right channel for a narrower run.

A channel on the left (mi 3.8) splits off to rejoin below the NC 210 bridge. Access at the NC 210 bridge (mi 4.6) is difficult because of guardrails and little parking space on the road shoulder. Nearby roads leading to the bank are private.

The channel that splits off above the bridge rejoins (mi 5.0), and many houses line the right bank at Long Bluff Landing (mi 5.5).

At a right bend, Moores Creek (mi 8.2) enters from the left. Turn into it to reach the take-out.

8	The Borough access on Moores Creek to confluence with the Cape Fear River and return		
Difficulty A		**Width**	125–400 ft
Distance 23.4 mi		**Gradient**	0 ft/mi
Scenery A		**Map**	page 48

Gauge USGS *Black River near Tomahawk*. Always above minimum. Tides affect this section and range about 2.5 feet at the confluence with the Cape Fear and lag Wilmington tides by about 2.5 hours. Wind affects paddling progress more than tide does.

Notes See Moores Creek (page 111) about The Borough access.

This section is usually run as a camper because of the distance. It is only 11.7 miles to the confluence with the Cape Fear, but there is no take-out. The options are to return to the put-in or paddle 14.4 more miles to Wilmington. See the Cape Fear River, Section 13 (page 58). If going on to Wilmington, time the trip to arrive on an outgoing tide.

This is the most remote part of the Black River because its swampy borders preclude access roads. Other than a few cabins on the scarce high ground, a swampy wilderness is the vista. Fishermen and hunters boat these waters, but few paddlers venture here.

The main channel is easy to follow, but there are four channels that split off and rejoin the main channel. They are Thorofare, east channel around D Island, Cross Way Creek, and Black River Cut. Together they comprise almost 5 miles of routes that can be explored to see new areas when doing a round-trip. Using these channels shortens the one-way distance by a half-mile. The trip notes below describe the main channel and mention some of the other channels. Do not explore off the main channel without topo maps and good navigation skills because it is easy to confuse side channels with many creeks, long coves, and even Lyon Thoroughfare, a shortcut to the Cape Fear River.

Turn left where Moores Creek joins the Black (mi 0.2).

The channel (mi 1.8) to the left is called Thorofare. It returns to the main Black (mi 2.9) not far above another channel (mi 3.3) going to the left around D Island. The term *island* in these parts does not imply dry ground. It is often a swampy area.

Hedden Bluff Landing (mi 3.9) is private property on the right where the ground rises several feet.

The channel from D Island rejoins (mi 4.2) just before Cross Way Creek (mi 4.4) splits off on the left.

A house is on a small bluff to the right at Rhyne Grave (mi 5.5).

In a 400-foot wide bay, Cross Way Creek (mi 6.7) rejoins the main channel.

Lyon Thoroughfare (mi 7.2) is a channel to the right connecting to the Cape Fear River. The large area downstream between the Black and Cape Fear is Roan Island. Most of it is swampy or a jungle of trees and vines.

Black River Cut (mi 8.8) to the left is a shortcut across a loop in the main channel, and returns (mi 9.5) just upstream of Peachtree Landing. Peachtree Landing (mi 9.7), on the left bank, is in a right bend past a long row of saw grass where a few tall pine trees are seen. It is easy to miss this rare high-ground campsite. Behind the trees near the bank is a small level clearing.

The river is straight until a few bends in the last mile before joining the Cape Fear River (mi 11.7).

■

Time is a sort of river of passing events, and strong is its current; no sooner is a thing brought to sight than it is swept by and another takes its place, and this too will be swept away.
— Marcus Aurelius, *Meditations* (121–180)

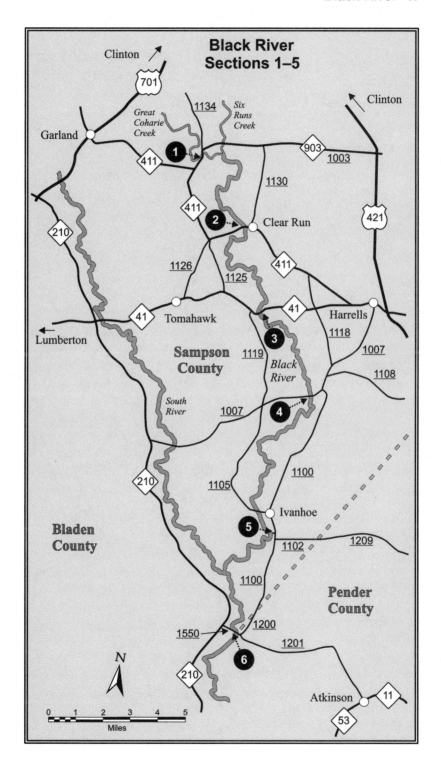

**Black River
Sections 1–5**

Clinton

701

1134 · Six Runs Creek

Great Coharie Creek

Clinton

Garland

411

903 · 1003

1130

411

2

Clear Run

411

421

1126

1125

411

41 · Tomahawk

41

Harrells

1118

1007

Lumberton

Sampson County

1119 · Black River

1007 · 1108

South River

1007 · 4

1100

1105

210

Ivanhoe

5

1102 · 1209

Bladen County

1100

Pender County

1550 · 1200

6 · 1201

N

210

Atkinson · 11

Miles · 0 1 2 3 4 5

53

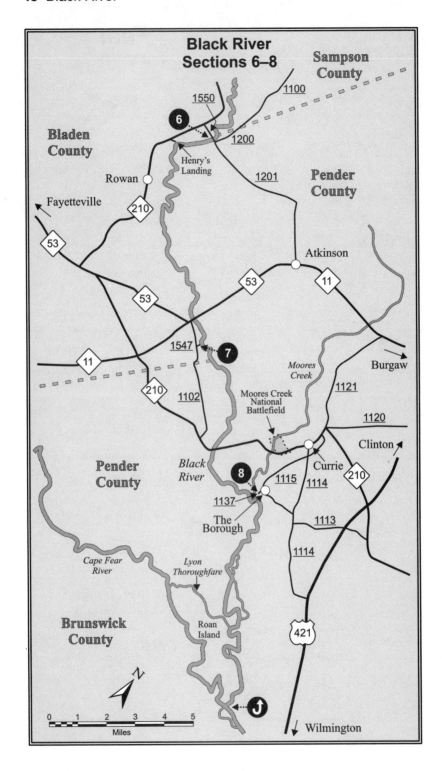

Black River
Sections 6–8

Sampson County

Bladen County

1550

1100

6

1200

Henry's Landing

1201

Pender County

Rowan

Fayetteville

210

53

Atkinson

53

53

53

11

11

Burgaw

1547

7

Moores Creek

1121

210

1102

Moores Creek National Battlefield

1120

Clinton

Pender County

Black River

Currie

210

8

1115

1114

Cape Fear River

1137

The Borough

1113

1114

Lyon Thoroughfare

Brunswick County

Roan Island

421

N

0 1 2 3 4 5
Miles

Wilmington

Cape Fear Basin

Cape Fear River

Counties	Chatham, Lee, Harnett, Cumberland, Bladen, Pender, Columbus, Brunswick, New Hanover
Topos	Merry Oaks, Moncure, Cokesbury, Mamers, Lillington, Coats, Erwin, Wade, Slocomb, Vander, Cedar Creek, Duart, Tar Heel, Dublin, Elizabethtown North, Elizabethtown South, Singletary Lake, Council, Kelly, Point Caswell, Acme, Leland, Castle Hayne, Wilmington

The Cape Fear River is formed by the confluence of the Haw and Deep Rivers, near Moncure and Haywood, 10 miles northeast of Sanford. It flows through Lillington, Fayetteville, Elizabethtown, Wilmington, and Southport.

The river is named for the dangerous Cape Fear shoals off Bald Head Island, near the river's mouth. The upper Cape Fear was known as "Sapona" by Indians. Italian explorer Verrazzano, backed by the French government to discover a westward passage to Asia, came to the lower Cape Fear in 1524.

The Cape Fear is the only large river in North Carolina flowing directly into the Atlantic Ocean instead of into a sound.

There are four dams on the river, and the lower three have locks to make the river navigable by large boats all the way to Fayetteville. The locks were built in the early 1900s for commercial traffic, but there has been none in many years.

The paddling sections described from Jordan Dam to Wilmington cover 172 miles.

 1 Jordan Dam Road (Chatham Co. 1970) access on the Haw River to Buckhorn Road (Chatham Co. 1921) access

Difficulty A		**Width** 175–1,000 ft	
Distance 10.2 mi		**Gradient** 0 ft/mi	
Scenery A (40%), B (40%), C (20%)		**Map** page 60	

Gauge USGS *Haw River below B. Everett Jordan Dam near Moncure*. Always above minimum.

Notes The access below Jordan Dam is the "Day Use Area." There is no boat ramp here. The bank is 40 feet above the Haw River, and it is lined with riprap, where a fall could be dangerous. It is safer to put in a few hundred yards downstream of the parking lot where the riprap ends.

This section is all flatwater because the backwater from Buckhorn Dam comes to the base of Jordan Dam. Eagles and osprey are often seen fishing this flatwater.

After passing US 1 (mi 1.5) and Old US 1 (Chatham Co. 1011) (mi 2.7), there are some factories on the left, and Progress Energy's Cape Fear plant smokestacks downstream can be seen and sound of its operation heard.

The Cape Fear River is born at the confluence where the Deep River (mi 4.2) enters from the right. The point of land where the rivers join is known as Mermaid's Point. Legend says mermaids gathered here on a sandy spit to sun themselves after swimming from the ocean to wash away the salt. The sandy spit is now under the backwater of Buckhorn Dam.

On the left bank, across from Mermaid's Point, are Progress Energy's plant and cooling lake.

McKay Island (mi 6.3) is almost a mile long and offers a choice of channels.

The NC 42 bridge (mi 8.1) can be seen from the end of McKay Island. A Wildlife boating access is upstream left of the bridge, and it makes for an easier take-out than at Buckhorn Dam.

Stay back from Buckhorn Dam because water flows over it. Take out on the left side, but be careful of current where water from the upstream cooling lake comes into the river on the left, just upstream of the dam.

2	Buckhorn Road (Chatham Co. 1921) access to Wildlife Road (Harnett Co. 2069) access near Lillington		
Difficulty I–II		**Width**	90–900 ft
Distance 16.7 mi		**Gradient**	2.7 ft/mi
Scenery A (60%), B (40%)		**Map**	page 61

Gauge USGS *Cape Fear at Lillington*. Minimum is 675 cfs (1.7 ft). Water in this section is from the Deep River and releases from the Haw's Jordan Dam.

Notes The access below Buckhorn Dam is rough road, but it is possible to drive close to the water where fishermen often launch.

A Wildlife boating access is at the end of Wildlife Road. To reach it from Lillington, take East McNeil Street (Harnett Co. 2016).

Class I rapids begin near islands (mi 0.8). The rapids continue for several hundred yards, ending in Class II rapids known as Buckhorn Falls. At high water these become Class III.

Lanier Falls (mi 5.7) is a river-wide Class II rapid with rocks on the right up to 15 feet above water. The flat rocks make a scenic lunch stop. The usual run is toward the center of the river, but there is a more abrupt drop of a few feet near the right bank. Be careful here because current flows toward undercut rocks on the right.

Raven Rock State Park starts on the right bank just before reaching Lanier Falls. Below the rapid, park property extends across the river, taking in land on the left bank. Farther downstream, the right bank is rocky and steep, rising more than 150 feet above the river. A rock outcropping near the next rapid is called Raven Rock.

A Class I$^+$ rapid (mi 6.8) is at Fish Traps. A lock and dam were constructed by the Cape Fear Navigation Company. It was one of many on the river allowing steamboat travel in the 1800s. Scattered stones from the dam are still evident.

On the right, a small white buoy (mi 8.1) marks the park's paddle-in campsites. A small dock (mi 8.5) is the entrance to the group campsites. Bring drinking water because there is none at the sites. Trails lead a few miles up to the park road. Call the park office, 910-893-4888, for campsite reservations. There is no park road leading to the river for boat access.

A few Class I rapids are found before reaching the US 401/421 bridge (mi 14.3) at Lillington. It can be used for access to shorten the trip, but the boat ramp downstream is an easier take-out.

3 Wildlife Road (Harnett Co. 2069) access near Lillington to NC 217 bridge near Erwin		
Difficulty I–II	**Width**	30–400 ft
Distance 7.9 mi	**Gradient**	5.2 ft/mi
Scenery A (75%), B (25%)	**Map**	page 61

Gauge USGS *Cape Fear at Lillington*. Minimum is 400 cfs (1.3 ft). Water here is from the Deep River and releases from the Haw's Jordan Dam.

Water is usually above minimum because the Corps of Engineers tries to release enough water to keep the Lillington flow at 600 cfs or above, but it can dip lower during dry times.

At flows from 1,000–2,000 cfs (2.2–3.2 ft), there are waves and many possible routes. As the water rises, waves are higher and some rapids wash out. Above 4,500 cfs (5 ft), rescue becomes more difficult.

Notes See the previous section about the Wildlife Road access.

This section contains the most rapids of the Cape Fear River. It is rated Class I–II, but this rating is not for high water. At high flows, it may appear to be only swift water at the put-in, but waves and current will be powerful downstream as water pours over boulders and islands. Inexperienced paddlers have died here during high water.

There are some small Class I rapids down to the first power line crossing (mi 4.5), and then the action picks up to Class II.

At Narrow Gap (mi 5.4), water flows through a 30-foot gap in the rocks and past Big Island. The set of rapids from Narrow Gap to the rapid at the take-out is known as Smylie's Falls. The gradient of the last 2 miles is 10 feet/mile.

Boulders are up to 8 feet above water near where the Upper Little River (mi 6.2) enters from the right.

A pump station (mi 6.6) is on the left bank, and there are many rapids in this area, with the best routes depending on water level.

The rapids diminish approaching the bridge, but Campbell's Falls starts under the bridge to the right of center. The river drops a few feet in a slope that kicks up waves. Avoid the far right side of this rapid near the bank because rebar has been seen at low water.

Downstream of the last rapid, the right bank is private property. Paddle upstream as far as possible and take out on the right bank near the bridge. Go under the bridge to the upstream right by walking up a goat trail, through poison ivy, and along the bridge right-of-way. Some paddlers take out on river left where the bank is steep but not as rutted.

 4 NC 217 bridge near Erwin to Old Bluff Church access on Old Bluff Church Road (Cumberland Co. 1709)

Difficulty	I, and one II	**Width**	80–200 ft
Distance	10.4 mi	**Gradient**	1.8 ft/mi
Scenery	A (80%), B (20%)	**Map**	page 62

Gauge USGS *Cape Fear at Lillington.* Always above minimum.

Notes Old Bluff Church is in a beautiful setting. Built in the late 1700s, it is now used only for special occasions.

The access to the river is past the church building where a sign notes "The Old Spring." This access is difficult because it drops 110 feet down to river level. There are wooden steps down the steepest part, and then the trail goes through woods. Walk to the river to be able to recognize the take-out. There are no signs marking the trail or church at the riverbank. Park outside the gate to the church grounds because it closes at 6 P.M.

At the put-in, there is a choice to run the rapid under the bridge, Campbell's Falls, or put in below it. See the previous section for a description.

Small rapids, formed by ledges of less than 2 feet, are scattered down this section at least every few miles.

After houses in the first mile, little development is seen, and banks often reach over 100 feet above the river.

The Lower Little River (mi 4.5) enters on the right.

5	Old Bluff Church access on Old Bluff Church Road (Cumberland Co. 1709) to Person St. access in Fayetteville		
Difficulty A–I⁻		**Width** 150–175 ft	
Distance 15.9 mi		**Gradient** 0.6 ft/mi	
Scenery A (85%), B (15%)		**Map** page 62	

Gauge See Section 4.

Notes See the previous section about the Old Bluff Church access.

The Person Street access is at Riverside Sports Center, and the fee is $4 per boat. Coming from north of Fayetteville, go south on Business I-95/US 301 and cross the Cape Fear River. Cross NC 24 and turn left on Person Street. Riverside Sports Center is on the right just after crossing the Cape Fear. Their ramp is upstream of the railroad bridge. Person Street becomes Clinton Road (Cumberland Co. 1006) a few blocks east of Riverside Sports Center. To take out at a free access, continue to the next section.

There are Class I⁻ rapids in the first half of this section. The backwater from the dam at the end of Section 7 creates flatwater extending upstream of Fayetteville.

After passing the I-95 Business/US 301 bridge (mi 15.1), the Cape Fear Botanical Garden is on the right bank just upstream of Cross Creek and the NC 24 bridge (mi 15.7). A future whitewater course has been proposed for Cross Creek.

6	Person Street access in Fayetteville to Wilmington Highway (Cumberland Co. 2337) access	
Difficulty A	**Width**	150–200 ft
Distance 3.6 mi	**Gradient**	0 ft/mi
Scenery B	**Map**	page 63

Gauge USGS *Cape Fear at Fayetteville*. Always above minimum. This is in the backwater of the Huske Lock and Dam.

Notes See the previous section about the Person Street access.

Off Wilmington Highway (Cumberland Co. 2337), there is a Wildlife boating access. It is 1.1 miles south of East Mountain Drive (Cumberland Co. 2283) and 1.1 miles north of I-95. Look for the Wildlife sign near the road leading to the ramp.

Derelict equipment, used when Fayetteville had commercial boat traffic, is seen on the banks.

On warm weekends, paddling requires dodging wakes from jet skis and powerboats pulling water-skiers.

7	Wilmington Highway (Cumberland Co. 2337) access to Huske Lock access on Glengerry Hill Rd. (Bladen Co. 1355)	
Difficulty A	**Width**	150–170 ft
Distance 16.4 mi	**Gradient**	0 ft/mi
Scenery A (75%), B (25%)	**Map**	page 63

Gauge USGS *Cape Fear River at Wilm O Huske Lock near Tarheel*. Always above minimum. This section is in the backwater of the Huske Lock and Dam.

Notes See the previous section about Wilmington Highway access.

The Huske Lock and Dam is sometimes called Lock #3, as it is the third and last lock coming upriver from Wilmington. Portage trails are provided around each lock and dam, and there is a boat ramp downstream. For paddlers continuing downstream, it is possible to go through the locks on Monday–Friday, 8 A.M.–5 P.M., except on holidays. Life jackets (PFDs) are required to be worn in the locks. Call the lockmaster in advance to be sure someone will be there when you arrive. Groups of five or more boats can make reservations to be locked through on weekends and holidays, when staff is available. Reservations must be made by 5 P.M. Thursday. Huske Lock and Dam office telephone is 910-483-7746.

After passing I-95 (mi 1.0), there are no bridges until the next section.

Rockfish Creek (mi 3.0) enters on the right.

Camping sites below Fayetteville are generally difficult to find without going up steep banks. The deep water from the dams covers the usual sandbars and flat ground found in free-flowing rivers.

A large "105" sign (mi 6.5) on a tree marks the number of river miles from Wilmington. Signs are posted at most five-mile points.

When approaching the dam, stay to the right. Water flows over the dam, and people have drowned in its hydraulic. A portage trail is to the right of the lock.

8	Huske Lock access on Glengerry Hill Rd. (Bladen Co. 1355) to Tar Heel Ferry Road (Bladen Co. 1316) access		
Difficulty A		**Width** 150–175 ft	
Distance 7.0 mi		**Gradient** 0 ft/mi	
Scenery A		**Map** page 64	

Gauge USGS *Cape Fear River at Wilm O Huske Lock near Tarheel.* Always above minimum. This section is in the backwater of Lock and Dam #2.

Notes There is a boat ramp at Huske Lock operated by the Corps of Engineers.

At Tar Heel Ferry Road bridge, a Wildlife boating access is upstream left. It is reached via a small service road (Wildlife Landing Drive) connecting with Tar Heel Ferry Road, 0.8 miles east of the river.

Little development is seen on this section, but the tree buffer is thin at times, and fishing boats are common. The banks range from 10–30 feet.

9	Tar Heel Ferry Road (Bladen Co. 1316) access to US 701 access at Elizabethtown		
Difficulty A		**Width** 150–190 ft	
Distance 14.4 mi		**Gradient** 0 ft/mi	
Scenery A (85%), B (15%)		**Map** page 64	

Gauge See Section 8.

Notes See the previous section about the Tar Heel Ferry Road access.

A Wildlife boating access is at US 701.

Many cypress knees are on the right bank (mi 2.2), and farther downstream, cypress trees have Spanish moss.

A creek (mi 3.7) entering from the right has built a sandbar 2 feet above the river. It is one of the few sandbar campsites on the lower Cape Fear. Sharks' teeth can be found in the creek.

The banks in this section range from a few feet to 100 feet above the river.

A wastewater disposal plant (mi 12.0) on the right can be heard but neither seen nor smelled.

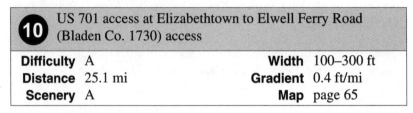

10 US 701 access at Elizabethtown to Elwell Ferry Road (Bladen Co. 1730) access		
Difficulty A	**Width**	100–300 ft
Distance 25.1 mi	**Gradient**	0.4 ft/mi
Scenery A	**Map**	page 65

Gauge USGS *Cape Fear River at Lock #1 near Kelly.* Always above minimum. This section is in the backwater of the Lock #2 and Lock #3 dams.

Notes The put-in and take-out are Wildlife boating access areas.

Instead of a bridge at Elwell Ferry Road, the river is crossed in one of the state's three remaining two-car ferryboats. The diesel-powered ferry uses a cable for guidance, saving a 20-mile trip to cross by the nearest bridge. The boat ramp is on the right (west) bank.

When approaching Lock and Dam #2 (mi 1.7), stay to the right. Water flows over the dam, and people have drowned in its hydraulic. A portage trail is to the right of the lock. See Section 7 for information about paddling through the lock. The Lock and Dam #2 office telephone is 910-862-2347.

This section can be shortened and the lock bypassed by starting at the boat ramp (mi 1.9) below the lock and dam. The ramp is off NC 87 at the end of Lock #2 Road (Bladen Co. 1703).

Where the river flows to the north for a mile, an abrupt right turn to the south marks Big Sugar Loaf (mi 7.2), a pure sandbank on the right. The upstream end rises 20 feet above the river, and a sandbar extends 300 feet downstream. This is a prime campsite, but in good weather, and especially on weekends, solitude is unlikely. It is a popular spot for people arriving by motorboat to fish and camp.

Across from Big Sugar Loaf, the left bank rises up to 30 feet and is always wet. Ground water moving down through sand hits the hard clay layers and then moves laterally until coming to the cut made by the river. Here it weeps out, and in a few places water is concentrated into springs falling to the river.

Walkers Bluff (mi 13.0) rises over 75 feet above the river and is home to large pines. It also displays well-exposed clay and sand layers of different geological periods.

At the take-out, watch out for the ferry and cables which cross the river.

11 Elwell Ferry Road (Bladen Co. 1730) access to Lock #1 Road (Bladen Co. 1734) access			
Difficulty A		**Width** 160–300 ft	
Distance 8.7 mi		**Gradient** 0 ft/mi	
Scenery A		**Map** page 65	

Gauge USGS *Cape Fear River at Lock #1 near Kelly.* Always above minimum. This section is in the backwater of the Lock and Dam #1.

Notes See the previous section about the Elwell Ferry Road access.

A boat ramp at Lock #1 is managed by the Corps of Engineers.

This section winds through farmland, and the banks are lower than in most of the upstream sections.

When approaching Lock and Dam #1, stay to the right. Water flows over the dam, and people have drowned in its hydraulic. Take out at the portage trail to the right of the lock.

If proceeding on to the next section, see Section 7 for information about paddling through the lock. The Lock and Dam #1 office telephone is 910-655-2605.

12 Lock #1 Road (Bladen Co. 1734) access to Riegel Course Road (Columbus Co. 1816) access			
Difficulty A		**Width** 150–200 ft	
Distance 8.1 mi		**Gradient** 0 ft/mi	
Scenery A (50%), B (50%)		**Map** page 66	

Gauge USGS *Cape Fear River at Lock #1 near Kelly.* Always above minimum. This is the beginning of the tidal part of the river.

Notes A boat ramp at Lock #1 is managed by the Corps of Engineers.

The Riegel Course Road access is managed by Columbus County. To reach it, take Riegel Course Road past the golf course and continue to the river.

NC 11 (mi 2.1) is the only bridge between Elizabethtown and Wilmington.

International Paper Company's Riegelwood mill can be heard for over a mile and seen a half-mile before reaching it at the take-out.

13	Riegel Course Road (Columbus Co. 1816) access to Dram Tree Park access in Wilmington		
Difficulty A		**Width**	140–600 ft
Distance 26.1 mi		**Gradient**	0 ft/mi
Scenery A (75%), B (15%), C (10%)		**Map**	page 66

Gauge USGS *Cape Fear River at Lock #1 near Kelly.* Always above minimum. Tides range from about 2 feet at the beginning of this section up to 5.5 feet in Wilmington. Near the confluence with the Black River, the tides are about 2.5 hours delayed from Wilmington tides. Wind can be a problem. Plan this trip according to tide tables and wind predictions.

Notes See the previous section about the Riegel Course Road access.

The Dram Tree Park access is managed by Wilmington Parks and Recreation. It is upstream left of the US 17 bridge. US 74/76/421 also pass over this bridge. From Third Street (Business US 17) turn on Castle Street toward the river (west). After crossing South Front Street, Dram Tree Park is one block ahead.

The sounds of the paper mill at the put-in can be heard in the first few miles.

There are many places where the original river channel makes a loop for more than a mile and comes back to a point less than a half-mile away from the start of the loop. To assist navigation, channels were dug across the loops to straighten the river. The loops remain, and paddling them rather than the shortcuts adds almost 4 miles, making this section 30 miles long.

Because of the distance, this section is usually done as an overnight camper, but finding a dry campsite becomes increasingly difficult downstream as the river flows into marshes. Lyon Thoroughfare (mi 6.1) enters from the left and connects with the Black River. Land on the left bank, Roan Island, has some dry ground but is a jungle of trees and vines. If a campsite has not been found by the confluence with the Black River (mi 11.7), go back upstream and find one. It is very swampy from here down.

Near where the Black River joins, there is an industrial plant on the right. Little of it can be seen, but it can be heard long before reaching it.

Signs of the Cape Fear estuary start to show downstream. Saw grass is abundant, fiddler crabs roam over mud flats, ospreys dive for fish, and alligators are often seen.

Large smokestacks (mi 19.6) signal the approach to the development near Wilmington. After going under a railroad bridge (mi 22.3), stay to the left. The channel to the right, Brunswick River, leads back to the Cape Fear River below Wilmington.

After passing the US 421/NC 133 bridge (mi 25.0), the Northeast Cape Fear joins from the left. Paddle past the waterfront development of Wilmington, Battleship North Carolina, and take out at Dram Tree Park, upstream left of the bridge.

Camping at the end of Big Sugar Loaf
Cape Fear River, Section 10

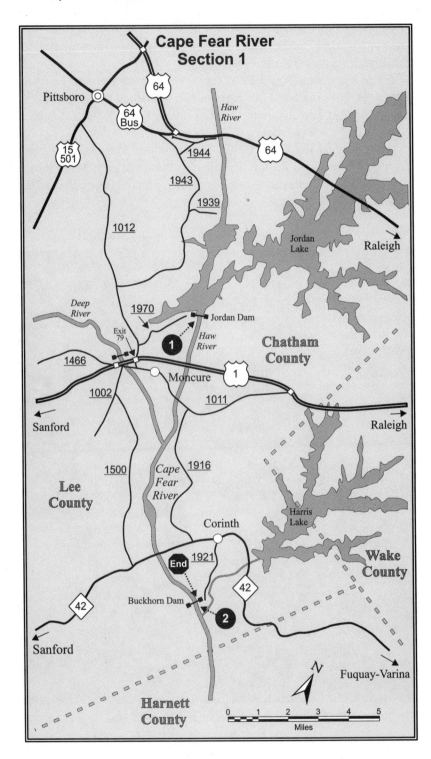

Cape Fear Basin

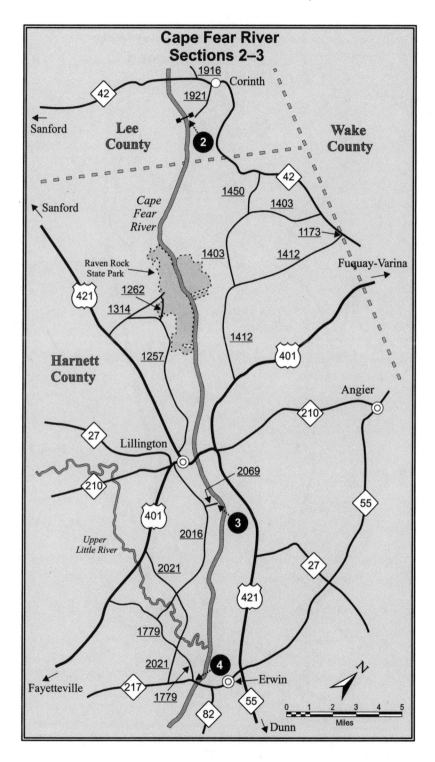

**Cape Fear River
Sections 2–3**

1916

Corinth

42

1921

Sanford

**Lee
County**

2

**Wake
County**

42

1450

1403

*Cape
Fear
River*

1173

1403

1412

Raven Rock
State Park

Fuquay-Varina

Sanford

421

1262

1314

1412

**Harnett
County**

1257

401

Angier

210

27

Lillington

55

210

2069

401

3

*Upper
Little River*

2016

27

2021

421

1779

2021

Erwin

Fayetteville

217

1779

4

55

82

Dunn

0 1 2 3 4 5
Miles

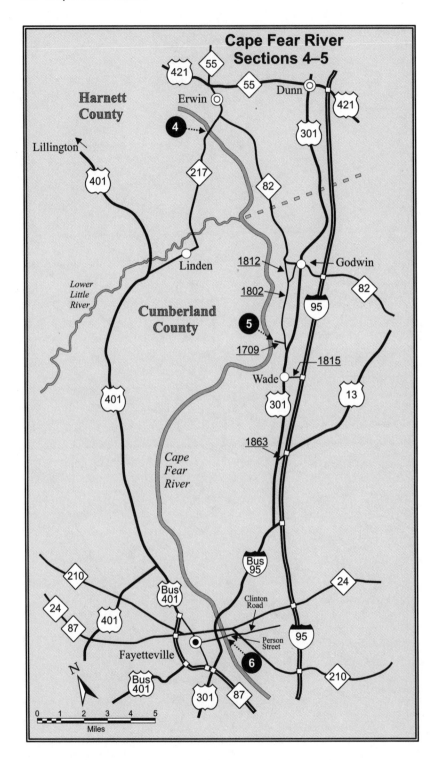

Cape Fear Basin

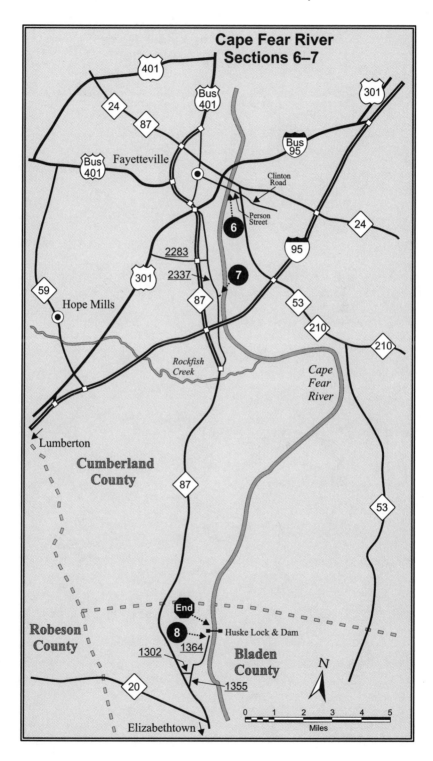

Cape Fear River
Sections 6–7

Clinton Road

Person Street

6

7

2283

2337

Fayetteville

Hope Mills

Rockfish Creek

Cape Fear River

Lumberton

Cumberland County

End

8

Huske Lock & Dam

1302

1364

Bladen County

1355

Robeson County

Elizabethtown

N

0 1 2 3 4 5
Miles

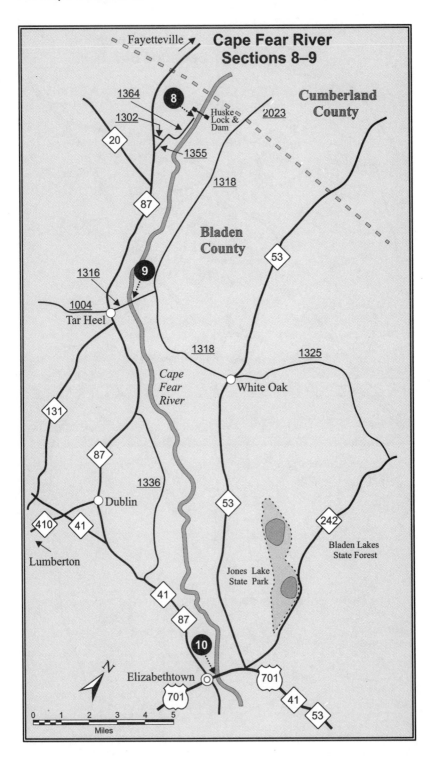

Cape Fear Basin

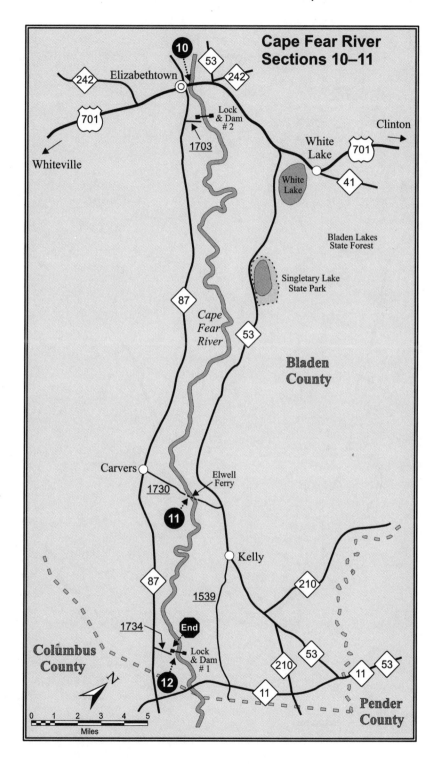

Cape Fear River
Sections 10–11

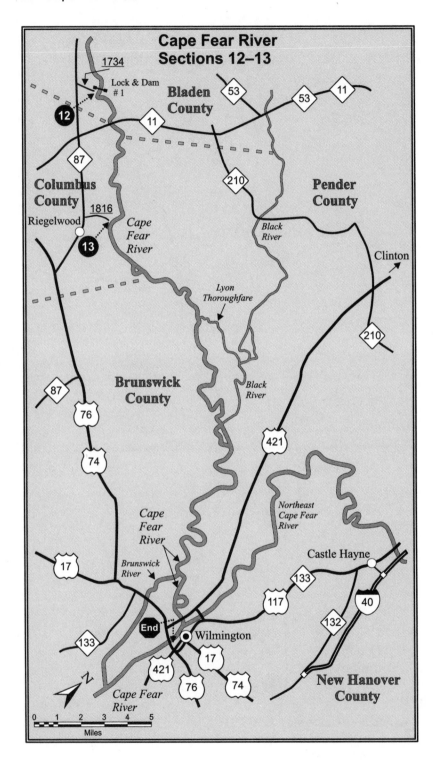

Cape Fear Basin

Deep River

Counties   Randolph, Moore, Lee, Chatham

Topos   Randleman, Grays Chapel, Ramseur, Coleridge, Bennett, Robbins, Putnam, White Hill, Goldston, Colon, Moncure, Merry Oaks

The Deep River begins west of Greensboro and above High Point. It flows southeast passing near Asheboro and turning east near High Falls, one of many small mill towns built on the banks of the Deep. It forms the border between Chatham and Lee Counties, and below Moncure the Deep meets the Haw to form the Cape Fear.

In the 87 miles of paddling sections described from Worthville to Moncure, there are eight intact dams requiring portage. Many of them are used today to generate hydroelectric power.

Iron and coal deposits along the Deep River in Chatham and Lee Counties were known to early settlers in the 1700s. Plans were made to exploit these deposits using locks and dams to make the river navigable down to the Cape Fear and on to the coast. The minerals proved to be difficult to extract in quantity, and making the river navigable so far upstream was beyond the resources available. Ruins of locks, dams, and furnaces can still be seen on the river.

 Worthville Road (Randolph Co. 2122) bridge to Loflin Pond Road (Randolph Co. 2221) bridge at Cedar Falls

Difficulty II–III	**Width** 70–350 ft
Distance 6.2 mi	**Gradient** 8.9 ft/mi
Scenery A (30%), B (70%)	**Map** page 77

Gauge USGS *Deep River at Ramseur*. Minimum is 180 cfs (1.4 ft). The rapids at Cedar Falls increase to Class IV as flow goes above 600 cfs (2.5 ft).

Notes The put-in is 100 yards below the Worthville Dam and is in the backwater of the next dam at Central Falls.

Old Liberty Road (Randolph Co. 2261) (mi 3.0) can be used as a put-in to eliminate some flatwater and combine the remainder of this section with the next section for a 7.5-mile run.

Stay back from the 25-foot high Central Falls Dam (mi 4.5). Portage on the left side around the hydroelectric building. A long rope is useful to help lower boats down the steep bank.

Downstream of the dam are Class I rapids and a Class II, followed by the backwater of the next dam.

Portage the Cedar Falls Dam (mi 5.8) on the right. The mill is on the left. The best of the Deep River whitewater is in the next quarter-mile where it drops 20 feet (80 ft/mi) through a boulder garden with ledges. There is little space between rapids. The best route depends on water level, but it is usually to the center, then left, and back toward the right side for the steepest ledge. Scout from the right bank. Downstream, the gradient slows and the route becomes more obvious.

2 Loflin Pond Road (Randolph Co. 2221) bridge at Cedar Falls to US 64 access at Ramseur			
Difficulty I–II		**Width** 90–500 ft	
Distance 4.3 mi		**Gradient** 16.3 ft/mi	
Scenery A (50%), B (50%)		**Map** page 77	

Gauge USGS *Deep River at Ramseur*. Estimated minimum is 180 cfs (1.4 ft).

Notes A Wildlife boating access is at US 64. The ramp is on Sandy Creek, 100 feet upstream from the Deep River.

There are several Class I–II rapids before reaching the 20-foot dam (mi 2.0) at Franklinville. Portage on the right where there is an eroded path from high water. The boulders and rugged terrain make one wonder what rapids were covered by this dam.

Water passing through the dam gates is returned to the main river channel on the left, downstream of Andrew Hunter Road (Randolph Co. 2235) bridge (mi 2.2). A rapid dropping 2 feet just under the bridge may be too low, depending on the amount of water being diverted into the left side of the river.

On the right bank, a 60-foot sloping rock outcropping is Faith Rock (mi 2.4), named for a daring escape on horseback in 1782. Andrew Hunter eluded his British Loyalist pursuers by riding his horse down the rock to a ledge where he leaped his horse into the turbulent river to reach safety on the other side.

A high pedestrian bridge (mi 2.5) provides access to the right bank and trail to Faith Rock. The bridge begins on the left bank at the upper end of Franklinville's Riverside Park. A parking lot off NC 22 is at the downstream end (mi 2.7) of the park, and it offers easy river access.

A small dam (mi 2.8) is broken out on the left. Maneuvering is required to work from left to right in Class I–II rapids around islands and remnants of old structures.

Just before seeing US 64, there are small boulders (mi 3.7) in the river creating Class I$^+$ rapids for a few hundred feet.

After passing under US 64 (mi 4.2), the take-out is 0.1 miles downstream and to the left, up Sandy Creek.

3 US 64 access at Ramseur to NC 42 bridge at Coleridge		
Difficulty I–II	**Width** 80–350 ft	
Distance 9.1 mi	**Gradient** 5.3 ft/mi	
Scenery A (55%), B (45%)	**Map** page 77	

Gauge USGS *Deep River at Ramseur.* Estimated minimum is 150 cfs (1.3 ft).

Notes See the previous section about the US 64 access.

Brooklyn City Park (mi 1.0) is on the right bank and can be used as an alternative put-in. It is reached from Leonard Park Street off Brooklyn Avenue (Randolph Co. 2615).

Portage the 10-foot Ramseur Dam (mi 1.1) on the right. Water flows through a 6-foot wide slot in the dam on the left side. It may be tempting to run it, but rocks with imbedded metal can be seen at low flows.

There is little water below the dam on the right side because islands channel water down the left side. The left side has a Class II rapid a few hundred feet below the dam.

Past the Brooklyn Avenue bridge (mi 1.4), there are islands and Class I rapids down to the gauge on the right bank (mi 1.6).

Class I rapids and an occasional Class II are encountered down to the Hinshaw Town Road (Randolph Co. 2656) bridge (mi 6.4).

The rapids cease downstream of a large island (mi 7.5) where the backwater of the Coleridge Dam begins.

The take-out is downstream right of the NC 42 bridge.

For paddlers continuing to the next section, the Coleridge Dam is 0.2 miles downstream of the bridge. Portage on the right side, up a small hill to a path leading to the river, 100 feet beyond the dam. There are small rapids here, but water may be low for the next 0.1 miles until water used by the hydroelectric plant rejoins the river.

> **4** NC 22 mill at Coleridge to N. Howard Mill Road (Moore Co. 1456) bridge

Difficulty I–II	**Width** 30–150 ft
Distance 12.7 mi	**Gradient** 4.3 ft/mi
Scenery A	**Map** page 78

Gauge See Section 3.

Notes The put-in is off NC 22, downstream left of the mill. From the small parking area, carry boats 50 feet downstream. The parking area is owned by the mill, but paddlers have been allowed to use it.

At the N. Howard Mill Road bridge, there is a gate to farmland on upstream left. Ask for permission at the adjacent house to use this property for access. Close the gate to keep in cattle, carry boats, and do not drive on the grass. Ask permission to park at the army surplus store across the road.

Many boulders and small ledges create Class I–II rapids in the first few miles. The rapids become less frequent farther downstream.

A small channel (mi 3.1) splits off to the right behind a large island. Several more channels split to the right leaving the left channel low and only 30 feet wide until all channels reunite (mi 3.5).

Downstream of Bennett Road (Randolph Co. 1002) (mi 7.8), there are a few Class I rapids before reaching the ruins of Howard's Milldam (mi 12.5), a Class II. At low water, it can be run on the left side. The drop is a few feet over a run of 25 feet.

> **5** N. Howard Mill Road (Moore Co. 1456) bridge to NC 22 bridge at High Falls

Difficulty I–II, and one II$^+$	**Width** 40–800 ft
Distance 6.8 mi	**Gradient** 6.6 ft/mi
Scenery A (60%), B (40%)	**Map** page 78

Gauge USGS *Deep River at Ramseur.* Estimated minimum is 200 cfs (1.5 ft).

Notes See the previous section about access at N. Howard Mill Road.

At the NC 22 bridge, guardrails prevent parking on the right side of the river. Upstream left of the bridge, Deep River Mill's gate is closed to traffic, but paddlers have been permitted to carry boats the quarter-mile between the upstream dam area and the gate.

It is possible to take out downstream left of NC 22 off River Road (Moore Co. 1606), but the bank drops abruptly and there is no path. It is only a thicket of briars and bushes. A narrow channel between the bank and a long island carries outflow from the hydroelectric plant. Paddling downstream on the right side of the island requires portaging over the island or going to the island's end and paddling upstream in strong current for 300 feet.

It is best to read the description below about portaging the dam, inspect the paths to the road, and evaluate water conditions before deciding where to take out.

At a left bend (mi 1.2), islands begin, and Class I–II rapids are in the next mile.

A horizon line (mi 2.5) marks the end of Johnson's Ford Rapid, a Class II⁺, where the river drops 5–6 feet over about 60 feet. The final drop is not abrupt but should be scouted. Downed trees can lodge in this area. It is also possible to paddle to the left side of small islands where the drop is a bit more gradual.

Bear Creek (mi 3.0) enters from the right, and the Deep River is flatwater until reaching the downstream dam.

High Falls Dam (mi 6.5) is 10–15 feet high and 800 feet wide. The portage on the right side is over large rock slabs and boulders. Taking out on the left side, upstream of the sluice gates, requires walking a quarter-mile to NC 22. Except at high levels, water does not flow over the dam. Toward the left side, it is possible to climb onto the top of the dam, lower boats over it, and climb down using rocks for footing. Use caution here because a fall would be onto rock.

There are a few Class II rapids and islands below the dam. Work toward the left side if taking out near the NC 22 bridge.

6	NC 22 bridge at High Falls to Glendon-Carthage Road (Moore Co. 1006) bridge at Glendon		
Difficulty I–II⁻		**Width** 60–500 ft	
Distance 10.5 mi		**Gradient** 4.1 ft/mi	
Scenery A		**Map** page 78	

Gauge USGS *Deep River at Ramseur*. Minimum is 110 cfs (1.1 ft). The gauge is over 30 miles upstream of this section, and water at the gauge takes over a half-day to reach the put-in.

Notes See the previous section about access at NC 22. Use downstream left of the NC 22 bridge off River Road or put in a quarter-mile upstream near the dam. Walk past the mill gate about 400 feet to a path to the left where a small bridge crosses the sluice. This path leads up the island and down to a beach below the dam. Putting in here allows running Class I–II rapids before reaching the bridge.

Getting to the river at the Glendon-Carthage Road bridge is difficult. There is little parking space, and guardrails are only a nuisance compared to the 70-foot steep bank on the right. A long rope is useful here. The left bank is less steep but is posted and has a barbed-wire fence.

The banks often rise to over 100 feet, and many long islands split the river into channels. There are more than a dozen small rapids scattered down this section. The first half of the trip has ten rapids, with a few reaching Class II⁻.

7	Glendon-Carthage Road (Moore Co. 1006) bridge at Glendon to Carbonton access near NC 42 bridge		
Difficulty A, and one I		**Width** 80–120 ft	
Distance 11.1 mi		**Gradient** 0.2 ft/mi	
Scenery A		**Map** page 78	

Gauge USGS *Deep River at Moncure*. Always above minimum.

Notes See the previous section about Glendon-Carthage Road.

A Wildlife boating access is 0.3 miles upstream left of the NC 42 bridge at Carbonton. A road (no number or name) near the railroad track leads to the boat ramp.

The only rapid (mi 0.1) is just past the bridge. The backwater of the Carbonton Dam below the take-out makes this run almost all flatwater.

The Carbonton Road (Moore Co. 1621) bridge (mi 5.2) is near the middle of a large horseshoe bend, and upstream left is the ground of House in the Horseshoe, a historic site. The home was built in 1772 and has scars and bullet holes from a skirmish during the Revolutionary War.

8	Carbonton access near NC 42 bridge to Plank Road (Chatham Co. 1007) access at Gulf		
Difficulty A–I		**Width** 65–100 ft	
Distance 6.5 mi		**Gradient** 3.1 ft/mi	
Scenery A (70%), B (30%)		**Map** page 79	

Gauge See Section 7.

Notes See the previous section about the Carbonton access.

Downstream left of the Plank Road bridge, just off US 421, is known as McIver Landing. It is Triangle Land Conservancy property and includes a boat access.

After passing under NC 42 (mi 0.3), paddle to the right bank to portage the 15-foot Carbonton Dam (mi 0.4). It is possible to put in here and avoid this portage. A dirt road leads from NC 42 to downstream right of the dam.

There are a few Class I rapids in this section, and some appear to have been part of old navigation locks or mills.

The banks are up to 25 feet, and rocks can be seen at low water on the banks near the riverbed.

From the left bank (mi. 1.4) and extending for the next 2.6 miles is the La Grange Riparian Reserve, a Triangle Land Conservancy property. It includes 308 acres and was part of the La Grange farm, dating from the 1700s. The protected land ends where the river goes through a right turn, reversing direction from northwest to southeast.

9	Plank Road (Chatham Co. 1007) access at Gulf to Deep River Park access off R. Jordan Road (Chatham Co. 2145)		
Difficulty A–I		**Width** 80–100 ft	
Distance 6.3 mi		**Gradient** 0.9 ft/mi	
Scenery A		**Map** page 79	

Gauge See Section 7.

Notes See the previous section about the Plank Road access.

The Deep River Park access is upstream left of the Rosser Road (Chatham Co. 2153) bridge. Its entrance is off R. Jordan Road.

Rock from the left bank (mi 0.3) extends into the river and the channel narrows, creating a Class I rapid under an overhanging willow tree.

US 421 (mi 4.2) is not often used for river access because of guardrails and high banks. Downed trees occasionally collect at the bridge piers and block the route.

At two railroad bridges (mi 5.3), Cumnock is off the right bank. It was known as Egypt in the 1800s and was the site of a large coal mine.

At the Deep River Park take-out, historic Camelback Bridge (mi 6.3) spans the river. It was once part of the Lillington bridge over the Cape Fear in the early 1900s. It now serves as a pedestrian bridge. Steps for boat access are downstream left of the bridge.

> ⑩ Deep River Park access off R. Jordan Road (Chatham Co. 2145) to US 15/501 bridge

Difficulty A, and one I⁺   **Width** 40–150 ft
Distance 5.8 mi   **Gradient** 0.9 ft/mi
Scenery A   **Map** page 79

Gauge See Section 7.

Notes See the previous section about the Deep River Park access.

The only rapid (mi 2.7) is at an old navigation lock at the end of a left bend. Water drops over the dam's rocks, making a sloping 1-foot drop on the left side.

The impressive remains of Endor Iron Furnace (mi 3.0) are on the right. It was named after the Bible's Witch of Endor. The bank is 15 feet high, and the furnace is behind trees, about 100 feet back, nestled next to a bluff. It can only be seen from the river when the leaves have fallen, and even then it is easy to miss. The Confederates erected this 35-foot high stone structure to smelt iron ore. The ore was brought upriver by barge through navigation locks from the Cape Fear River, a few miles downstream of Buckhorn Dam.

The furnace and 425 acres of surrounding land, including about 3.5 miles of stream frontage, have been preserved. The Triangle Land Conservancy manages the property for the state, and Lee County has plans to manage the area around the furnace.

In a left bend (mi 4.1), the river heads north, and for the next half-mile the right bank rises to 100 feet with rock outcroppings.

> ⑪ US 15/501 bridge to Old US 1 (Lee Co. 1466) bridge at Moncure

Difficulty I–II   **Width** 90–800 ft
Distance 7.9 mi   **Gradient** 5.1 ft/mi
Scenery A (75%), B (25%)   **Map** page 79

Gauge USGS *Deep River at Moncure*. Minimum is 200 cfs (1.6 ft) except for the short stretch of rapids below the left side of the dam near US 1, where the estimated minimum is 400 cfs (1.9 ft).

Notes Upstream right of the Old US 1 bridge can be used for a take-out. A dirt drive leads upstream through the woods to a ramp, which was used by an old marina. It is on private property but is not posted, and boaters have been using the ramp.

After a small rapid (mi 0.7), it is flatwater until reaching the Rocky River on the left (mi 3.8). A 228-acre tract between the Deep and Rocky Rivers is part of the White Pines Nature Preserve. The terrain here rises 200 feet above the river. See the Rocky River, Section 4 (page 134).

Downstream of the confluence with the Rocky River, there are many Class I–II rapids through rock gardens and over small ledges. Below the USGS gauge (mi 6.1) on the right, rapids are fairly constant for 0.7 miles.

Stay back from the 15-foot Lockville Dam (mi 7.3). Water flows over the dam, and it is especially dangerous at high flows. The dam can be portaged right or left.

The right side portage requires going up a steep bank and then several hundred feet downstream to put in below rocks. A long rope is useful for getting boats up the bank. At high flows, large waves are between the dam and US 1 bridge (mi 7.6).

Paddling to the left side above the dam can be difficult because the area collects a tremendous number of downed trees. At high flows, a large eddy becomes a magnet for flotsam. On the left bank, a sluice takes water into the old hydroelectric building downstream. This area is posted and should not be entered. Stay away from the gates letting water into the sluice. The right bank of the sluice is a large island. Between the sluice and the left side of the dam is a dirt embankment rising about 20 feet above the dam. It is possible to go up the embankment to a flat area on top, then down the backside to the island. There are rapids in constricted areas between islands before reaching the US 1 bridge (mi 7.6). Watch for strainers.

To continue beyond the take-out, it is 2.7 miles in the backwater of Buckhorn Dam before reaching the confluence with the Haw River, where the Cape Fear begins. See the Cape Fear River, Section 1 (page 49).

■

And the river bank talks of the waters of March
It's the end of all strain, it's the joy in your heart
   —Antonio Carlos Jobim, *Waters of March* (song, 1972)

Paul Ferguson at Endor Iron Furnace
Deep River, Section 10

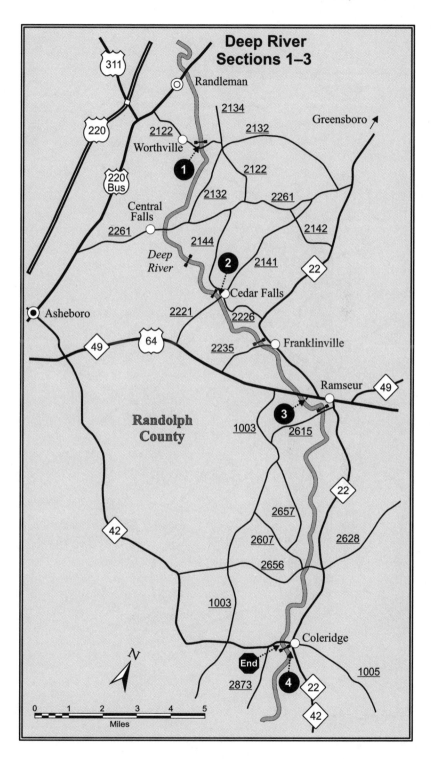

**Deep River
Sections 1–3**

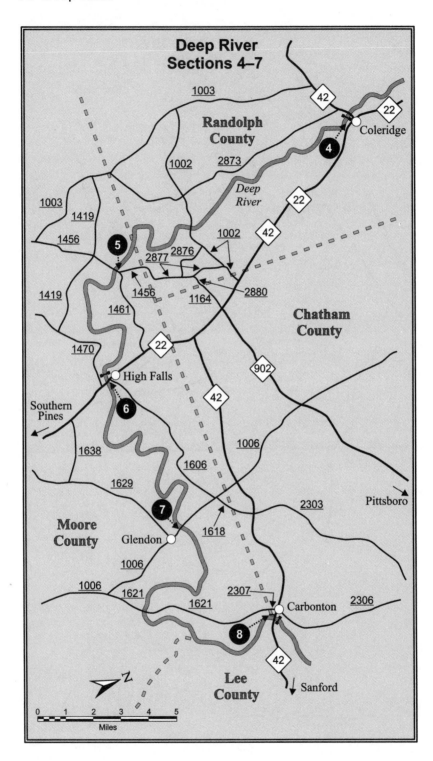

Cape Fear Basin

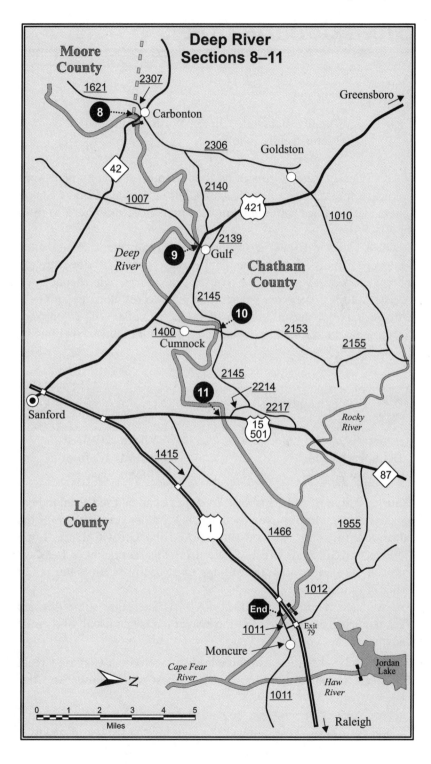

Great Coharie Creek

County	Sampson
Topos	Timothy, Bearskin, Clinton North, Bonnetsville, Clinton South, Ingold

Great Coharie Creek begins in northern Sampson County and flows south, passing a few miles west of Clinton. It adds Little Coharie Creek, and 15 miles south of Clinton, it joins Six Runs Creek to form the Black River.

Great Coharie Creek is swampy in its headwaters, as are most Sampson County rivers. The banks rise somewhat downstream, where it becomes a blackwater river confined to a single channel.

The Nature Conservancy purchased 4,858 acres along upper Great Coharie Creek, preserving 16 continuous miles of floodplain, swamps, and bottomland. The protected corridor includes Sections 1–3 described below.

---

1 Keener Road (Sampson Co. 1746) bridge to US 421 bridge

Difficulty A		**Width**	20–55 ft
Distance 9.3 mi		**Gradient**	1.9 ft/mi
Scenery A		**Map**	page 84

Gauge USGS *Black River near Tomahawk* can be used as an indicator of water conditions even though it is 45 miles downstream of the put-in and measures the combined flow from Great Coharie, Little Coharie, and Six Runs Creeks. Water from this section takes 1–2 days to reach the gauge, making readings most useful when water is not rising or falling rapidly.

Estimated minimum is 700 cfs (6.0 ft). There are some downed trees requiring lifting over, but the beaver dams can usually be run at this minimum.

Notes At US 421 there are three bridges over Great Coharie Creek. The clearest channel is at the bridge farthest south (closest to Clinton).

The creek is narrow just beyond the put-in. Long, green, hairy, underwater weeds wave in the current, giving the feeling of paddling in an aquarium. There are few trees beyond a thin buffer along the banks. Many channels connect and split off. The route to choose is usually the one with evidence of downed trees having been cut.

A large farm (mi 3.6) with many buildings is a quarter-mile off to the left where land rises 50 feet. It is one of the few signs of development visible in this section.

A large blue heron rookery (mi 4.6) was seen. Rookeries are common sights in the swampy areas of Sampson County rivers.

Downstream, beaver dams are more frequent and aquatic weeds on the surface impede paddling.

The water flows through stands of trees (mi 6.1) for the next mile, and the closed-in swamp-forest contrasts with the rest of this more open section.

2 US 421 bridge to NC 24 bridge near Clinton	
Difficulty A	**Width** 10–70 ft
Distance 4.6 mi	**Gradient** 2.6 ft/mi
Scenery A	**Map** page 84

Gauge See Section 1.

The gauge is 35 miles downstream. Estimated minimum is 550 cfs (5.2 ft). There are some downed trees requiring lifting over, but the beaver dams can usually be run at this minimum. Aquatic weeds are dense in areas.

Notes See the previous section about US 421.

Beaver dams back up water to the put-in, and there are many dead trees in the ponds.

Five Bridge Road (Sampson Co. 1311) (mi 2.0) can be used for access.

A blue heron rookery (mi 2.9), larger than the one mentioned in Section 1, was seen in an old tree near the main channel.

Near power lines (mi 4.1), water pennywort and alligator weed are dense enough to make paddling difficult. Allow extra time for this trip.

> **3** NC 24 bridge near Clinton to Boykin Bridge Road (Sampson Co. 1214) bridge

Difficulty A	**Width** 35–70 ft
Distance 6.1 mi	**Gradient** 2.5 ft/mi
Scenery A	**Map** page 84

Gauge See Section 1.

The gauge is 31 miles downstream. Estimated minimum is 550 cfs (5.2 ft). There are some downed trees requiring lifting over, but the beaver dams can usually be run at this minimum. Aquatic weeds are dense in areas.

Notes Beaver dams and aquatic weeds continue from the previous section. The weeds cause the most problem in parts of the first mile. Be prepared to turn back if new growth blocks too much of the route.

The only sign of development is a fence and private road (mi 1.9) on the left.

Some cypress trees have a diameter greater than 3 feet. There is little dry ground until the second half of this section where banks rise up to a few feet, and the character changes from swamp to a blackwater creek.

> **4** Boykin Bridge Road (Sampson Co. 1214) bridge to Wright Bridge Road (Sampson Co. 1206) bridge

Difficulty A	**Width** 25–70 ft
Distance 9.2 mi	**Gradient** 2.3 ft/mi
Scenery A	**Map** page 84

Gauge See Section 1.

The gauge is 25 miles downstream. Estimated minimum is 500 cfs (4.9 ft). Downed trees become an increasing problem at lower water levels.

Notes The banks are typically a few feet high, and there are several drainage channels entering the creek. Some appear to be connected to farm ponds.

Trees make a canopy over the creek in the beginning of this section.

A large farm (mi 2.3) can be seen on the right. The farmhouse is over a half-mile away where the land rises 50 feet.

Ebenezer Forest Road (Sampson Co. 1211) (mi 6.1) can be used to shorten this run. Downstream, there are often few trees behind a thin buffer along the banks.

5 Wright Bridge Road (Sampson Co. 1206) bridge to NC 903 (Sampson Co. 1003) bridge

Difficulty A		**Width** 45–70 ft	
Distance 8.8 mi		**Gradient** 1.3 ft/mi	
Scenery A		**Map** page 84	

Gauge See Section 1.

The gauge is 16 miles downstream. Estimated minimum is 500 cfs (4.9 ft). Downed trees become an increasing problem at lower water levels.

Notes It is also possible to put in on Little Coharie Creek at Riley Town Road (Sampson Co. 1207), where access is a little easier than at Wright Bridge Road. It is 0.4 miles to reach Great Coharie Creek.

Little Coharie Creek (mi 0.3) joins from the right, adding water and width to the run below.

The banks are up to 10 feet, and some large cypress trees are draped with Spanish moss. Parts of the river are covered by a tree canopy. There are a few houses and areas of cleared land.

US 701 (mi 1.9) can be used for access.

Len Felton stuck in weeds at low water
Six Runs Creek, Section 1

Cape Fear Basin

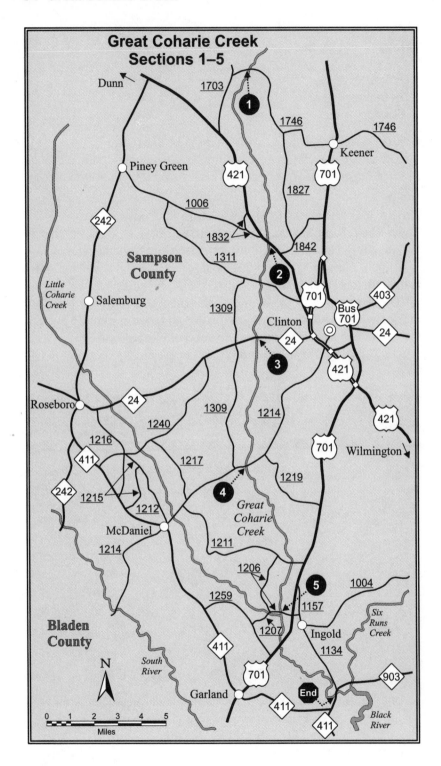

Great Coharie Creek
Sections 1–5

Cape Fear Basin

Haw River

Counties   Alamance, Orange, Chatham

Topos   Ossipee, Lake Burlington, Burlington, Mebane, Saxapahaw, White Cross, Bynum, Silk Hope, Farrington, Merry Oaks

The Haw River begins near Kernersville and flows northeast before turning south below Reidsville. Many of the towns on its southerly course grew from the industry provided by mills. Altamahaw, Glencoe, Burlington, Swepsonville, Saxapahaw, and Bynum were all centered around mills. From just above Altamahaw to Bynum, there are five dams large enough to require portaging, and several smaller or broken dams that can be run depending on conditions.

The most recent dam on the Haw is Jordan Dam, but less than 5 miles of the Haw is lake. Most of Jordan Lake backs up into the flatter valley of New Hope Creek. Downstream of Jordan Dam where the Haw meets the Deep, the Cape Fear begins its journey to the sea.

The Haw River has suffered from development. In the 1970s the water often ran denim-blue from dyes discharged. In more recent years, there have been problems with city wastewater treatment plants not meeting standards and releasing untreated water when floods occur.

The Haw River Assembly was formed in 1982 to restore and protect the beauty and health of the Haw River and Jordan Lake. Its main efforts are concentrated in education and monitoring. The group purchased four acres of marsh north of Kernersville that surround the source of the Haw and gave the land to the Piedmont Land Conservancy for preservation and management.

The Haw River is popular for paddling because of its variety of scenery, whitewater, and proximity to the Triangle and Triad population centers. Many rivers are dangerous during high water levels, but the Haw is especially so. Islands and boulders are numerous on many sections. Powerful currents flow over tree-covered islands creating many strainers. There have been deaths and high profile helicopter rescues.

With increased development, there has been pressure on many of the old access points. The Carolina Canoe Club has worked to improve access in the Chatham County sections. It has been largely through the diligent efforts of Cleo Smith that formal access areas have been established. In Alamance County, Graham Parks and Recreation established an access at NC 54, and Mike Holland has worked on creating access areas and a Haw River Trail.

1	NC 87 bridge at Altamahaw to NC 62 bridge at Glencoe	
Difficulty I–II		**Width** 40–200 ft
Distance 8.2 mi		**Gradient** 7.0 ft/mi
Scenery B		**Map** page 96

Gauge USGS *Haw River at Haw River*. Estimated minimum is 350 cfs (2.7 ft). This gauge is about 13 miles downstream of the put-in and may not reflect water conditions near the put-in.

Reedy Fork joins the Haw River 1.2 miles downstream of NC 87. Its watershed includes Buffalo Creek and is larger than the Haw River watershed above the confluence. The flows indicated by USGS gauges *Buffalo Creek near McLeansville* and *Reedy Fork near Gibsonville* added together give an approximation of the flow Reedy Fork delivers to the Haw.

Notes The Glencoe Mills area is owned by Preservation North Carolina, and the mill houses are available for restoration. The Glencoe Mills Dam is 0.4 miles upstream of the NC 62 bridge. There are take-out points upstream and downstream of the dam.

To take out upstream of the dam, take River Road (Alamance Co. 1600) at the NC 62 bridge. River Road goes upriver for 0.2 miles, passing the mill along the left bank. Where the road turns right to become Glencoe Street, go straight ahead on a gravel drive for 0.2 miles to a gate. Park outside the gate and walk 350 feet to the bank, 100 feet upstream left of the dam. If water conditions make getting close to the dam unsafe, there is a beach 700 feet farther upstream, off the old roadbed.

Downstream of the dam, just upstream right of the NC 62 bridge can be used for access. There is also a drive off River Road on private property, but it is not posted and has been used by paddlers.

At the put-in, a Class I rapid under the bridge can be used to judge if there is adequate water, but Glen Raven Mills diverts some water from the dam upstream of the put-in. The diverted water is returned 0.1 miles downstream of the put-in.

A rapid below Hub Mill Road (Alamance Co. 1561) bridge (mi 0.5) has a 2-foot drop on the left side of an island that formed a mill sluice. It is narrow and makes a turn, so make sure the channel is clear if running it. The right side of the island is a Class II rock garden.

Reedy Fork (mi 1.2) joins from the right and is wider than the Haw. There are several small rapids downstream, and the longest set is near an island (mi 1.8) where Class I–II rapids run for about 100 yards.

After Gerringer Mill Road (Alamance Co. 1530) (mi 2.7) and Burch Bridge Road (Alamance Co. 1530) (mi 5.2), a golf course is on the left bank.

Stonework (mi 6.6) on the left marks an old 2-foot dam across the river, which can be portaged on the right. It can be run at low water levels, but at higher water levels, it could present a hydraulic. Scout and portage if there is any doubt.

The backwaters of Glencoe Mills Dam are entered below the golf course dam.

Stay back, especially at high water, from the 12-foot Glencoe Mills Dam (mi 7.7). Portage it on the left side or use the left bank as a take-out.

There is a long series of Class I–II rapids between the dam and NC 62.

---

2 NC 62 bridge at Glencoe to NC 54 access near Graham

Difficulty I–II	**Width** 65–125 ft	
Distance 7.9 mi	**Gradient** 7.3 ft/mi	
Scenery A (25%), B (50%), C (25%)	**Map** page 96	

Gauge USGS *Haw River at Haw River.* Minimum is 280 cfs (2.5 ft).

Notes See the previous section about possible put-ins at NC 62 and River Road.

The access at NC 54 is downstream right of the bridge, and the entrance is from Cooper Road (Alamance Co. 2109). It is managed by Graham Parks and Recreation.

Just below the put-in, the river drops about 3 feet over 75 feet, creating Class I–II rapids. Rapids up to Class II continue past the large Copeland Fabric plant near the Hopedale Road (Alamance Co. 1712) bridge (mi 1.3) and extend to the head of a mile-long island (mi 2.3).

After passing US 70 (mi 4.2), the high Cone Mills smokestack can be seen downstream on the left. Adjacent to the mill buildings, a broken dam (mi 4.6) has a drop of about 3 feet over a 30-foot run. At low levels, the left side has the most water. Metal bolts still protrude from the debris. Scout this area because swimming could be dangerous.

NC 49 (mi 4.8) at the town of Haw River crosses below the dam rapid. It can be used as a put-in to provide a shorter run without rapids because the remaining portion of this section is fairly flat as it goes under I-40/85 (mi 6.4) and to NC 54 at the take-out.

3	NC 54 access to Boy Scout access at Saxapahaw Dam off Swepsonville-Saxapahaw Road (Alamance Co. 2158)		
Difficulty I–II		**Width** 80–500 ft	
Distance 7.7 mi		**Gradient** 2.9 ft/mi	
Scenery A (25%), B (75%)		**Map** page 96	

Gauge USGS *Haw River at Haw River.* Minimum is 220 cfs (2.3 ft).

Notes See the previous section about the NC 54 access.

The take-out is upstream left of Saxapahaw Dam. From the Community Center building upstream left of the Church Street (Alamance Co. 2171) bridge, take Swepsonville-Saxapahaw Road 0.1 miles and turn left into a small unmarked road. Go 0.1 miles to a gate leading into the Boy Scout camp. The gate is usually locked to keep out vehicles. A pier is 700 feet upstream of the gate and may be used as a take-out. Boats must be carried around the gate.

It is also possible to take out on the bank just downstream of the camp gate. A 75-foot path from the river is often muddy and covered in poison ivy.

There is no space for parking along the access road leading to the dam and camp. Parking is allowed behind the Community Center building.

There are a few Class I rapids down to the Swepsonville-Saxapahaw Road (Alamance Co. 2158) bridge (mi 1.8), and downstream are the remains of an old dam (mi 1.9).

The right bank, just upstream of the dam, can be used for boat access. It is reached from Boy Wood Road (Alamance Co. 2116). Going south on Boy Wood Road, go 0.3 miles past where Swepsonville-Saxapahaw Road connects. A "Powell-Bason Access" sign is 75 feet before guardrails begin. Steps and a trail lead to the river.

The dam can be portaged on the left or right. The Class II run over the dam's remains drops about 3 feet and has rocks, wooden posts, and metal bolts to avoid. It is often run toward the left, but scout to make sure there is a clear path well within your paddling ability. Some of the hazardous bolts are difficult to spot.

Alamance Creek (mi 2.5) enters from the right and joins the backwater of the high dam downstream.

Stay back from the 10-foot Swepsonville Dam (mi 3.1). The portage is not easy on either side. On the left side, water runs through a gate, and there is turbulence below with strainers in the outflow. To the left of the water flow is the old building which housed the hydroelectric turbines. The channel below it is dry and requires dragging down the channel bed before reaching the river. The Southwick Golf Course is on the right bank. Portaging here requires negotiating steep banks. It is best to inspect conditions on both sides before making a choice.

A Class II rapid is just below the dam. Use caution because rebar is embedded in some of the rocks. The remainder of this section is in the backwater of the Saxapahaw Dam at the take-out.

At the Boy Scout camp pier, a sign says "Danger - Dam Spillway Ahead - Mandatory Canoe Portage - No Boating Beyond This Point." Water flows over the dam at high water. Stay back from the dam and do not approach the water intakes on the left side.

4	Church Road (Alamance Co. 2171) bridge to East Greensboro-Chapel Hill Road (Alamance Co. 1005) bridge		
Difficulty I–II		**Width** 40–125 ft	
Distance 5.5 mi		**Gradient** 4.7 ft/mi	
Scenery A		**Map** page 97	

Gauge See Section 3.

Notes Church Road crosses the river at Saxapahaw where a large island divides the river into two channels. A bridge connects each side of the river to the island, and there is a break in the guardrails at the island on the downstream side. The island is private property, but access has been allowed for paddlers to put in. A cable blocks vehicle entry, leaving little space to stop and unload boats without interfering with bridge traffic. Put in on the left channel. The right channel is usually too low because water taken into the hydroelectric plant is released into the left channel.

Park behind the Community Center building, upstream left of the bridge. It is possible to put in behind the Community Center, but it is not recommended. The sluice here is narrow and carries the outflow from water used for power generation. It can be fast, and the steep bank is lined with riprap.

This section has little development near the river, and hills close to the banks rise up to 100 feet. Pastureland occasionally reaches the banks.

A few Class I rapids are encountered before reaching a large island (mi 2.5) which extends for 0.3 miles.

The best set of rapids (mi 3.3) begins as Class I ledges and builds to a couple of Class II ledges (mi 3.5), with the last one dropping 2.5 feet.

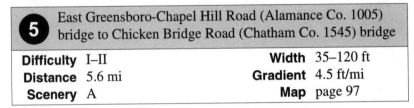

5	East Greensboro-Chapel Hill Road (Alamance Co. 1005) bridge to Chicken Bridge Road (Chatham Co. 1545) bridge		
Difficulty I–II		**Width** 35–120 ft	
Distance 5.6 mi		**Gradient** 4.5 ft/mi	
Scenery A		**Map** page 97	

Gauge USGS *Haw River near Bynum.* Estimated minimum is 300 cfs (3.4 ft).

Notes The main concentration of rapids is in the latter part of this section. There are three Class I rapids scattered in the first few miles. A Class I (mi 3.2) marks a point where other rapids can be seen downstream. This series ends with a Class II (mi 3.6).

Rocks resembling tombstones (mi 4.3) are just before many islands. The islands rise up to 10 feet above the riverbed. Rapids are Class I$^+$–II$^-$ depending on the route chosen. Passages between islands are narrow with strainers possible.

Chicken Bridge can be seen at the end of the last island (mi 5.2), and there is a short run of ledge rapids.

6	Chicken Bridge Road (Chatham Co. 1545) bridge to Bynum Dam US 15/501 access		
Difficulty I–II		**Width** 30–800 ft	
Distance 6.7 mi		**Gradient** 8.8 ft/mi	
Scenery A		**Map** page 97	

Gauge USGS *Haw River near Bynum.* Minimum is 200 cfs (3.1 ft).

Notes The take-out is near the US 15/501 bridge on the left bank, upstream of the dam. A new bridge is under construction, and an access area is planned, which will be managed by Chatham County. A portage path of several hundred feet will lead to parking at the bridge.

The first rapid (mi 1.3) marks the start on many Class I rapids interspersed with Class II rapids until the backwater of the dam at the take-out. This section is roughly half flatwater and half whitewater.

A large island (mi 1.7) is normally run to the right where the channel curves left then right. On the backside of the island, Class II Sawtooth Ledge has many rocks to dodge over a 75-foot run. Paddlers with marginal skills often have trouble here.

It is mostly flat down to the next rapid, where a low, rocky area on the right is a popular lunch stop (mi 2.7).

The next 2 miles have the most rapids and least flatwater. Hills near the river rise more than 100 feet. Describing a route is difficult because the maze of islands and channels present many options. Generally the best run is where the most water flows.

It is easy to mistake long islands (mi 3.0) on the left for the left bank of the river. The far left channel makes a 1.5-mile run before reuniting with the main river near the pipeline crossing. This route requires more water and is best done at a minimum of 600 cfs (4 ft).

Little Nantahala rapid (mi 3.6) is to the center and has noticeable gradient as water flows 200 feet and passes old, brick bridge piers. Another 200 feet downstream, the channel narrows to 30 feet as it turns right.

A ledge (mi 4.3) makes a sloping drop of several feet into a wave at the bottom. It is run to the left of center where the most water flows.

A clearing on both banks marks an underground pipeline (mi 4.5). Downstream, a 100-yard long rock garden ends in calm water above the last rapid, Final Solution (mi 4.7). At low flows, it is often run by heading toward the right bank and turning sharply left immediately past a boulder to go with the downstream current. If the turn is not made tightly enough, the boat will be heading into rocks. This is a good rapid to scout the first time because boulders obscure the path. Many boats have broached here. Scout from rocks on the left of the chute. Water below this rapid is deep from the dam backwater.

Stay to the left side of the islands downstream and take out on the left bank before the dam. Do not approach the gate area where water flows into the mill sluice.

If continuing downstream to the next section, it is 0.4 miles to the put-in. Portage the dam on the left side. Do not put in at the left channel because it is the water intake for power generation. There are Class I–II rapids between the dam and Bynum Road bridge.

7 Bynum Road (Chatham Co. 1713) access to US 64 access

Difficulty I–II		**Width**	40–500 ft
Distance 3.6 mi		**Gradient**	11.7 ft/mi
Scenery A		**Map**	page 97

Gauge USGS *Haw River near Bynum*. Minimum is 340 cfs (3.5 ft).

Notes The put-in is downstream right of Bynum Road bridge. The area is managed by Chatham County. The bridge is open only to pedestrians.

A canoe access is at the US 64 bridge on downstream right, managed by Chatham County.

Numerous islands make for many possible routes down this section. At low flows, the left side of the first islands downstream is the better run.

The USGS gauge (mi 0.6) is on the right bank. The usual route downstream near islands (mi 1.0) is to the left.

Where the main channel (mi 1.6) angles to the left and islands are to the right, go to the right through small islands into the next channel and proceed downstream. This leads a few hundred yards through Class II rapids to a right turn (mi 1.9) dropping 2 feet with a boulder in the outflow to avoid. The end of the rapid is in the rightmost river channel.

Where there are many rocks straight ahead, the main channel angles to the left (mi 3.1). When there is sufficient water, a route to the right through rocks and rock islands contains the more challenging rapids. When flow is near minimum, staying with the main (left) channel is best, but islands extending to just below the US 64 bridge prevent paddling directly to the take-out on the right without having to paddle upstream. Getting to the right bank may require some dragging at low levels. It is also possible to take out on the left bank.

> **8** US 64 access to Robeson Creek Canoe Access off Hanks Chapel Road (Chatham Co. 1943)

Difficulty	II–III	**Width**	50–500 ft
Distance	1.3 mi	**Gradient**	28.5 ft/mi
Scenery	A	**Map**	page 97

Gauge USGS *Haw River near Bynum*. Minimum is 600 cfs (4.0 ft). A paddling gauge is painted on a bridge support visible from the US 64 access. The approximate relationship is:

Paddling Gauge	USGS Gauge	
-1.0 ft	3.4 ft	300 cfs
-0.5 ft	4.0 ft	600 cfs
0.0 ft	4.7 ft	1,100 cfs
0.5 ft	5.4 ft	1,900 cfs
1.0 ft	6.0 ft	2,700 cfs
1.5 ft	6.7 ft	3,700 cfs
2.0 ft	7.2 ft	4,600 cfs
2.5 ft	8.0 ft	6,000 cfs
3.0 ft	8.8 ft	7,800 cfs
5.0 ft	11.2 ft	14,500 cfs

Notes See the previous section about the US 64 access.

To reach the take-out from the US 64 canoe access, turn left where the access road meets Chatham Co. 1991. Go 0.4 miles and turn left on Dee Farrell Road (Chatham Co. 1944). Go to the T-intersection, and turn left on Hanks Chapel Road (Chatham Co. 1943). Go 1.0 miles to a gravel road on the left sign-posted "Robeson Creek Canoe Access." Turn left and it is 0.8 miles to the parking lot. The access is managed by Jordan Lake State Recreation Area.

From the put-in, a foot trail goes down the right side of the river to Gabriel's Bend Rapid. Most of the rapids can be scouted from the bank.

In late 1981, Jordan Lake inundated 1.2 miles of whitewater below the current take-out. Many fine rapids such as S-Turn, Finders Keepers, and Pipeline were silenced. Now the section is only half its former length, but it is still a good run. Many paddlers spend hours here playing the waves and holes.

This section has the highest gradient of the Haw. The combination of gradient, boulders, islands, and trees can make it deadly at high levels. As the water rises, it flows over tree-covered islands. A swimming paddler faces many hazards with no calm spots for recovery.

There have been deaths and helicopter rescues here. High water greatly increases the skills required to paddle this section safely.

A few hundred feet from the put-in is Lunchstop Rapid, named for its frequent use by paddlers starting at the previous section. At low flows, Lunchstop has many exposed rocks to cause problems. At higher flows, there are big waves with open routes down the middle.

Going to the left through islands (mi 0.3) after Lunchstop leads to Ocean Boulevard. The river is wide with many boulders and large waves at high flows.

At the end of Ocean Boulevard, a rapid (mi 0.5) off the right bank drops into a long pool of water just upstream of Gabriel's Bend. The right bank rises steeply to 150 feet above the river.

The entrance to Gabriel's Bend (mi 0.6) is where the high right bank curves left, preventing a view of the rapid until entered. The bend runs for 200 feet and contains many boulders and eddies. The easier path is to the left, off the inside bend. Gabriel's Bend is a popular place for surfing and catching eddies.

Only 75 feet downstream of the end of Gabriel's Bend is Moose Jaw Falls (mi 0.7) off the right bank. It is a sloping 4-foot drop through boulders with a path difficult to see without scouting. It is not a good route at low flows. There are at least two other options to running Moose Jaw Falls.

To the left of Moose Jaw Falls and about 75 feet downstream is Black 'n Blue, a slot angling to the right bringing one in below Moose Jaw Falls.

From the end of Gabriel's Bend, 125 feet downstream and a bit to the left, but still to the right of very small islands is the start of The Maze. It is a series of three rapids, starting with a straight-ahead drop of a few feet, followed by a tight S-turn from right to left, and ending with a smaller drop. It all occurs within 100 feet. The Maze ends (mi 0.8) on the right side of the river about 300 feet below Moose Jaw Falls.

A few Class I–II rapids are downstream before meeting Jordan Lake (mi 1.1) near the take-out. The beginning of the lake depends on the lake level.

For paddlers on an extended trip down the Haw, it is another 4.5 miles to Jordan Lake Dam. The section below the dam is described under the Cape Fear River, Section 1 (page 49). A portage around the dam requires gaining about 50 feet in elevation to the top, dropping 100 feet to the bottom, and covering about 0.3 miles.

Len Felton running the entrance to The Maze
Haw River, Section 8

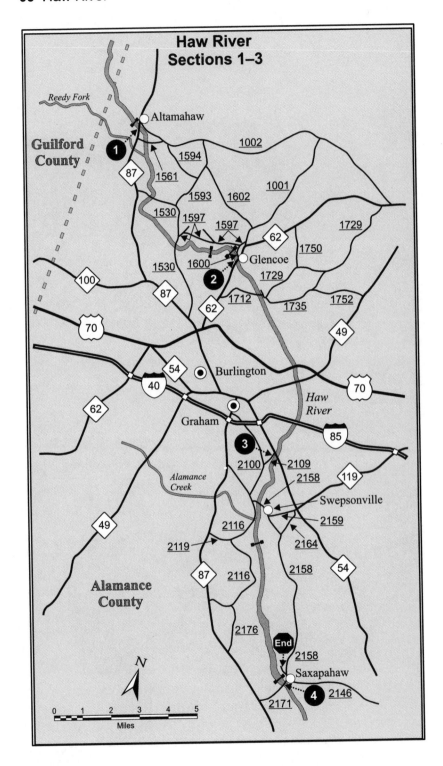

Haw River
Sections 1–3

Reedy Fork

Guilford
County

Altamahaw

1

87

1594

1561

1002

1593   1602

1001

1530

1597   1597

62

1729

1750

1530   1600

Glencoe

2

1729

100

87

1712

62

1735   1752

70

49

54

Burlington

40

62

Graham

Haw
River

70

3

85

2100   2109

2158

119

Alamance
Creek

Swepsonville

2159

49

2116

2119

2164

87   2116

2158

54

Alamance
County

2176

End   2158

2146

Saxapahaw

2171   **4**

N

0   1   2   3   4   5
Miles

Cape Fear Basin

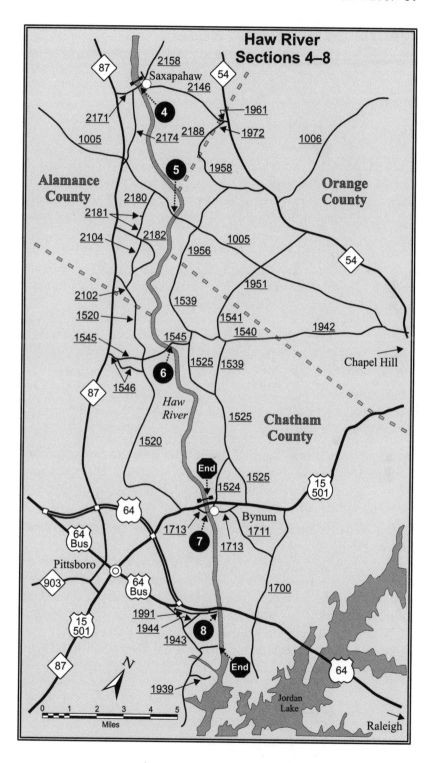

Holly Shelter Creek

County   Pender

Topos   Maple Hill, Maple Hill SW, Stag Park, Pin Hook

Holly Shelter Creek (also known as Shelter Creek) begins in Onslow County, just over the northeast border of Pender County. It is a small blackwater stream with a large beaver population in the headwaters, and a small tidal influence near its confluence with the Northeast Cape Fear River.

Angola Bay Game Land is north of Holly Shelter Creek, and Holly Shelter Game Land is south. These two large tracts were linked by land purchased by The Nature Conservancy. The link extends across Holly Shelter Creek along Shaken Creek, a tributary.

1 NC 50 bridge to Old Maple Hill Highway (Pender Co. 1520) bridge

Difficulty A	**Width** 10–35 ft
Distance 4.5 mi	**Gradient** 2.4 ft/mi
Scenery A	**Map** page 101

Gauge None. This is a narrow stream with enough beaver dams and downed trees to make for a long day. A trip here at low water took 6 hours. A high water level is recommended to help paddle over beaver dams and downed trees.

Notes Cattails, aquatic plants, cypress trees, and beaver dams make for interesting viewing.

In the paddling guidebook *Blackwater Paradise*, rocky walls are reported where water has cut through limestone sides. They were not seen, probably because the water level must be lower, or beaver dams submerged them.

Water flows through a large culvert (mi 2.2) under a gravel road. Paddling through the culvert is possible if it is clear of obstructions.

Sandy Run Swamp (mi 2.7) enters from the left. Downed trees continue to the take-out.

Cape Fear Basin

2 Old Maple Hill Highway (Pender Co. 1520) bridge to Old Maple Hill Highway bridge over Shaken Creek

Difficulty A	**Width** 15–60 ft	
Distance 6.2 mi	**Gradient** 0.5 ft/mi	
Scenery A	**Map** page 101	

Gauge See Section 1.

Notes The take-out is at the Maple Hill Highway bridge over Shaken Creek. From Holly Shelter Creek, it is a few hundred feet upstream on Shaken Creek to the bridge. Inspect the area so the take-out will be recognized.

Many downed trees were found, but progress was better than in the previous section. A trip here at low water took 4 hours. Unless downed trees have been cleared, allow extra time.

There is some beaver activity, and banks vary from 2–15 feet.

3 Old Maple Hill Highway (Pender Co. 1520) bridge over Shaken Creek to Shaw Highway (Pender Co. 1523) access

Difficulty A	**Width** 30–80 ft	
Distance 5.5 mi	**Gradient** 0.6 ft/mi	
Scenery A (35%), B (30%), C (35%)	**Map** page 101	

Gauge None. Always above minimum.

Notes See the previous section about Shaken Creek.

A Wildlife boating access is at Shaw Highway.

Turn left where Shaken Creek meets Holly Shelter Creek.

Many houses and cabins (mi 2.2) are on the right bank and continue for the next 1.5 miles.

The banks are often steep and up to 15 feet high. Cypress knees are abundant.

4 Shaw Highway (Pender Co. 1523) access to Whitestocking Road (Pender Co. 1512) access on NE Cape Fear River

Difficulty A	**Width** 40–125 ft	
Distance 6.3 mi	**Gradient** 0.6 ft/mi	
Scenery A (70%), B (30%)	**Map** page 101	

Gauge None. Always above minimum. This section is influenced by tides from the Northeast Cape Fear River of about 1.5 feet.

Notes The put-in and take-out are Wildlife boating access areas.

The take-out for this section is the put-in for the Northeast Cape Fear River, Section 8 (page 121) and requires paddling 0.4 miles upstream. Check the current below the take-out. If it is too fast to paddle against, go 4.1 miles downstream once reaching the Northeast Cape Fear to the Section 8 take-out off Old Plantation Road (Pender Co. 1520).

Holland's Shelter Creek Restaurant (mi 0.7) is on the right. It is a popular spot for a meal after a river trip. Cabins and boats are available for rent (910-259-5743).

The river swings away from the road (mi 1.0). There is little development downstream where the river changes course in many tight switchbacks.

Banks are up to 10 feet high in the beginning but turn swampy for much of the trip.

At the confluence with the Northeast Cape Fear (mi 5.9), turn right and paddle upstream to the take-out. Much of the land here has been logged.

Cleo Smith on Holly Shelter Creek, Section 1

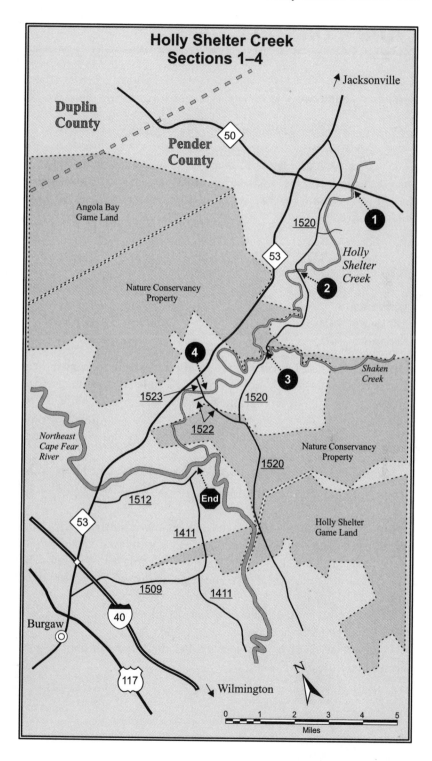

Holly Shelter Creek
Sections 1–4

Jacksonville

Duplin County

Pender County

50

Angola Bay Game Land

1520

Holly Shelter Creek

53

Nature Conservancy Property

Shaken Creek

1523

1520

1522

Northeast Cape Fear River

1520

Nature Conservancy Property

1512

End

Holly Shelter Game Land

53

1411

1509

1411

40

Burgaw

117

Wilmington

N

0 1 2 3 4 5
Miles

Cape Fear Basin

Little Coharie Creek

County	Sampson

Topos	Roseboro, Bonnetsville, Garland, Ingold

Little Coharie Creek begins in northwest Sampson County between the South River and Great Coharie Creek watersheds. It flows south, passing just east of Roseboro, and joins Great Coharie Creek 12 miles south of Clinton.

1 NC 242 bridge to Boykin Bridge Road (Sampson Co. 1214) bridge

Difficulty A	**Width** 10–60 ft
Distance 9.0 mi	**Gradient** 2.2 ft/mi
Scenery A (55%), B (45%)	**Map** page 104

Gauge USGS *Black River near Tomahawk* can be used as an indicator of water conditions even though it is 33 miles downstream of the put-in and measures the combined flow from Great Coharie, Little Coharie, and Six Runs Creeks. Water from this section takes about a day to reach the gauge, making readings most useful when water is not rising or falling rapidly.

Minimum is 250 cfs (3.3 ft). At this level there are likely to be some trees and beaver dams to lift over. A higher level of 500 cfs (4.9 ft) will eliminate most obstacles.

Notes There are some houses and junked cars near the creek in the first half-mile, but downstream the scenery improves. Banks are up to a few feet and the channel is constantly twisting and turning. The banks show evidence of a great number of downed trees removed from across the water.

NC 24 (mi 2.7) and Fleet Cooper Road (Sampson Co. 1240) (mi 5.3) can be used for access.

There are signs of beaver activity, but their dams did not require portage at a flow of 500 cfs.

2 Boykin Bridge Road (Sampson Co. 1214) bridge to Riley Town Road (Sampson Co. 1207) bridge	
Difficulty A	**Width** 20–55 ft
Distance 8.9 mi	**Gradient** 2.4 ft/mi
Scenery A	**Map** page 104

Gauge See Section 1.

Notes There are no bridges in this section. Banks are up to a few feet, and the channel continues twisting and turning.

Little development is seen. There are farms nearby, but few can be seen except for one large farm (mi 1.9) with several long factory-style buildings.

The banks show many stumps from downed trees removed from across the water, but one area is different. Where the stream widens (mi 3.9) and there are many cypress trees, no signs are seen of old downed trees. The lack of logging around this area protected trees near the water from the big storms of past years.

Kim Warren dog paddling
Rocky River (Cape Fear Basin), Section 4

Cape Fear Basin

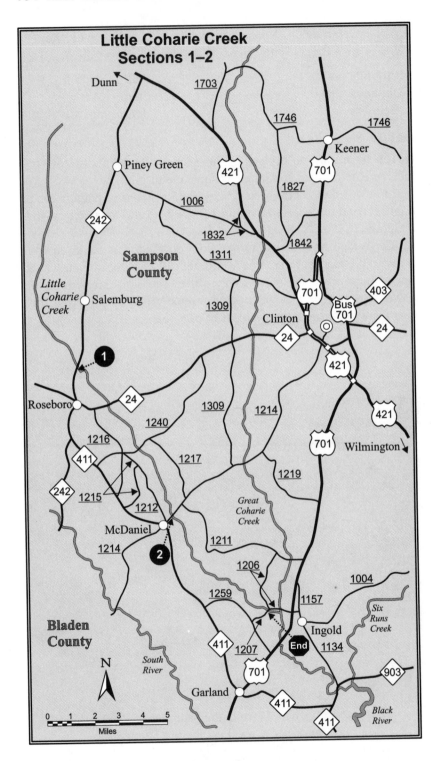

Cape Fear Basin

Lower Little River

Counties   Moore, Hoke, Cumberland, Harnett

Topos   Lobelia, Overhills, Manchester, Slocomb, Bunnlevel,
            Erwin

The Lower Little River is noted on some maps as simply the Little River, but it is more commonly called the Lower Little River to distinguish it from the Upper Little River, only 5 miles to the north.

The Lower Little begins in the Sandhills region, about 6 miles northwest of Pinehurst, and flows east through several reservoirs.

At the confluence with James Creek, the Lower Little River becomes the northern border of Fort Bragg Military Reservation and then flows through military property. Paddling through military property is allowed, but there are restrictions on use of the roads. See Section 1 for more information.

The Lower Little River becomes the Harnett and Cumberland County border before joining the Cape Fear River, 5 miles south of Erwin.

The river has a good gradient and a variety of scenery including old hydroelectric dams, high banks, and interesting vegetation.

1 Morrison Bridge Road (Moore Co. 2021) bridge to John Neil Shaw Road bridge off NC 690 (Vass Road)

Difficulty B, and one I		**Width** 20–110 ft	
Distance 10.4 mi		**Gradient** 3.6 ft/mi	
Scenery A (60%), B (20%), C (20%)		**Map** page 109	

Gauge USGS *Little River at Manchester.* Estimated minimum is 125 cfs (6.0 ft).

Notes NC 690 is Vass Road in Cumberland County and Lobelia Road in Moore County. Traveling west on Vass Road, 0.2 miles before crossing into Cumberland County, John Neil Shaw Road connects on the left. It is a gravel road going into Fort Bragg property. Travel on John Neil Shaw Road about 0.7 miles to a bridge. On the south side of the river, there is a military gate that can be closed. The north (left) bank has been used for paddling access in the past. A Fort

Bragg official said roads on their property are open to anyone to use to get to the river if they have a Fort Bragg permit for fishing or hunting. Permits may be purchased Wednesday–Sunday, 8:30 A.M.–4:30 P.M. A one-year permit costs $15. The permit allows access to military roads. A permit is not required to paddle the river through Fort Bragg. For more information and a map, see: http://www.bragg.army.mil/wildlife/

The river is narrow over a gravel and sand bottom with a current that often exceeds 2 miles per hour because the gradient is relatively high.

Property on the right bank is part of Fort Bragg. Many houses are seen on the left bank in the first 4 miles.

An old 15-foot dam (mi 1.0) does not back up water because the left side is open where small rocks create a Class I rapid. Stay away from the dam's right side where water flows through open gates. The gates are about 3 feet high and usually clogged with debris.

A 10-foot wide creek (mi 6.0) enters on the left. A culvert under a gravel road can be seen about 100 feet up the creek. This is close to the point where Fort Bragg property extends over the left bank. For about the next 10 miles, both sides of the river are military property.

Lower River Road (mi 6.3) comes close to the left bank, but it is difficult to see because of trees and brush. It is a possible access point, but the permit previously mentioned is required. Traveling west on NC 690, after crossing into Moore County, go 1.7 miles. Turn left on Flat Road (gravel) and go 0.6 miles. Turn right on Gravel Pit Road and go 0.3 miles. Turn left on Lower River Road and go 0.2 miles to where the river comes close to the road.

An old 15-foot dam (mi 8.9) should be portaged on the right. On the left side of the dam, large round holes probably housed turbines for electric power generation. Avoid approaching the dam closely because water flows through holes underwater. Right of center, a section of the dam is broken, and water pours over slabs of concrete, dropping about 4 feet. Do not be tempted to paddle here because rebar is waiting below.

2 John Neil Shaw Road bridge off NC 690 (Vass Road) to NC 210 bridge

Difficulty	B, and one I	**Width**	50–80 ft
Distance	10.6 mi	**Gradient**	2.7 ft/mi
Scenery	A (60%), B (20%), C (20%)	**Map**	page 109

Gauge See Section 1.

Notes See the previous section about John Neil Shaw Road.

The banks range 5–35 feet with many cypress trees near the water and tall pines on higher ground.

A bridge (mi 2.8) is used by the military, and is not open to the public.

A 2-foot low-head dam (mi 3.7) spans the river. It has been run by paddlers but is not recommended because it has a powerful hydraulic. Portage on the right side.

Another dam (mi 4.5) is where the river makes a sharp turn to the left. This 7-foot dam creates a powerful hydraulic at the base. A Fort Bragg water treatment plant is on the right bank. Portage on the left.

At concrete piers near where a railroad crossing existed, a 6-inch ledge (mi 6.4) creates a Class I rapid. Downstream, Fort Bragg property does not cover both banks, but it does own property on one bank or the other for much of the remainder of this section.

The NC 24/87 bridge (mi 7.6) is just upstream of the Manchester Road (Cumberland Co. 1451) bridge (mi 7.7). Under the Manchester Road bridge, a pipe crosses about 6 feet above the river at low flows. At high flows, the pipe would be a hazard. A similar low pipe (mi 10.1) crosses before reaching the take-out.

3 NC 210 bridge to West Reeves Bridge Road (Cumberland Co. 1609) bridge

Difficulty	B	**Width**	40–90 ft
Distance	10.6 mi	**Gradient**	3.9 ft/mi
Scenery	A	**Map**	page 110

Gauge See Section 1.

Notes West Reeves Bridge Road banks have steep sides with riprap. A long rope is useful for raising boats.

Cypress and pine trees are found in this section along with mountain laurel. The banks are typically 30 feet or higher, giving the feeling of being in a small gorge. In spring when the blooms are out, it is a colorful trip.

McCormick Bridge Road (Cumberland Co. 1600) (mi 1.7) and Elliott Bridge Road (Harnett Co. 2045) (mi 5.9) can be used for access. Access near Elliott Bridge Road is easier at a private ramp where usage can be arranged through Denton Ridge. See the next section for more information.

The right bank rises 100 feet above the river (mi 7.8) for most of the next mile.

4	West Reeves Bridge Road (Cumberland Co. 1609) bridge to NC 217 bridge		
Difficulty B		**Width**	40–70 ft
Distance 7.2 mi		**Gradient**	3.1 ft/mi
Scenery A (70%), B (30%)		**Map**	page 110

Gauge See Section 1.

Notes See the previous section about West Reeves Bridge Road.

The banks are typically 30–40 feet or higher. Cypress trees are common, and a few Atlantic white cedar trees are on the banks. Mountain laurel, wild azaleas, and wildflowers make this an especially scenic springtime trip. A few side creeks enter in small waterfalls of 4–8 feet.

Just before a sharp, right bend (mi 0.9), a steel cable hangs only 2 feet above water at low flows. Watch for the cable and portage if it presents a problem.

A campground (mi 2.8) is on the right bank. Usage can be arranged through Denton Ridge (910-980-0125). They also rent canoes and run shuttles.

At the US 401 bridge (mi 3.7), there is an abandoned USGS gauge.

From the take-out, it is 2.8 miles to where the Lower Little River enters the Cape Fear River, Section 4 (page 52).

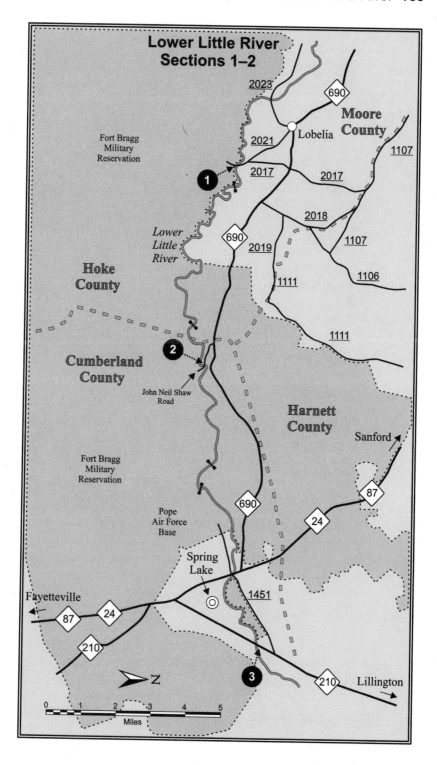

Lower Little River
Sections 1–2

2023

690

Moore County

Lobelia

1107

Fort Bragg
Military
Reservation

2021

2017

2017

1

2018

1107

*Lower
Little
River*

690

2019

1106

Hoke County

1111

1111

Cumberland County

2

John Neil Shaw
Road

Harnett County

Sanford

Fort Bragg
Military
Reservation

87

690

24

Pope
Air Force
Base

Spring
Lake

Fayetteville

1451

87

24

3

210

210

Lillington

N

0 1 2 3 4 5
Miles

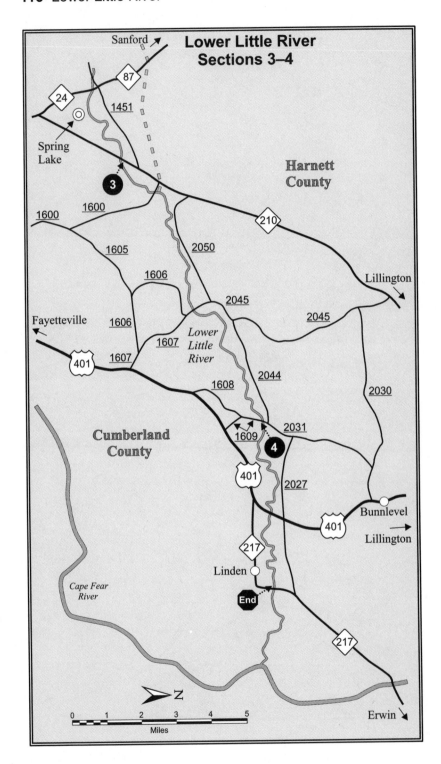

Lower Little River
Sections 3–4

Cape Fear Basin

Moores Creek

County   Pender

Topo   Currie

Moores Creek begins in northwest Pender County and flows south, passing Moores Creek National Battlefield near Currie before joining the Black River.

Moores Creek National Battlefield is a half-mile from the put-in. The 88-acre park commemorates the decisive February 27, 1776 victory by 1,000 Patriots over 1,600 Loyalists at the Battle of Moores Creek Bridge. The battle ended the Royal Governor's hopes of regaining control of the colony for the British crown. This first decisive Patriot victory of the Revolutionary War raised morale for Patriots throughout the colonies. The colony of North Carolina voted to declare independence from the British two weeks after the Moores Creek victory.

1 NC 210 bridge to The Borough access off Borough Spur Road (Pender Co. 1137)			
Difficulty A		**Width** 35–125 ft	
Distance 3.7 mi		**Gradient** 0 ft/mi	
Scenery B		**Map** page 113	

Gauge None. Always above minimum. There is a tidal influence of about 2 feet. The tide delay is about 2 hours from the Castle Hayne tides on the Cape Fear River.

Notes The access at The Borough is private. From Borough Road (Pender Co. 1115) turn on Borough Spur Road. State maintenance ends 100 yards ahead. Proceed on and take the third drive to the right. There are "No trespassing" and "Private property" signs here, but instructions from residents of the house to the left said usage of the access is allowed. Go 100 yards to the dirt ramp on Moores Creek and deposit the $4 fee in the honor box.

A landing downstream of the last house in The Borough was used for access in the past, but it is now posted.

An alternative to using the private access at The Borough is to make a round-trip and paddle back to the put-in.

This is a blackwater stream with many houses built on the banks after the first mile. The banks vary from swampy to 20 feet high.

At the take-out, the confluence with the Black River is only 0.2 miles downstream.

Cleo Smith below first old dam
Lower Little River, Section 1

Cleo Smith portaging second dam
Lower Little River, Section 1

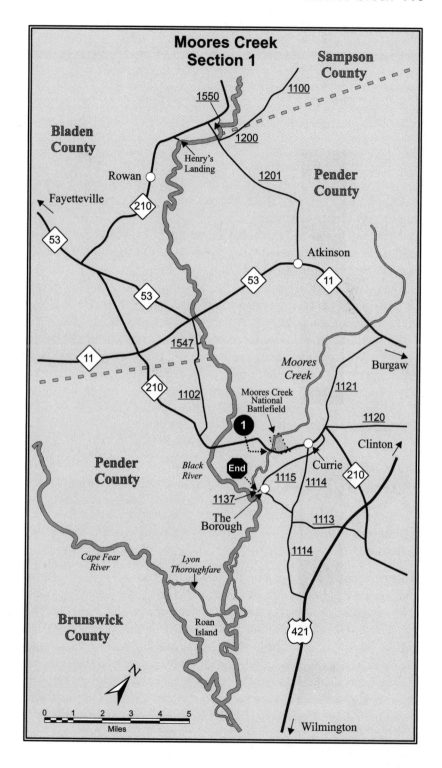

New Hope Creek

County   Orange

Topo   Chapel Hill

New Hope Creek begins about 5 miles south of Hillsborough. It flows generally eastward toward Durham and winds through Duke Forest, a research forest owned by Duke University. The terrain is rolling, with sharp bluffs along the stream.

Near the Orange and Durham County line, New Hope Creek flows south between Durham and Chapel Hill, and the sharp bluffs disappear to be replaced by a swampy valley.

Below US 15/501, land near the creek is part of Jordan Game Land. Just before crossing into Chatham County, New Hope Creek empties into Jordan Lake.

Preservation of the New Hope watershed has been assisted by the Triangle Land Conservancy's addition of three tracts along New Hope Creek, including the 296-area Johnston Mill Nature Preserve. The preserve extends over a mile along the creek from Mount Sinai Road to the put-in for the section described below, where most land is within Duke Forest.

---

1   Turkey Farm Road (Orange Co. 1730) bridge to Erwin Road (Orange Co. 1734) bridge

Difficulty I–II⁺, and one III	**Width** 10–50 ft
Distance 4.9 mi	**Gradient** 27.6 ft/mi
Scenery A (50%), B (50%)	**Map** page 116

Gauge Concrete footings on the left of the Turkey Farm Road one-lane bridge can be used to gauge water levels. The top of the wider lower concrete footing is about 1.5 feet above the creek bed. A 3.5-foot high concrete footing sits on top of the bottom footing. The bottom footing needs to be covered by at least 3 inches of water, placing minimum at 39 inches below the top of the upper footing.

The watershed drains only about 15 square miles above the put-in. Water is above minimum only after heavy rain. The USGS *New Hope Creek near Blands* gauge is 11 miles below the take-out and not very useful because water conditions upstream change quickly.

Notes Most of the land along this section is part of the Korstian Division of Duke Forest, but there are areas of private property. Two trail bridges cross New Hope Creek, and there are many hiking and biking trails.

This is a hazardous run because it is a narrow stream with many sharp bends, and there are usually many downed trees. As water rises above a foot higher than minimum, speed increases the danger. Excellent boat control is required, and scouting for strainers is mandatory.

Many trees have been downed by storms, but Duke does not clear them because the forest is used for teaching and research projects that require a natural system of large woody debris that will remain and undergo normal degradation, decay, and ultimate movement downstream. It is best to hike along the creek and scout it before deciding to paddle.

After several homes and flatwater, the first small rapid, Class I$^+$, (mi 0.6) is reached.

Just after passing under power lines (mi 1.2), there are two steel cables hanging across the stream, one at minimum paddling level and the other 4 feet higher.

A trail bridge (mi 1.4) on Wooden Bridge Road crosses the stream.

The banks frequently rise over 70 feet, and some rocky outcroppings display colors of yellow lichen.

Class II rapids are found in the half-mile before a low-water concrete trail bridge (mi 2.9). At minimum water level, the 2-foot drop on the downstream side of the bridge is too low to run.

Several rapids lead to a left turn where a creek enters on the right (mi 3.2). There are large rocks (mi 3.5) on the right for a lunch stop. The Big Rapid, Class III, is a few hundred feet downstream around the bend and can be scouted from the right bank. It is a series of rapids spread over 100 feet, with the larger drops at the end.

Piney Mountain (mi 3.8) rises 150 feet on the left bank. Piney Mountain Rapid, Class II$^+$, runs 50 feet through boulders and is only 10 feet wide at the narrowest slot.

At a left bend (mi 4.4), a ledge of several feet creates a good surfing wave, and an old stone wall (mi 4.8) juts into the creek from the right, but the left side is clear. A wide basin is formed behind the wall.

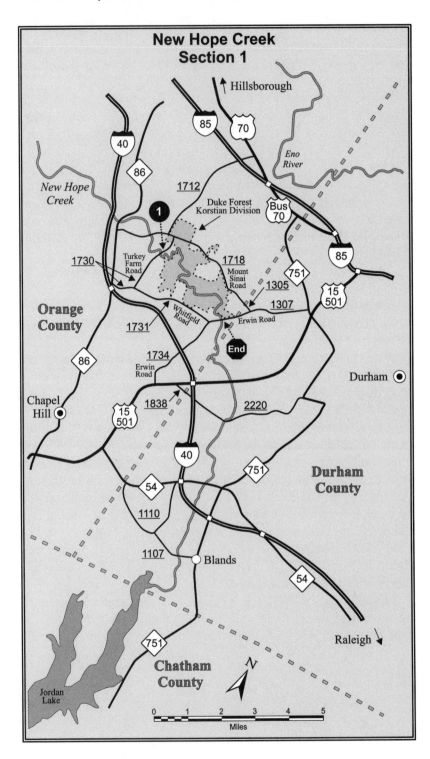

New Hope Creek
Section 1

↑ Hillsborough

85

70

Eno
River

40

86

New Hope
Creek

1712

Duke Forest
Korstian Division

Bus
70

1

85

1730

Turkey
Farm
Road

1718

Mount
Sinai
Road

751

1305

15
501

Orange
County

1731

Whitfield
Road

1307

Erwin Road

End

Durham

86

1734

Erwin
Road

Chapel
Hill

15
501

1838

2220

40

Durham
County

751

54

1110

751

1107

Blands

54

Raleigh ↓

751

Chatham
County

N

Jordan
Lake

0   1   2   3   4   5
Miles

Cape Fear Basin

Northeast Cape Fear River

Counties	Duplin, Pender, New Hanover
Topos	Albertson, Beulaville, Chinquapin, Charity, Wallace East, Pin Hook, Stag Park, Burgaw, Mooretown, Scotts Hill, Castle Hayne, Rocky Point, Wilmington

The Northeast Cape Fear River begins near Mount Olive as a small blackwater stream. It flows southeast before taking on a more southerly course and passes through few towns as it makes its way to join its larger northwest arm, the Cape Fear River, at Wilmington.

There is little development in the upper watershed where the land is largely agricultural, including dense poultry and swine farms. Waste has spilled into the river following major floods.

The first written record of exploration was in 1664 by English explorer William Hinton. His men anchored their ship and rowed its longboat about 40 miles upstream. They reported rich land suitable for settlements.

In the early 1700s, the Northeast Cape Fear River was a prime route for transportation and trade, supplying timber and turpentine to the port of Wilmington.

The sections described here cover 112 miles of paddling. Much of it is through undeveloped areas, making it popular for camping, but there are few public camping areas available.

The river has been paddled from several bridges above Section 1, but there are many downed trees. Do not be deceived by open channels at the bridges. Following major storms, trees are often cleared but only near the bridges. A memorable adventure here resulted in being challenged by aggressive water moccasins and unexpectedly spending a night sleeping between cypress knees.

❶ NC 11 bridge to Sarecta Road (Duplin Co. 1700) bridge

Difficulty	A	**Width**	10–60 ft
Distance	6.7 mi	**Gradient**	2.0 ft/mi
Scenery	A	**Map**	page 125

Gauge USGS *NE Cape Fear near Chinquapin.* Estimated minimum is 300 cfs (3.5 ft).

Notes The river braids into several channels through swampy land. The channel most clear of trees swings close to NC 11 (mi 1.0) for a half-mile.

Goshen Swamp (mi 2.5) joins from the right, and the river widens to about 50 feet.

At low to medium water levels, a large number of trees (mi 5.0) on the river bottom have stumps and limbs above water, requiring a search for the best route.

The snags end (mi 6.0), and the river character changes with banks on the left rising up to 4 feet.

❷ Sarecta Road (Duplin Co. 1700) bridge to NC 24 access

Difficulty	A	**Width**	50–75 ft
Distance	5.0 mi	**Gradient**	1.3 ft/mi
Scenery	A	**Map**	page 125

Gauge USGS *NE Cape Fear near Chinquapin.* Estimated minimum is 125 cfs (2.3 ft).

Notes At the NC 24 bridge, a Wildlife boating access is upstream left. The entrance is from Wildlife Road (Duplin Co. 2037), 0.3 miles east of the bridge.

After the first mile, there has been logging near the river for much of this section.

The banks rise to 8 feet, and the swampy nature of the previous section is not seen here. At low flows, sandbars are up to 3 feet above water. Cypress and large river birch trees are numerous.

3 NC 24 access to Hallsville Road (Duplin Co. 1961) bridge

Difficulty A		**Width** 50–75 ft	
Distance 4.1 mi		**Gradient** 1.6 ft/mi	
Scenery A		**Map** page 125	

Gauge See Section 2.

Notes See the previous section about the NC 24 access.

A large beach is on downstream right at Hallsville Road (Duplin Co. 1961). It is reached by a sandy drive, 200 feet west of the bridge.

There is high ground available for stops. Much logging has been done near the river.

4 Hallsville Road (Duplin Co. 1961) bridge to NC 41/50 bridge at Chinquapin

Difficulty A		**Width** 65–125 ft	
Distance 9.8 mi		**Gradient** 0.9 ft/mi	
Scenery A		**Map** page 125	

Gauge See Section 2.

Notes See the previous section about Hallsville Road.

At the NC 41/50 bridge, there is a beach upstream right. It is reached by a rough drive, 150 feet west of the bridge.

Many cypress trees and only a few cabins are seen on this stretch. Banks range up to 10 feet, and there are many sandbars at low flow.

A large loop (mi 5.1) almost doubles back on itself. A half-mile can be saved by taking the channel to the left, cutting off the loop.

5 NC 41/50 bridge at Chinquapin to Wayne's Landing access off Cypress Hole Road (Duplin Co. 1925)

Difficulty A		**Width** 50–100 f	
Distance 8.0 mi		**Gradient** 0.6 ft/mi	
Scenery A		**Map** page 125	

Gauge See Section 2.

Notes See the previous section about NC 41/50.

Wayne's Landing, at the end of Cypress Hole Road, is a Wildlife boating access. A shelter and small camping area is managed by the Northeast Ruritan Club. To camp here or for picnicking groups of ten or more, permission must be obtained from Hanchey's Store (910-285-1157), 1.5 miles west on NC 41.

Access at Deep Bottom Road (Duplin Co. 1827) (mi 4.1) is possible on downstream right. It is private but not posted. A drive leads to a high beach. Across from the beach, the left bank rises to 60 feet.

Some farms and cabins are near the river before reaching Wayne's Landing.

6	Wayne's Landing access off Cypress Hole Road (Duplin Co. 1925) to Croomsbridge Road (Pender Co. 1318) bridge	
Difficulty A	**Width**	70–125 ft
Distance 20.0 mi	**Gradient**	0.5 ft/mi
Scenery A (80%), B (20%)	**Map**	page 126

Gauge See Section 2.

Notes See the previous section about Wayne's Landing access.

Because of the distance, this section is often done as a camper. There are no public camping areas, but high ground is available.

Angola Bay Game Land, over 21,000 acres covering Angola Swamp, is on the left for most of this section, but it is mostly more than a half-mile away. There has been some logging along the left bank.

River Landing golf course and community (mi 5.8) begins and runs along the right bank. Many of the large homes overlooking the river were flooded during Hurricane Floyd (1999).

The Horseshoe (mi 6.8) is a large oxbow to the left, but it is dry except at high water. When it can be explored, it adds a mile to the trip.

Rockfish Creek (mi 10.5) joins from the right, marking passage into Pender County. From here to the take-out, the river does not meander as it does upstream.

7	Croomsbridge Road (Pender Co. 1318) bridge to Whitestocking Road (Pender Co. 1512) access	
Difficulty A	**Width**	70–130 ft
Distance 8.9 mi	**Gradient**	0.6 ft/mi
Scenery A (25%), B (25%), C (50%)	**Map**	page 126

Gauge USGS *NE Cape Fear near Burgaw*. Always above minimum. This section has tides of about 1–1.5 feet. Refer to tide tables for Cape Fear River at Bannermans Branch of the Northeast River.

Notes A Wildlife boating access is at Whitestocking Road.

Many homes and cabins are along the bank, especially after the first 2 miles.

NC 53 (mi 5.2) can be used to shorten the trip, but access is much easier at Whitestocking Road, where the Wildlife ramp is in a small cove to the right.

8	Whitestocking Road (Pender Co. 1512) access to Old Plantation Road (Pender Co. 1520) access		
Difficulty A		**Width** 110–250 ft	
Distance 4.5 mi		**Gradient** 0 ft/mi	
Scenery A		**Map** page 126	

Gauge See Section 7.

Notes Whitestocking Road and Old Plantation Road have Wildlife boating access areas.

Holly Shelter Creek (mi 0.4) enters from the left. See Holly Shelter Creek, Section 4 (page 99).

There are few houses, and banks range up to 6 feet.

9	Old Plantation Road (Pender Co. 1520) access to NC 210 Lanes Ferry access		
Difficulty A		**Width** 80–500 ft	
Distance 11.6 mi		**Gradient** 0 ft/mi	
Scenery A (40%), B (50%), C (10%)		**Map** page 127	

Gauge USGS *NE Cape Fear near Burgaw.* Always above minimum. This section has tides of 1.5–2 feet. Tides on the Cape Fear River at Castle Hayne are delayed about 2.5 hours at the put-in, 1 hour at the take-out. The river is wide, making wind a problem.

Notes A Wildlife boating access is at Old Plantation Road.

The access at NC 210, upstream right, is owned by Lanes Ferry Grocery. Pay the $2 per boat fee at the store.

Many houses and docks (mi 2.7) are along the left bank. This is typical of several areas along this section, where many homes and cabins overlook the river.

The river enters a large cove (mi 3.7). The channel to the left is the main river channel.

The main channel (mi 6.4) splits, and the slightly larger channel bears right. The left channel picks up a few small tributaries before rejoining (mi 8.2). If paddling the right channel, there could be confusion where the channels rejoin because a right turn is required to go downstream. An incoming tide could be mistaken for downstream current, and paddling directly ahead instead of bearing right goes up the left channel.

10	NC 210 Lanes Ferry access to US 117 access at Castle Hayne		
Difficulty A		**Width** 275–500 ft	
Distance 9.1 mi		**Gradient** 0 ft/mi	
Scenery A (65%), B (35%)		**Map** page 127	

Gauge USGS *NE Cape Fear near Burgaw*. Always above minimum. This section has tides of about 2 feet. For the take-out, use tide tables for the Cape Fear River at Castle Hayne. Tides at the put-in are delayed about 1 hour. The river is wide with long straight runs, making wind a problem.

Notes See the previous section about the NC 210 Lanes Ferry access.

A Wildlife boating access is upstream left of the US 117 bridge. From US 117, take Orange Street a few hundred feet to the access entrance.

Several straight stretches (mi 2.2) begin where one can see a mile ahead.

Alligators frequent these waters and are often seen near the marsh grass and lily pads. Cypress trees with Spanish moss are common.

Occidental Chemical operates the large plant (mi 5.8) on the left, and its property extends downstream for the next mile.

The high I-40 bridges (mi 8.7) mark the approach to Castle Hayne.

11	US 117 access at Castle Hayne to Cowpen Landing at Armstrong Road (Pender Co. 1428) end		
Difficulty A		**Width** 300–500 ft	
Distance 10.8 mi		**Gradient** 0 ft/mi	
Scenery A (80%), C (20%)		**Map** page 127	

Gauge USGS *NE Cape Fear near Burgaw*. Always above minimum. This section has tides of about 2 feet at the put-in and 2.5–3 feet at the take-out. Use tide tables for the Cape Fear River at Castle Hayne for the put-in. At the take-out, tides will be about 1.5 hours ahead. The river is wide with long straight runs, making wind a problem.

Notes See the previous section about the US 117 access.

Cowpen Landing is private. Permission to cross private property must be obtained from either of the two homes at the end of Armstrong Road.

An alternative to Cowpen Landing is Clarks Landing on Long Creek. From the end of Clarks Landing Road (Pender Co. 1408), a one-lane sandy drive continues 0.3 miles to a ramp. To reach the ramp from the Northeast Cape Fear River, paddle 2.4 miles upstream on Long Creek, making this section an 11.6-mile trip. Long Creek is subject to the same tides as the Northeast Cape Fear River.

It is possible to combine this section with the next for a long run of 23.9 miles from Castle Hayne to Wilmington. To paddle it in one day requires favorable wind, tide, and long daylight. Plan the trip to arrive in Wilmington as an outgoing tide ends. This requires starting in Castle Hayne against the tide and catching an outgoing tide downstream. Camping is difficult because there are houses on most of the high ground.

After passing many houses in the first 2 miles, there is little development.

At a large loop (mi 3.5), a 50-foot wide channel to the left cuts off the loop. Taking the shortcut saves a mile.

Prince George Creek (mi 6.9) enters from the left, and past it is dry ground (mi 7.9) on the left, owned by a timber company and leased to a hunting club.

Turkey Creek (mi 8.4) and Long Creek (mi 9.2) both enter from the right.

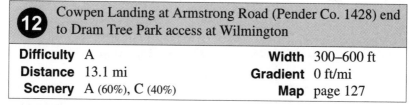

12 Cowpen Landing at Armstrong Road (Pender Co. 1428) end to Dram Tree Park access at Wilmington

Difficulty A	**Width** 300–600 ft
Distance 13.1 mi	**Gradient** 0 ft/mi
Scenery A (60%), C (40%)	**Map** page 127

Gauge USGS *NE Cape Fear near Burgaw*. Always above minimum. This section has tides of about 2.5–5.5 feet. Use tide tables for the Cape Fear River at Wilmington for the take-out. At the put-in, tides will be delayed about 1.5 hours. The river is wide with long straight runs, making wind a problem.

Notes See the previous section about Cowpen Landing and Clarks Landing as an alternative.

Cape Fear Basin

For directions to Dram Tree Park, see the Cape Fear River, Section 13 (page 58).

The banks are tidal flats with saw grass until reaching power lines (mi 5.8) where the left bank rises steeply to 30 feet.

Banks on the right (mi 8.5) rise steeply to 50 feet, and from here downstream much industry is on the banks.

After the US 117/NC 133 bridge (mi 11.3), the Cape Fear River (mi 12.1) comes in on the right.

Waterfront development of Wilmington is on the left and the Battleship North Carolina is on the right.

Take out at Dram Tree Park, upstream left of the bridge.

■

It is difficult to find in life any event which so effectually condenses intense nervous sensation into the shortest possible space of time as does the work of shooting, or running an immense rapid. There is no toil, no heart breaking labour about it, but as much coolness, dexterity, and skill as man can throw into the work of hand, eye, and head; knowledge of when to strike and how to do it; knowledge of water and rock, and of the one hundred combinations which rock and water can assume—for these two things, rock and water, taken in the abstract, fail as completely to convey any idea of their fierce embracings in the throes of a rapid as the fire burning quietly in a drawing-room fireplace fails to convey the idea of a house wrapped and sheeted in flames.

—Sir William Francis Butler, *The Great Lone Land* (1872)

Cape Fear Basin

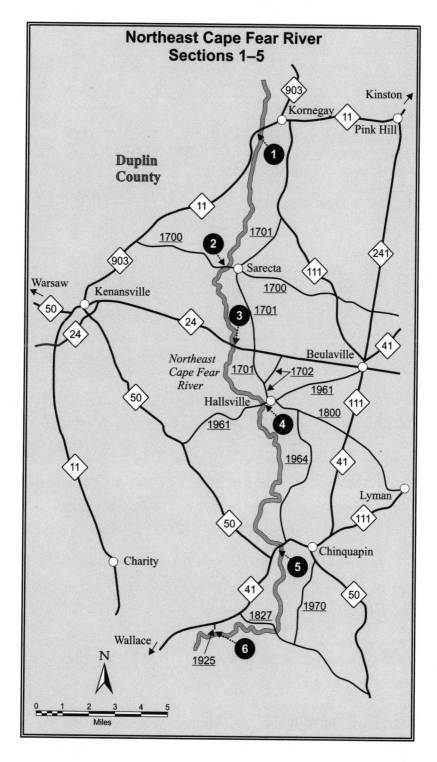

Northeast Cape Fear River
Sections 1–5

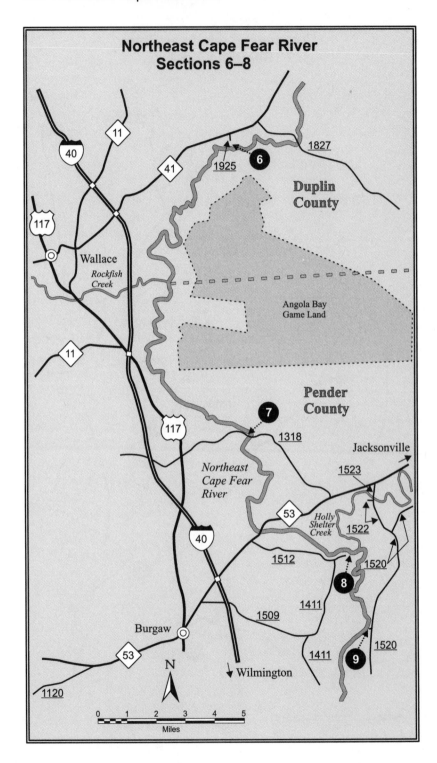

Northeast Cape Fear River
Sections 6–8

Duplin County

Wallace

Rockfish Creek

Angola Bay Game Land

Pender County

Northeast Cape Fear River

Jacksonville

Holly Shelter Creek

Burgaw

N

Wilmington

Miles

0 1 2 3 4 5

Cape Fear Basin

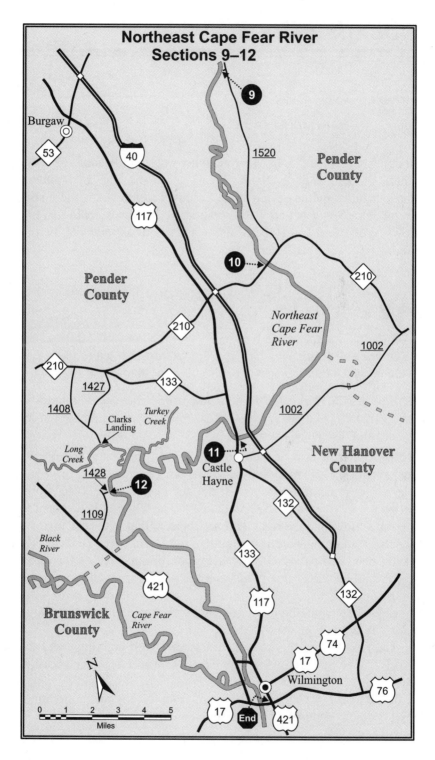

**Northeast Cape Fear River
Sections 9–12**

Rockfish Creek

County   Cumberland

Topos   Hope Mills, Cedar Creek

Rockfish Creek begins in Moore County only a mile south of Weymouth Woods Sandhills Nature Preserve, on the edge of Southern Pines. It flows southeast into Hoke County, entering the western border of Fort Bragg Military Reservation. It continues southeast and flows by Raeford and Hope Mills, just south of Fayetteville, before joining the Cape Fear River.

---

1 NC 59 (South Main Street) bridge near Hope Mills to NC 87 bridge

Difficulty A–B, and one II	**Width** 40–60 ft	
Distance 9.3 mi	**Gradient** 3.8 ft/mi	
Scenery A (55%), B (45%)	**Map** page 130	

Gauge *USGS Rockfish Creek at Raeford.* Estimated minimum is 80 cfs (3.4 ft). The gauge is about 20 miles upstream of the put-in. Water from the gauge takes about a day to reach this section.

Notes Slabs of broken concrete (mi 1.3) in the water and on the banks mark the site of an old dam. The river narrows, and there is a Class I$^+$–II rapid at low water. At the end of this rapid, water flows between concrete walls 15–20 feet apart. The left wall is diagonal to the water flow, and the right wall has rebar jutting out. This area is a popular swimming hole even though swimming here is illegal. A young man was paralyzed after being swept into underwater rebar. The hazard increases greatly as water rises. The rapid can be portaged on the right.

Below the rapid, there is a good view upstream of part of the high dam still standing on the right bank.

The first half of this section has several road crossings, and the first is Calico Street (Cumberland Co. 1127) (mi 1.5) where access is possible.

Little Rockfish Creek (mi 2.3) joins from the left, just upstream of the US 301/I-95 Business bridge, and the terrain becomes steeper.

Research Drive (Cumberland Co. 2350) bridge (mi 3.7) is followed by I-95 (mi 4.4). There are no more bridges until reaching the take-out, and there is less development seen in the last 3 miles.

The take-out at NC 87 is steep and requires going up 70 feet.

From the take-out, it is 2.0 miles to where Rockfish Creek enters the Cape Fear River, Section 7 (page 54).

Paul Ferguson walking the Narrows
Black River, Section 6

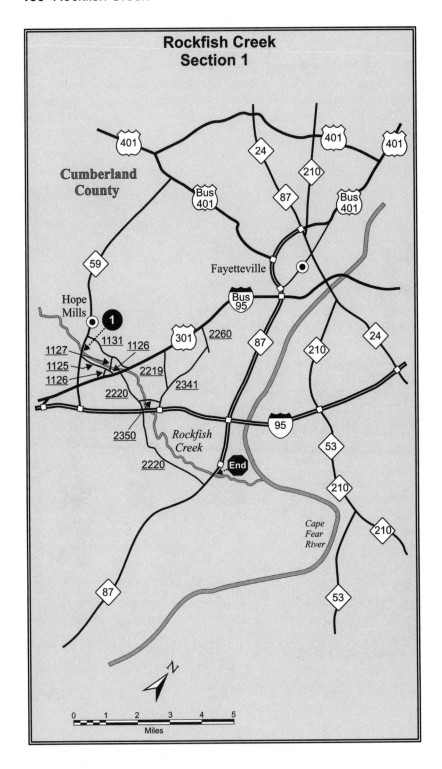

Rocky River

County   Chatham

Topos   Crutchfield Crossroads, Siler City, Siler City NE,
           Pittsboro, Colon, Moncure, Merry Oaks

The Rocky River begins near Liberty and is impounded for use as a
Siler City water supply. It flows southeast, and after crossing US 64 it
does not pass near any towns before joining the Deep River, 4 miles
upstream of US 1.

Since the late 1700s, over thirty mills were built on the Rocky
River. Most were gristmills, but there were also cotton mills and saw-
mills. Remains of these can be seen on the river.

The Cape Fear Shiner fish is on the endangered species list and
has been found in the Rocky River near the confluence with the Deep
River.

The Rocky River's whitewater is a popular alternative when the
Haw River is too high.

1 Snow Camp Road (Chatham Co. 1004) bridge to Carolina
Hill Road (Chatham Co. 2168) roadside

Difficulty I–II	**Width**	35–100 ft
Distance 7.9 mi	**Gradient**	8.9 ft/mi
Scenery A (50%), B (25%), C (25%)	**Map**	page 136

Gauge USGS *Rocky River at SR 1300 near Crutchfield Crossroads.*
The gauge is 10 miles above the put-in and measures drainage from
only 7.4 square miles. Estimated minimum is 20 cfs (1.5 ft).

There is also a gauge strapped to the left pier of the put-in bridge,
where estimated minimum is 2.0 feet.

Notes The take-out is off Carolina Hill Road. From Rives Chapel
Church Road (Chatham Co. 2170) bridge, take Carolina Hill Road
0.4 miles to a creek crossing. The Rocky River is 100 feet from the
roadside.

Dam backwater starts within the first mile, and there are many
houses and pastures. The 8-foot milldam (mi 2.8) should be portaged
on the left.

The river narrows below the dam, and the right side offers a Class II rapid. Remains of the old mill are just around the right bend.

US 64 (mi 3.0) can be used as a put-in to avoid the dam portage.

Few houses are seen, and the banks are generally wooded with steep hills. Class I rapids (mi 4.0) run for 100 feet. More rapids are found downstream with a few Class II rapids until a flat stretch (mi 6.4).

A Class I is at Rives Chapel Church Road (Chatham Co. 2170) bridge (mi 7.5), followed by flatwater to the take-out.

2	Carolina Hill Road (Chatham Co. 2168) roadside to NC 902 bridge		
Difficulty II–III		**Width** 20–80 ft	
Distance 6.0 mi		**Gradient** 18.3 ft/mi	
Scenery A (35%), B (65%)		**Map** page 136	

Gauge USGS *Rocky River at SR 1300 near Crutchfield Crossroads* and *Tick Creek near Mount Vernon Springs* measure only small drainage areas, but they can be used as indicators of water in this section. With more than 20 cfs on each gauge, the Rocky is usually above minimum.

A paddling gauge is painted on the NC 902 bridge. Minimum is 20 inches below zero. This gauge was repainted when the bridge was replaced. The gauge on the old bridge was set for a minimum of 6 inches below zero.

The last rapid can be seen from the NC 902 bridge at the take-out. It is a good indicator of water conditions in this section.

As water rises above 2 feet on the NC 902 paddling gauge, the difficulty becomes Class IV because of narrow channels, islands, and high gradient. Downed trees are common.

Notes See the previous section about Carolina Hill Road.

At the NC 902 bridge, the landowner on upstream left has allowed paddlers to park in the driveway if nothing is blocked, including the mailbox. Downstream left has been used as a portage path.

There are several islands in this section with blind turns. Caution should be used to avoid downed trees.

A rapid (mi 0.1) dropping 1.5 feet is the first of many in this section.

Continuous Class II rapids begin (mi 0.6) and end with a sloping drop through boulders at the site of an old mill (mi 0.8). Rebar can be seen on the sides of the main channel when water is low. Rapids separated by flat stretches continue.

Tick Creek (mi 2.3) enters on the right.

A 5-foot dam (mi 2.9) is just below a large island. It can be scouted from the left bank. The left side of the dam is broken making the drop less here, but this route requires turning to the right to miss large rocks. The most common run is to the right of the dam's middle, but at low water there are rocks to avoid. At high water, a swim will sweep one through downstream rapids. Portage the dam if not confident.

The next few hundred feet below the dam have several rapids closely spaced with fairly steep gradient. The final drop has a hole and boulder to avoid. This series of rapids is a Class III at low water levels.

There are scattered Class II rapids mixed with flatwater until a creek (mi 5.6) enters on the right. Class II rapids extend from here to the bridge. The final drop has a boulder to avoid in the outflow.

3	NC 902 bridge to Chatham Church Road (Chatham Co. 1953) bridge		
Difficulty I–II⁻		**Width** 60–200 ft	
Distance 8.5 mi		**Gradient** 7.1 ft/mi	
Scenery A (70%), B (30%)		**Map** page 136	

Gauge A paddling gauge is painted on the NC 902 bridge. Minimum is 22 inches below zero.

Notes See the previous section about NC 902.

Class I–II⁻ rapids are found in the first 4 miles. Most are separated by flat stretches, but in two areas the rapids run for a few hundred yards.

Backwaters from a dam start near Pittsboro-Goldston Road (Chatham Co. 1010) (mi 4.3). Take out here to shorten the trip and bypass the dam portage.

Stay back from the 20-foot Woody Dam (mi 7.4). The portage is on the left and covers a few hundred yards over an old roadbed. A fence on the right bank prevents access to the road passing near the dam.

A Class I is below the dam, and Bear Creek (mi 7.8) enters from the right. Another Class I is before reaching the take-out.

> **4** Chatham Church Road (Chatham Co. 1953) bridge to Old
> US 1 (Lee Co. 1466) bridge over Deep River at Moncure

Difficulty I–II, and one III		**Width** 45–800 ft
Distance 8.6 mi		**Gradient** 13.0 ft/mi
Scenery A (75%), B (25%)		**Map** page 136

Gauge A paddling gauge is painted on the US 15/501 bridge's center pier. It can be seen from the bank, downstream right. Minimum is 9 inches below zero.

Use the USGS *Deep River at Moncure* gauge for the Deep River.

Notes See the Deep River, Section 11 (page 74) about the take-out near the Old US 1 bridge.

After a right bend (mi 0.7), Class I–II rapids run for several hundred yards. The left bank is steep and rocky, rising to 100 feet.

A 4-foot ledge (mi 1.0) is within sight of the US 15/501 bridge. The steepest run is Class III on the left side where care must be used to avoid rocks at the bottom. The drop is more gradual on the right side. There are two smaller ledges before the US 15/501 bridge (mi 1.2).

Class I–II rock gardens (mi 1.6) are found in the next half-mile followed by flatwater.

After a right turn (mi 2.7), the riverbed gradient is noticeable as the view reveals a straight channel for 0.3 miles, with continuous rock gardens and ledges. The river drops 40 feet over the next mile.

One of the better ledge rapids (mi 3.0) is near the left side. When water is at minimum, it is difficult to find a route with enough water.

Class II rapids continue with only short stretches of flatwater. The banks are steep and rocky, especially on the right where they rise up to 150 feet above the river, displaying rhododendron.

The rapids on the Rocky end (mi 3.9) before reaching the Deep River. Land on the right bank is the White Pines Natural Area, 258 acres owned by the Triangle Land Conservancy. The preserve supports several stands of white pines, a tree that is normally found in the cooler mountain region of North Carolina. Hiking trails are open to the public. It is possible to take out here and portage about a half-mile up the rough road to the preserve parking lot.

The Rocky joins the Deep River (mi 4.5), and the remainder of the trip is described under the Deep River, Section 11 (page 74). Add 0.7 miles to the mileage given in the Deep River description to correct for distances from the Rocky River put-in.

Reed Bumgarner stuck on an old dam at low water
Rocky River (Cape Fear Basin), Section 2

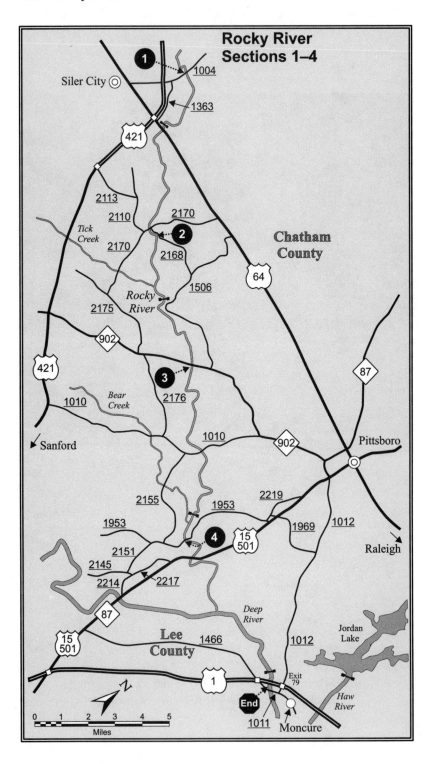

Rocky River
Sections 1–4

Cape Fear Basin

Six Runs Creek

County   Sampson

Topos   Faison, Turkey, Delway, Ingold

Six Runs Creek is a blackwater stream beginning in swamps north-east of Clinton in Sampson County. It flows south and joins Great Coharie Creek to form the Black River, 14 miles south of Clinton.

Six Runs Creek is swampy in its headwaters, as are most Sampson County rivers. The banks rise somewhat downstream, and it becomes a blackwater river confined to a single channel.

Sections 4–5 of Six Runs Creek were designated Outstanding Resource Waters in 1994. There has been some decrease in water quality in recent years, and the high concentration of hog farms in the Sampson County watersheds has caused concern.

1 Pine Ridge Road (Sampson Co. 1904) bridge to NC 24 bridge

Difficulty A	**Width**	5–60 ft
Distance 4.6 mi	**Gradient**	2.6 ft/mi
Scenery A	**Map**	page 140

Gauge USGS *Black River near Tomahawk* can be used as an indicator of water conditions even though it is 35 miles downstream of the put-in and measures the combined flow from Great Coharie, Little Coharie, and Six Runs Creeks. Water from this section takes 1–2 days to reach the gauge, making readings most useful when water is not rising or falling rapidly.

Estimated minimum is 700 cfs (6.0 ft). There are many beaver dams and much aquatic weed, but the beaver dams can usually be run at this minimum. A trip at 140 cfs (2.4 ft) took almost 6 hours.

Notes Beavers have been very active here—eighteen dams were seen on one trip. Their dams are separated in places by only a few hundred feet. Large ponds behind beaver dams are so numerous that the section becomes a swamp where the channel is often not so obvious. Wildlife is abundant and signs of human activity are rare—one bridge and one set of power lines.

Just below Old Warsaw Road (Sampson Co. 1919) bridge (mi 2.1), aquatic weeds become denser in spots, slowing progress.

A power line right-of-way (mi 2.9) provides a rare view of land a half-mile away rising 50 feet above the swamp.

On one trip, a large heron rookery with twenty-two nests was seen in a dead tree (mi 3.2). Rookeries are often sighted in the swampy areas of Sampson County rivers.

The swamps give way to actual banks (mi 4.4) up to a few feet high and extending to the take-out.

2	NC 24 bridge to Needmore Road (Sampson Co.1004) bridge		
Difficulty A		**Width** 25–50 ft	
Distance 5.5 mi		**Gradient** 3.5 ft/mi	
Scenery A (65%), B (35%)		**Map** page 140	

Gauge See Section 1. The gauge is 30 miles downstream. Estimated minimum is 250 cfs (3.3 ft).

Notes The banks in this section run from 2–8 feet, and the swampy character of the previous section is not seen here.

A railroad bridge (mi 0.4) is followed by Rowan Road (Sampson Co. 1924) (mi 1.2), and there is some development in the next half-mile.

The banks are tree-lined, but there are few trees beyond the banks. Many mussel shells are scattered on sandbars.

3	Needmore Road (Sampson Co.1004) bridge to River Road (Sampson Co. 1960) bridge		
Difficulty A		**Width** 45–60 ft	
Distance 6.6 mi		**Gradient** 3.5 ft/mi	
Scenery A		**Map** page 140	

Gauge See Section 1. The gauge is 25 miles downstream. Estimated minimum is 250 cfs (3.3 ft).

Notes Some cypress trees are along the banks, but there are few trees behind the thin buffer of trees near the water.

Stewarts Creek (mi 2.6) joins from the left.

The take-out road (mi 6.2) runs close to the river and can be seen on the right. Access and parking is much better at the bridge.

Quewhiffle Swamp joins from the left, a few hundred feet before reaching the take-out.

4 River Road (Sampson Co. 1960) bridge to Moores Bridge Road (Sampson Co. 1130) bridge

Difficulty A	**Width** 25–60 ft
Distance 7.8 mi	**Gradient** 0.9 ft/mi
Scenery A	**Map** page 140

Gauge See Section 1. The gauge is 18 miles downstream. Estimated minimum is 250 cfs (3.3 ft).

Notes The banks vary from 3–10 feet. Much of the land near the river has been logged, but few signs of development are seen.

After the US 421 bridge (mi 2.5), there is a narrow area where a large cypress tree grows in the stream.

5 Moores Bridge Road (Sampson Co. 1130) bridge to NC 903 (Sampson Co. 1003) bridge

Difficulty A	**Width** 25–60 ft
Distance 3.7 mi	**Gradient** 1.4 ft/mi
Scenery A	**Map** page 140

Gauge See Section 1. The gauge is 10 miles downstream. Estimated minimum is 250 cfs (3.3 ft).

Notes The banks range 3–8 feet at low water, and as in previous sections, there has been much logging near the banks.

The left channel at an island (mi 3.4) is the widest, but it is full of downed trees. The right channel, 25 feet wide, is clear and has small waves caused by a sloping streambed. Other than beaver dams and downed trees at water level, this is the closest thing to a rapid on Six Runs Creek.

Only 0.3 miles downstream of the take-out, Six Runs Creek joins Great Coharie Creek to form the Black River. A longer trip can be made by continuing 5.8 miles to the take-out for the Black River, Section 1 (page 40).

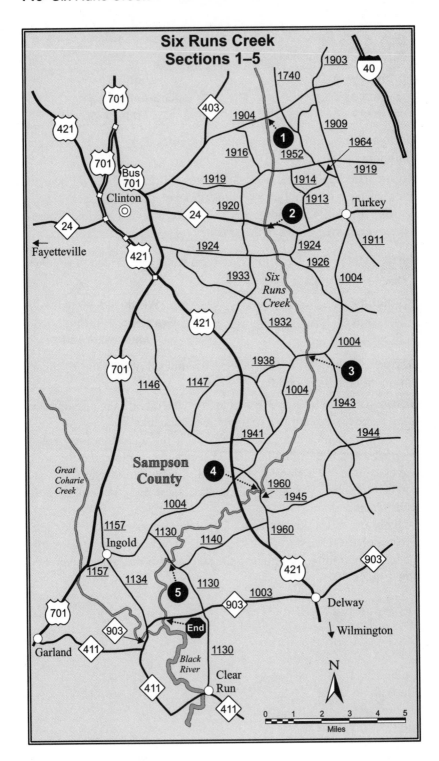

Cape Fear Basin

South River

Counties   Cumberland, Sampson, Bladen

Topos   Wade, Stedman, Autryville, Roseboro, Ammon, Garland,
             White Lake, Tomahawk, Rowan

The South River flows along the western border of Sampson County. It begins 7 miles south of Dunn at the confluence of its headwaters, Mingo Swamp and the Black River. This Black River, beginning in Harnett County near Angier, is often called the Little Black so that it is not confused with the much larger and more well-known Black River beginning in southern Sampson County.

Near its beginning, the South River is less than 4 miles east of the Cape Fear River. It is a blackwater stream with low to swampy banks and significant stands of cypress trees. The South River empties into the Black River, 30 miles south of Clinton. Falcon and Autryville are the only small towns to border the river. Occasional homes, farms, and logged land are seen, but a trip down the 85 miles of sections described is mainly one of splendid isolation.

The lower 50 miles of the South River were designated Outstanding Resource Waters in 1994.

① Green Path Road (Sampson Co. 1005) bridge at Falcon to Hayes Mill Road (Sampson Co. 1445) bridge		
Difficulty A	**Width** 10–100 ft	
Distance 6.8 mi	**Gradient** 1.2 ft/mi	
Scenery A (60%), B (40%)	**Map** page 147	

Gauge A local paddler uses old trestle pilings from an abandoned railroad a few hundred feet downstream of the NC 24 bridge. His rules: pilings submerged is plenty of water; a half-foot showing is enough water; a foot showing is too low.

The USGS *Black River near Tomahawk* gauge is usually a good indicator of water conditions on the South River even though the South River joins the Black River downstream of the gauge. The Black River gauge measures the combined flows from Little Coharie, Great Coharie, and Six Runs Creeks. These creeks are centered only about 15 miles east of the South River. Water takes 1–2 days to reach the gauge, making readings most useful when water is not rising or falling rapidly.

Estimated minimum is 700 cfs (6.0 ft).

Notes The river often braids into several channels through the swampy land. The best choice is where downed trees have been cleared. Look for old stumps on the side. Often the channel that was cleared is not the largest. Newly downed trees are common. Look beyond new downfalls to determine the best route.

Knees from the many cypress trees provide obstacles to avoid, especially where the channel is very narrow. Dense tree stands provide shade and often a closed canopy. Blackberry bushes are along the borders and can be picked while floating by.

Access is possible at US 13 (mi 4.3), but it is a busy highway with limited parking and long guardrails.

2 Hayes Mill Road (Sampson Co. 1445) bridge to Maxwell Road (Cumberland Co. 1006) bridge		
Difficulty A	**Width**	10–100 ft
Distance 5.7 mi	**Gradient**	1.2 ft/mi
Scenery A (65%), B (35%)	**Map**	page 147

Gauge See Section 1. Estimated minimum is 600 cfs (5.4 ft).

Notes See Section 1 for information about choosing the best channel. This section is similar, but more high ground and houses are seen.

The largest channel (mi 0.7) goes to the right, but the left is the best route. Clearing down the right channel stops after it passes a farm on the right bank.

Downstream of a wide area with several houses (mi 3.8) on the left, the downed tree saw cuts lead to a left turn and a narrow channel. Alligator weed is close to growing over the channel for a short distance.

3 Maxwell Road (Cumberland Co. 1006) bridge to Hollow Bridge Road (Cumberland Co. 2030) bridge at Autryville		
Difficulty A	**Width**	20–100 ft
Distance 8.7 mi	**Gradient**	1.0 ft/mi
Scenery A (70%), B (30%)	**Map**	page 147

Gauge See Section 1. Estimated minimum is 400 cfs (4.3 ft).

Notes Hollow Bridge Road is named South Gray Street (Sampson Co. 1414) on the east (left) side of the river.

A few farm roads are in this section, but the only houses seen are at Autryville. There is little high ground except where farm roads approach the river.

Logged land is often close to the stream, but cypress trees are still abundant. Poison ivy vines grow on many trees near the water.

Faircloth Bridge Road (Sampson Co. 1426) (mi 2.9) and NC 24 (mi 7.7) cross this section. Access is much easier at Hollow Bridge Road than at NC 24.

4 Hollow Bridge Road (Cumberland Co. 2030) bridge to Butler Island Bridge Road (Cumberland Co. 2035) bridge	
Difficulty A	**Width** 15–90 ft
Distance 9.4 mi	**Gradient** 1.7 ft/mi
Scenery A	**Map** page 148

Gauge See Section 1. Estimated minimum is 300 cfs (3.6 ft).

Notes See the previous section about Hollow Bridge Road.

The ground is swampy in most of the previous sections, but here there are usually banks a few feet above water. Tall trees line the banks, providing shade and a closed tree canopy.

Where a choice in routes must be made, choose where stumps, from the clearing of trees blocking the channel, are seen.

Where the land was logged, leaving a thin buffer of trees on the bank, many trees were blown down by storms because nothing remained to divert the force of the wind on trees near the river.

The cleared channel (mi 4.7) becomes very narrow for a short distance. Cypress knees must be avoided and tree limbs are at face level.

5 Butler Island Bridge Road (Cumberland Co. 2035) bridge to NC 242 bridge	
Difficulty A	**Width** 30–80 ft
Distance 4.4 mi	**Gradient** 1.4 ft/mi
Scenery A	**Map** page 148

Gauge See Section 1. Estimated minimum is 300 cfs (3.6 ft).

Notes Tall trees line the bank to form a closed canopy providing shade. When cloudy, it seems almost dark in densely-covered areas.

At low water, sandbars are exposed, and banks range from swampy to 8 feet high.

Downstream of the confluence with Big Swamp (mi 2.9), the South River is designated Outstanding Resource Waters.

6 NC 242 bridge to Boykin Bridge Road (Sampson Co. 1214) bridge

Difficulty A	**Width** 30–60 ft
Distance 6.2 mi	**Gradient** 1.3 ft/mi
Scenery A	**Map** page 148

Gauge See Section 1. Estimated minimum is 300 cfs (3.6 ft).

Notes A farm (mi 2.0) is one of the few signs of development, but there are several areas where logging has come close to the river.

The blackwater course meanders with banks swampy to several feet high. There are numerous places where other channels appear to join, but these are usually only small coves.

7 Boykin Bridge Road (Sampson Co. 1214) bridge to NC 701 access

Difficulty A	**Width** 25–90 ft
Distance 10.4 mi	**Gradient** 1.6 ft/mi
Scenery A	**Map** page 148

Gauge See Section 1. Estimated minimum is 300 cfs (3.6 ft).

Notes A Wildlife boating access is at NC 701.

There are few signs of development, some logged land, and occasional sandy banks up to 8 feet high.

Green Sea Road (Bladen Co. 1503) (mi 3.4) can be used for access. Helltown Road (Bladen Co. 1528) (mi 7.7) can also be used for access but requires going through heavy brush.

8 NC 701 access to NC 41 bridge

Difficulty A	**Width** 35–65 ft
Distance 8.6 mi	**Gradient** 1.2 ft/mi
Scenery A	**Map** page 149

Gauge See Section 1. Estimated minimum is 300 cfs (3.6 ft).

Notes A Wildlife boating access is at NC 701.

After the first few miles, the banks rise to 5–10 feet. More houses and cabins are seen than in the previous section. Many oaks and cypress trees shade the river.

> ⑨ NC 41 bridge to Ennis Bridge Road (Bladen Co. 1007) access

Difficulty	A	**Width**	25–90 ft
Distance	9.4 mi	**Gradient**	1.1 ft/mi
Scenery	A	**Map**	page 149

Gauge See Section 1. Estimated minimum is 300 cfs (3.6 ft).

Notes A Wildlife boating access entrance is 0.1 miles west of the Ennis Bridge Road bridge. The ramp is 0.2 river miles upstream right of the bridge.

At low water, many sandbars are available for lunch and rest stops. The river is confined to one channel with banks ranging 1–12 feet high.

There are a few houses in the first 1.5 miles where roads approach the river on the right.

The river continues twisting and turning. A rare straight stretch (mi 6.6) gives a view for 0.3 miles downstream.

> ⑩ Ennis Bridge Road (Bladen Co. 1007) access to Beattys Bridge Road (Bladen Co. 1550) bridge on Black River

Difficulty	A	**Width**	55–110 ft
Distance	13.4 mi	**Gradient**	1.1 ft/mi
Scenery	A (85%), B (15%)	**Map**	page 149

Gauge See Section 1. Estimated minimum is 300 cfs (3.6 ft).

Notes See the previous section about the Ennis Bridge Road access.

Many large coves are off the main channel.

Land on the left bank is part of a conservation easement (mi 7.7) from International Paper Company and managed by the Coastal Land Trust. The easement protects a narrow buffer of 271 acres, running to the confluence with the South River and extending 5 miles up the right bank of the Black River.

The South River joins the Black River (mi 9.7). A primitive campsite is 0.5 miles upstream on the Black River and is available by reservation. For campsite information and a description of the remainder of this section, see the Black River, Section 5 (page 42). Add 5.8 miles to the mileage given in the Black River description to correct for distance from the South River put-in.

Steve Henderson paddling South River, Section 3

Cape Fear Basin

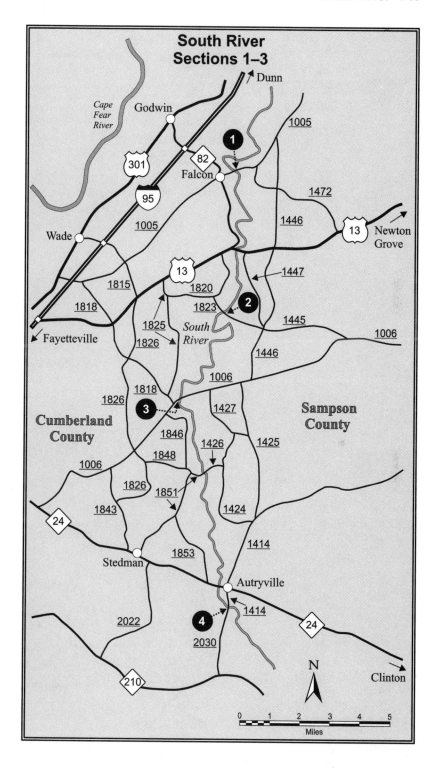

South River
Sections 1–3

Dunn

Cape
Fear
River

Godwin

1005

1

301

82

95

Falcon

1472

1446

13

Newton
Grove

Wade

1005

13

1447

1815

1820

1818

1823

2

1445

1006

Fayetteville

1825

South
River

1826

1446

1006

1818

1006

1826

3

1427

Sampson
County

Cumberland
County

1846

1426

1425

1848

1006

1826

1424

1843

1851

24

1414

Stedman

1853

Autryville

2022

4

1414

24

Clinton

2030

N

210

0   1   2   3   4   5
Miles

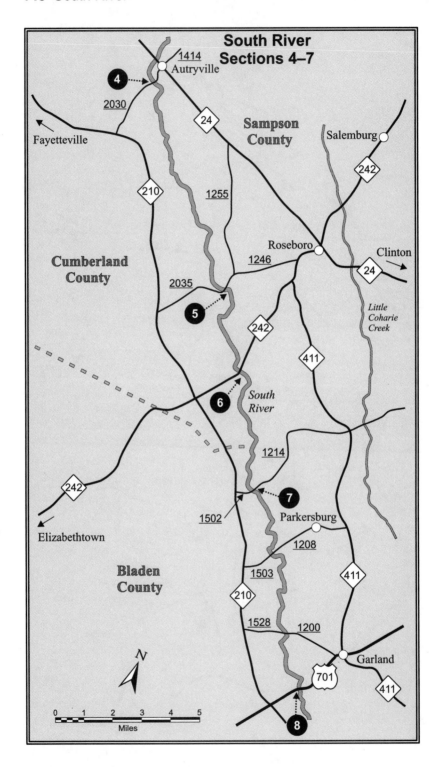

South River
Sections 4–7

1414
Autryville

4

2030

24

Sampson
County

Salemburg

242

Fayetteville

210

1255

Cumberland
County

Roseboro

1246

Clinton

24

2035

5

242

Little
Coharie
Creek

411

South
River

6

1214

242

1502

7

Parkersburg

Elizabethtown

1208

Bladen
County

1503

210

1528   1200

N

701

Garland

411

411

8

0   1   2   3   4   5
Miles

Cape Fear Basin

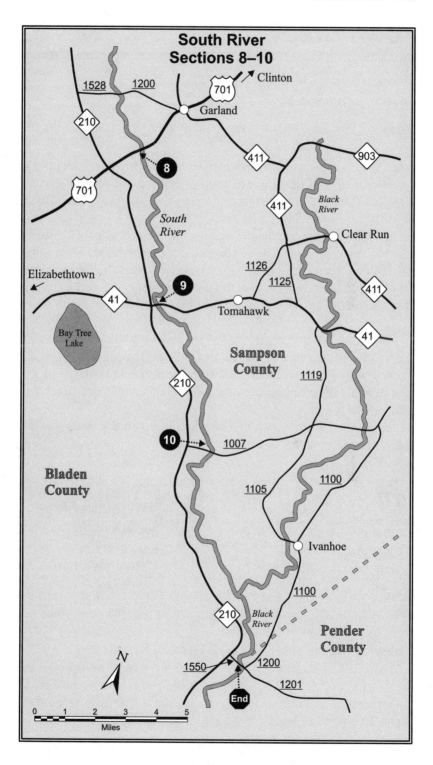

South River
Sections 8–10

Clinton

701

1528   1200

Garland

210

411

903

701

411

Black
River

South
River

8

Clear Run

Elizabethtown

1126

411

41

1125

9

Tomahawk

41

Bay Tree
Lake

Sampson
County

1119

210

10   1007

Bladen
County

1105   1100

Ivanhoe

1100

210   Black
River

Pender
County

N

1550   1200

0 1 2 3 4 5
Miles

1201

End

Town Creek

County   Brunswick

Topos   Lewis Swamp, Winnabow, Wilmington, Carolina Beach

Town Creek begins as a blackwater stream in Brunswick County at the eastern edge of the Green Swamp. It flows to the southeast, passing US 17 and NC 133 before emptying into the Cape Fear River, downstream from Wilmington.

In 1664 a group of English settlers from Barbados established Charles Town on Town Creek near the Cape Fear River. Their effort failed three years later because of hostile coastal Indians, pirates, weak supply lines, mosquitoes, and other problems that drove the residents south, where they founded the city of Charleston, South Carolina.

Town Creek is prime wildlife habitat and wetlands, and much of it is protected for the future. The North Carolina Coastal Land Trust has worked with state and federal agencies, timber companies, and private individuals to protect almost 6,000 acres along Town Creek and tributaries.

Alligators are often seen in Town Creek, especially along the last few miles before reaching the Cape Fear.

 Rock Creek Road (Brunswick Co. 1411) bridge to Gordon Lewis Road (Brunswick Co. 1567) access on Rice Creek

Difficulty A		**Width** 25–300 ft	
Distance 6.9 mi		**Gradient** 0 ft/mi	
Scenery A (70%), B (30%)		**Map** page 153	

Gauge None. Always above minimum. There are a few downed trees and beaver dams in the first 1.5 miles. Farther downstream, a small tidal influence is noticeable.

Notes A Wildlife boating access is on Gordon Lewis Road.

The creek is narrow for the first 2 miles. There are cypress and tupelo-gum trees and many palmetto plants.

Some trees require squeezing under and a few require portage, depending on water level. Near a 2-foot beaver dam (mi 0.4), land on the left bank for the next mile is part of the Ev-Henwood Nature Preserve. It is open to the public, with an entrance on Rock Creek Road. The preserve has hiking trails but no boat access.

An area with lakes (mi 2.3) is on the left, and the creek channel becomes 80 feet wide.

Town Creek Pottery is upstream left of the US 17 bridge (mi 3.0). They allow parking and boat access for $2. Canoe rentals are also available. Downstream left of the bridge is also often used for boat access.

The creek swings left and runs close to US 17 (mi 3.3) for a few hundred yards.

A 60-foot wide channel (mi 4.3) on the right, where Town Creek is 100 feet wide, should not be mistaken for Rice Creek. It leads back upstream.

Turn into the mouth of Rice Creek on the right (mi 4.9). Town Creek is 300 feet wide, and Rice Creek is about 80 feet wide. There are no signs marking Rice Creek. If the turn into Rice Creek is missed, 0.5 miles downstream on Town Creek, the left bank rises 25 feet and has many homes. Turn back to find Rice Creek.

On Rice Creek, a channel is to the left (mi 5.5). Taking it goes through a loop, adding 0.3 miles to the trip.

---

2 Gordon Lewis Road (Brunswick Co. 1567) access on Rice Creek to NC 133 bridge

Difficulty A		**Width**	85–200 ft
Distance 16.5 mi		**Gradient**	0 ft/mi
Scenery A (75%), B (25%)		**Map**	page 153

Gauge None. Always above minimum. There is a tidal influence from the Cape Fear River. Tide tables are available for Campbell Island, near the mouth of Town Creek, where the tide range is about 3–5 feet. In the beginning of this section, the tide is estimated to lag the Campbell Island tide by about 5–6 hours. At the NC 133 bridge, the tide runs about 2 feet with a 2-hour lag. Since this is a long section, it is best to time the trip to paddle with an outgoing tide in the last half.

Notes A Wildlife boating access is on Gordon Lewis Road.

This is a long section, but a Wildlife boating access is planned at mile 10.3. It will allow this section to be divided into 10.3 and 5.2-mile trips. Completion is expected during 2003.

From the put-in, go left on Rice Creek. Turn right at the confluence with Town Creek (mi 2.0).

The banks are mainly swampy with occasional privately-owned high ground. Cypress trees, palmetto plants, and marsh grass are common.

After high ground (mi 2.5) on the left with houses, the creek widens (mi 3.0), and there is a channel straight ahead and one to the right. Take the channel to the right because going straight ahead leads upstream on Morgan Branch.

A railroad (mi 6.8) crosses, and downstream the creek takes large loops and folds back on itself many times. In paddling the next 5 miles, the course only advances a mile in a straight line.

3	NC 133 bridge to Cape Fear River's Campbell Island and return		
Difficulty A		**Width**	65–8,000 ft
Distance 9.0 mi		**Gradient**	0 ft/mi
Scenery A (50%), B (50%)		**Map**	page 153

Gauge See Section 2.

Notes The creek passes a few points of higher ground, but it is mainly tidal flats with marsh grass. Alligators are frequently seen along this section.

At the mouth of Town Creek (mi 3.9), there are several islands visible in the wide Cape Fear River. Campbell Island is 0.5 miles downstream and 0.2 miles off the right bank. The island makes a remote lunch stop. If wind is too strong on the Cape Fear, it is easy to skip visiting the island.

Campbell Island (mi 4.5) was used for bombing practice in the 1940s. A paddling trip around the island adds 3.2 miles to the trip.

■

(Bobby) *Yeah, we beat it didn't we? Didn't we beat that?*
(Lewis) *You don't beat it. You don't beat this river.*
                    —*Deliverance* (the movie, 1972)

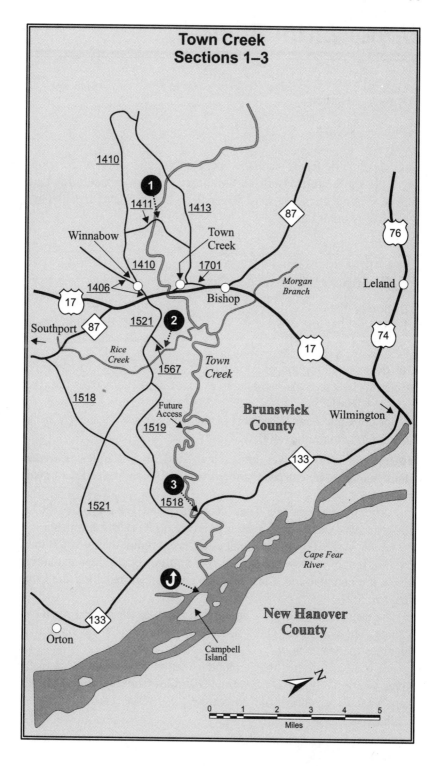

**Town Creek
Sections 1–3**

1410

1

1411   1413

87

76

Winnabow   Town
Creek

1410   1701   *Morgan
Branch*

17   1406   Bishop   Leland

Southport   87   1521   **2**

74

*Rice
Creek*   1567   *Town
Creek*   17

1518   Future
Access   **Brunswick
County**   Wilmington

1519

133

1521   1518   **3**

Cape Fear
River

133   **New Hanover
County**

Orton   Campbell
Island

N

0   1   2   3   4   5
Miles

Cape Fear Basin

Upper Little River

County   Harnett

Topo   Erwin

The Upper Little River watershed begins in Lee County on the southeast side of Sanford. It flows southeast through agricultural land. Before joining the Cape Fear River near Erwin, it has rock ledges, which form small rapids.

> **1** Ross Road (Harnett Co. 2016) bridge to NC 217 bridge over the Cape Fear River near Erwin

Difficulty B–I–II		**Width** 30–400 ft	
Distance 6.9 mi		**Gradient** 6.5 ft/mi	
Scenery A (70%), B (30%)		**Map** page 155	

Gauge A paddling gauge is on the put-in bridge, downstream right. Minimum is 0 feet. At levels above 2 feet, tree limbs over the river become hazards.

For the Cape Fear River part of the trip, use USGS *Cape Fear at Lillington*. Minimum is 400 cfs (1.3 ft).

Notes Water flows over gravel and sand at 2–4 miles per hour. Many trees jut over the river, and good boat control is needed to avoid them.

Farmland is near the Titan Roberts Road (Harnett Co. 2021) bridge (mi 2.4), and farms border the river in the next 1.5 miles.

A half-foot ledge (mi 3.4) makes a Class I rapid, then it is flat until a 1-foot ledge (mi 4.4). There are five similar rock ledges extending across the channel and a few smaller ones before reaching the Cape Fear (mi 5.2).

The transition from the Upper Little River to the Cape Fear River is huge. The Cape Fear is ten times wider and usually has more than ten times the water flow.

For a description of the remainder of this trip, see the Cape Fear River, Section 3 (page 51). Subtract 0.9 miles from the mileage in the Cape Fear River description to correct for distances from the Upper Little River put-in.

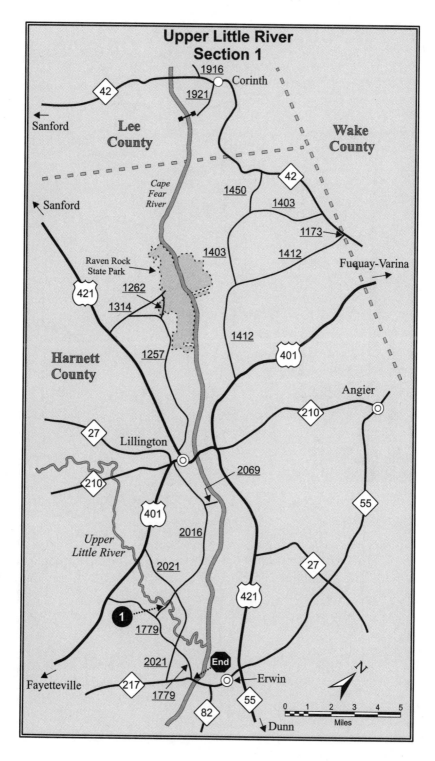

Upper Little River
Section 1

1916

Corinth

42

← Sanford

1921

Lee County

Wake County

42

← Sanford

Cape Fear River

1450

1403

1173

1403

1412

Fuquay-Varina

Raven Rock State Park

421

1262

1314

1412

1257

401

Harnett County

Angier

210

27

Lillington

210

2069

55

401

2016

Upper Little River

2021

421

27

1

1779

2021

End

Erwin

Fayetteville

217

1779

55

82

Dunn

N

0 1 2 3 4 5
Miles

Cape Fear Basin

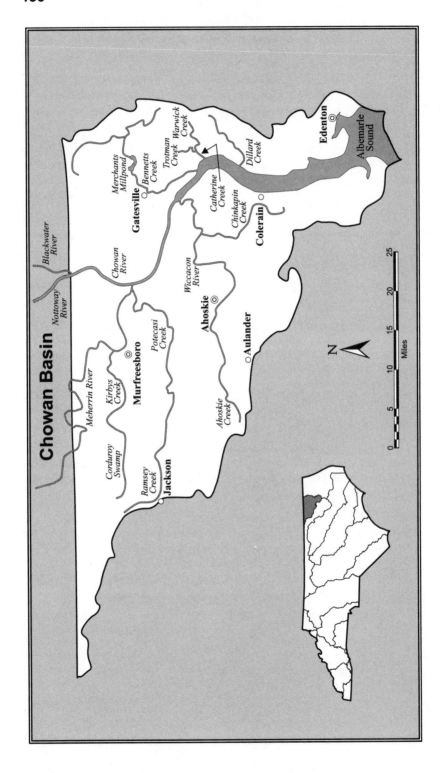

Chowan Basin

The Chowan Basin begins in southeastern Virginia. The Blackwater River and Nottoway River, major tributaries in Virginia, meet at the North Carolina border to form the Chowan River. The entire watershed is 5,439 square miles, but only twenty-five percent (1,378 square miles) is in North Carolina. The North Carolina portion of the Chowan Basin is located in the Coastal Plain.

Major tributaries of the Chowan River are Bennetts Creek, Meherrin River, Potecasi Creek, and Wiccacon River.

The Chowan River empties into Albemarle Sound near Edenton. The Chowan Basin is part of the Albemarle-Pamlico estuary, the second largest estuary in the United States.

The basin contains large cypress and tupelo-gum tree swamps. Merchants Millpond State Park, 3,252 acres, is an excellent example of a blackwater swamp in this area. The Chowan Swamp Game Land protects almost 11,000 acres and borders the Chowan River.

For many centuries, Algonquin Indians lived on the banks of the Chowan. Colonists migrated from Virginia in the late 1600s and established farms. Commercial boats ventured up the Chowan and tributaries for trade.

Herring fishing was a major source of income. Each spring, herring swim from the sea, into coastal waters and upriver to spawn. Millions per year were netted and processed until water quality declined. In the early 1970s algae blooms caused massive fish kills, and brought the basin problems to the public's attention.

In recent years, with the help of citizen volunteers and government agencies, action has been taken to reduce nitrogen and phosphorus runoff and discharges from entering the water. Dioxin from some commercial plants has also been a problem; it is being reduced and monitored. The Chowan has shown improvement, but more is needed.

Bennetts Creek

Counties   Gates, Hertford, Chowan

Topos   Merchants Millpond, Gatesville, Mintonsville

Bennetts Creek's headwaters are in northeastern Gates County, just west of the Great Dismal Swamp National Wildlife Refuge. Near Sunbury, two swamps converge to form Bennetts Creek. It flows west through Lassiter Swamp and into Merchants Millpond State Park (page 173).

Below Merchants Millpond, Bennetts Creek turns to the south, passes by Gatesville, and flows through the Chowan Swamp and into the Chowan River.

The Stewards of Bennetts Creek is a group of volunteers who watch over Bennetts Creek and assist the Merchants Millpond staff. Several times a year, they remove trash and clear a path through downed trees on Bennetts Creek below Merchants Millpond. They have also provided the labor to construct the steps and dock at the put-in.

1 Millpond Road (Gates Co. 1400) access to NC 37 access at Gatesville

Difficulty A	**Width** 20–80 ft
Distance 5.8 mi	**Gradient** 0 ft/mi
Scenery A	**Map** page 160

Gauge None. Always above minimum.

Notes At the Millpond Road bridge, across the road from the small dam on the millpond, there are wooden steps and a dock. This access is part of Merchants Millpond State Park.

A picnic area and dock at the NC 37 bridge are provided by Gatesville.

The creek quickly narrows to 25 feet as blackwater flows through dense stands of tupelo-gum and cypress trees. For about the first mile, the creek is within the boundaries of Merchants Millpond State Park.

The banks are mainly swampy, but ground rises as high as 25 feet in places.

2 NC 37 access at Gatesville to Cannons Ferry Road (Chowan Co. 1231) access on Chowan River

Difficulty A	**Width** 70–7,500 ft
Distance 15.9 mi	**Gradient** 0 ft/mi
Scenery A (75%), B (25%)	**Map** page 160

Gauge None. Always above minimum. On the Chowan River, there is a slight tidal influence. The Chowan River is wide, and wind can whip up whitecaps.

Notes See the previous section about the NC 37 access.

A Wildlife boating access is off Cannons Ferry Road at the end of a small channel, a quarter-mile off the river.

Most of the land between the right bank and the Chowan River is part of the Chowan Swamp Game Land.

Camping is difficult because rare high ground on the left bank is private, and the right bank is mostly swampy. A creek (mi 1.6) on the right contains Hermit Island, high ground 500 feet up the creek, which is often used as a campsite.

Nixon's Ditch (mi 5.9) is a channel on the left leading 0.3 miles to a fishing club's property bordering Carter Road (Gates Co. 1100).

The channel widens to 300 feet (mi 9.6), and water lilies are along the sides. It is 1,000 feet wide just before the confluence with the Chowan River (mi 12.5.). The Chowan is a mile wide here and broadens to 1.5 miles at the take-out.

If wind is anticipated to be a problem on the Chowan, protection from the open water can be had by using Warwick Creek (page 178) as a take-out. Stay close to the left bank, and just before reaching the head of Holiday Island (mi 13.5), turn left to go up Catherine Creek. At the fork with Trotman Creek, bear to the right up Warwick Creek. This option adds 1.2 miles to the trip.

Continuing on to Cannons Ferry, depending on wind direction, it is often best to pass to the left of Holiday Island (mi 13.5) for protection. The large, scenic island has many cypress trees with hanging moss but no dry ground.

At the end of Holiday Island (mi 14.9) move to the left bank. A small channel (mi 15.6) is on the left past a few houses. A "No-Wake" buoy is just in front of wooden windbreaks. The ramp is a quarter-mile up this 30-foot wide channel.

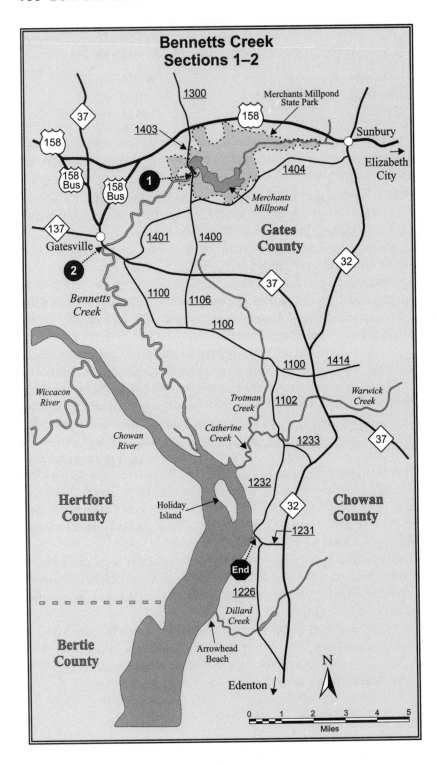

**Bennetts Creek
Sections 1–2**

Merchants Millpond
State Park

Sunbury

Elizabeth
City

Merchants
Millpond

Gates
County

Gatesville

Bennetts
Creek

Wiccacon
River

Chowan
River

Trotman
Creek

Catherine
Creek

Warwick
Creek

Hertford
County

Holiday
Island

Chowan
County

End

Dillard
Creek

Bertie
County

Arrowhead
Beach

Edenton

N

0 1 2 3 4 5
Miles

Chowan Basin

Chowan River

Counties   Southampton (Virginia), Hertford, Gates, Chowan

Topos   Riverdale, Winton, Gatesville, Harrellsville, Mintonsville

The Chowan River begins as a large river on the North Carolina border at the confluence of the Nottoway and Blackwater Rivers, 10 miles northeast of Murfreesboro and 10 miles south of Franklin, Virginia. It flows southeast to Albemarle Sound. There is occasional high ground, but it flows through mostly swampy land with cypress and tupelo-gum trees along the banks.

Because the Chowan is large and has several public boat ramps, motorboats are frequently seen plying its waters. Groups of poles in the river are used to string nets when herring are in season.

Wind can be a major obstacle for paddlers because the river is up to 2 miles wide.

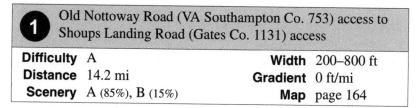

1 Old Nottoway Road (VA Southampton Co. 753) access to Shoups Landing Road (Gates Co. 1131) access

Difficulty A	**Width** 200–800 ft
Distance 14.2 mi	**Gradient** 0 ft/mi
Scenery A (85%), B (15%)	**Map** page 164

Gauge USGS *Blackwater River near Franklin, VA* and *Nottoway River near Sebrell, VA*. Always above minimum. There is a slight tidal influence. This is a wide river where wind can whip up whitecaps.

Notes The put-in is in Virginia at Battle Beach on the Nottoway River, less than a mile from the start of the Chowan River. Dockside Restaurant, on Old Nottoway Road, has a ramp. Pay $3 at the honor box.

A Wildlife boating access is at Shoups Landing Road, downstream left of the US 13/158 bridge near Winton.

The Nottoway River crosses into North Carolina (mi 0.6) and meets the Blackwater River (mi 0.9) to become the Chowan River.

The banks are mainly swampy with cypress and tupelo-gum trees. Occasional high banks are mostly private property.

The Meherrin River (mi 11.7) enters from the right. Parkers Ferry is 0.5 miles upstream and can be used as an access point. See the Meherrin River, Section 4 (page 171).

Decaying buildings at Chowan Beach (mi 12.7) on the right were once a part of an amusement park which closed in the 1970s. A mannequin peering from the Laff Land building adds an eerie flavor.

The take-out is just beyond the US 13/158 bridge (mi 14.0).

---

2 Shoups Landing Road (Gates Co. 1131) access to New Ferry Road (Gates Co. 1111) access

Difficulty A	**Width**	700–2,200 ft
Distance 9.8 mi	**Gradient**	0 ft/mi
Scenery A (40%), B (40%), C (20%)	**Map**	page 165

Gauge See Section 1.

Notes See the previous section about Shoups Landing Road access.

A Wildlife boating access is at New Ferry Road reached from Gatesville.

Channel markers (mi 1.2) begin marking the deep water for large boats.

Tunis (mi 2.8) is on the right before reaching power lines. A Wildlife boating access is at the end of Hertford Co. 1402.

Spanish moss hangs from many of the trees, and ospreys have large nests in some of the cypress trees.

Sarem Creek (mi 9.5) enters on the left, near the take-out.

---

3 New Ferry Road (Gates Co. 1111) access to Cannons Ferry Road (Chowan Co. 1231) access

Difficulty A	**Width**	800–7,500 ft
Distance 8.9 mi	**Gradient**	0 ft/mi
Scenery A (45%), B (55%)	**Map**	page 165

Gauge See Section 1.

Notes See the previous section about the New Ferry Road access.

A Wildlife boating access is off Cannons Ferry Road at the end of a small channel, a quarter-mile off the river.

The Wiccacon River (mi 1.6) enters on the right.

A private boat ramp (mi 3.5) can be used for access. See the take-out for the Wiccacon River, Section 2 (page 181).

Bennetts Creek (mi 5.9) joins from the left at a back angle. In the previous few miles, the Chowan is about a half-mile wide, but here it widens to a mile and reaches 1.5 miles at the take-out.

Catherine Creek enters from the left, across from the head of Holiday Island (mi 6.6). Depending on wind direction, it is often best to pass to the left of Holiday Island for protection. The large scenic island has many cypress trees with hanging moss but no dry ground.

At the end of Holiday Island (mi 8.0) move to the left bank. A small channel (mi 8.7) is on the left, past a few houses. A "No-Wake" buoy is just in front of wooden windbreaks. The ramp is a quarter-mile up this 30-foot wide channel.

From the take-out, it is 17.3 miles to the Wildlife boating access at US 17 near Edenton. The Chowan broadens to over 2 miles wide before entering Albemarle Sound.

Shells embedded in the bank of the Meherrin River

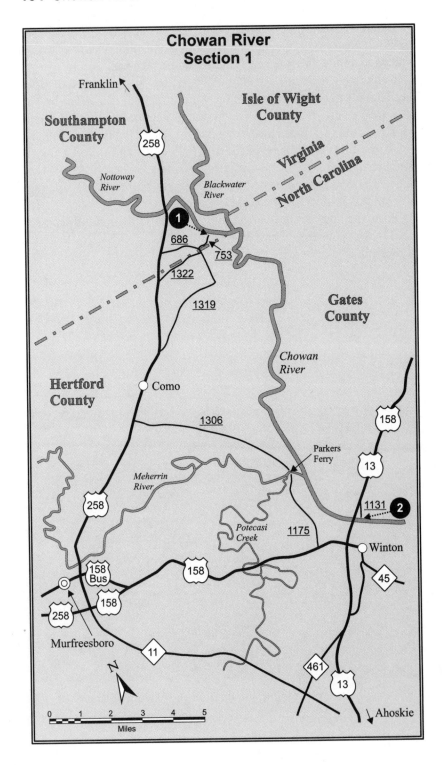

Chowan Basin

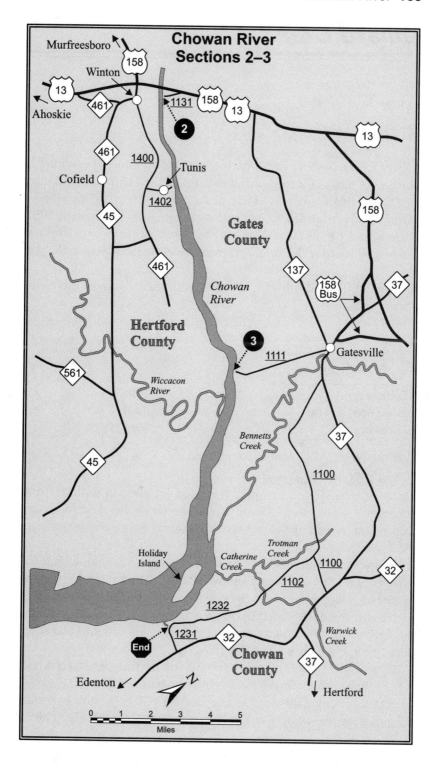

Dillard Creek

County   Chowan

Topo   Vahalla

Dillard Creek is shown on topo maps as Indian Creek, beginning in northeast Chowan County. It flows southwest into Dillard's Millpond.

Dillard's Millpond was built in the early 1700s and powered a sawmill and gristmill. The gristmill was operated by water until 1952, when a tractor motor was installed and is still in use today. Cornmeal can be purchased at the building upstream left of the bridge at the put-in.

From Dillard's Millpond, Dillard Creek makes a short run to the Chowan River.

1	Dillard's Mill Road (Chowan Co. 1226) bridge to Chowan River and return		
Difficulty A		**Width** 35–80 ft	
Distance 5.9 mi		**Gradient** 0 ft/mi	
Scenery B		**Map** page 168	

Gauge None. Always above minimum.

Notes Dillard's Millpond is 0.1 miles upstream of the bridge at the put-in. It is possible to explore the pond for about a mile before it becomes a small creek. The bridge at the put-in has low clearance. Depending on water level and boat size, it may not be possible to paddle under the bridge.

Below the put-in, Dillard Creek is a blackwater stream with many cypress trees, Spanish moss, and water lilies. The banks are swampy in the beginning, but ground rises up to 20 feet in places.

Houses and docks (mi 2.0) on the left for the next mile are part of the Arrowhead Beach community. The boat ramp (mi 2.5) and small dock (mi 2.7) are only for use by residents.

Cypress trees stand in a cove (mi 2.9) on the Chowan River where it is 1.6 miles wide. This is the return point for the trip.

Instead of doing this section as a round-trip, it is possible to paddle 2.7 miles up the wide Chowan River to the Cannons Ferry Road access. See the take-out for the Chowan River, Section 3 (page 162). Consider this possibility only if the wind and current are favorable. A strong wind will cause whitecaps on the Chowan.

Holiday Island on Chowan River, Section 3

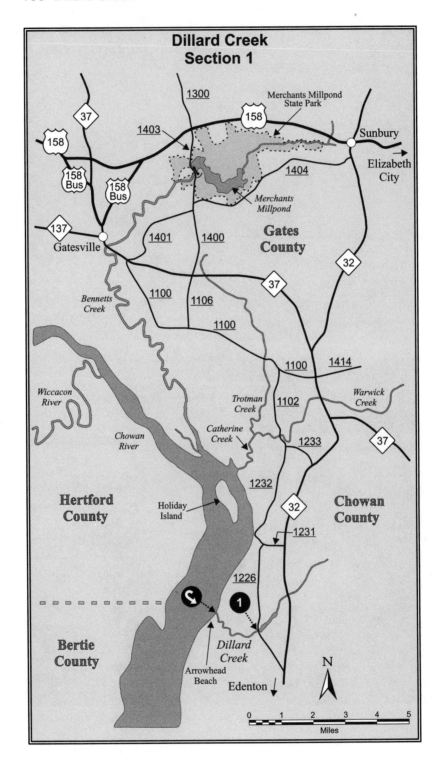

Dillard Creek
Section 1

37

158

1300

1403

158

Merchants Millpond
State Park

Sunbury

Elizabeth
City

158
Bus

158
Bus

1404

Merchants
Millpond

137

Gatesville

1401

1400

Gates
County

32

1100

1106

37

1100

Bennetts
Creek

1100

1414

Wiccacon
River

Warwick
Creek

Trotman
Creek

1102

Chowan
River

Catherine
Creek

1233

37

1232

Hertford
County

Holiday
Island

Chowan
County

32

1231

1226

Bertie
County

Dillard
Creek

Edenton

N

Arrowhead
Beach

0   1   2   3   4   5
Miles

Chowan Basin

Meherrin River

Counties   Northampton, Southampton (VA), Hertford

Topos   Margrettsville, Boykins, Sunbeam, Murfreesboro,
            Winton

The Meherrin River begins in south central Virginia, about 50 miles northwest of Emporia. It travels over 100 miles in Virginia, flowing past Lawrenceville and through Emporia, where a reservoir created by a 20-foot dam is used for hydroelectric power. Below the dam, it flows southeast into North Carolina, passing Murfreesboro on its way to the Chowan River.

The river has a sandy bottom, some swampy areas, but mainly dry banks. The sections described below have occasional high banks embedded with shells, telling of the time that this was an ancient seabed.

At low water, there are many downed trees exposed as well as large sandbars. It is relatively undeveloped and suitable for wildlife viewing and camping trips.

In *Virginia Whitewater*, Roger Corbett says remoteness is the Meherrin's middle name. It continues to live up to its name in North Carolina.

---

1 Branchs Bridge Road (Northampton Co. 1339) roadside to NC 35 bridge

Difficulty	A	**Width**	30–100 ft
Distance	12.6 mi	**Gradient**	0.8 ft/mi
Scenery	A	**Map**	page 172

Gauge USGS *Meherrin River at Emporia, VA*. Estimated minimum is 75 cfs (2.3 ft). The gauge is 37 miles upstream from the put-in.

Notes The put-in is where Branchs Bridge Road turns east and runs close to the river, 0.8 miles from the bridge. Branchs Bridge (mi 1.1) can be used for access, but banks are steep and covered in poison ivy.

The banks range from 10–60 feet high. There are many downed trees. A few trees span the river, and large sandbars at low water narrow the channel to make it more likely that passage is blocked. High sandbars make fine campsites if there is little chance of rising water.

Few signs of development are seen, although there are many farm fields near the banks.

The river makes a run to the north and enters Virginia (mi 4.5) for the next 4 miles. Roads shown on topo maps approaching the river in this area are private and not available for access.

The supports on a railroad bridge (mi 11.9) are closely spaced and often collect downed trees.

2	NC 35 bridge to Boones Bridge Road (Hertford Co. 1355) bridge		
Difficulty A		**Width**	70–100 ft
Distance 4.5 mi		**Gradient**	0.4 ft/mi
Scenery A		**Map**	page 172

Gauge See Section 1.

Notes As in the previous section, the river swings into Virginia (mi 1.3) but only for a half-mile.

Many willow trees hang over sandbars exposed at lower water levels. At low water, a few downed tree blockages are likely.

3	Boones Bridge Road (Hertford Co. 1355) bridge to US 258 access at Murfreesboro		
Difficulty A		**Width**	40–200 ft
Distance 17.0 mi		**Gradient**	0.2 ft/mi
Scenery A (90%), B (10%)		**Map**	page 172

Gauge See Section 1. There is a tidal influence starting about halfway down.

Notes Downstream left of the US 258 bridge is a Wildlife boating access. The ramp is 500 feet from the river, connected by a narrow channel.

The distance makes for a long day, especially at low water because downed trees in the beginning of the trip can block the route.

A large island (mi 5.2) is where the channel narrows to 40–50 feet. It widens in a sharp left bend (mi 6.9).

The channel (mi 10.1) broadens to 100 feet wide where a tidal influence can be detected, water lilies are along the edges, and motorboats often come for fishing.

4	US 258 access at Murfreesboro to Parkers Ferry Road (Hertford Co. 1306) end		
Difficulty A		**Width** 175–500 ft	
Distance 11.7 mi		**Gradient** 0 ft/mi	
Scenery A (50%), B (50%)		**Map** page 172	

Gauge None. Always above minimum. Tides from the Chowan River influence this section but are easy to paddle against. Wind can be a problem.

Notes See the previous section about the US 258 access.

The take-out is where Parkers Ferry, a two-car diesel-powered boat, provides transportation across the river. The north side of the river is recommended for a take-out because parking space is available near the ferry operator's office.

Many cypress and tupelo-gum trees line the banks, and water lilies grow at the water's edge.

Houses and cabins are near the water in the first half of this section.

In a left turn, a high, eroded right bank (mi 0.9) displays seashells. It is an example of similar banks upstream showing evidence of the ancient seabed.

A channel (mi 5.6) on the right is a shortcut. Taking it cuts off a large loop, saving 2.0 miles.

Staying with the main channel, the shortcut channel (mi 7.8) comes in on the right.

Many groups of poles in the river are used to string nets to catch herring.

Potecasi Creek (mi 11.4) joins on the right, and the ferry landings are just downstream. A half-mile below the take-out, the Meherrin becomes part of the Chowan River.

■

We work hard at doing nothing: we seek happiness in boats . . .
—Horace (Quintus Horatius Flaccus) (65–8 B.C.)

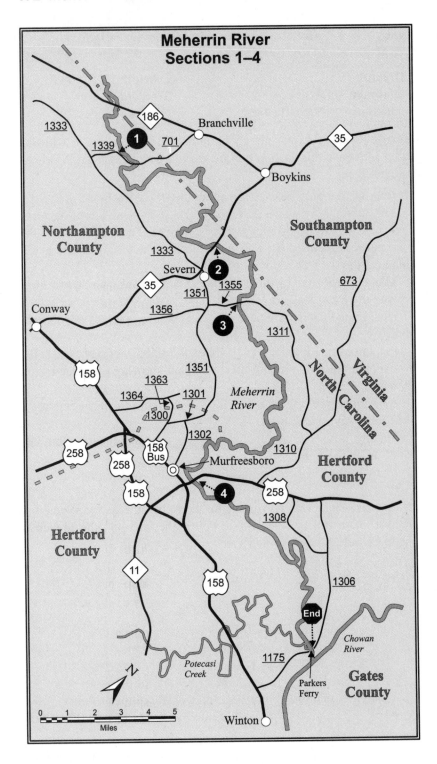

**Meherrin River
Sections 1–4**

1333

1339 701

186 Branchville

35

①

Boykins

**Northampton
County**

**Southampton
County**

1333

Severn 673

35 ② 1355

1351

Conway 1356

③

1311

1351

158

1363

1364 1301

1300

*Meherrin
River*

1302

1310

258

158
Bus

258 — Murfreesboro

**Hertford
County**

158

④

158 258

1308

**Hertford
County**

11

158

1306

End

*Chowan
River*

*Potecasi
Creek*

1175

Parkers
Ferry

**Gates
County**

N

0 1 2 3 4 5
Miles

Winton

Virginia

North Carolina

Chowan Basin

Merchants Millpond

County   Gates

Topo   Merchants Millpond

Norfleets Millpond, built in 1811, became a center of trade in Gates County and became known as Merchants Millpond.

· A.B. Coleman, a paddler and lover of nature, thought the area too beautiful for development. He bought the property and donated 919 acres, including the millpond, to the state. The Nature Conservancy contributed an additional 925 acres of woodlands, and Merchants Millpond State Park was established in 1973.

Today the park is more than 3,250 acres. The millpond itself covers 760 acres. Old bald cypress and tupelo-gum trees, displaying Spanish moss and resurrection ferns, grow in and around the pond's blackwater. Many aquatic plants thrive in the pond. Floating duckweed and water fern often cover much of the water's surface.

Over 200 species of birds have been recorded in the park. Beaver and otter are common, and alligators are occasionally seen.

The east side of the park includes Lassiter Swamp, containing remnants of an ancient bald cypress swamp, and the eerie "enchanted forest" of tupelo-gum trees whose trunks and branches have been distorted into fantastic shapes by mistletoe.

1 Park access off Millpond Road (Gates Co. 1400) and return

Difficulty A	**Width**	20–1,500 ft
Distance 1–10 mi	**Gradient**	0 ft/mi
Scenery A	**Map**	page 175

Gauge None. Always above minimum.

Notes The park entrance is off Millpond Road near the bridge over Bennetts Creek. A boat ramp is provided and canoes can be rented. For information on hours and rates, call the park at 252-357-1191.

The millpond is about 2 miles long and up to 0.3 miles wide. On the west side, near the road, is the dam and spillway where water flows into Bennetts Creek. On the northeast side of the millpond is

Lassiter Swamp and headwaters of Bennetts Creek. The park owns property extending about 2.5 miles from the millpond upstream on Bennetts Creek.

The paddle from the boat ramp can be as short or long as one desires. The millpond can be explored with its many coves, or one can paddle upstream on Bennetts Creek into Lassiter Swamp.

A compass and map are useful for exploring. Paddling on the millpond is different from paddling most lakes because the many trees standing in the millpond make it difficult to see more than a few hundred feet in any direction.

From the boat ramp, orange buoys lead 0.7 miles to the family canoe camp with seven sites. Yellow buoys lead 1.1 miles to the group canoe camp with three sites. Pit toilets are available, but campers must carry in all supplies, including water. Family sites are available on a first-come basis. Group sites can be reserved by organized groups providing their own canoes.

Mosquitoes are always a problem during warm weather months, and the area is heavily infested with ticks. Take precautions or visit during the cooler months.

Merchants Millpond

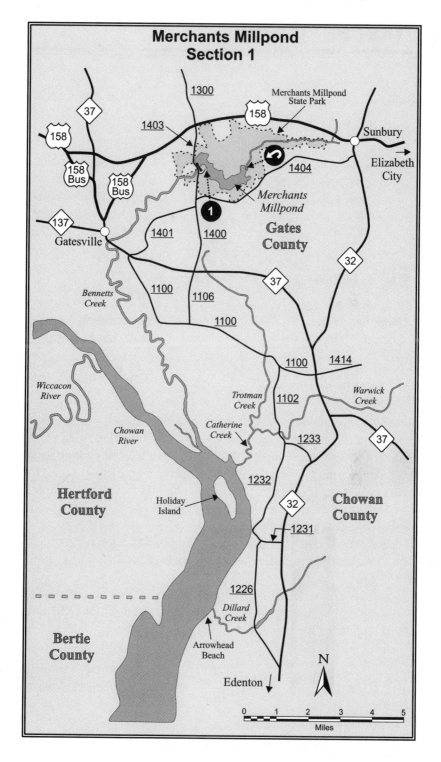

**Merchants Millpond
Section 1**

Potecasi Creek

County   Hertford

Topos   Union, Murfreesboro, Winton

Potecasi Creek is the largest tributary of the Meherrin River in North Carolina. Its headwaters begin in creeks and swamps just to the east of the Roanoke River watershed, east and southeast of Roanoke Rapids.

> **1** US 158 bridge to Parkers Ferry Road (Hertford Co. 1306) ferry landing on the Meherrin River
>
> | | | |
> |---|---|---|
> | **Difficulty** A | **Width** | 40–200 ft |
> | **Distance** 11.3 mi | **Gradient** | 0 ft/mi |
> | **Scenery** A | **Map** | page 177 |

Gauge USGS *Potecasi Creek near Union*. Minimum is 90 cfs (4.5 ft) to paddle over most of the downed trees in the beginning of the section.

Notes At the take-out, Parkers Ferry, a two-car diesel-powered boat, provides transportation across the river. The north (left) side of the Meherrin River is recommended for a take-out because parking space is available near the ferry operator's office. There is little parking space at the ferry landing on the south side of the Meherrin at Parkers Ferry Road. If driving in from the south side, take the ferry to the north side to leave a vehicle.

Blackwater flows through swampy land with cypress and tupelo-gum trees, but there are many areas having high banks, rising as much as 35 feet.

Potecasi Creek enters the Meherrin (mi 10.7), but an old channel to the right continues around an island and reenters the Meherrin (mi 11.2) just before reaching the ferry crossing.

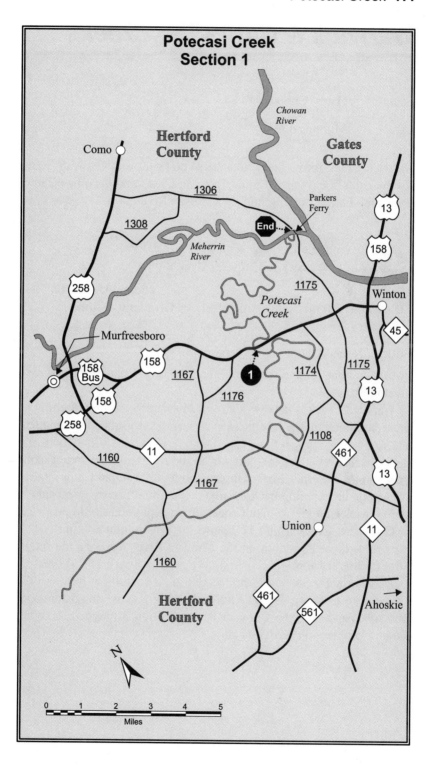

Potecasi Creek
Section 1

Chowan
River

Hertford
County

Gates
County

Como

1306

Parkers
Ferry

13

1308

End

158

Meherrin
River

258

1175

Winton

Potecasi
Creek

45

Murfreesboro

158

1

158
Bus

1167

1174

1175

158

1176

13

258

1108

11

461

1160

13

1167

Union

11

1160

461

Hertford
County

561

Ahoskie

N

0   1   2   3   4   5
Miles

Chowan Basin

Warwick & Catherine Creeks

Counties   Gates, Chowan

Topo   Mintonsville

Warwick Creek forms the border between Gates and Chowan Counties and runs southwest. It joins Trotman Creek and becomes Catherine Creek before flowing into the Chowan River.

1 Cannons Ferry Road (Chowan Co. 1232) access over Warwick Creek to Chowan River and return		
Difficulty A	**Width** 35–500 ft	
Distance 7.0 mi	**Gradient** 0 ft/mi	
Scenery A	**Map** page 179	

Gauge None. Always above minimum.

Notes A boat ramp is at the Cannons Ferry Road bridge, downstream left.

Warwick Creek is narrow with low to swampy banks. Other than a house and dock on the left, the trip is through an isolated swamp forest.

Trotman Creek (mi 1.3) joins from the right and the stream name changes to Catherine Creek. Observe how the Trotman Creek branch will look when coming back upstream because it is easy to mistake it for Warwick Creek. Trotman Creek can be explored as a side trip.

Catherine Creek (mi 2.7) begins to widen quickly until it is 500 feet wide at its mouth on the Chowan River (mi 3.5), the return point for this section.

An alternative to doing this section as a round-trip is to paddle 2.4 miles to Cannons Ferry Wildlife boating access, downstream of Holiday Island. See the Chowan River, Section 3 (page 162). Wind can be a problem on the Chowan.

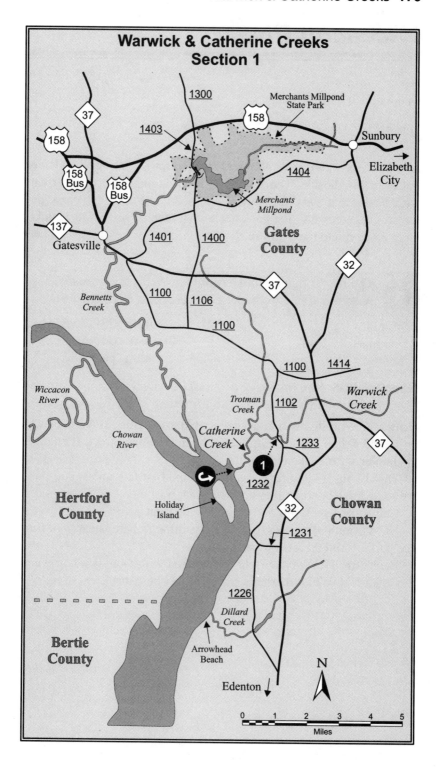

Wiccacon River

Counties   Hertford, Gates

Topos   Ahoskie, Harrellsville, Mintonsville

Ahoskie Creek joins several other creeks to form the Wiccacon River, northeast of Ahoskie. The Wiccacon is a winding blackwater stream with banks that vary from swampy to 35 feet high. Cypress and tupelo-gum trees line the banks. The Wiccacon gains width quickly on its short run to the Chowan River.

1	Thomas Bridge Road (Hertford Co. 1427) bridge to Old Ferry Road (Hertford Co. 1433) access at Harrellsville	
Difficulty A	**Width** 30–175 ft	
Distance 12.5 mi	**Gradient** 0 ft/mi	
Scenery A	**Map** page 182	

Gauge USGS *Ahoskie Creek at Ahoskie*. Always above minimum. There is a small tidal influence in this section.

Notes A Wildlife boating access is at Harrellsville. Traveling south on NC 45 (Main Street), turn left at North Quebec Street. It changes to Old Ferry Road and ends at the access.

The stream has multiple channels in the first few miles, and there are some large cypress trees and abundant mistletoe.

Chinkapin Creek (mi 5.9) enters on the right.

NC 45 (mi 8.9) crosses, but access is difficult here because of limited parking and private property.

Banks (mi 11.2) on the right are covered with mountain laurel and rise to 35 feet. White seashells can be seen where dirt is exposed.

> **2** Old Ferry Road (Hertford Co. 1433) access to Apache Road
> (Hertford Co. 1460) access on the Chowan River

Difficulty	A	**Width**	120–3,000 ft
Distance	9.8 mi	**Gradient**	0 ft/mi
Scenery	A (80%), B (20%)	**Map**	page 182

Gauge See Section 1. The take-out is on the Chowan River, where wind can be a problem.

Notes See the previous section about the Old Ferry Road access.

The take-out is private. The fee is $3 paid to the honor box. Take Pawnee Road (Hertford Co. 1450) to a left turn on Apache Road. Follow Apache Road to the stop sign, and go straight ahead, down the hill to the access on the right.

This section of the Wiccacon requires some paddling on the Chowan because there is no access at the confluence. An option to paddling the 2.2 miles down the Chowan to the private access is to paddle 1.6 miles upstream and across the Chowan to the Wildlife boating access at the end of New Ferry Road (Gates Co. 1111). The choice should be made based on wind direction and current, but note that driving to the east side of the Chowan requires a 56-mile round-trip from the put-in.

Regardless of the take-out chosen, the Chowan is up to 0.6 miles wide here. Strong winds can make for difficult and dangerous paddling conditions.

The banks range from swampy to 35 feet high. As with the high banks in the previous section, white shells can be seen where dirt is exposed.

The river widens to 300 feet before joining the Chowan River (mi 7.6). The take-out is 2.2 miles down the Chowan, just past the farthest point of land that can be seen on the right bank.

■

When you get out on one of those lakes in a canoe like this, you do not forget that you are completely at the mercy of the wind, and a fickle power it is. The playful waves may at any time become too rude for you in their sport, and play right over you.
    —Henry David Thoreau, *The Allegash and East Branch* (1864)

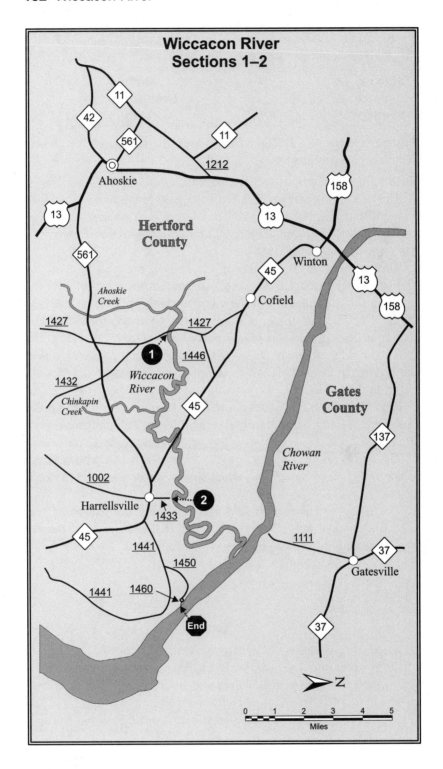

Wiccacon River
Sections 1–2

Chowan Basin

Wiccacon River, Section 1

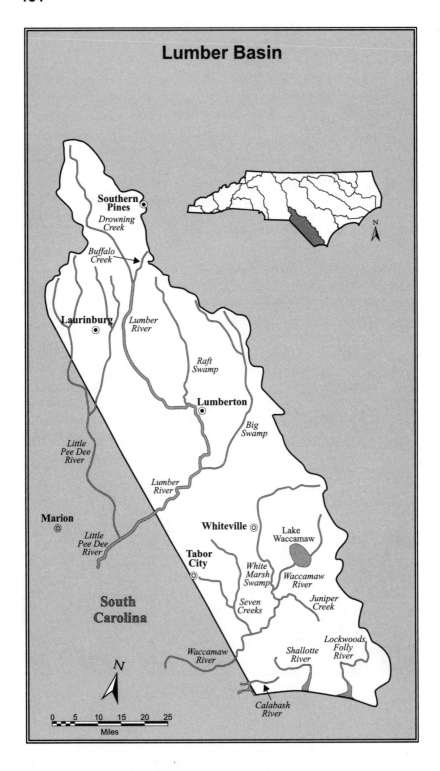

Lumber Basin

Southern Pines

Drowning Creek

Buffalo Creek

Laurinburg

Lumber River

Raft Swamp

Lumberton

Big Swamp

Little Pee Dee River

Lumber River

Marion

Little Pee Dee River

Whiteville

Lake Waccamaw

Tabor City

White Marsh Swamp

Waccamaw River

South Carolina

Seven Creeks

Juniper Creek

Lockwoods Folly River

Waccamaw River

Shallotte River

Calabash River

N

N

0   5   10   15   20   25
Miles

Lumber Basin

The Lumber Basin begins in the Coastal Plain in the southeast corner of North Carolina and extends into South Carolina. The North Carolina portion of the basin contains 3,343 square miles.

The Lumber Basin is composed of four separate watersheds: Lumber River watershed, Waccamaw River watershed, Little Pee Dee headwaters watershed, and Coastal Area watershed.

The watersheds in the Lumber Basin, except for the Coastal Area watershed, flow into South Carolina and are tributaries of the Great Pee Dee River, which flows into the Atlantic Ocean near Georgetown, South Carolina.

The Lumber River, one of the largest blackwater rivers in the state, begins as Drowning Creek in the Sandhills region in southern Moore and Montgomery Counties. It is a state Natural and Scenic River, and 81 miles of the river are designated a National Wild and Scenic River. Lumber River State Park protects land along some of the river.

The Waccamaw River watershed includes the rare and unique fauna of Lake Waccamaw, making it one of the state's most significant biological resources. Lake Waccamaw State Park borders part of the lake, and the Waccamaw River begins at the lake's outflow. Juniper Creek drains the Green Swamp to the Waccamaw River. Over 15,000 acres of the Green Swamp have been preserved by The Nature Conservancy. The Green Swamp straddles two watersheds and also drains to Lockwoods Folly River in the Coastal Area watershed.

The Little Pee Dee River headwaters watershed originates in the Sandhills region above Laurinburg where there are extensive natural communities of longleaf pine. The aquatic and wetland communities in the Sandhills are different in character from the large floodplains of the Lumber and Waccamaw Rivers. The wetlands contain small stream swamps and Atlantic white cedar forests.

The Coastal Area watershed is made up of several small stream systems including Lockwoods Folly River, Shallotte River, and Calabash River. These streams flow southward to inlets through barrier islands and into the Atlantic Ocean.

Big Swamp

Counties   Robeson, Columbus

Topo   Evergreen

Big Marsh Swamp, Little Marsh Swamp, and Gallberry Swamp are the headwaters of Big Swamp. They begin from just southeast of Raeford to south of Hope Mills and join about 15 miles south of Fayetteville to form Big Swamp.

As Big Swamp flows south near Tarheel, it is only 4 miles west of the Cape Fear River. After passing between Bladenboro and Lumberton, it flows southwest to join the Lumber River.

1	Old Lumberton Road (Robeson Co. 1002) access to US 74 access on Lumber River near Boardman		
Difficulty A		**Width** 30–150 ft	
Distance 6.5 mi		**Gradient** 1.4 ft/mi	
Scenery A		**Map** page 187	

Gauge USGS *Big Swamp near Tarheel*. Hurricane Floyd (1999) downed many trees on Big Swamp. Blockages were removed on the Lumber River but not on Big Swamp. Unless they are cleared, paddle this at high water when there are paths around most trees. Estimated minimum is 550 cfs (11.0 ft).

USGS *Lumber at Boardman* should be used for the Lumber River portion of this section.

Notes The put-in is a Wildlife boating access. The take-out has an access managed by Lumber River State Park.

At high water, there are many possible routes. A compass and map are useful.

The banks are swampy and heavily wooded with some cypress trees displaying Spanish moss.

Lumber River State Park owns a small amount of land bordering Big Swamp, near its mouth.

At the Lumber River (mi 4.8), there are many channels, and the confluence area is known as Net Hole Swamp. Follow the current and take the most open channel. See the Lumber River, Section 12 (page 201).

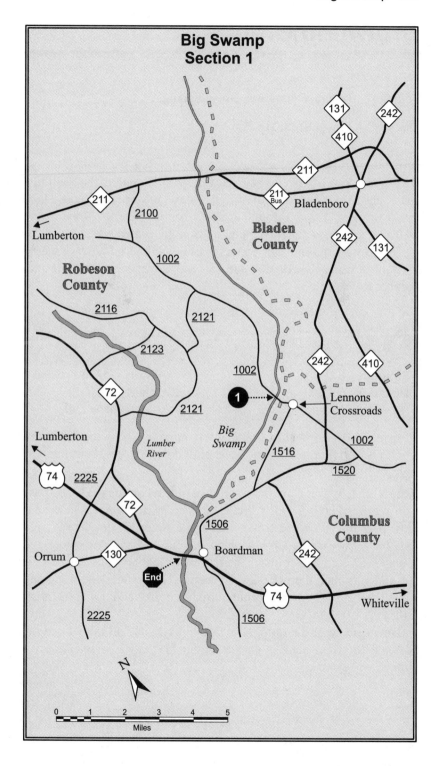

Drowning Creek

Counties   Moore, Richmond, Hoke, Scotland

Topos   Pinebluff, Silver Hill

Drowning Creek is a blackwater stream forming the headwaters of the Lumber River. It begins at an elevation of 700 feet in the Sandhills near Candor and becomes the Montgomery and Moore County border. It flows southeast through sparsely populated land. Much of the 58,000 acres of Sandhills Game Land is in this watershed.

Near Southern Pines, the creek forms the northern border of Camp Mackall Military Reservation and 15 miles downstream becomes the Lumber River.

1 US 1 bridge near Pinebluff to US 15/501 bridge	
Difficulty B	**Width** 25–50 ft
Distance 6.2 mi	**Gradient** 3.4 ft/mi
Scenery A	**Map** page 190

Gauge USGS *Drowning Creek near Hoffman*. Estimated minimum is 300 cfs (4.8 ft) to reduce the number of downed trees requiring portage.

Notes The first half of this section is not recommended for those who want a relaxing trip. A great number of tree limbs and bushes grow over the creek and sometimes to the water. Often there is only time for a few paddle strokes before having to bend down to avoid being raked out of your boat. The narrow channel is constantly twisting and turning. A small saw is useful. High water allows going around some trees, but the faster current requires additional paddling skill.

Downstream of the railroad bridge (mi 1.5) and all the way to the take-out, the right bank is part of Camp Mackall Military Reservation.

A dredged channel (mi 2.1) goes to the right, leaving the natural course for a half-mile. There is a bulkhead and signs of military usage. The right bank rises 10 feet and has stands of large pine trees. The dredged channel is the more open route.

The Ashemont Road (Hoke Co. 1225) bridge (mi 3.5) can be used for access on the left bank. The right bank is military property. There are far fewer downed trees and low limbs from here to the take-out.

Another dredged channel (mi 3.8) goes to the right, leaving the natural course for a half-mile. It is similar to the previous dredged channel and is the more open route.

There are many tupelo-gum trees, some cypress trees, and little development.

2	US 15/501 bridge to Turnpike Road (Scotland Co. 1412) access		
Difficulty B		**Width** 35–60 ft	
Distance 7.6 mi		**Gradient** 3.6 ft/mi	
Scenery A		**Map** page 190	

Gauge See Section 1.

Notes The take-out has a "NC Trail System, Lumber River Canoe Trail" sign.

The course is easy to follow but winds constantly. Trees requiring portage are common, and there are many low limbs. The current is faster than found downstream on the Lumber River. Good boat control is necessary to maneuver around and under obstacles.

Cypress, tupelo-gum, laurel oak, and large pine trees are dense along the corridor.

A home (mi 1.1) is on the left bank where the ground rises 40 feet. Little other high ground is found.

Near the latter part of this section, the channel becomes wider and the bends are spaced out.

To continue downstream of the take-out, see the Lumber River, Section 1 (page 196).

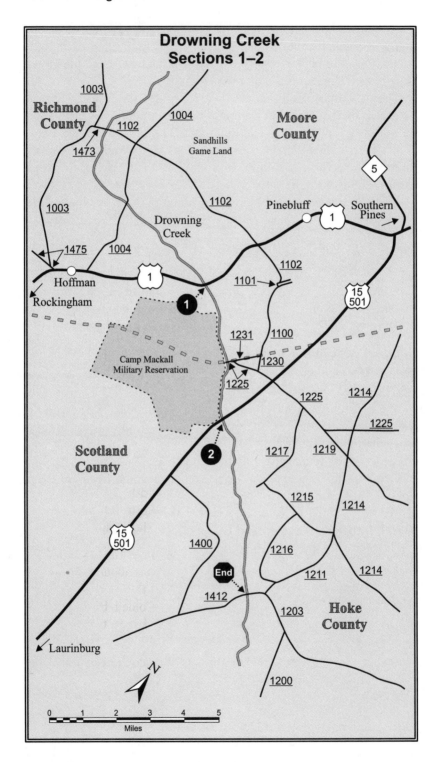

Lumber Basin

Lockwoods Folly River

County   Brunswick

Topos   Bolivia, Supply, Holden Beach, Lockwoods Folly

Lockwoods Folly River (also known as Lockwood Folly River) drains a small watershed in south central Brunswick County, about 25 miles southwest of Wilmington. It begins on the southeastern edge of the Green Swamp and flows south through low land. It empties into the Atlantic Ocean through Lockwoods Folly Inlet near Holden Beach.

The Intracoastal Waterway crosses just above Lockwoods Folly Inlet. During the waterway's construction in the 1930s, water flow through the inlet was altered by diverting the original channel and dredging and widening a new channel.

The coastal area has had much urban growth and development since the 1980s. Water quality in Lockwoods Folly River deteriorated, and closing of areas for harvesting shellfish has been relatively common. Studies are underway to determine the causes and possible remedies.

1 Gilbert Road (Brunswick Co. 1501) bridge to NC 211 bridge near Supply			
Difficulty A		**Width**	20–80 ft
Distance 5.9 mi		**Gradient**	0 ft/mi
Scenery A		**Map**	page 194

Gauge None. This section is tidal up to near the put-in. Refer to tide tables for Lockwoods Folly Inlet. The tide delay is about 3–4 hours at the NC 211 bridge where tides range about 2 feet.

Downed trees in the first mile can be avoided by starting at NC 211 and going upstream until reaching blockages, then returning to NC 211.

Notes From the put-in bridge, it looks clear downstream, but the channel splits (mi 0.1), going both left and right where it is narrow with downed trees. The best route is not obvious because a large beaver dam, 0.3 miles downstream of the put-in, has turned the whole area above it into a swamp.

Both channels were examined for a short distance, and the right seemed more open and is described below. Topo maps show only the left channel.

The channels rejoin (mi 0.8). Downed trees were not found in the rest of the section, but they are likely because the stream is only 20–50 feet wide in the next mile.

Power lines (mi 1.5) cross over swampy ground, and the first high ground (mi 1.8) is on the left bank, where it rises briefly to 10 feet high at a right turn.

There are many tall cypress trees, palmetto plants are often dense, and mistletoe is common in tupelo-gum trees.

Homes (mi 4.3) are on the right along with a few docks and boats.

2	NC 211 bridge near Supply to Fisherman Road (Brunswick Co. 1123) access near Varnamtown		
Difficulty A		**Width** 40–300 ft	
Distance 9.8 mi		**Gradient** 0 ft/mi	
Scenery A (40%), B (40%), C (20%)		**Map** page 194	

Gauge None. This section is tidal. Refer to tide tables available for Lockwoods Folly Inlet, about 3 miles downstream of the take-out. At the put-in, tides range about 2 feet and are delayed by 3–4 hours. At the take-out, tides range 3–6 feet and are delayed about 1 hour. Plan the trip to go with favorable wind and tide.

Notes A public boat ramp is next to Garlands Seafood. Take Varnamtown Road (Brunswick Co. 1122). Where it angles to the left, continue straight ahead on Fisherman Road for 0.3 miles to the road's end.

In the first few miles, there is little dry ground at high tide. Small cypress trees and many palmetto plants are along the banks. Farther downstream, tall marsh grass grows on the tidal flats.

This is good territory to see alligators near the marsh grass and osprey in large nests built in old trees.

The Winding River Plantation golf community (mi 4.1) is on the left where the bank rises 20 feet.

A channel (mi 5.2) to the right makes a shortcut of a river loop and goes by high ground at Sand Hill Landing. Taking the shortcut saves 0.6 miles and goes away from denser development on the left bank.

A side channel (mi 7.7) to the right makes a long loop around an island at the entrance and returns to the main channel a few hundred feet downstream. This channel can be paddled when the tide is not too low, adding 0.8 miles to the trip. The island rises 20 feet and has pine trees.

The channel (mi 8.6) goes right and straight ahead. The channel to the right goes by Wildcat Landing, and going straight saves 0.7 miles.

Fishing boats and docks are on the right bank near the take-out.

Laura Wright on the Lumber River, Section 2

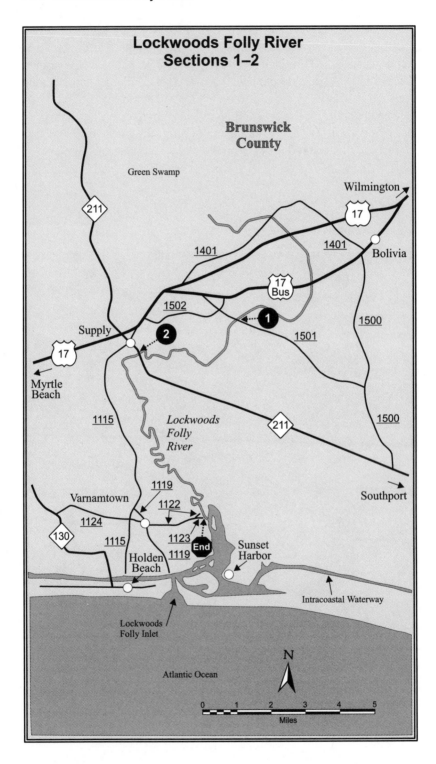

Lockwoods Folly River
Sections 1–2

Brunswick
County

Green Swamp

Wilmington

211

1401

1401

Bolivia

17
Bus

1502

1500

Supply

2

1

1501

17

Myrtle
Beach

1115

*Lockwoods
Folly
River*

211

1500

Southport

1119

Varnamtown

1122

1124

1123

130

1115

1119

End

Sunset
Harbor

Holden
Beach

Intracoastal Waterway

Lockwoods
Folly Inlet

N

Atlantic Ocean

0   1   2   3   4   5
Miles

Lumber Basin

Lumber River

Counties	Hoke, Scotland, Robeson, Columbus, Dillon (SC), Horry (SC), Marion (SC)
Topos	Silver Hill, Wagram, Wakulla, Maxton, Pembroke, McDonald, SW Lumberton, NW Lumberton, SE Lumberton, Evergreen, Fairmont, Fair Bluff, Lake View, Nichols (SC)

The Lumber River was known to the Indians as *Lumbee*—thought to be an Indian word for *black water*. The Lumber meanders tightly through the southeastern part of the state, flowing over a sandy bottom. It joins the Little Pee Dee River in South Carolina before flowing into the Atlantic as the Great Pee Dee River.

The Lumber River was recognized as a valuable resource in 1978 when it was designated as North Carolina's first recreational water trail. In 1981, it was made a national canoe trail. In 1989, 115 miles of the river were added to the North Carolina Natural and Scenic River System, and the state created the Lumber River State Park. In 1998, 81 miles of the Lumber were accepted into the National Wild and Scenic Rivers System. The river segment from near Maxton to the confluence with Back Swamp above Lumberton was left to be added after an adequate management plan is developed to protect it.

Included in the national system are paddling Sections 1–3 and Section 8, from the confluence with Back Swamp, through Section 15 to the border with South Carolina.

Much credit for the Lumber's protection goes to the many local people who formed conservation groups and worked for years to give it the recognition it deserves.

Lumber River State Park owns more than 7,000 acres along the river. The park has a major access area at Princess Ann and has plans for others.

The floodplain is mainly a cypress, tupelo-gum, and water oak swamp forest. Above the perennially wet lands, loblolly pine and many varieties of hardwoods are found. Rare and endangered plants grow in the river corridor. The insect-eating Venus flytrap also grows here.

Wildlife is diverse. Deer, beaver, mink, raccoon, ducks, and wild turkey are common. Alligators and black bear are sometimes seen. The area is an important habitat for the endangered bald eagle and red-cockaded woodpecker.

Newly fallen trees are common. At low water, there are often downed trees across the river that would be submerged at higher flows; but at higher flows the current increases, and good boat control is necessary to avoid being swept into overhanging trees and bushes.

Overnight canoe camping is popular. Lumber River State Park provides seven paddle-in camping areas, and their master plan calls for others to be developed. Except at Princess Ann, there is no fee or permit required to use the paddle-in camping areas.

---

1 Turnpike Road (Scotland Co. 1412) access to US 401 access

Difficulty A–B		**Width**	40–60 ft
Distance 8.3 mi		**Gradient**	1.8 ft/mi
Scenery A		**Map**	page 205

Gauge USGS *Drowning Creek near Hoffman*. Estimated minimum is 200 cfs (3.8 ft).

Notes The put-in has a "NC Trail System, Lumber River Canoe Trail" sign.

A Wildlife boating access is at US 401.

The put-in is commonly considered the beginning of the Lumber River, but the topo map shows it as Drowning Creek, with the Lumber River actually beginning about a mile below the put-in, at the confluence of Drowning Creek and Buffalo Creek.

Many cypress trees overhang the water to provide a paddling canopy. Downed trees are common, and there are signs of beaver activity on the banks.

After the first few miles, the river often splits into channels.

There is little high ground until Chalk Banks (mi 5.5) on the right. Lumber River State Park owns land here, and a paddle-in campsite area is available with picnic table and fire-ring.

> ② **US 401 access to McGirts Bridge Road (Scotland Co. 1433) bridge**

Difficulty A–B	**Width** 25–70 ft
Distance 10.1 mi	**Gradient** 2.0 ft/mi
Scenery A (80%), B (20%)	**Map** page 205

Gauge USGS *Lumber River near Maxton*. Estimated minimum is 200 cfs (7.4 ft).

Notes A Wildlife boating access is at US 401.

River Road (Scotland Co. 1404) bridge (mi 2.4) is a popular hangout in the warmer months. It is not recommended as a place to leave a vehicle.

The Lumber River State Park's Jasper Memory paddle-in campsite (mi 6.5) is on the right bank. It has a picnic table and fire-ring.

Riverton Road (Scotland Co. 1403) (mi 6.9) comes within 40 feet of the river and can be used for access. This road also goes by the J.P. Stevens Company's water intake (mi 7.8) where public access has been allowed for fishing and boating.

> ③ **McGirts Bridge Road (Scotland Co. 1433) bridge to NC 71 bridge**

Difficulty A–B	**Width** 40–60 ft
Distance 5.5 mi	**Gradient** 2.5 ft/mi
Scenery A	**Map** page 205

Gauge See Section 2.

Notes The river winds through cypress, pine, and holly trees. The banks are 1–6 feet high.

Laurinburg-Maxton Airport is near the right bank for most of this section.

> ④ **NC 71 bridge to Alma Road (Robeson Co. 1393) bridge**

Difficulty A	**Width** 40–60 ft
Distance 6.4 mi	**Gradient** 1.3 ft/mi
Scenery A (40%), B (60%)	**Map** page 206

Gauge USGS *Lumber River near Maxton*. Estimated minimum is 150 cfs (6.8 ft).

Notes This section is similar to the previous section, but more development is seen near the river.

Old Red Springs Road (Robeson Co. 1303) bridge (mi 3.3) can be used for access.

---

5 Alma Road (Robeson Co. 1393) bridge to Recreation Center Road (Robeson Co. 1354) bridge

Difficulty A	**Width**	25–70 ft
Distance 6.7 mi	**Gradient**	2.1 ft/mi
Scenery A (70%), B (30%)	**Map**	page 206

Gauge See Section 4.

Notes A building and property, upstream right of the bridge at Recreation Center Road, is owned by the Indian Cultural Center and may be used for access. Some paddlers have reported being charged arbitrary fees. Downstream right of the bridge is recommended.

The channel splits around islands in many places and runs close to a railroad bridge in the first mile. The main channel is easy to follow by watching the current.

US 74 runs parallel to the river, bringing in the sound of truck traffic.

---

6 Recreation Center Road (Robeson Co. 1354) bridge to Three Bridges Road (Robeson Co. 1554) bridge

Difficulty A	**Width**	25–60 ft
Distance 7.9 mi	**Gradient**	1.4 ft/mi
Scenery A (25%), B (75%)	**Map**	page 206

Gauge See Section 4.

Notes See the previous section about Recreation Center Road.

The sounds of traffic from nearby US 74 continue on this section.

Harpers Ferry Church (mi 2.9) is upstream right of Harpers Ferry bridge, where NC 710 crosses. Paddlers have been allowed to use the church parking lot and ramp for access.

---

7 Three Bridges Road (Robeson Co. 1554) bridge to Lowe Road (Robeson Co. 1550) bridge

Difficulty A	**Width**	35–75 ft
Distance 8.8 mi	**Gradient**	1.7 ft/mi
Scenery A (75%), B (25%)	**Map**	page 206

Gauge See Section 4.

Notes Apartments and Pine Lake Park (mi 0.5) are on the left bank. Campsites are available April–mid-September (910-521-2545).

The sounds of traffic from nearby US 74 continue on this section.

Chicken Road (Robeson Co. 1003) bridge (mi 3.1) can be used for access.

The channel splits in several places and becomes narrow until the channels rejoin.

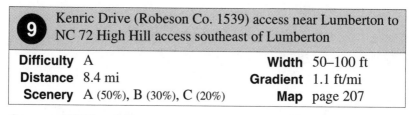

8	Lowe Road (Robeson Co.1550) bridge to Kenric Drive (Robeson Co. 1539) access near Lumberton		
Difficulty A		**Width** 30–75 ft	
Distance 9.3 mi		**Gradient** 1.8 ft/mi	
Scenery A (80%), B (20%)		**Map** page 207	

Gauge USGS *Lumber River at Lumberton.* Estimated minimum is 200 cfs (7.5 ft).

Notes A Wildlife boating access is off Kenric Drive. From I-95 in Lumberton, take Exit 17 for NC 72. Go west 0.3 miles to Kenric Drive (Robeson Co. 1539). Turn left and go 0.1 miles to the access area on the left. It is also called McNeil's Bridge access; but McNeil's Bridge, upstream of the ramp, has been removed.

After a few houses and private docks in the first few miles, development lessens.

Back Swamp (mi 3.9) enters from the right, and the Lumber River resumes its National Wild and Scenic River designation.

Tom Avent Landing (mi 8.2), on the right bank, is part of Lumber River State Park and has a paddle-in campsite equipped with a fire-ring and picnic table.

Traffic can be heard from I-95, only a half-mile from the river for most of the trip.

9	Kenric Drive (Robeson Co. 1539) access near Lumberton to NC 72 High Hill access southeast of Lumberton		
Difficulty A		**Width** 50–100 ft	
Distance 8.4 mi		**Gradient** 1.1 ft/mi	
Scenery A (50%), B (30%), C (20%)		**Map** page 207	

Gauge USGS *Lumber River at Lumberton.* Estimated minimum is 250 cfs (7.8 ft) to the first railroad bridge (mi 1.3), and 100 cfs (6.7 ft) downstream of the railroad bridge.

Notes See the previous section about the Kenric Drive access.

A Wildlife boating access is at the NC 72 bridge southeast of Lumberton.

This section has many access points and can be divided into shorter trips.

In the first few miles, the experience varies, from floating under a tree canopy with large cypress trees in an area seemingly remote from the city of Lumberton to running along I-95 and billboards.

There are many downed trees in the river until reaching a railroad bridge (mi 1.3). A path has been cleared through the trees, but they still cause problems at low water.

McMillan's Beach (mi 2.8) is on the left, just before passing under I-95. It has a locked gate, but camping and access is allowed by making reservations with the Lumberton Recreation Commission (910-671-3869).

Downstream, the river becomes straighter and wider as it runs through residential areas. Jet skis are sometime encountered on the lower parts of this section.

Stephens Park (mi 4.6) is off Riverside Drive and can be used for access. The gate is open from 8 A.M. until dusk.

Just past the Fifth Street bridge is the NC 41/72 (Second Street) bridge (mi 5.1). There is a boat ramp downstream left, at the end of First Street.

A few hundred yards past the Chestnut Street (Robeson Co. 2289) bridge is the Noir Street Playground (mi 6.1) on the left. There is no ramp, but access is easy from the bank.

Soon after passing Chippewa Street/Hestertown Road (Robeson Co. 2202) bridge (mi 6.5), sounds of Progress Energy's coal-fired Weatherspoon plant in the next section can be heard.

Less than a half-mile before reaching the take-out, the river bends right, and the left bank rises to over 35 feet. This area is known locally as High Hill.

10	NC 72 access southeast of Lumberton to Matthew Bluff Road (Robeson Co. 2123) bridge		
Difficulty A		**Width** 20–100 ft	
Distance 9.3 mi		**Gradient** 1.0 ft/mi	
Scenery A (80%), C (20%)		**Map** page 207	

Gauge USGS *Lumber River at Lumberton*. Estimated minimum is 600 cfs (9.6 ft). This section requires more water than most because of downed trees and braided channels.

Notes See the previous section about the NC 72 access.

Sounds from Progress Energy's Weatherspoon plant (mi 0.5) can be heard for at least a mile up and down the river. A sign at the plant warns of turbulent water from the cooling lake. Releases are infrequent and occur in times of heavy rain when the cooling lake has risen too high.

After passing the plant, the river character changes to remote, swampy, and braided into many smaller channels. At low flows, some of the smaller channels may require dragging for short distances. There are many large, moss-covered cypress trees.

Camping is difficult because most of the sparse high ground is posted.

11 Matthew Bluff Road (Robeson Co. 2123) bridge to Willoughby Road (2121) bridge

Difficulty A	**Width**	20–100 ft
Distance 4.0 mi	**Gradient**	1.3 ft/mi
Scenery A	**Map**	page 207

Gauge USGS *Lumber River at Boardman*. Estimated minimum is 600 cfs (5.0 ft). Aquatic weeds and downed trees cause problems at low flows.

Notes This section is similar to the latter half of the previous section. In several areas, the river braids into many smaller channels, leaving little water in the channels for paddling at low flows. Aquatic weeds have grown over some of the narrow channels.

Cypress trees are dense in areas, and cypress knees cover the low banks. The river is constantly bending, making it rare to see far ahead.

There is little high ground for camping.

12 Willoughby Road (Robeson Co. 2121) bridge to US 74 access near Boardman

Difficulty A	**Width**	30–150 ft
Distance 8.1 mi	**Gradient**	1.7 ft/mi
Scenery A	**Map**	page 207

Gauge USGS *Lumber River at Boardman*. Estimated minimum is 500 cfs (4.5 ft).

Notes An access at US 74 is managed by Lumber River State Park. Heading east on US 74, turn right on V.C. Britt Road (Robeson

Co. 2245) 0.1 miles before going over the bridge. Turn left at the drive to the access.

In places where there are numerous channels, the best route is usually where a narrow path has been cut through downed trees.

Lumber River State Park owns high ground on the left at Buck Landing (mi 2.7). Camping is allowed, and the area has a picnic table, small shelter, and fire-ring.

The park's Piney Island primitive paddle-in camping area (mi 4.8) on the right has a dock, picnic tables, and stone fire-ring. Groups can make reservations (910-628-9844), but exclusive use is not granted, so the area may be shared with others.

Farther downstream are old wooden pilings—remains of railroad trestles used for logging. In the late 18th and 19th centuries the river corridor was an important source of timber for the logging industry.

The confluence with Big Swamp (mi 6.2) can be difficult to recognize because there are numerous channels here. The area is known as Net Hole Swamp, one of twelve Natural Heritage Priority Areas in the Lumber corridor. Net Hole covers 1,242 acres, and is known for being an excellent example of a swamp dominated by cypress and tupelo-gum trees, as well as being prime wildlife habitat.

13 US 74 access near Boardman to Lumber River State Park Princess Ann access		
Difficulty A	**Width**	50–150 ft
Distance 8.4 mi	**Gradient**	0.8 ft/mi
Scenery A	**Map**	page 208

Gauge USGS *Lumber River at Boardman*. Estimated minimum is 175 cfs (2.3 ft). Many sandbars are exposed below flows of 350 cfs (3.5 ft).

Notes See the previous section about the US 74 access.

Lumber River State Park has a ramp at their Princess Ann access.

The USGS gauge is near the US 74 boat ramp.

Downstream right is the park's Pea Ridge Rest Stop (mi 0.5). It can be used for camping, but it is close to developed areas.

There are houses to the left where Williamsons Crossroads (Columbus Co. 1504) (mi 6.3) approaches the river. It can be used for access, but Lumber River State Park's Princess Ann access area is only 2 miles downstream where there is parking, boat ramp, and camping. The campsites are downstream from the ramp. Reservations are not accepted.

At the approach to the take-out, the river bends left sharply at a 40-foot bluff (mi 8.2). At high water, a large eddy to the right is known as Griffin Whirl.

---

14 Lumber River State Park Princess Ann access to NC 904 access at Fair Bluff

Difficulty A	**Width**	50–100 ft
Distance 11.3 mi	**Gradient**	0.4 ft/mi
Scenery A	**Map**	page 208

Gauge See Section 13.

Notes See the previous section about the Princess Ann access.

At the take-out in Fair Bluff, a boat ramp is 100 yards upstream left of the NC 904 bridge. The access is managed by Robeson County, and there is a donation box for contributions to help support it. The ramp is next to River Bend Outfitters (910-649-5998). They rent boats and run shuttles. See: http://whitevillenc.com/rbo/

At the put-in, there is a straight vista downstream of 0.3 miles that is uncommon on the Lumber River.

The banks are generally low to swampy, with some areas of dry ground up to a few feet high at low flows.

A line of wooden posts (mi 11.0) runs across the river. These are remains of small bridges built to support logging.

---

15 NC 904 access at Fair Bluff to Rice Field Cove Landing access off US 76 near Nichols, South Carolina

Difficulty A	**Width**	60–100 ft
Distance 16.4 mi	**Gradient**	1.3 ft/mi
Scenery A	**Map**	page 208

Gauge See Section 13.

Notes See the previous section about the Fair Bluff access.

To reach Rice Field Cove Landing from the US 76 bridge, go east 0.5 miles and turn right on Drowning Creek Drive. Bear right on River Road and go to the road's end.

The houses of Fair Bluff are not seen for long. The river continues its meandering through a primitive setting.

There are no signs to mark the river's passage into South Carolina (mi 3.7), where the National Wild and Scenic designation ends.

Griffins Landing (mi 4.7) is on the left and 0.2 miles up a small canal. This section can be divided into two sections of 4.7 and

11.7 miles by using Griffins Landing access. It is reached by going south from Fair Bluff on Causey Road (Robeson Co. 1360). The road changes to unpaved as it crosses into South Carolina. Continue 0.6 miles to Griffins Landing Road and turn right. The ramp into the canal is where the road turns left.

The river passes under an old railroad bridge (mi 13.6) with a center swing section, which was turned parallel to the river to allow large boats to pass when commercial traffic used the river.

At the US 76 bridge (mi 15.8), Rice Field Cove Landing access is two bends downstream on the left.

Pete Peterson on Lumber River, Section 3

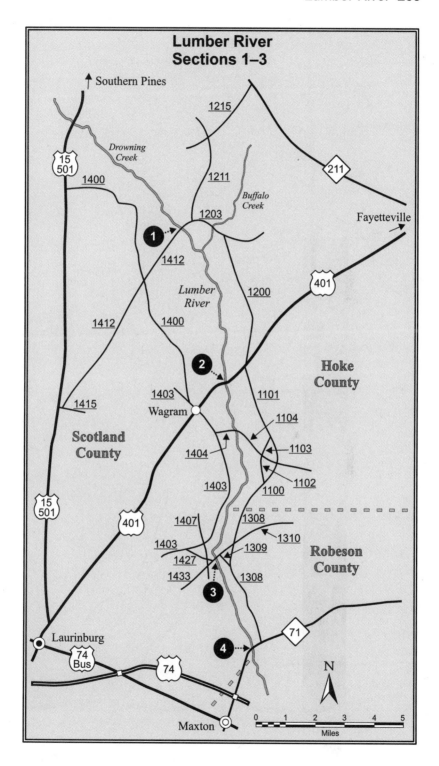

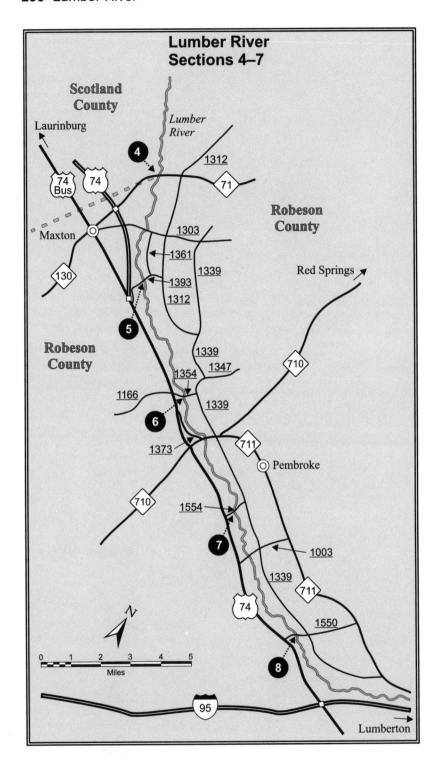

Lumber River
Sections 4–7

Scotland County

Laurinburg

Lumber River

4

1312

71

74 Bus

74

Robeson County

Maxton

130

1303

1361

1393

1339

1312

Red Springs

5

Robeson County

1339

1347

710

1354

1166

1339

6

1373

711

710

Pembroke

1554

7

1003

1339

711

74

1550

8

N

0 1 2 3 4 5
Miles

95

Lumberton

Lumber Basin

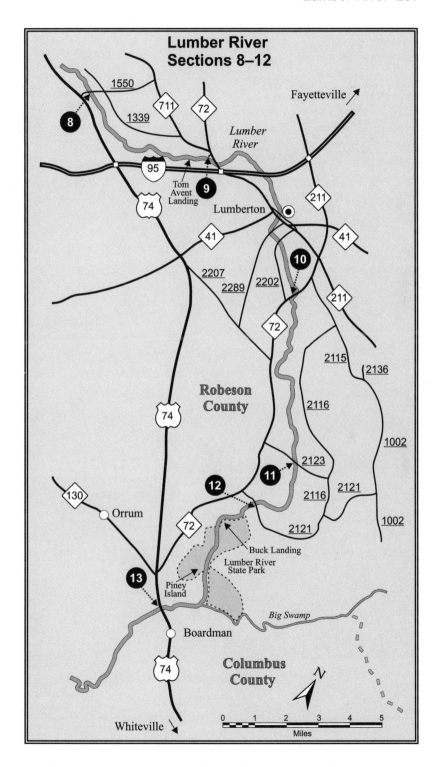

Lumber River
Sections 8–12

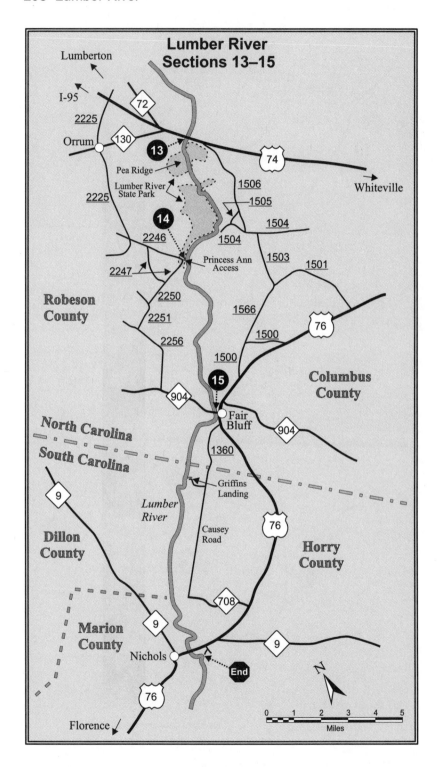

**Lumber River
Sections 13–15**

Lumberton

I-95

2225

Orrum

130

72

74

Whiteville

Pea Ridge

Lumber River
State Park

1506

1505

1504

13

14

2225

2246

1504

Princess Ann
Access

2247

1503

1501

2250

2251

2256

1566

1500

76

**Robeson
County**

**Columbus
County**

1500

15

904

North Carolina

South Carolina

Fair
Bluff

904

1360

Griffins
Landing

*Lumber
River*

9

**Dillon
County**

Causey
Road

76

**Horry
County**

708

**Marion
County**

9

9

Nichols

End

76

Florence

N

0 1 2 3 4 5
Miles

Lumber Basin

Large cypress base on the Lumber River

Lumber Basin

Waccamaw River

Counties   Columbus, Brunswick, Horry (SC)

Topos   Lake Waccamaw West, Old Dock, Freeland, Pireway,
             Longs

The Waccamaw River begins at the outflow of Lake Waccamaw near Whiteville. Below the lake, it flows through the largest remaining cypress/tupelo-gum blackwater swamp in North Carolina. On the east side is the vast Green Swamp. The Waccamaw flows on to South Carolina to join the Great Pee Dee River near the Atlantic Ocean at Georgetown.

Lake Waccamaw is the largest of the *Carolina Bays*—elongated oval-shaped depressions with the long axis generally running along a northwest to southeast line. The name Carolina Bay is from evergreen bay trees often found in and near the depressions. Hundreds of thousands of these depressions exist in the sandy Coastal Plain soil. The largest concentration is in North and South Carolina, but they are found from Florida to New Jersey.

Most Carolina Bays are small and contain water only in wet periods. Lake Waccamaw is unique for its large size and for containing a number of fish and mollusks found only in its waters. Other Carolina Bay lakes are highly acidic and support little life. Lake Waccamaw is close to a neutral pH because of limestone.

More than a dozen theories have been proposed to explain the origin of the Carolina Bays. A popular explanation was that they were formed by meteors, but no meteorite material has been found. Another possibility is that a comet passed close enough to heat and explode wet areas. An earth-based explanation is they were natural round or irregular-shaped depressions in an emerging sea floor. Prevailing winds caused currents in the water, changing the basins to oval-shaped. Scientific debate continues, leaving the big mystery unsolved.

There is little development on the Waccamaw River as it flows through wilderness and past a few small communities. Lake Waccamaw State Park owns land on the eastern side of the lake, but most of the land along the river corridor in North Carolina is owned by timber companies. More protection is afforded in South Carolina where much of the river is protected by the Waccamaw National Wildlife Refuge and a state Natural Heritage Preserve.

A research team from East Carolina University studied the Waccamaw River watershed and found it to be in jeopardy from severe and conflicting pressures. Ditching, draining, and increasing sediment are part of the problem, but there are many more. The team's report concluded that the ecosystem must be managed as a single entity with a focus on the main component that drives the wetland system—water.

The Waccamaw is a popular choice for overnight camping, but the only public land where camping is allowed is in the South Carolina Natural Heritage Preserve (see Section 5). Suitable campsites can be found in other areas, but it is often several miles between possible sites on dry ground.

---

1 Waccamaw Shores Road (Columbus Co. 1967) end to Dock Road (Columbus Co. 1928) bridge

Difficulty A		**Width**	20–90 ft
Distance 11.5 mi		**Gradient**	1.0 ft/mi
Scenery A		**Map**	page 215

Gauge USGS *Waccamaw River at Freeland*. Estimated minimum is 200 cfs (5.2 ft). Downed trees are common. Higher flows lessen problems with trees.

Notes The put-in is where Waccamaw Shores Road ends on the south side of the lake. There is a sandy area here near the small dam at the lake's outlet. It is not a managed access but has been used for many years. Boat ramps are on the northeast and northwest lakeshores, but using them requires several miles of lake paddling to reach the river.

At flows above about 1,300 cfs (12.3 ft), the dam is underwater. Below the dam, the river channel is not obvious because the river flows through trees, but a few hundred feet downstream the channel is more defined.

For the first few miles, the river is as narrow as 20 feet. Cypress and tupelo-gum trees cover the banks and provide a closed canopy.

A logging road (mi 2.8) comes to the left bank just upstream of power lines. Another logging road (mi 4.9) crossed the river, but the bridge has been washed downstream. The wooden support pilings remain.

The channel becomes wide, straight, and deep in an area known as the Fishponds (mi 5.7).

A private dock (mi 6.3) on the left is at Fishponds Landing on Crusoe Island. Thomas Spivey used this landing to hunt and fish the river, sometimes using his handmade canoes hewn from old cypress logs. Until his death in 1999, he kept this section open for paddlers by sawing a narrow path through downed trees.

The small community at Crusoe Island has remained relatively isolated for 200 years, and the residents have an unusual dialect. There are many stories about their descendents, including that they were from the Lost Colony. The most common story is they were French settlers who left Haiti during the slave insurrections.

White Marsh Swamp (mi 9.5) enters on the right. A crew under contract to clear downed trees from the Waccamaw during the summer of 2000 also cleared up White Marsh Swamp for over a mile. They told of snakes in the tree canopy "hanging like Christmas tree ornaments."

The take-out road runs close to the river (mi 9.9) until the bridge is reached.

---

② Dock Road (Columbus Co. 1928) bridge to NC 130 access

Difficulty A		**Width** 20–90 ft	
Distance 11.4 mi		**Gradient** 0.5 ft/mi	
Scenery A (80%), B (20%)		**Map** page 215	

Gauge See Section 1.

Notes At NC 130, parking and access at the bridge are difficult because of guardrails, but there is a private access with a boat ramp downstream left of the bridge. Deposit the $2 fee in the honor box.

Cypress, river birch, and pine trees are abundant. The river narrows (mi 2.0) to channels only 20 feet wide.

The river takes an abrupt right turn (mi 2.0) where Juniper Creek joins from the left. Juniper Creek drains the Green Swamp to the Waccamaw River. It is wide and runs straight ahead, making the Waccamaw appear to be the tributary.

Columbus Co. 1333 (mi 5.9) comes close to the river where there are several houses, but the only access to the river is through private property.

3 NC 130 access to Reeves Ferry Road (Columbus Co. 1943) end

Difficulty	A	**Width**	50–100 ft
Distance	7.6 mi	**Gradient**	0.5 ft/mi
Scenery	A	**Map**	page 216

Gauge See Section 1.

Notes See the previous section about the NC 130 access.

Just beyond where Reeves Ferry Road maintenance ends, the river can be reached for boat access.

Some land on the right bank has been logged.

Gore Creek (mi 5.6) enters on the right. A side trip can be made by going up Gore Creek a quarter-mile into Gore Lake. The lake is almost a mile long and up to 200 feet wide.

4 Reeves Ferry Road (Columbus Co. 1943) end to NC 904 access

Difficulty	A	**Width**	70–200 ft
Distance	8.6 mi	**Gradient**	0.5 ft/mi
Scenery	A (75%), B (25%)	**Map**	page 216

Gauge See Section 1.

Notes See the previous section about Reeves Ferry Road.

A Wildlife boating access is at NC 904.

Groups of houses are near the beginning and end of this section. There are many cypress and oak trees. The banks range from swampy to several feet above water.

The river widens near the end, and motorboats are common.

5 NC 904 access to SC 9 access near Longs, South Carolina

Difficulty	A	**Width**	50–200 ft
Distance	17.9 mi	**Gradient**	0.3 ft/mi
Scenery	A (80%), B (10%), C (10%)	**Map**	page 216

Gauge USGS *Waccamaw River near Longs, SC*. Estimated minimum is 200 cfs (5.0 ft).

Notes There is a Wildlife boating access at NC 904.

At the SC 9 bridge, there is a choice of two landings. Downstream left has a public boat access operated by South Carolina. Upstream left has a free, private access next to Horrys Restaurant. Their sign

Lumber Basin

says it all: "Horrys Landing, private property, to be used only by those who respect and wish to maintain the beauty of nature."

The river is wide and the banks are residential for the first few miles. Houses fade away (mi 3.1) as the banks turn swampy. Downstream are many loops and old channels marking where the winding river has changed its course.

The channel narrows to as little as 50 feet (mi 6.6) in contrast to the wide, developed river at the put-in. The banks are low and swampy with many palmetto plants.

Cawcaw Swamp (mi 7.8) enters from the left.

After the South Carolina border (mi 8.6) is crossed, signs on the banks mark land in the state's Natural Heritage Preserve. The preserve contains over 5,000 acres in the Waccamaw floodplain and extends down the next 29 miles. Camping is allowed on these lands. The preserve consists of several different tracts. In places, only one side of the river is within the preserve, and there are a few gaps where neither side is within the preserve.

The left bank rises to 30 feet at Worthams Ferry (mi 12.3) where there are several houses and a public boat ramp. It can be used to shorten this section. It is reached by taking SC 111 from Brooksville toward the river. At the end of SC 111 continue straight ahead on a small road, then bear right to reach the ramp.

Motorboats become more common on the latter part of this section.

■

In time of freshet, the water could spread out horizontally for miles, and so rose very little. At present, the floor of the swamp was out of the water, although you would stop short of calling it dry land. It was dank and oozing, and when I made my one portage, each footprint had filled immediately with water.
—Franklin Burroughs, *The River Home* (1992)

Lumber Basin

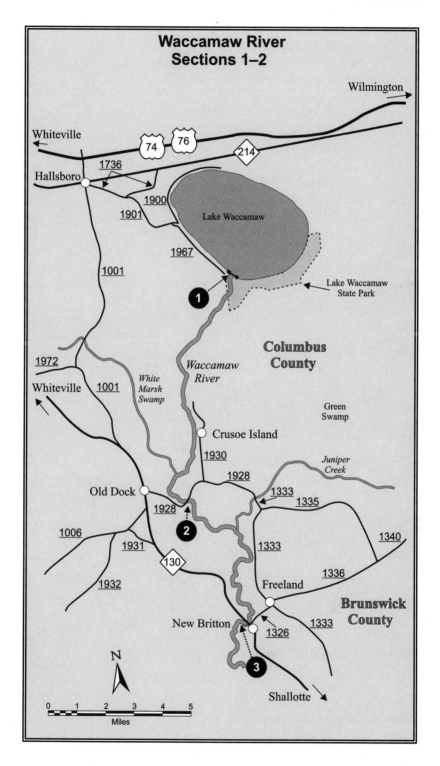

Waccamaw River
Sections 1–2

Wilmington

Whiteville

74 76 214

1736

Hallsboro

1900

1901

Lake Waccamaw

1967

1001

1

Lake Waccamaw
State Park

**Columbus
County**

*Waccamaw
River*

1972

*White
Marsh
Swamp*

Green
Swamp

Whiteville 1001

Crusoe Island

1930

*Juniper
Creek*

1928

Old Dock

1333

1335

1928

2

1006

1333

1340

1931

1336

130

Freeland

1932

**Brunswick
County**

New Britton

1326

1333

3

N

Shallotte

0 1 2 3 4 5
Miles

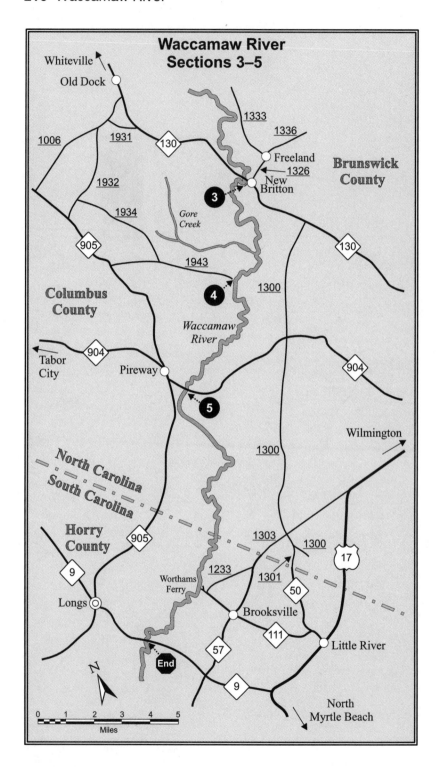

**Waccamaw River
Sections 3–5**

Whiteville

Old Dock

1333

130

1336

1006   1931

Freeland

1326   **Brunswick
County**

1932

New
Britton

3

1934

*Gore
Creek*

905

1943

1300

**Columbus
County**

4

130

*Waccamaw
River*

904

Tabor
City

Pireway

904

5

Wilmington

1300

North Carolina

South Carolina

**Horry
County**   905

1303   1300

17

9   1233   1301

Worthams
Ferry   50

Longs   Brooksville

End   111   Little River

N   57

9

North
Myrtle Beach

0 1 2 3 4 5
Miles

Lumber Basin

Lake Waccamaw Dam at high water
Waccamaw River, Section 1

■

The little lake, out of which the long and crooked river with its dark cypress waters flowed to the sea. The paper canoe shot into the whirling current which rushes out of the lake through a narrow aperture into a great and dismal swamp. Down the tortuous, black, rolling current went the paper canoe with a giant forest covering the great swamp and screening me from the light of day. Festoons of gray Spanish moss hung from the weird limbs of monster trees, giving a funeral aspect to the gloomy forest, while owls hooted as though it were night. The creamy, wax-like berries of the mistletoe gave a Druidical aspect to the woods.

Such is the character of the Waccamaw, this most crooked of rivers.

—N.H. Bishop, *Voyage of the Paper Canoe* (1878)

Lumber Basin

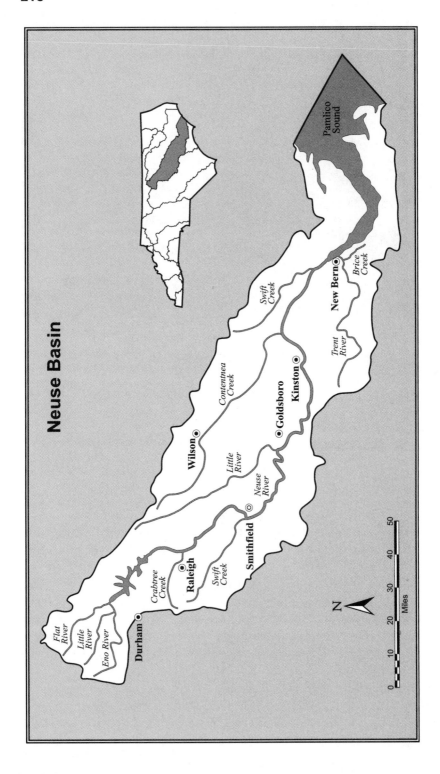

Neuse Basin

Neuse Basin

The Neuse Basin is North Carolina's third largest river basin, draining 6,235 square miles, and is one of only four major river basins whose boundaries are located entirely within the state.

The Neuse Basin originates in Person and Orange Counties where the Eno, Little, and Flat Rivers begin above Hillsborough and Durham. The Neuse River begins at the confluence of the Flat and Eno Rivers where the next 24 miles are part of Falls Lake. Falls Dam is about 10 miles northeast of Raleigh.

Below the dam, the Neuse River flows southeasterly past Smithfield, Goldsboro, and Kinston until it reaches tidal waters near New Bern. Major tributaries of the Neuse River below Falls Lake include Crabtree Creek, Swift Creek (near Smithfield), Little River (near Goldsboro), Contentnea Creek, Swift Creek (near New Bern), and Trent River.

At New Bern, the river broadens dramatically and changes from a free-flowing river to a tidal estuary, which eventually flows into Pamlico Sound as the widest-mouthed river in the continental United States. The Neuse River is one of three large rivers that flow into Albemarle and Pamlico Sounds, forming the second largest estuary in the United States.

The Neuse Basin spans both the Piedmont and Coastal Plain regions. The upper third of the basin, generally west of I-95, is in the Piedmont, and the remainder of the basin to the east is part of the Coastal Plain.

Four state parks are within the Neuse Basin: Eno River State Park, William B. Umstead State Park, Cliffs of the Neuse State Park, and Waynesborough State Park. Part of Croatan National Forest drains to the Neuse Basin.

A large growth in population and development in the Neuse Basin has not been good for water quality. See the Neuse River (page 263).

Brice Creek

County   Craven

Topo   New Bern

Brice Creek (also known as Brices Creek) begins in Croatan National Forest and flows north, forming the northeast border of the forest. It joins the Trent River, 3 miles southwest of New Bern.

This blackwater stream is popular for fishing and observing wildlife.

Portions of the creek upstream of Section 1 can only be paddled at high water levels because there are many downed trees.

---

1   Old Airport Road (Craven Co. 1111) bridge to Croatan National Forest Route 610 access

Difficulty A	**Width** 30–110 ft
Distance 5.4 mi	**Gradient** 0 ft/mi
Scenery A	**Map** page 222

Gauge None. Always above minimum. There is a small tidal influence.

Notes A Wildlife boating access is at the end of Croatan National Forest Route 610. From Brices's Creek Road (Craven Co. 1004), take Perrytown Road (Craven Co. 1143) 1.6 miles south. Turn left on Forest Route 121-A and continue 0.5 miles. Go straight where Forest Route 170 bears off to the right. The road is now Forest Route 610, leading 0.7 miles to the ramp.

Starting on the left bank (mi 1.7), Croatan National Forest property begins and continues for the remainder of this section. The right bank is privately-owned.

Blackwater winds through lily pads where the banks are swampy to 15 feet high. Many cypress trees and some tall pines are along the course, and ospreys have nests overlooking the creek.

A channel (mi 4.8) to the right can be explored for a half-mile before it dead-ends.

2 Croatan National Forest Route 610 access to Merchants Store access off Perrytown Road (Craven Co. 1143)	
Difficulty A	**Width** 75–500 ft
Distance 4.2 mi	**Gradient** 0 ft/mi
Scenery A (50%), C (50%)	**Map** page 222

Gauge See Section 1.

Notes See the previous section about the Forest Route 610 access.

Merchants Store, a service station and grocery at the intersection of Brices's Creek Road (Craven Co. 1004) and Perrytown Road, operates a boat ramp a few hundred yards down Perrytown Road. Use of their ramp is $3, paid at the store, but usually only charged for boats on trailers.

Motorboats and jet skis are common on this section during warm weather.

Craven County's Creekside Park (mi 0.9) is on the right bank. A long dock and canoe/kayak launch are planned. Access to the park is from Old Airport Road (Craven Co. 1111).

Croatan National Forest property ends (mi 2.3) on the left bank. Many homes are along the banks downstream.

The trip can be extended by continuing past Merchants Store's ramp for 1.4 miles to the Trent River and another 1.7 miles to Lawson Creek Park in New Bern. See the Trent River, Section 6 (page 285). Wind can be a problem because the Trent is up to 0.4 miles wide.

Len Felton at entrance to Bobbitt Hole
Eno River, Section 3

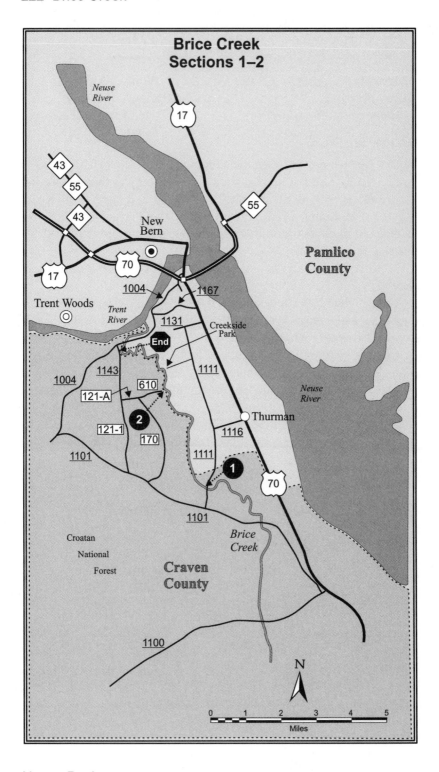

**Brice Creek
Sections 1–2**

Neuse
River

43

55

43

55

17

New
Bern

70

17

Pamlico
County

Trent Woods

1004

1167

Trent
River

1131

Creekside
Park

End

1143

1111

1004

610

121-A

Neuse
River

2

Thurman

121-1

170

1116

1101

1111

1

70

1101

Croatan

National

Forest

Brice
Creek

Craven
County

1100

N

0   1   2   3   4   5
Miles

Contentnea Creek

Counties   Wilson, Greene, Lenoir, Pitt, Craven

Topos   Lucama, Wilson, Saratoga, Stantonsburg, Walstonsburg, Snow Hill, Hookerton, Ayden, Grifton

The headwaters of Contentnea Creek begin near Moccasin Creek, northeast of Raleigh and north of Zebulon. After flowing into Buckhorn Reservoir, west of Wilson, Contentnea Creek is born and continues into Wiggins Mill Reservoir, a few miles southeast of Wilson. It then flows southeast through Snow Hill and Grifton before joining the Neuse River.

Water flowing into Contentnea Creek from Wilson's wastewater treatment plant had a history of exceeding its discharge permit limits on certain pollutants. Because the state's enforcement actions were deemed too lenient, the American Canoe Association (ACA) filed a lawsuit in 1996 on behalf of its members. The City of Wilson entered into a consent decree in 1999. The settlement provided that the city would meet its permit limits, allow the ACA to monitor the results, and provided money for the purchase and preservation of riparian land and wetlands along Contentnea Creek.

Contentnea Creek flows mostly through farmland and undeveloped land, providing 100 miles of paddling opportunities.

1 NC 581 bridge near Buckhorn Reservoir to Saint Rose Church Road (Wilson Co. 1154) bridge

Difficulty A–I, and one II$^+$		**Width** 30–100 ft	
Distance 7.1 mi		**Gradient** 2.3 ft/mi	
Scenery A (70%), B (30%)		**Map** page 230	

Gauge USGS *Contentnea Creek near Lucama*. Minimum is 40 cfs (2.0 ft). During dry conditions, almost all flow is from water released at Buckhorn Reservoir.

Notes The USGS gauge is 250 feet upstream of the put-in, and Buckhorn Reservoir Dam is 0.8 miles upstream of the gauge.

At low flows, there are a few Class I rapids over gravel bars. The first rapid at the put-in is a good indicator of water conditions.

Many trees hang over the creek, and holly trees are especially abundant.

At the Sadie Road (Wilson Co. 1144) bridge (mi 1.1), the right bank rises 50 feet.

After a creek (mi 2.0) enters from the right, water becomes deeper from the backwater of the downstream milldam.

Portage the 6-foot milldam (mi 4.6) on the right where a section of the dam is broken. The break is a jumble of large pieces of concrete and brickwork, making a 6-foot drop over a 40-foot run. It is a Class II$^+$ rapid at good flows, but rough edges of the debris are hazardous if one swims here.

NC 42 (mi 4.7) is just below the dam.

After passing the I-95 bridges (mi 5.4), beavers have been active downstream. Their dams provide drops of 1–2 feet, which can be paddled over.

2	Saint Rose Church Road (Wilson Co. 1154) bridge to Wiggins Mill Road (Wilson Co. 1103) access		
Difficulty A		**Width**	35–2,600 ft
Distance 9.1 mi		**Gradient**	1.3 ft/mi
Scenery A (80%), B (20%)		**Map**	page 230

Gauge See Section 1.

Notes Wiggins Mill Dam is a few hundred feet upstream of US 301. An access area off Wiggins Mill Road has no signs, but is used by the public to reach the reservoir above the dam or the river below the dam.

Twin bridges (mi 3.3) are part of the future US 264 to the southwest of Wilson.

Quaker Road (Wilson Co. 1162) (mi 3.6) can be used for access, but the banks are steep.

There are many downed trees below Quaker Road, but most can be paddled around. The water is deeper downstream of Quaker Road because of backwater from Wiggins Mill Reservoir.

Downing Road (Wilson Co. 1163) (mi 7.0) comes within 50 feet on the left. A dirt ramp here makes for easier boat access than downstream at Downing Road bridge (mi 7.7).

The reservoir has many islands and trees. It narrows approaching the 12-foot dam. Take out on the right above the dam. If continuing into the next section, a portage trail leads below the dam.

3 Wiggins Mill Road (Wilson Co. 1103) access to Evansdale Road (Wilson Co. 1622) bridge

Difficulty A–I⁺		**Width** 35–90 ft	
Distance 6.0 mi		**Gradient** 2.2 ft/mi	
Scenery A (30%), B (70%)		**Map** page 230	

Gauge USGS *Contentnea Creek near Lucama*. Estimated minimum is 75 cfs (2.4 ft).

Notes See the previous section about the Wiggins Mill Road access. The put-in is below the dam, almost under the US 301 bridge.

In the first 0.2 miles below the US 301 bridge, four rock ledges extend across the river making Class I⁺ rapids at low water levels. The drops are about a half-foot and require some maneuvering.

An elephant-size boulder (mi 0.8) in the water is far bigger than any other boulders seen in Contentnea Creek.

Twin bridges (mi 2.5) are part of the future US 264 to the southwest of Wilson.

Old Black Creek Road (Wilson Co. 1606) (mi 2.9) is a possible access point.

The creek is generally narrow, and there are some gravel bar riffles at low flows.

4 Evansdale Road (Wilson Co. 1622) bridge to NC 222/111 access at Stantonsburg

Difficulty A		**Width** 25–70 ft	
Distance 10.3 mi		**Gradient** 1.7 ft/mi	
Scenery A (80%), B (20%)		**Map** page 230	

Gauge See Section 3.

Notes At NC 222/111, a road on downstream right leads to a parking area and concrete ramp managed by Stantonsburg.

An island (mi 0.7) splits the river, causing the main channel to be only 25 feet wide. A few more islands are found in the first 3 miles.

Woodbridge Road (Wilson Co. 1628) (mi 3.5) runs along the right side of the creek until reaching the bridge (mi 4.2). It can be used for access.

Pelt Road (Wilson Co. 1632) (mi 6.1) is on the right bank for 0.1 miles.

The creek is 65-70 feet wide in the last few miles and flows through farmland.

5	NC 222/111 access at Stantonsburg to Speights Bridge Road (Greene Co. 1225) access		
Difficulty A		**Width** 35–90 ft	
Distance 10.6 mi		**Gradient** 0.7 ft/mi	
Scenery A		**Map** page 231	

Gauge See Section 3.

Notes See the previous section about the NC 222/111 access.

At Speights Bridge Road, a ramp is upstream left. It is managed by Greene County.

The NC 58 bridge (mi 3.4) can be used for access, but there is little parking space. From downstream left of the bridge, it is about 200 feet to the river.

River birch and sycamore trees are common. Farmland is occasionally seen near the banks.

The banks are typically only 3 feet high, but approaching the take-out at a right bend (mi 10.0), the left bank rises 50 feet.

6	Speights Bridge Road (Greene Co. 1225) access to Sheppard Ferry Road (Greene Co. 1222) bridge		
Difficulty A		**Width** 35–80 ft	
Distance 8.2 mi		**Gradient** 1.3 ft/mi	
Scenery A		**Map** page 231	

Gauge USGS *Contentnea Creek at Hookerton*. Estimated minimum is 125 cfs (4.4 ft).

Notes See the previous section about the Speights Bridge Road access.

Large river birch trees continue into this section, and there are cypress trees with dense rows of knees.

Discarded tires are seen in the water at low flows. Where Beaman Run (mi 2.5) enters on the left, more than fifty tires litter the river bottom.

7 Sheppard Ferry Road (Greene Co. 1222) bridge to Mill Street access at Snow Hill

Difficulty A	**Width** 50–70 ft	
Distance 10.5 mi	**Gradient** 0.4 ft/mi	
Scenery A (75%), B (25%)	**Map** page 231	

Gauge See Section 6.

Notes A Wildlife boating access is at the end of Mill Street in Snow Hill. Going north on US 258 (Southeast Second Street), turn right at Mill Street.

The stream winds through farmland, and cypress trees are along low banks.

The US 13 bridge (mi 9.9) marks the development of Snow Hill on the right, and the take-out is just downstream of the US 258 bridge (mi 10.4).

8 Mill Street access at Snow Hill to NC 123 bridge at Hookerton

Difficulty A	**Width** 60–80 ft	
Distance 10.3 mi	**Gradient** 0.5 ft/mi	
Scenery A (80%), B (20%)	**Map** page 232	

Gauge See Section 6.

Notes See the previous section about the Mill Street access.

The banks start off low but rise to 40 feet on the right (mi 3.5).

There is little development seen until near the end of the trip, but the creek comes within 0.2 miles of Greene Co. 1400 (mi 5.8) where traffic can be heard.

9 NC 123 bridge at Hookerton to Edwards Bridge Road (Greene Co. 1004) bridge

Difficulty A	**Width** 50–75 ft	
Distance 8.4 mi	**Gradient** 0.7 ft/mi	
Scenery A	**Map** page 232	

Gauge See Section 6.

Notes Contentnea Creek continues its winding course with mostly low banks and little development except for a few signs of nearby farms.

The second half of the run has some large stands of cypress trees.

---

10 Edwards Bridge Road (Greene Co. 1004) bridge to South Street access at Grifton

Difficulty A   **Width** 50–110 ft
Distance 9.2 mi   **Gradient** 1.1 ft/mi
Scenery A (65%), B (20%), C (15%)   **Map** page 233

Gauge See Section 6.

Notes A Wildlife boating access is at the end of South Street in Grifton. Going east on NC 118 (Queen Street), turn right on South Street.

Spanish moss hangs from some of the many cypress trees in this section.

Little Contentnea Creek (mi 2.1) enters on the left.

The channel narrows to 50 feet with low banks (mi 4.3) and broadens a mile downstream.

The NC 11 (mi 7.3) and NC 118 (mi 8.4) bridges are passed before reaching the take-out.

---

11 South Street access at Grifton to Maple Cypress Road (Craven Co. 1470) bridge on Neuse River

Difficulty A   **Width** 50–200 ft
Distance 10.1 mi   **Gradient** 0.1 ft/mi
Scenery A (80%), C (20%)   **Map** page 233

Gauge See Section 6. For the Neuse River portion of this section, use USGS *Neuse River at Fort Barnwell.*

Notes See the previous section about the South Street access.

Two miles downstream of Grifton, homes are no longer seen on the banks.

After a channel (mi 2.3) to the left from a wastewater treatment plant, the stream character changes in the next half-mile. Several smaller channels branch off into swamp, and the stream narrows from 150 feet to 50 feet as it winds through cypress knees.

A take-out is possible at Jolly Ole Field Road (Pitt Co. 1914) roadside (mi 4.0), but it is easy to miss. A small cove on the left comes in at a back angle, and 0.3 miles up the cove it ends near the road. If the flow is below 600 cfs (7.5 ft) on the Hookerton gauge, some walking will be required. To use this take-out, scout it to make sure it will be recognized.

There are many large cypress trees before reaching the Neuse River (mi 4.5).

For the remainder of the trip, see the Neuse River, Section 18 (page 273). Add 4.2 miles to the mileage given in the Neuse River description to correct for distances from the Contentnea Creek put-in.

Pete Peterson running a broken dam
Flat River, Section 1

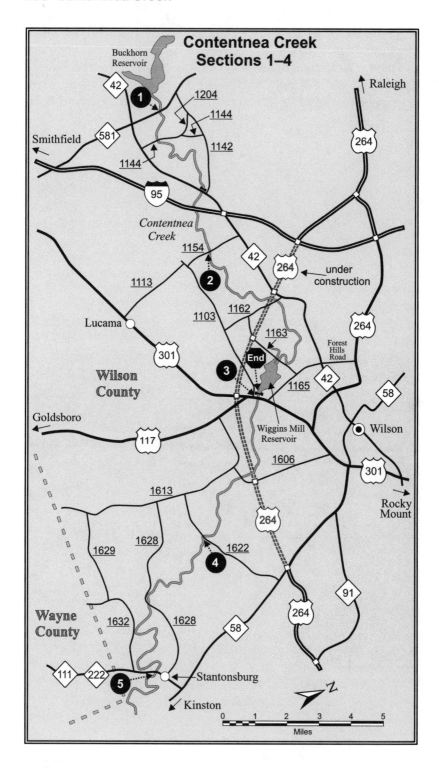

Contentnea Creek
Sections 1–4

Buckhorn Reservoir

Raleigh

42

1204

1144

581

Smithfield

1142

1144

95

Contentnea Creek

1154

42

264

under construction

1113

2

Lucama

1103

1162

1163

Forest Hills Road

264

301

Wilson County

3

End

1165

42

58

Goldsboro

117

Wiggins Mill Reservoir

Wilson

1606

301

Rocky Mount

1613

264

1629

1628

1622

4

91

Wayne County

1632

1628

58

264

111

222

5

Stantonsburg

Kinston

0 1 2 3 4 5
Miles

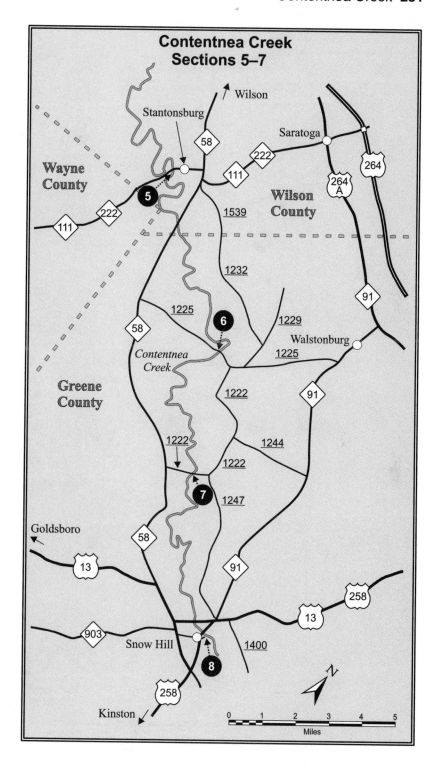

Contentnea Creek
Sections 5–7

Wilson

Stantonsburg

Saratoga

58

222

111

264
A

264

Wayne
County

5

222

111

Wilson
County

1539

91

1232

1225

6

1229

58

Walstonburg

1225

*Contentnea
Creek*

1222

91

Greene
County

1222

1244

1222

7

1247

Goldsboro

58

13

91

258

13

903

Snow Hill

1400

8

258

Kinston

N

0 1 2 3 4 5
Miles

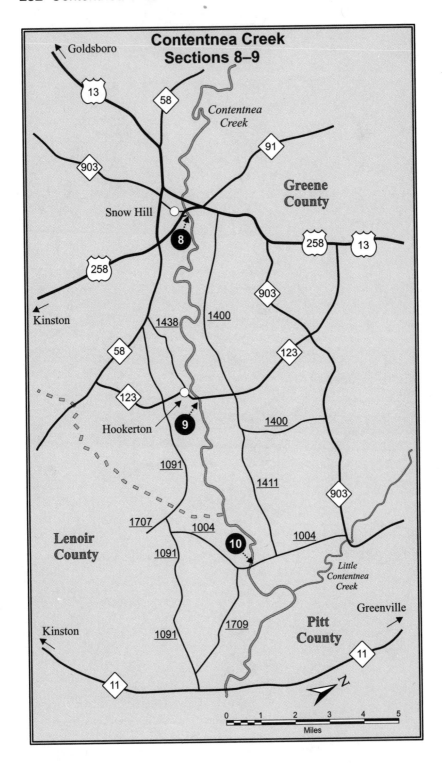

Neuse Basin

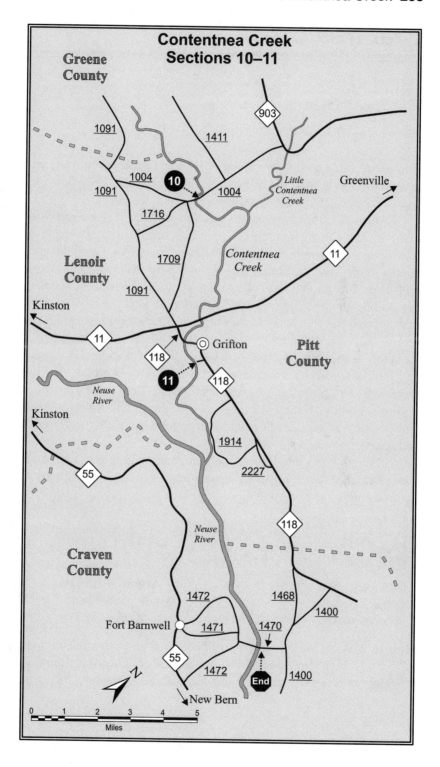

Contentnea Creek
Sections 10–11

Greene County

1091

1411

903

1004 · **10** · 1004

Little Contentnea Creek

Greenville

1091

1716

1709

Contentnea Creek

11

Lenoir County

1091

Kinston

11

118

Grifton

Pitt County

11

118

Neuse River

1914

Kinston

55

2227

118

Neuse River

Craven County

1472

1468

1400

Fort Barnwell

1471

1470

1400

55

End

1472

New Bern

0   1   2   3   4   5
Miles

Crabtree Creek

County   Wake

Topos   Cary, Raleigh West, Raleigh East

Crabtree Creek's headwaters include Crabtree Creek west of Cary and several creeks starting east of Research Triangle Park. They flow into Lake Crabtree, a 520-acre flood-control lake in Cary.

Downstream, the creek passes through William B. Umstead State Park. It flows on to Raleigh's Crabtree Valley, a prime example of unwise development in a floodplain. Before the 1970s, the valley was almost empty, but the state's largest shopping mall was soon to be built here. Floods that the valley used to absorb continued, but now the mall began absorbing the muddy waters. It was not only the mall that suffered but also many homes built in floodplains downstream as the city developed rapidly.

Dams were built on creeks to help control flooding. For homes and businesses in the floodplain, it has meant fewer floods, but the dams cannot stop the largest ones, as Hurricane Fran (1996) proved.

From Crabtree Valley, the creek continues through Raleigh's residential and business development before joining the Neuse River in southeastern Raleigh.

A Raleigh Parks and Recreation hiking and biking greenway runs along Crabtree Creek for most of paddling Sections 2–3 and part of Section 4 described below.

1 Old Reedy Creek Road (Wake Co. 1795) bridge to Ebenezer Church Road (Wake Co. 1649) bridge

Difficulty A–I, and one II	**Width**	10–50 ft
Distance 5.3 mi	**Gradient**	5.5 ft/mi
Scenery A	**Map**	page 238

Gauge USGS *Crabtree Creek at Ebenezer Church Road*. Minimum is 75 cfs (4.3 ft). It can be paddled down to 30 cfs (3.6 ft) but requires dragging over rapids at the ruins of the old Company Milldam. Downed trees are common.

Water picks up speed as flow increases above 175 cfs (5.3 ft), making downed trees an increasing hazard in the narrow stream.

Notes To reach the put-in from I-40, take Harrison Avenue (Exit 287). Go 0.5 miles west on Harrison Avenue and turn right on Weston Parkway. Continue 0.6 miles and turn right on Old Reedy Creek Road. It is 0.5 miles to the one-lane bridge. Lake Crabtree is to the left.

After passing under I-40 (mi 0.1), land on the right bank rises 100 feet. A quarry operation is just over the ridge for the next 2 miles.

The creek enters William B. Umstead State Park property (mi 1.3), but the park owns little land on the right bank until the creek makes a left bend (mi 1.8). The remainder of this section is through park property, giving the paddler a view of a rare undeveloped haven in a rapidly growing area. Mountain laurel, rhododendron, and rock outcroppings are common.

Hurricane Fran (1996) downed a tremendous number of trees in the park. Trees across the creek were cleared, but there are always newly downed trees in such a heavily forested area. Many trees can be ducked under at low water but at higher water become hazards.

There is a Class I$^+$ rapid formed by ledges before reaching a hiking trail bridge (mi 2.3), upstream of the ruins of the Company Milldam (mi 2.6). Rocks from the dam are scattered in the channel for about 50 feet, making a Class I$^+$–II rapid. The Company Mill hiking trail borders the left bank.

Reedy Creek Road bridge (mi 3.4) is part of a hiking, biking, and bridle trail.

2	Ebenezer Church Road (Wake Co. 1649) bridge to Old Lassiter Mill Road access	
Difficulty A–I	**Width** 35–50 ft	
Distance 5.4 mi	**Gradient** 5.2 ft/mi	
Scenery C	**Map** page 238	

Gauge USGS *Crabtree Creek at Ebenezer Church Road.* Minimum is 30 cfs (3.6 ft).

There is always water to paddle in the backwater of the Lassiter Milldam. Putting in above the dam allows paddling upstream to Crabtree Valley and return, making a 3-mile trip.

Notes At the Lassiter Mill Road (Wake Co. 1808) bridge, Old Lassiter Mill Road connects on the upstream right and leads to a small park managed by Raleigh Parks and Recreation. A greenway borders the creek on the right, and there is parking downstream of the dam.

A large quarry (mi 0.4) is active on the left and owns land on the right. A ledge (mi 0.7) forms a 1-foot drop, and a similar one is downstream before going under the Duraleigh Road (Wake Co. 1664) bridge (mi 0.8).

Mountain laurel thickets are on the right bank with some rhododendron. A small creek (mi 1.0) drops over rocks, making a waterfall of a few feet. Many houses are on the banks throughout the rest of this section.

As the creek runs behind hotels and the mall at Crabtree Valley, there are many bridges, including private and pedestrian bridges, before going under US 70. The major bridges are on Creedmoor Road (mi 2.8) and Blue Ridge Road (mi 3.4).

A greenway runs along the creek on the right. To cross Blue Ridge Road and US 70, the trail dips halfway down into the creek channel and is supported by a terrace.

After passing under US 70 (mi 3.6) and a smaller bridge, the creek swings under the I-440 beltline (mi 4.3). The backwater of Lassiter Mill Dam begins in this area.

From Yadkin Drive (mi 4.6) to the end of this section, there are many homes on the banks.

Take out on the right, about 75 feet before reaching the 12-foot Lassiter Milldam. If continuing into the next section, portage on the right.

3	Old Lassiter Mill Road access to Raleigh Boulevard (Wake Co. 2921) access	
Difficulty A	**Width**	35–80 ft
Distance 3.8 mi	**Gradient**	2.9 ft/mi
Scenery C	**Map**	page 238

Gauge USGS *Crabtree Creek at Highway 70*. Minimum is 40 cfs (4.9 ft).

Notes See the previous section about the Old Lassiter Mill Road access. Put in on the gravel bar below the dam.

At the Raleigh Boulevard bridge, there is a greenway access on downstream right, but no motor vehicles are allowed. Parking for the greenway is 500 feet away on Crabtree Boulevard. This requires carrying boating equipment across the street, but there is a stop light at this intersection.

Lassiter Mill Road (Wake Co. 1808) bridge (mi 0.1) is just downstream of the put-in.

There are many houses in the beginning of this section and many businesses in the latter part. Banks are about 15 feet high and often steep, reducing the amount of development seen from the water.

The other bridges passed before the take-out are Anderson Drive (mi 1.4), Wake Forest Road (mi 2.0), Atlantic Avenue (mi 2.5), and Capital Boulevard (US 401) (mi 3.2).

4	Raleigh Boulevard (Wake Co. 2921) access to Poole Road (Wake Co. 1007) access on Neuse River		
Difficulty A–I, and one II		**Width** 25–100 ft	
Distance 7.5 mi		**Gradient** 3.6 ft/mi	
Scenery A (45%), B (55%)		**Map** page 238	

Gauge USGS *Crabtree Creek at US 1*. Minimum is 40 cfs (1.1 ft).

Notes See the previous section about the Raleigh Boulevard access.

The Poole Road access is managed by Raleigh Parks and Recreation.

Before reaching the Neuse River, there are a few Class I rapids dropping up to a foot over ledges or piles of rock.

Less development is seen in this section than in the previous two sections.

Before reaching New Bern Avenue (mi 2.5), the channel winds and becomes as narrow as 25 feet.

After passing under the I-440 beltline (mi 4.0) and the high bridge of South New Hope Road (mi 4.6), Crabtree Creek joins the Neuse River (mi 6.5).

For the remainder of this trip, see the Neuse River, Section 4 (page 266). The Class II rapid is at mile 6.9 from the Crabtree Creek put-in.

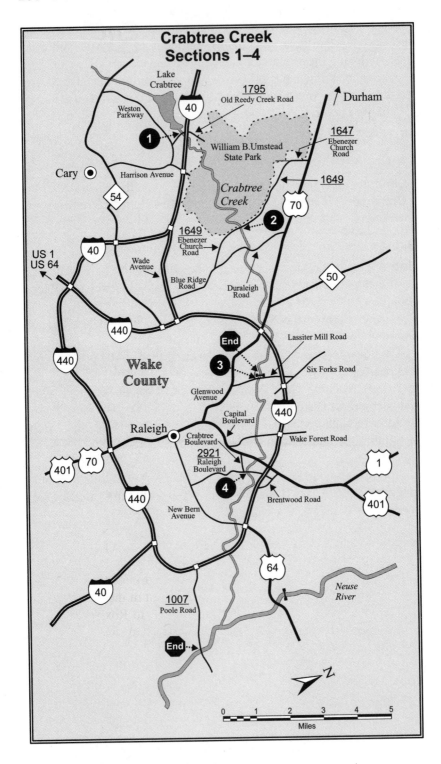

Neuse Basin

Eno River

Counties   Orange, Durham

Topos   Hillsborough, Northwest Durham, Northeast Durham

The Eno River begins northwest of Hillsborough and flows to the south. On the west side of Hillsborough, it turns east and passes across the northern part of Durham, where most of the river corridor is part of Eno River State Park. East of Durham, the Little River joins the Eno followed by the Flat River, where the Neuse River begins. The backwater of Falls Lake extends up the Eno for a short distance.

Shakori, Occaneechi, and Eno Indians lived in the Eno River Valley. The Great Indian Trading Path crossed the Eno near Hillsborough. It connected the area of present-day Petersburg, Virginia to near Charlotte and was used by the native traders long before European explorers and traders arrived.

The Eno River is an outstanding example of a beautiful natural river corridor in a fast-developing urban area, saved from development by community activism. In the 1960s, the Eno was being considered for a reservoir as a Durham water supply that would flood part of the valley. A group of citizens formed the Association for the Preservation of the Eno River Valley. Margaret Nygard was their tireless and visionary leader. They worked for many years to educate the public and political leaders on the value of preserving this natural area. A broad-based coalition was formed of people with many interests: paddling, hiking, photography, birding, and others who saw the value of preservation.

Property along the river has been acquired through purchases and gifts. In 1975 the Eno River State Park opened with 1,000 acres of land. It now contains almost 3,000 acres. The park starts a few miles above Few's Ford access and extends along most of the river corridor to Guess Road. The corridor from Guess Road to Roxboro Road is part of Durham's West Point on the Eno Park. There are many hiking trails along the Eno.

The Eno River Association continues to protect the Eno and preserve it as a natural river. Since the reservoir proposal, there have been other threats from roads, landfills, and sewer systems. The organization raises money for adding land to the park, and the most popular fund-raising event is the Eno River Festival, held during the Fourth of July holiday.

---

1 US 70 bridge to Eno River State Park Few's Ford access

Difficulty I–II, and one III		**Width** 25–75 ft	
Distance 5.4 mi		**Gradient** 13 ft/mi	
Scenery A (65%), B (35%)		**Map** page 245	

Gauge USGS *Eno River at Hillsborough*. Minimum is 90 cfs (2.6 ft).

Notes The Eno crosses US 70 twice. The put-in is at US 70 Bypass, east of Hillsborough, upstream left of the bridge. A long rope is useful to safely lower boats down the 50-foot bank.

To reach Few's Ford access, enter the park from Cole Mill Road (Durham Co. 1569). Take the second right into the parking lot for Buckquarter Creek Trail and canoe access. A 500-foot trail leads down to the river. The last rapid can be seen upstream and can be scouted from a trail leading upstream. For an access closer to the river, continue to the next section take-out.

Eno River State Park gates are open November–February, 8 A.M.– 6 P.M.; March and October, 8 A.M.–7 P.M.; April and September, 8 A.M.– 8 P.M.; May–August, 8 A.M.–9 P.M. The park is closed Christmas Day.

Downed trees are more common in this section than in following ones because it is more narrow and less traveled.

There are a few Class I rapids before reaching the Lawrence Road (Orange Co. 1561) bridge (mi 1.0). Putting in here is possible, but the land is posted on three sides of the bridge. The homeowners on downstream left have allowed paddlers to cross their land when asked.

Rapids (mi 1.5) become more frequent, and there are more than a dozen Class I–II rapids before the take-out.

At a power line crossing (mi 4.3), sloping rocks on the left make a convenient lunch stop. A Class II rapid is downstream, followed by a rapid with a car-size boulder on the right and a ledge dropping 2 feet. Another rapid drops 3–4 feet over a 50-foot run through a rock garden.

Handrails and steps, part of a park trail, go over a 10-foot rock wall (mi 5.3) on the left. Near the left bank is an abrupt 4-foot drop, the steepest drop of the river. Scout from the left bank. A more gradual series of rapids is on the right half of the river.

> ## 2 Eno River State Park Few's Ford access to Eno River State Park Pleasant Green access
>
> | | |
> |---|---|
> | **Difficulty** A–I | **Width** 70–80 ft |
> | **Distance** 2.8 mi | **Gradient** 3.6 ft/mi |
> | **Scenery** B | **Map** page 245 |

Gauge See Section 1.

Notes See the previous section about Few's Ford access and park hours.

Eno River State Park Pleasant Green access is off Pleasant Green Road (Orange Co. 1567). It opens at 8:30 A.M. and closes 30 minutes earlier than the park.

After a few Class I rapids in the first mile, the backwater begins from the old Duke Power dam, upstream of Pleasant Green Road.

Many sets of power lines from Duke Power's distribution network cross this section.

Take out on the right, upstream of the 6-foot dam. Do not get too close to the dam. At high water, it forms a dangerous hydraulic.

Most of the Eno River has enough water to paddle only after rain, but it is always possible to put in at Pleasant Green access, make a 2-mile trip upstream in the dam's backwater, then return.

> ## 3 Eno River State Park Pleasant Green access to Eno River State Park Cole Mill access
>
> | | |
> |---|---|
> | **Difficulty** I–II | **Width** 40–100 ft |
> | **Distance** 3.6 mi | **Gradient** 13.1 ft/mi |
> | **Scenery** A | **Map** page 245 |

Gauge USGS *Eno River near Durham*. Minimum is 120 cfs (2.2 ft). There are also paddling gauges at Pleasant Green Road and Cole Mill Road bridges, where minimum is 0.5 feet.

Notes See the previous section about the Pleasant Green access. See Section 1 for park hours.

Cole Mill access opens at 9 A.M. and closes 30 minutes earlier than the park. Heading north on Cole Mill Road (Durham Co. 1401), cross the river and take the first left on Old Cole Mill Road. The access is at the road's end.

Rocky banks, covered with mountain laurel and rhododendron, rise over 100 feet in many parts of this section.

A pile of dark boulders (mi 1.5) on the right bank is near an old quarry.

The first Class II rapid (mi 1.7) has a 5-foot high boulder splitting the river.

A Class II (mi 2.5) is at the entrance to Bobbitt Hole, a wide cove where the river takes a sharp bend to the right. At low water, it is usually run through a slot angling to the left and dropping 2 feet into the pool below.

The take-out at Cole Mill access has wooden steps on the left bank.

4	Eno River State Park Cole Mill access to West Point on the Eno Park at Roxboro Road (US 501)		
Difficulty I–II		**Width** 40–150 ft	
Distance 4.9 mi		**Gradient** 13.7 ft/mi	
Scenery A		**Map** page 245	

Gauge See Section 3.

Notes See the previous section about the Cole Mill access.

West Point on the Eno Park, operated by the city of Durham, is open daily from 8 A.M. until dusk. Traveling north on Roxboro Road, Seven Oaks Road is to the right, across from the park. Turn left into the park entrance. The park has a reconstructed water-powered gristmill, 388 acres, and hiking trails. Park in the designated spaces, but boats can be loaded at the park road near the take-out.

Cole Mill Road (Durham Co. 1401) bridge (mi 0.2) is just beyond the put-in.

Remains of a dam from Old Pump Station (mi 1.3) are on the right bank at the beginning of a Class II rapid formed by a sloping ledge. At the pool below the rapid, the river makes a sharp left turn.

A Class II rapid (mi 1.9) drops about 3 feet over a 50-foot run and creates large waves as water rises.

A wide pool is formed where part of the Guess-Geer Milldam (mi 3.2) extends into the river from the left. The right side is broken out, and the channel bears to the right over a Class II rapid at low water. It becomes a powerful cauldron at high water and was the site of a helicopter rescue for unskilled paddlers attempting the river at very high water.

Access at Guess Road (Durham Co. 1003) (mi 3.4) is difficult because the banks are steep, and parking is restricted. A Class II rapid begins under the bridge, and rapids continue in the next quarter-mile.

Boulders (mi 4.4) across the river mark the last Class II rapid in this section and the entrance to Sennett Hole. The best route at low flows is near the left bank, to the left of a rocky island. The drop is several feet through a narrow channel with rocks at the bottom to avoid.

At Sennett Hole, the river widens to 150 feet. A mill was here in the 1700s, and legend says it fell into the river and disappeared into a bottomless hole. The mill owner is said to have buried a hoard of gold here. It is now a popular swimming hole.

The backwater of the dam at West Point on the Eno Park is entered below Sennett Hole. Stay back from the dam because water flows over it. From the take-out on the right, a path leads a few hundred feet to the park road.

5 West Point on the Eno Park at Roxboro Road (US 501) to Penny's Bend Nature Preserve access		
Difficulty I	**Width** 40–65 ft	
Distance 4.6 mi	**Gradient** 4.1 ft/mi	
Scenery A (55%), C (45%)	**Map** page 246	

Gauge See Section 3.

Notes See the previous section about West Point on the Eno Park. A trail downstream of the mill leads to a put-in.

Penny's Bend Nature Preserve access is at the intersection of Snow Hill Road (Durham Co. 1631) and Old Oxford Road (Durham Co. 1004).

Many small Class I rapids are in this section at low water. They wash out as water rises.

The banks are 10–40 feet high, and even though there are houses and development near the banks, it does not give the feeling of paddling through a city. Many hardwood trees line the banks.

A steel cable (mi 1.6), crossing the river and hanging 4 feet above the river bottom, is a hazard when the river is a few feet above minimum paddling level.

At a right turn (mi 3.2), the river enters the 84-acre Penny's Bend Nature Preserve and runs for over a mile through a large loop, ending at a small rapid and site of an old mill. The parking lot for the take-out is on the left.

6	Penny's Bend Nature Preserve access to Akzo Avenue (Durham Co. 2602) access		
Difficulty A, and one I		**Width** 40–150 ft	
Distance 4.7 mi		**Gradient** 0.4 ft/mi	
Scenery A		**Map** page 246	

Gauge See Section 3.

When the river is too low, paddling is always possible in the backwater of Falls Lake by putting in at the Akzo Avenue access and paddling a round-trip.

Notes See the previous section about Penny's Bend Nature Preserve access.

A Wildlife boating access is at the end of Akzo Avenue. Traveling north on Old Oxford Road (Durham Co. 1004), bear right on Teknika Parkway (Durham Co. 1794), and turn right on Akzo Avenue.

It is possible to put in above or below the small rapid formed by the old mill. The only rapid downstream is under Old Oxford Road, only a few hundred feet from the put-in.

A rocky bank (mi 0.7) on the right rises over 50 feet, and another high bank is across from the confluence with the Little River (mi 1.3).

The backwater of Falls Lake usually comes up to near the Little River when the lake is at pool elevation of about 250 feet.

An oxbow (mi 3.7) on the right makes a loop of 0.6 miles off the main channel.

After the Red Mill Road (Durham Co. 1632) bridge (mi 3.9), the take-out ramp is a few bends downstream on the left.

The Flat River joins from the left, 0.8 miles downstream of the take-out, forming the beginning of the Neuse River. From here it is a 24-mile paddle across Falls Lake to the dam, northeast of Raleigh.

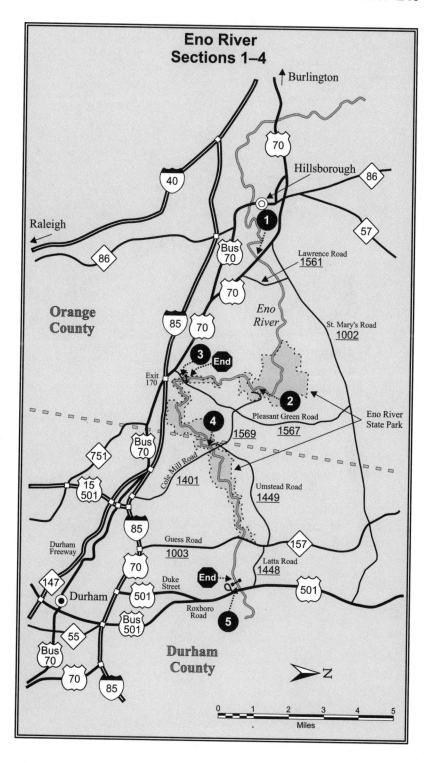

Eno River
Sections 1–4

↑Burlington

70

Hillsborough

86

40

57

Raleigh

1

Bus
70

Lawrence Road
1561

70

**Orange
County**

85   70

*Eno
River*

St. Mary's Road
1002

3   End

Exit
170

2

Pleasant Green Road
1567

Eno River
State Park

4

1569

Cole Mill Road

1401

Umstead Road
1449

Bus
70

751

15
501

85

Guess Road
1003

157

Latta Road
1448

Durham
Freeway

70

501

Duke
Street

End

501

147   ⊙Durham

Roxboro
Road

5

Bus
501

**Durham
County**

N

55

Bus
70

70   85

0   1   2   3   4   5
Miles

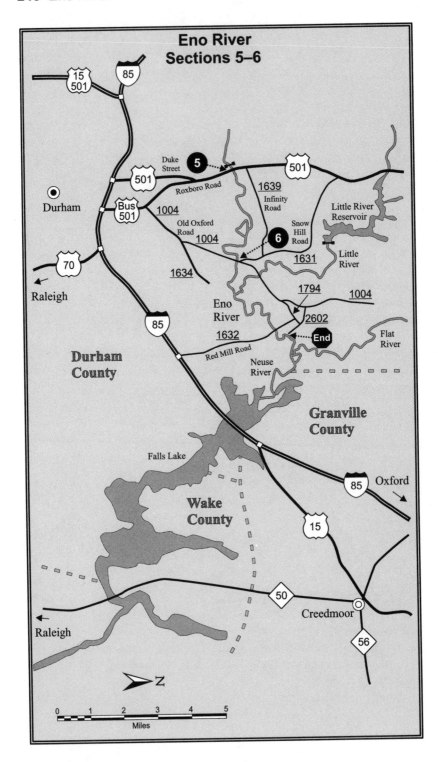

Eno River
Sections 5–6

Neuse Basin

Flat River

Counties   Person, Durham

Topos   Timberlake, Rougemont, Lake Michie

The North Fork of the Flat River gathers water from south of Roxboro. The South Fork drains southeastern Person County. The two forks join just east of US 501, near the Person and Durham County border.

The Flat must not have been named by someone looking at the sections described here. The gradient is typical of rivers with Class I–II whitewater, and a couple of old dams provide Class III.

Before reaching Lake Michie, the Flat flows through a scenic gorge, part of Hill Forest.

Downstream of Lake Michie, the Flat does become flat. It is joined by the Eno River, forming the beginning of the Neuse River, in the backwater of Falls Dam.

---

1   US 501 bridge at the South Fork of the Flat River to Moore's Mill Road (Durham Co. 1601) roadside

Difficulty	II, and one III	**Width**	40–60 ft
Distance	4.0 mi	**Gradient**	13.5 ft/mi
Scenery	B	**Map**	page 250

Gauge USGS *Flat River at Bahama*. Minimum is 230 cfs (2.2 ft).

Notes At the US 501 bridge, upstream left, it is possible to drive behind the guardrail and park near the bank. The put-in is on the South Fork of the Flat. The North Fork crosses US 501 4.4 miles to the north.

The take-out is where Moore's Mill Road (Durham Co. 1601) comes close to the river. There are no-parking signs until the road crosses into Durham County.

A Class II ledge (mi 1.1) is before the confluence with the North Fork (mi 1.4). Downed trees are usually less of a problem downstream.

Harris Mill (mi 2.3) still stands on the right bank, and Harris Mill Road (Person Co. 1739) ends close to it. This was a popular put-in but requires crossing private property, and permission has been refused in recent years.

After several Class I⁺ rapids and flatwater, an old dam (mi 3.3) creates the most formidable rapid of the Flat. The dam is broken on the left side, making an abrupt 4-foot drop. It should be scouted. Rocks in the outflow present an additional hazard. The easiest portage is on the left, but a house is here. Request permission to cross the owner's land. The right side can also be portaged but is more difficult.

A few hundred yards below the dam is a 2-foot ledge, and just downstream under Moore's Mill Road bridge (mi 3.6) is another small ledge followed by a boulder splitting the flow, requiring a quick decision in choosing a route.

Several more Class I–II rapids are downstream before the take-out on the right where the road is close. It is possible to paddle another mile to the Bowen Road (Durham Co. 1602) bridge to take out, but there is no room to park near the bridge.

2	Moore's Mill Road (Durham Co. 1601) roadside to State Forest Road (Durham Co. 1614) bridge	
Difficulty I–II	**Width** 50–80 ft	
Distance 4.2 mi	**Gradient** 8.6 ft/mi	
Scenery A (50%), B (50%)	**Map** page 250	

Gauge USGS *Flat River at Bahama*. Minimum is 100 cfs (1.8 ft).

Notes See the previous section about Moore's Mill Road.

There are a few Class I–II rapids before reaching the Bowen Road (Durham Co. 1602) bridge (mi 1.0).

Deep Creek (mi 1.7) joins from the left, where water drops over a steep ledge before entering the Flat.

Remnants of an old dam (mi 2.1) create a Class II rapid just before Red Mountain Road (Durham Co. 1471) bridge (mi 2.2). The road can be used for access, but guardrails prevent parking near the river.

Hill Forest, an educational forest managed by North Carolina State University, begins on the left bank (mi 2.9) and takes in both banks (mi 3.5) for the remainder of the section.

There are a few Class I rapids before the low-water bridge at the take-out. At minimum flow, the bridge has only 4–5 feet of clearance. At higher flows, be prepared to take out before reaching the bridge.

③	State Forest Road (Durham Co. 1614) bridge to Wilkins Road (Durham Co. 1613) access at Lake Michie		
Difficulty II, and one III		**Width** 50–400 ft	
Distance 3.4 mi		**Gradient** 11.5 ft/mi	
Scenery A		**Map** page 250	

Gauge USGS *Flat River at Bahama*. Minimum is 190 cfs (2.1 ft).

Notes The take-out is at a Lake Michie picnic area, upstream left of Wilkins Road bridge. The area closes at sunset. Lake rules require boaters using the lake to pay a fee and launch at the ramp near the boathouse. Over the years, a few paddlers have been told they cannot use the picnic area as a take-out, but no tickets have been issued. Signs here say "Canoe, sailboat, and boat launch at boathouse only." If use of the picnic area as a take-out is restricted, paddlers will need to seek a rule change or clarification.

Hill Forest, an educational forest managed by North Carolina State University, borders the river on both sides down to mile 0.7, then runs down the right bank, ending at the USGS gauging station.

The view in this section is of rugged tree-covered banks rising over 200 feet above the river gorge.

Rapids are Class I$^+$ until a left turn (mi 1.3) where the right bank is steep near the river. A Class II$^+$ is formed where ledges jut from the right. These ledges sometimes have trees washed down in high water. Staying to the left in the turn is the safest run.

At a right turn (mi 1.6) where the left bank is rocky and steep, Class I–II rapids extend downstream to a round, flat rock-island (mi 1.9) which makes an easy lunch stop. It is about 25 feet in diameter and 2 feet above water at minimum flow.

Just below the lunch stop, the river splits to the right around an island. The left route cannot be paddled at low flows. The right channel is constricted and can contain downed trees.

A USGS gauge (mi 2.3) built of native stone on the right bank marks the remains of an old dam and a Class III rapid, depending on water level. At low flows, there is only sufficient water in the right side of the rapid.

After a few more Class I–II rapids, the lake (mi 2.7) begins.

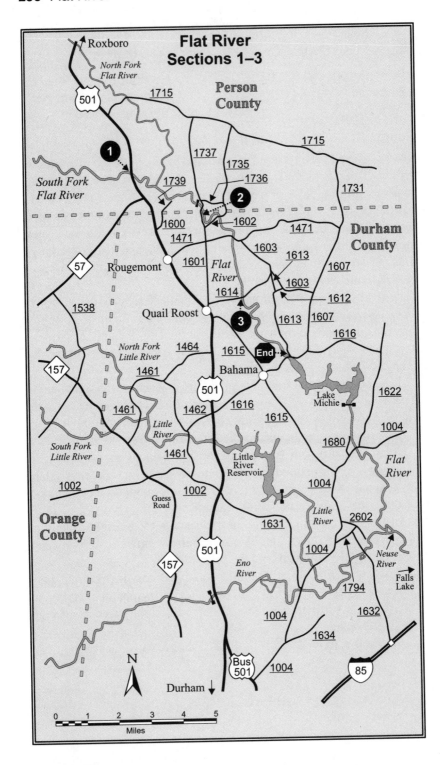

Flat River
Sections 1–3

Neuse Basin

Little River (near Durham)

County   Durham

Topo   Rougemont

Little River is one of the most common river names, and two are in the Neuse Basin. The largest Little River (page 255) in the upper Neuse Basin joins the Neuse near Goldsboro.

The Little River described here begins as the North Fork and South Fork in northern Orange County. The forks flow southeast and join after crossing into Durham County. The Little River Reservoir, a Durham water supply, begins near US 501 at Bahama. Downstream of the reservoir, the Little River joins the Eno River.

Upstream of the reservoir, the river runs through a gorge reminiscent of a western North Carolina mountain stream. Steep, rocky bluffs on north-facing slopes display rhododendron and mountain laurel. The riverbed has a high gradient for a Piedmont river, with rocks and ledges forming many rapids.

The beauty and environmental significance of the area has been recognized in the *Little River Corridor Open Space Plan*, published in 2001 by the Durham City-County Planning Department. Unlike the Eno and Flat Rivers, permanently protected natural areas along the Little River are scarce. The plans include future parks, nature trails, and canoe access areas.

A 390-acre tract on the Orange and Durham County border is being made into the Little River Regional Park and Natural Area. It will border the south bank of the North Fork for 1.2 miles and end about a half-mile upstream of the Section 1 put-in.

In 1975 the Little River made the news because of an important discovery. Jim Wright, a graduate student at North Carolina State University, and his thesis advisor were doing research on rocks of the Carolina Slate Belt. At a lunch stop on a rocky ledge over the river, Jim noticed odd imprints and scraped away moss to reveal fossils. The imprints were deemed to be the tracks of large worms moving along the shore 620 million years ago when this area was a volcanic island.

The discovery was reported in *American Scientist* and celebrated as the earliest animal fossils found in North America. A large slab was quarried and is now housed at the Smithsonian Institute. A smaller specimen is on display at the North Carolina Museum of Natural Sciences in Raleigh.

The famous fossils were challenged in a paper published in *Geology*. Researchers asserted that the patterns found are not fossils at all, but were formed by particles rolled between rock beds over time.

The scientific debate may continue, but a trip down the Little River is made more interesting when considering that one is paddling by rocks formed 620 million years ago where a volcanic island stood.

When the Little River Reservoir was constructed in 1987, private boats were not permitted because of fears they could bring in hydrilla, an aquatic weed. Since the reservoir extended just above US 501, flooding some of the lower rapids of the Little River gorge, paddlers could not legally reach a take-out.

The Carolina Canoe Club took the issue up with the Durham City Council on behalf of recreational paddlers and won a change to the city code. Now paddlers coming down the river are allowed to paddle into the reservoir waters and go directly to the US 501 bridge to take out, provided they obtain a permit. A permit costs $5 per year and can be obtained at the Little River Reservoir or Lake Michie boathouses. The boathouses are closed in the winter. For information, call Durham Parks and Recreation at 919-560-4355.

---

1 South Lowell Road (Durham Co. 1461) bridge over North Fork to Johnson Mill Road (Durham Co. 1461) bridge

Difficulty I–II	**Width**	20–60 ft
Distance 4.1 mi	**Gradient**	20.0 ft/mi
Scenery A (50%), B (50%)	**Map**	page 254

Gauge USGS *Little River at SR 1461 near Orange Factory*. Minimum is 120 cfs (2.3 ft).

Notes At Johnson Mill Road, parking is not permitted near the bridge. Park beyond the no-parking signs.

The first mile has a gradient of over 40 feet/mile, but there are no big drops. It is fairly constant Class I–II rapids and fast water over rock gardens. The channel is often less than 30 feet wide, and downed trees are common.

Many homes are seen from the river above the rhododendron and mountain laurel covered banks.

The gradient lessens, the South Fork (mi 1.7) enters from the right, and the river becomes generally 50–60 feet wide.

Class I–II rapids (mi 3.0) increase in frequency, and there are a few small ledges in the approach to the take-out bridge.

2	Johnson Mill Road (Durham Co. 1461) bridge to US 501 bridge at Little River Reservoir

Difficulty III	**Width** 35–500 ft
Distance 0.9 mi	**Gradient** 25.6 ft/mi
Scenery A	**Map** page 254

Gauge USGS *Little River at SR 1461 near Orange Factory*. Minimum is 120 cfs (2.3 ft). The Class III rating is for low levels. The difficulty greatly increases as water rises. At 400 cfs (3.4 ft), the flow is fast and decisions must be made quickly. Above 1,000 cfs (4.6 ft), the run becomes Class IV and higher with extremely powerful holes.

Notes See the previous section about Johnson Mill Road.

A permit is required to enter the reservoir and take out at US 501 (see page 252). Parking at the take-out is upstream right on the old roadbed. Do not block the homeowner's driveway and keep vehicles on the hard surface to avoid rutting the grass.

When the reservoir is full, its backwater begins only 0.5 miles from the put-in. The river gradient to this point is 45 feet/mile. This is where the river gorge is most mountain-like. Large boulders are in and along the river, and steep banks rise up to 150 feet.

Class II rapids lead from the put-in to a Class III ledge a few hundred feet downstream. Scout it from the rocky left bank.

Several Class II and two more Class III rapids are met in the short run down to the beginning of the reservoir (mi 0.5).

Paddle across the tip of the reservoir to the take-out, upstream right of the US 501 bridge.

■

A man is rich in proportion to the number of things which he can afford to let alone.

—Henry David Thoreau, *Walden* (1845)

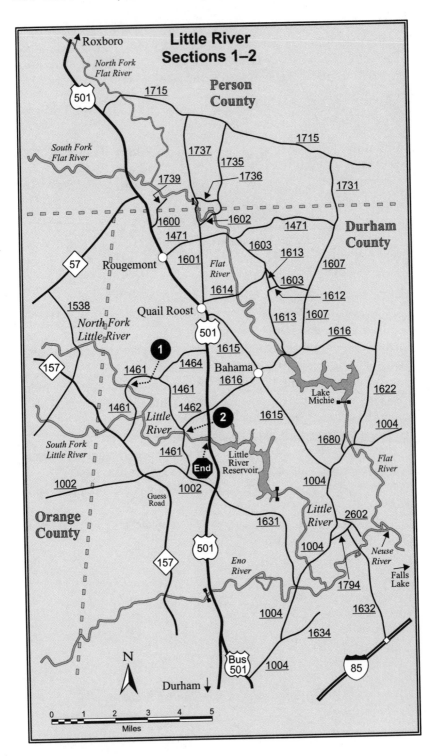

Neuse Basin

Little River (near Goldsboro)

Counties   Johnston, Wayne

Topos   Flowers, Stancils Chapel, Kenly West, Princeton,
Northwest Goldsboro, Southwest Goldsboro

Little River is one of the most common river names, and two are in
the Neuse Basin. A Little River in the upper Neuse Basin joins the
Eno River near Durham (page 251).

The Little River described here has a long run, but the watershed
is fairly narrow. It begins in Franklin County near Youngsville, northeast of Wake Forest, and flows south to southeast into Wake County,
passing between Wendell and Zebulon. The Little River flows under
I-95 to the east of Smithfield and Selma, and it joins the Neuse River
on the west side of Goldsboro.

The Little River is one of the Neuse River's largest and cleanest
tributaries. It flows through rural land with no towns on its banks. The
Triangle Land Conservancy completed a two-year inventory and
declared the river Nationally Significant. It contains two federally
endangered species of mussels.

Wake County has plans to build a water supply reservoir on the
river near Zebulon by 2005.

Two dams were removed from the Little River in 1998, opening
about 50 miles of the river to spawning opportunities for fish that
migrate up inland waters before returning to the ocean. Fish can now
migrate from the ocean, up the Neuse River, and up the Little River to
Atkinson's Mill at the beginning of Section 1.

---

1 Atkinson's Mill at NC 42 to Shoeheel Road (Johnston Co.
2127) bridge

Difficulty A	**Width** 30–60 ft
Distance 6.2 mi	**Gradient** 2.1 ft/mi
Scenery A (30%), B (70%)	**Map** page 261

Gauge USGS *Little River near Princeton*. Estimated minimum is
100 cfs (1.6 ft). The gauge is 23 miles downstream from the put-in.

Notes Atkinson's Mill is a few hundred yards upstream of the NC 42 bridge. The put-in at the bridge is difficult, but the mill owner has allowed paddlers to put in between the mill buildings and the bridge. Ask permission at the office and do not block the driveways.

The original Atkinson's Mill was built in 1757, when North Carolina was a colony. The mill was rebuilt after being destroyed by fire in 1950, and its millstones are still producing cornmeal and other products for sale in many counties. The mill can be toured during the week.

There are several houses and cabins on the banks, and farmland is often near the river. The banks are mostly 3–25 feet high.

Downstream of NC 39 (mi 0.4), there are many holly trees, and they are especially noticeable in the winter.

Old Dam Road (Johnston Co. 2123) (mi 2.8) runs near the right bank until reaching the bridge (mi 3.1). Downstream left of the bridge can be used as an access point.

A 50-foot bank (mi 5.6) is on the right near the take-out.

2	Shoeheel Road (Johnston Co. 2127) bridge to Weaver Road (Johnston Co. 2144) access near Bagley		
Difficulty A		**Width** 35–70 ft	
Distance 7.7 mi		**Gradient** 2.3 ft/mi	
Scenery A (75%), B (25%)		**Map** page 261	

Gauge See Section 1. The gauge is 17 miles downstream from the put-in.

Notes A Wildlife boating access is a quarter-mile downstream of the Weaver Road bridge. From US 301 take Weaver Road north. After crossing the bridge, a gravel drive leading to the ramp is 0.1 miles ahead on the right.

This section is similar to the previous section, but there are fewer houses and cabins. Farmland borders some of the river, and banks range from 2–25 feet high.

In the latter part of this section, the backwaters of the dam in the next section are entered.

There are three bridges that can be used as alternative access points: Micro Road (Johnston Co. 2130) (mi 2.2), Woodruff Road (Johnston Co. 2129) (mi 3.3), and Beulah Road (Johnston Co. 1934) (mi 4.4).

Weaver Road (Johnston Co. 2144) access near Bagley to Rains Crossroads (Johnston Co. 2320) bridge

Difficulty A

Distance 8.8 mi

Scenery A (55%), B (45%)

Width 45–100 ft

Gradient 2.4 ft/mi

Map page 261

Gauge See Section 1.

Notes See the previous section about the Weaver Road access.

At Rains Crossroads bridge, the vacant land extending downstream left is private, and the landowner lives in the nearby house. Take out near the bridge.

At the put-in, water is deep from the backwaters of the dam in this section.

Downstream of the put-in, the right bank rises up to 40 feet and is covered in mountain laurel. Several other high banks with mountain laurel are along this section.

Little Buffalo Creek (mi 0.5) enters from the left in a swampy area where the river makes a right turn near US 301 (mi 0.7).

After passing I-95 (mi 1.7), Lowell Milldam (mi 2.0) should be approached with caution. It is 6–8 feet high, and water flows over it. A short portage path is on the left, but reaching the left side can require paddling close to the dam, depending on water level. The right side can be portaged but requires going up a hill to a small drive where there is a "No Trespassing" sign near the bank. Lowell Mill Road (Johnston Co. 2335) makes a loop by a house on the right bank, just upstream of the dam. Permission may be required to take out here.

Bagley Road (Johnston Co. 2339) (mi 3.2) or Hinnant-Egerton Road (Johnston Co. 1001) (mi 5.4) can be used to shorten this section.

4 Rains Crossroads (Johnston Co. 2320) bridge to Capps Bridge Road (Wayne Co. 1234) bridge

Difficulty A–I, and one II

Distance 10.3 mi

Scenery A (50%), B (50%)

Width 50–150 ft

Gradient 1.8 ft/mi

Map page 262

Gauge USGS *Little River near Princeton*. Estimated minimum is 150 cfs (1.9 ft).

Notes See the previous section about Rains Crossroads.

As in the previous section, some banks are covered with mountain laurel.

The USGS gauge (mi 0.1) is on the left bank.

An island (mi 0.9) splits the river. Both channels tend to catch floating trees and may require portage.

A private bridge (mi 1.1) seems to be used for access to farmland on the left.

A quarry (mi 3.4) is near the right bank, and the left bank has some of the highest land on the river, rising as much as 75 feet.

Rock gardens form a few sets of Class I rapids (mi 3.8) extending downstream a few hundred yards.

In view of the bridge downstream, large boulders and rocks (mi 4.4) span the river, creating a Class II ledge rapid. At the estimated minimum, water may be too low to run the rapid.

Just downstream of Rains Mill Road (Johnston Co. 1002) bridge (mi 4.6) was the site of Rains Milldam, removed in 1998. At low water, rocks from the dam create a Class I rapid that can only be run on the right side. The public has been using private drives on downstream left and right of the Rains Mill Road bridge for fishing and boat access.

At 600 cfs (4.0 ft), water flows straight ahead and also down a channel (mi 7.5) to the right. The right channel cuts off a loop and is 0.9 miles shorter.

5	Capps Bridge Road (Wayne Co. 1234) bridge to NC 581 bridge (north of US 70)	
Difficulty A	**Width** 35–85 ft	
Distance 6.3 mi	**Gradient** 1.6 ft/mi	
Scenery A	**Map** page 262	

Gauge USGS *Little River near Princeton.* Minimum is 130 cfs (1.8 ft). At lower flows, submerged logs become exposed.

Notes Many trees overhang the river and provide shade. Only a few houses are seen.

The banks generally range from 2–10 feet high but rise 30 feet on the right (mi 3.0).

The channel has many bends, but a straight stretch (mi 5.2) allows a view of about 0.3 miles downstream.

6	NC 581 bridge (north of US 70) to Clairidge Nursery Road (Wayne Co. 1326) at US 70 bridge near Goldsboro

Difficulty A, and one II	**Width** 40–60 ft
Distance 8.2 mi	**Gradient** 2.2 ft/mi
Scenery A (25%), B (75%)	**Map** page 262

Gauge USGS *Little River near Princeton* and *Neuse River near Goldsboro.* Always above minimum.

Notes From Clairidge Nursery Road, a drive leads into a vacant lot adjacent to the river, upstream right of the US 70 bridge.

Clairidge Nursery Road (mi 3.9) is close to the right bank, where there are a few homes and businesses.

A golf course (mi 4.8) is on the left, and signs of it are seen over the next half-mile.

The banks are generally 2–15 feet high near the river. A 50-foot bank (mi 5.6) on the left is covered with mountain laurel.

At a left turn (mi 6.7), an old quarter-mile loop runs to the right around an island.

The two-story vacant building (mi 7.1) on the left is an old water pump station. A broken dam is a few hundred feet downstream. It can be scouted or portaged easily on the right side. The drop is about 3 feet over a run of 25 feet. Rocks to avoid make it a Class II rapid at low levels.

7	Clairidge Nursery Road (Wayne Co. 1326) at US 70 bridge to US 117 access on Neuse River at Goldsboro

Difficulty A	**Width** 30–130 ft
Distance 6.3 mi	**Gradient** 1.9 ft/mi
Scenery A (70%), B (30%)	**Map** page 262

Gauge See Section 6. A few downed trees are common on the Little River portion of this section. For the Neuse River, use USGS *Neuse River near Goldsboro.*

Notes See the previous section about Clairidge Nursery Road.

See Neuse River, Section 11 (page 269) about the US 117 access.

The Little River is 30–65 feet wide with many cypress and river birch trees. The banks range from a few feet to 20 feet high.

At an old pump station, a dam (mi 1.4) was removed in 1998 to open the river for fish migration.

Cherry Hospital, a psychiatric hospital serving many eastern counties, is downstream right of the NC 581 (mi 1.5) bridge.

A pipe (mi 1.6) on concrete supports spans the river only about 4 feet above the riverbed. At other than low water levels, it can be a hazard.

The Little River joins the Neuse River (mi 3.3) close to the middle of a 7-mile loop in the Neuse.

A cove (mi 4.3) on the left contains a floating dock, part of Waynesborough State Park. Access is possible from the parking lot, but requires a carry of a few hundred yards. The park is open 9 A.M.– 5 P.M., closed holidays.

Surfing below Falls Dam
Neuse River, Section 1

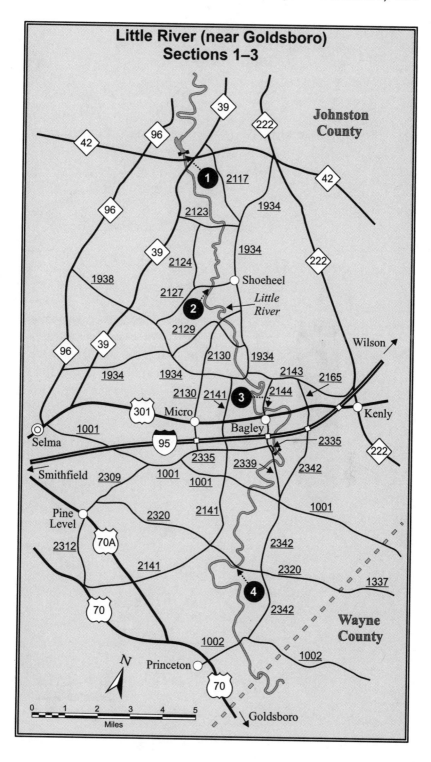

Little River (near Goldsboro)
Sections 1–3

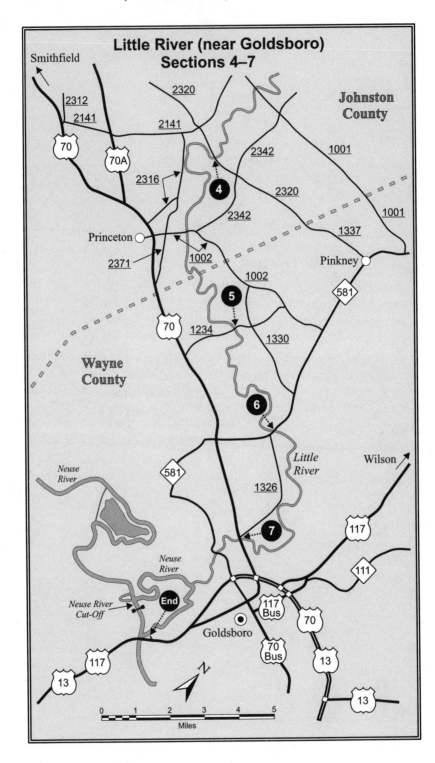

Neuse Basin

Neuse River

Counties	Wake, Johnston, Wayne, Lenoir, Pitt, Craven
Topos	Wake Forest, Raleigh East, Garner, Clayton, Flowers, Selma, Powhatan, Four Oaks, Four Oaks NE, Princeton, Grantham, Southwest Goldsboro, Northwest Goldsboro, Southeast Goldsboro, Williams, Seven Springs, Deep Run, Falling Creek, Kinston, Rivermont, Grifton, Fort Barnwell, Vanceboro, Jasper, Askin

The Neuse begins north of Durham at the confluence of the Eno and Flat Rivers. This is close to the beginning of Falls Lake. It is 24 miles to Falls Dam, northeast of Raleigh. Below the dam, the Neuse passes Raleigh, Smithfield, Goldsboro, and Kinston. It becomes a shallow, slow-moving, brackish estuary just upstream from New Bern. Where it empties into the Pamlico Sound, the Neuse has the widest river mouth in the continental United States.

The Neuse River empties into Pamlico Sound below New Bern. It is one of three large rivers that flow into the Albemarle and Pamlico Sounds. The estuarine system is the second largest in the United States.

The Neuse has received much publicity and national attention in the 1990s for its troubled waters. American Rivers, a nationally renowned environmental group, rated the Neuse as one of the twenty most threatened rivers in North America in 1995–1997. Fish kills caused by *Pfiesteria piscicida* were the subject of *And The Waters Turned To Blood*, a 1997 book by Rodney Barker. It is the story of an ancient organism, stimulated by phosphate and nitrate enrichment, causing massive fish kills in coastal waters. It is also the story of some people in the state government's environmental and health departments working against the public trust and scientific research.

The Neuse River Foundation, Rick Dove, Dr. JoAnn Burkholder, and the public outcry helped bring changes. The Neuse was the first river in the southeastern United States to have a Riverkeeper® to act as a caretaker and spokesman.

A paddling journey from Falls Dam to New Bern covers 193 miles.

1	Falls Dam Tailrace access to Falls of Neuse Road (Wake Co. 2000) access		
Difficulty II⁺		**Width** 60–80 ft	
Distance 0.4 mi		**Gradient** 20 ft/mi	
Scenery B		**Map** page 277	

Gauge USGS *Neuse River near Falls.* Estimated minimum is 250 cfs (1.6 ft). For surfing in the waves below the dam, most paddlers like 1,000–3,400 cfs (2.5–3.8 ft). Water is controlled by dam releases, and the dam usually releases sufficient water for this section only when the lake level rises above 251 feet.

Notes Upstream right of the Falls of Neuse Road bridge, a "Falls Tailrace Fishing Area" sign marks the entrance drive for the put-in. Carry down the bank from the parking lot. This area is managed by the Corps of Engineers.

The take-out, provided by Raleigh Parks and Recreation, is downstream right of the bridge where a "Falls of Neuse Canoe Launch" sign marks a road leading 0.2 miles to the parking area.

This short section provides rapids as the river flows through rock gardens and islands under and downstream of the bridge.

The big attraction is for practicing surfing skills in the waves below the dam. Many paddlers surfing here put in and take out at the Tailrace access area rather than paddle downstream.

2	Falls of Neuse Road (Wake Co. 2000) access to Buffaloe Road (Wake Co. 2215) access		
Difficulty A		**Width** 40–80 ft	
Distance 10.5 mi		**Gradient** 1.9 ft/mi	
Scenery A (80%), B (20%)		**Map** page 277	

Gauge USGS *Neuse River near Falls.* Minimum is 110 cfs (1.2 ft). Water is controlled by Falls Dam. Flow is usually above minimum but can drop below in times of drought.

Notes See the previous section about the Falls of Neuse Road access.

The Buffaloe Road access is downstream right of the Buffaloe Road bridge and is reached by turning on Elizabeth Road. The access is managed by Raleigh Parks and Recreation.

Paddling this section at low water requires searching for the deepest channels around sandbars. Many trees overhang the river channel, and there are sometimes a few downed trees to carry over. At high water, downed trees are a hazard. Considering that this section flows through Raleigh, there is not much development obvious from the river.

Access at the US 1 bridge (mi 3.2) is possible on the upstream left. It is private and managed by Pro Canoe & Kayak, an outfitter with a store on Falls of Neuse Road near the put-in. They also rent boats and run shuttles. To use the access, get permission from the outfitter (919-866-1954) and park outside of the gate.

The US 401 bridge (mi 7.4) was used for access, but a road-widening project made access difficult.

Before reaching the take-out, the water deepens from backwater of Milburnie Dam in the next section.

3 Buffaloe Road (Wake Co. 2215) access to Old Milburnie Road (Wake Co. 2217) access

Difficulty A	**Width** 50–120 ft
Distance 4.1 mi	**Gradient** 2.4 ft/mi
Scenery B (50%), C (50%)	**Map** page 277

Gauge USGS *Neuse River near Falls.* Always above minimum. This section is in the backwater of Milburnie Dam except for the last 100 yards downstream of the dam.

Notes See the previous section about the Buffaloe Road access.

To reach the Old Milburnie Road access from west of the river, take US 64 east (New Bern Avenue). Cross the Neuse River and turn left at the first light at Old Milburnie Road. Go 0.1 miles to the sign "Neuse River East Canoe Launch." Turn left on a dirt road and continue 0.2 miles to the parking area. The access is managed by Raleigh Parks and Recreation.

There are many houses along this section. Large islands (mi 2.5) are just above where the Beaverdam Lake outflow enters on the left.

Stay back from Milburnie Dam (mi 4.0). It is used to generate electricity, and water flows over it. The portage trail, 100–200 yards, is from the right bank to a dirt road and around the right side of the dam.

Put in below the dam and paddle to the take-out on the left, about 100 yards below the dam.

The portage can be avoided by turning around above the dam and paddling back to the put-in, making it an 8-mile round-trip.

---

4 Old Milburnie Road (Wake Co. 2217) access to Poole Road (Wake Co. 1007) access

Difficulty	I, and one II	**Width**	60–175 ft
Distance	3.5 mi	**Gradient**	1.7 ft/mi
Scenery	A (55%), B (45%)	**Map**	page 277

Gauge See Section 2. Crabtree Creek sometimes adds significant flow near the end of this section. See USGS *Crabtree Creek at US 1* gauge to determine the additional flow.

Notes See the previous section about Old Milburnie Road access.

The Poole Road access is upstream right of the bridge and is managed by Raleigh Parks and Recreation.

A Class I rapid is where the channel splits around an island (mi 0.2), and another Class I is at US 64 (mi 0.5). After passing the US 64 bridge, there are fewer signs of development.

A greenway runs along the right bank and ends at the Anderson Point Park (mi 1.8) off Rogers Lane (Wake Co. 2517). The park is managed by Raleigh Parks and Recreation and includes a boat ramp, 50 feet upstream of a railroad bridge.

Crabtree Creek (mi 2.5) enters on the right. After heavy rain, its flow is often greater than the Neuse's flow above the confluence because the Neuse is regulated by Falls Dam.

A house is on the right, and boulders (mi 2.9) are in the river on the right side. At minimum water level, the only way through is left of a small island near the middle. At 400 cfs of combined flow from Falls Dam and Crabtree Creek, the route through the boulders becomes a Class II. At 1,000 cfs of combined flow, this rapid is only small waves. Be especially careful of downed trees and tree limbs here.

---

5 Poole Road (Wake Co. 1007) access to Mial Plantation Road (Wake Co. 2509) bridge

Difficulty	A–I	**Width**	40–100 ft
Distance	6.9 mi	**Gradient**	1.9 ft/mi
Scenery	A (70%), B (30%)	**Map**	page 278

Gauge USGS *Neuse River near Clayton*. Always above minimum.

Notes See the previous section about the Poole Road access.

The bridge at Mial Plantation Road is not an easy take-out. The banks have dense brush and poison ivy. Reaching an easy take-out requires paddling on to the next section.

There are several small ledge rapids before reaching the Auburn-Knightdale Road (Wake Co. 2555) bridge (mi 2.8).

Another small rapid and a boulder island are passed before reaching a private bridge (mi 6.6) near the take-out.

6	Mial Plantation Road (Wake Co. 2509) bridge to NC 42 bridge	
Difficulty A–I		**Width** 80–120 ft
Distance 7.2 mi		**Gradient** 1.5 ft/mi
Scenery A (85%), B (15%)		**Map** page 278

Gauge See Section 5.

Notes See the previous section about Mial Plantation Road.

Upstream left of the NC 42 bridge, a rough dirt road leads to the bank.

At low flows, boulders and small ledges create a few Class I rapids with little drop.

Covered Bridge Road (Johnston Co. 1700) (mi 4.3) could be used for access, but it is easier at NC 42.

At a small island, there is a 1-foot ledge (mi 6.2) which appears to be remains of an old dam.

7	NC 42 bridge to Smithfield Town Commons Park access off US 70 Business	
Difficulty A–I		**Width** 50–120 ft
Distance 14.2 mi		**Gradient** 1.8 ft/mi
Scenery A (70%), B (15%), C (15%)		**Map** page 278

Gauge See Section 5. USGS *Neuse River at Smithfield* can be used, but it does not provide flow data.

Notes See the previous section about NC 42.

To reach the Smithfield Town Commons Park, going east on US 70 Business, cross the Neuse River, take the first left (North Front Street), and go 0.2 miles to the boat ramp.

In the first 3 miles, there are islands and old broken dams creating small rapids. There are also many homes and a golf course. Farther downstream, it is flatwater with fewer houses.

Parking and access is not good at either the Fire Department Road (Johnston Co. 1908) (mi 5.5) or US 70 (mi 10.6) bridges. A prison occupies the downstream right bank at US 70.

Banks are up to 40 feet high and covered with vegetation.

8	Smithfield Town Commons Park access to Richardson Bridge Road (Johnston Co. 1201) access		
Difficulty A		**Width** 50–100 ft	
Distance 27.5 mi		**Gradient** 1.1 ft/mi	
Scenery A (80%), B (20%)		**Map** page 279	

Gauge See Section 5.

Notes See the previous section about Smithfield Town Commons Park.

At Richardson Bridge Road, an entrance drive to a Wildlife boating access is 0.2 miles north (river left) of the bridge. There are no signs marking the turn into the drive. The access area cannot be seen from the bridge.

This section is usually done as a camper because of its length. After passing US 301/NC 96 (mi 3.8) and I-95 (mi 4.1), there are no bridges or public roads to the river for the next 23 miles. As the crow flies, it is only 12 miles between bridges, but the river twists and turns through the lowlands where many oxbows have been created. This remote section is known locally as Let'Lones. The Triangle Land Conservancy is working to preserve 1,000 acres here for a possible new state park.

The banks range from a few feet to 20 feet. There are occasional houses and cabins, and there are many possible campsites. At flows below 500 cfs (2.0 ft), sandbars with willow oaks offer good sites, but be prepared to move if the water should rise from rain or a Falls Dam release. One camping night here, the owls were loud, but they were outdone by beavers slapping their tails on the water.

9	Richardson Bridge Road (Johnston Co. 1201) access to Ferry Bridge Road (Wayne Co. 1224) access		
Difficulty A		**Width** 45–100 ft	
Distance 7.1 mi		**Gradient** 1.4 ft/mi	
Scenery A		**Map** page 279	

Gauge See Section 5.

Notes See the previous section about the Richardson Bridge access.

A Wildlife boating access is at Ferry Bridge Road.

The river flows through cleared lowlands until reaching where Mill Creek (mi 4.4) enters on the right. Downstream, the right bank rises abruptly to 70 feet and has stands of tall beech and poplar trees.

There are two islands (mi 6.3) near the take-out where the road comes close to the river. The right bank has many cypress trees covered with Spanish moss.

10 Ferry Bridge Road (Wayne Co. 1224) access to Stevens Mill Road (Wayne Co. 1008) bridge

Difficulty A–I⁻		**Width** 80–150 ft	
Distance 9.1 mi		**Gradient** 0.7 ft/mi	
Scenery A (70%), B (10%), C (20%)		**Map** page 279	

Gauge USGS *Neuse River near Goldsboro.* Always above minimum.

Notes A Wildlife boating access is at Ferry Bridge Road.

In the first few miles, cypress trees with large trunks are near the water, and there are a couple of Class I⁻ rapids.

After passing power lines (mi 3.3), Progress Energy's Quaker Neck plant is just around the bend. A side channel to the right enters plant property. Continue straight ahead in the main channel, under a private bridge. Quaker Neck Lake is on the right, but all that can be seen are 30-foot banks reinforced with riprap.

The side channel previously mentioned reenters from the right (mi 8.4). Just below it was the site of the Quaker Neck Dam, removed in 1997. The dam was a mandatory portage, but now there are no signs of its existence. Its removal opened up over 75 miles of river and 925 miles of tributaries to spawning saltwater fish. For the first time in 45 years, striped bass, sturgeon, American shad, and other types of fish have been able to complete their life cycles in the upper Neuse River.

11 Stevens Mill Road (Wayne Co. 1008) bridge to US 117 access at Goldsboro

Difficulty A		**Width** 70–160 ft	
Distance 10.1 mi		**Gradient** 0.9 ft/mi	
Scenery A (80%), B (20%)		**Map** page 279	

Gauge See Section 10.

Notes A Wildlife boating access is off US 117, 0.3 miles upstream left of the bridge. The entrance is not well-marked. Traveling south on US 117, just before guardrails begin, turn right on a gravel drive (Wayne Co. 2108). The gravel drive leads to a private club, Whitetail Landing, and the building can be seen from the highway. The boating access is just upstream of the club.

There are three channels (mi 3.4): straight ahead, left, and right. Going straight ahead is the Neuse River Cut-Off, a dredged channel containing a flood-control dam. At low water levels, the dam must be portaged. At high water levels, it will have a dangerous hydraulic where water flows over the dam. Going right is a short loop of the old natural channel leading back upstream. Take the left channel to stay in the long loop of the natural channel.

The Little River (mi 7.1) joins from the left, and a cove (mi 8.0) on the left contains a floating dock, part of Waynesborough State Park. Access is possible from the parking lot but requires a portage of a few hundred yards. The park is open 9 A.M.–5 P.M., closed holidays.

12	US 117 access at Goldsboro to NC 581 access		
Difficulty A		**Width** 80–150 ft	
Distance 6.8 mi		**Gradient** 0.7 ft/mi	
Scenery A (35%), B (35%), C (30%)		**Map** page 280	

Gauge See Section 10.

Notes See the previous section about the US 117 access.

A Wildlife boating access is at the NC 581 bridge closest to NC 111. Another bridge on NC 581 crosses the river in the beginning of this section.

The Neuse River Cut-Off, mentioned in the previous section, joins just before going under the US 117 bridges (mi 0.3).

Downstream of the first NC 581 bridge (mi 2.5), Seymour Johnson Air Force base is on the left bank for several miles. In the river channel, a few concrete towers with lights (mi 3.6) mark runway patterns. When jets are taking off and landing, they pass just overhead with thunderous roars.

13 NC 581 access at Goldsboro to NC 111 bridge

Difficulty A		**Width** 100–200 ft	
Distance 6.5 mi		**Gradient** 0.6 ft/mi	
Scenery A (70%), B (30%)		**Map** page 280	

Gauge See Section 10.

Notes See the previous section about the NC 581 access.

At NC 111 use downstream left of the bridge. Do not block the driveway leading into "Outdoors with Tony Daw," a paddling outfitter (919-734-2291). They are open on weekends and rent boats and run shuttles. Use of their access inside the gate is $2 per boat. Primitive camping is also available.

There are a few straight wide channels giving a view almost a mile downstream. The banks range 10–20 feet high.

14 NC 111 bridge to Main Street (Wayne Co. 1731) access at Seven Springs

Difficulty A		**Width** 85–135 ft	
Distance 8.4 mi		**Gradient** 0.8 ft/mi	
Scenery A		**Map** page 280	

Gauge See Section 10.

Notes See the previous section about NC 111 and the private access.

A Wildlife boating access is at Seven Springs.

Past power lines (mi 5.4) is the boundary for Cliffs of the Neuse State Park (mi 5.5). Pine trees appear ahead on the right bank. Around the bend, steep cliffs (mi 6.0) rise 70 feet above the river. The river has slowly carved the cliffs, exposing layers of sand, clay, seashells, shale, and gravel. The layers' different colors highlight the cliffs.

There are trails from the public facilities on top, but there is no boating access provided or camping allowed at river level.

The high ground occupied by the park was used by Indians as ceremonial ground.

On the right bank, an old building houses springs (mi 7.8) that gave the town its name. Years ago people came to the Seven Springs resort to take the curative waters. The springs were closed when Hurricane Fran (1996) contaminated them.

15 Main Street (Wayne Co. 1731) access at Seven Springs to Hardy Bridge Road (Lenoir Co. 1389) bridge

Difficulty A		**Width** 110–200 ft	
Distance 6.8 mi		**Gradient** 0.5 ft/mi	
Scenery A (70%), B (30%)		**Map** page 280	

Gauge See Section 10.

Notes A Wildlife boating access is at Seven Springs.

Hardy Bridge Road is Lenoir Co. 1389, but the green road signs still have its old number, 1152, next to the road name.

Most of this section is through swampy ground. Downstream of the NC 903 bridge (mi 2.0), the river makes several loops. When the water is high, a channel to the right bypasses the last loop.

16 Hardy Bridge Road (Lenoir Co. 1389) bridge to US 70 access at Kinston

Difficulty A		**Width** 80–200 ft	
Distance 15.1 mi		**Gradient** 0.6 ft/mi	
Scenery A		**Map** page 281	

Gauge USGS *Neuse River at Kinston*. Always above minimum.

Notes See the previous section about Hardy Bridge Road.

A boating access at US 70 is managed by Kinston. Markings on the bridge supports near the boat ramp show impressive peak water levels reached during major floods.

In this long section, there are no bridges or public roads to the river. The channel is seldom straight as it winds through swampy ground.

Few houses are seen except about halfway down (mi 7.1).

17 US 70 access at Kinston to NC 55 bridge east of Kinston

Difficulty A		**Width** 100–200 ft	
Distance 12.3 mi		**Gradient** 1.0 ft/mi	
Scenery A (30%), B (20%), C (50%)		**Map** page 281	

Gauge See Section 16.

Notes See the previous section about the US 70 access.

The first 5 miles of this section are heavily developed as the river winds through Kinston.

A state historic site is in the first right bend (mi 0.4), where a large open-sided shelter can be seen on the left bank. It housed remains of the ironclad gunboat CSS Neuse, from the Confederate navy's ill-fated attempt to regain control of the lower Neuse River and retake the city of New Bern during the Civil War. The vessel was recovered after spending nearly 100 years on the river bottom.

Because of flooding, the CSS Neuse has been moved a few hundred yards back from the river. There is no dock, but the bank can be climbed to take a walking tour of the boat. It can be viewed through a fence surrounding the new shelter. To go inside, check for hours (252-522-2091). The site can also be reached from Business US 70/258.

Neuseway Nature Park and Campground (mi 2.2) on the right bank is open all year. It has eight RV and six tent campsites and is managed by Kinston-Lenoir County Parks and Recreation (252-939-3367). Around the bend is the NC 11/55 bridge (mi 2.6).

Downstream of the NC 58 bridge (mi 3.9) and a railroad bridge (mi 5.5) with a center swing section, the river returns to its rural character.

18	NC 55 bridge east of Kinston to Maple Cypress Road (Craven Co. 1470) bridge		
Difficulty A		**Width** 100–200 ft	
Distance 14.3 mi		**Gradient** 0.3 ft/mi	
Scenery A		**Map** page 281	

Gauge USGS *Neuse River at Fort Barnwell.* Always above minimum.

Notes There are no bridges and little development in this long section. Cypress trees line the banks, but the largest and densest stands are around and up the mouth of Contentnea Creek (mi 8.7).

It is possible to paddle up Contentnea Creek less than a mile and take out, but this requires taking a side branch that is easy to miss. See Contentnea Creek, Section 11 (page 228).

A sandy bank (mi 12.5) is on the left where people often camp. On the right bank is a landing where cars can be driven. Both areas are probably private land but have not been posted.

On a trip down this section, a gang of dozens of wild turkeys were spotted feeding near the bank.

19 Maple Cypress Road (Craven Co. 1470) bridge to Cow Pen Landing Road (Craven Co. 1441) access

Difficulty A	**Width** 150–200 ft
Distance 11.4 mi	**Gradient** 0.2 ft/mi
Scenery A (80%), B (20%)	**Map** page 282

Gauge See Section 18. There is a small tidal influence in this section, but wind is far more important.

Notes The Cow Pen Landing Road access is managed by Craven County.

At several places where creeks enter, their mouths are as big as the main river channel. Quarter Creek (mi 9.5) is wide and enters from the right at a back angle. There is a private ($2 fee) boat ramp 200 feet up this creek at Shell Landing. It is reached from Craven Co. 1445.

Greens Thorofare (mi 9.7) is a channel to the right that returns to the main Neuse 0.7 miles downstream of the take-out.

20 Cow Pen Landing Road (Craven Co. 1441) access to Glenburnie Park access at New Bern

Difficulty A	**Width** 75–1,000 ft
Distance 10.8 mi	**Gradient** 0.2 ft/mi
Scenery A (55%), B (25%), C (20%)	**Map** page 282

Gauge See Section 18. Tides are about a foot. Wind is far more important.

Notes See the previous section about Cow Pen Landing Road access.

To reach New Bern's Glenburnie Park from US 70, take the NC 43/Glenburnie Road exit. Follow Glenburnie Road 2.2 miles and turn right on Oaks Road. Continue 0.4 miles on Oaks Road and turn left on Glenburnie Drive. Go to the wastewater treatment plant, and the park is to the left.

A public landing (mi 2.2) on the right bank is managed by Craven County. It is at the end of West Craven Middle School Road (Craven Co. 1423).

At the NC 43 bridge (mi 3.7), a Monsanto plant is downstream left.

The Gut (mi 5.1) is a 75-ft wide side channel to the right. It leads to Bachelor Creek and back to the Neuse before the take-out. Continuing down the Neuse to the take-out is 0.2 miles shorter but much wider. Paddle into The Gut, where there are many water lilies and stands of saw grass. The swampy land between The Gut and the Neuse is called Hog Island.

Bachelor Creek (mi 6.7) joins The Gut from the right. Continue straight ahead, where the combined channel is Bachelor Creek. Alligators are often sighted here.

Bachelor Creek joins the Neuse (mi 9.6). Paddle along the right shore to reach the Glenburnie Park ramp.

■

This River is near as large as Reatkin; the South-side having curious Tracts of good Land, the Banks high, and Stone-Quarries. The Tuskeruros being come to us, we ventur'd over the River, which we found to be a strong Current, and the Water about Breast-high. However, we all got safe to the North-Shore, which is but poor, white, sandy Land, and bears no Timber, but small shrubby Oaks. We went about 10 Miles, and sat down at the Falls of a large Creek, where lay mighty Rocks, the Water making a strange Noise, as if a great many Water-Mills were going at once. I take this to be the Falls of Neus-Creek, called by the Indians, Wee quo Whom.

—John Lawson, *A New Voyage to Carolina* (1701)
(at Falls of Neuse near Raleigh)

Len Felton and Elmer Eddy at Cliffs of the Neuse State Park
Neuse River, Section 14

Neuse Basin

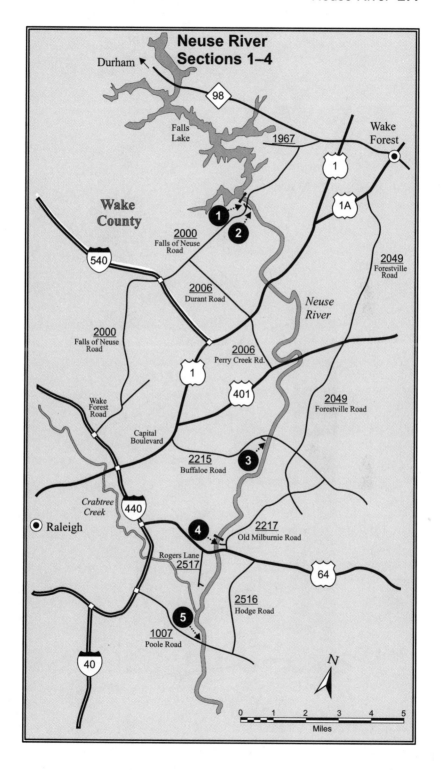

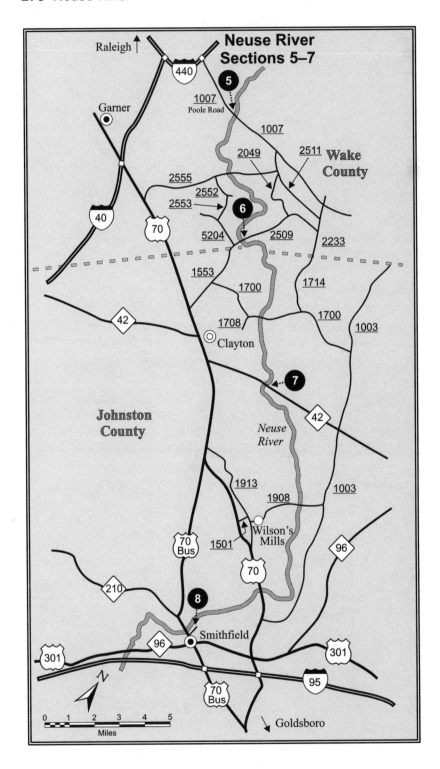

Neuse Basin

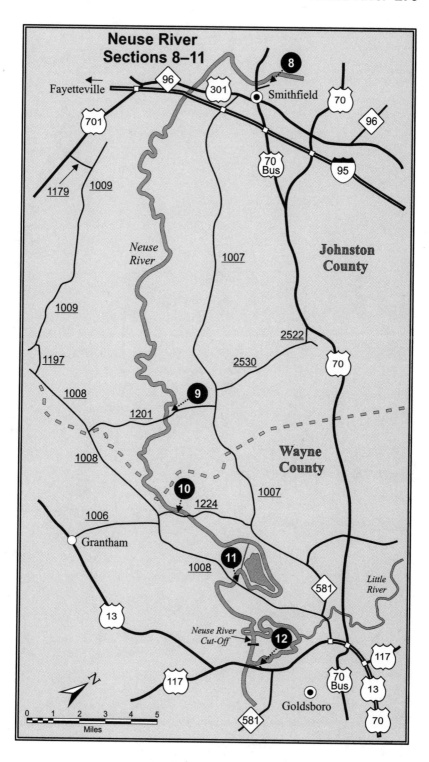

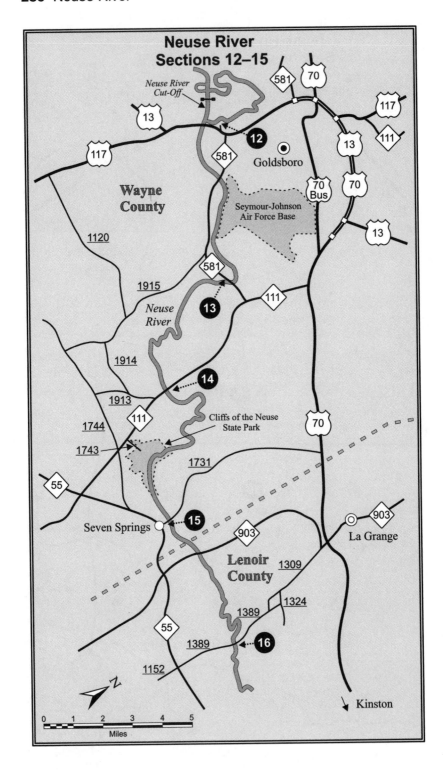

Neuse Basin

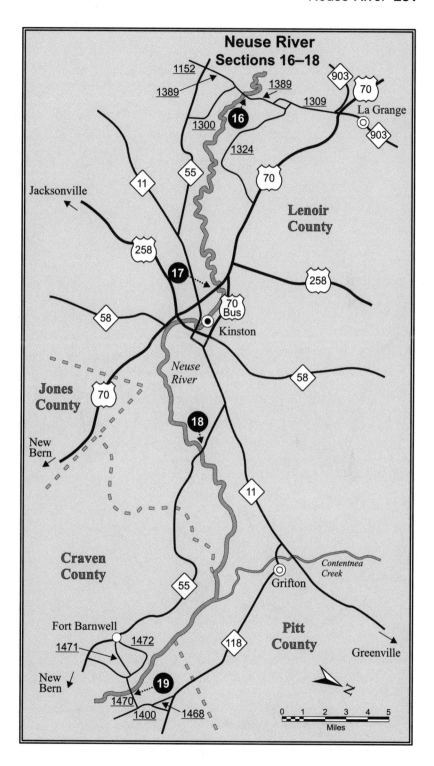

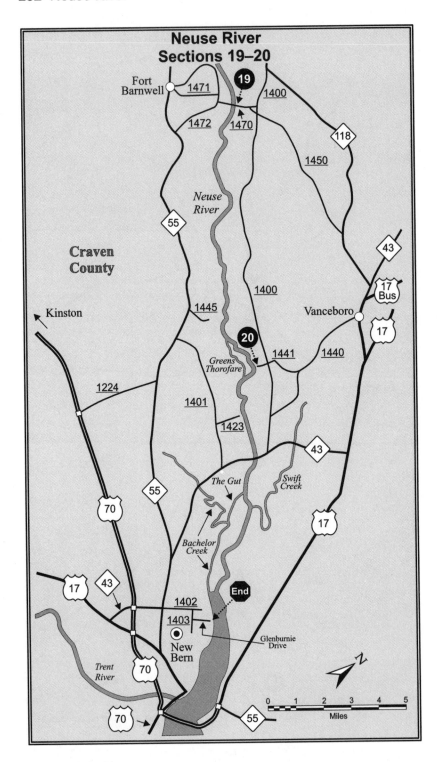

**Neuse River
Sections 19–20**

Fort Barnwell

1471

19

1400

1472 1470

118

1450

55

Neuse River

Craven County

43

17 Bus

1400

Kinston

1445

Vanceboro

17

20

1224

1441 1440

Greens Thorofare

1401

1423

43

The Gut

Swift Creek

55

70

17

Bachelor Creek

17

43

End

1402

70

1403

Glenburnie Drive

Trent River

New Bern

70

N

0 1 2 3 4 5
Miles

70

55

Neuse Basin

Trent River

Counties   Jones, Craven

Topos   Phillips Crossroads, Trenton, Pollocksville, New Bern

The Trent River headwaters begin 15 miles southwest of Kinston. Starting as a narrow blackwater stream, it takes a winding course making its way to the east. It goes through forest and farmland before flowing through the first town at Trenton.

Below Trenton, development is more frequent, and the river widens so that downed trees are seldom an obstacle. After going through Pollocksville, the Trent joins the Neuse River at New Bern.

1 Chinquapin Chapel Road (Jones Co. 1129) bridge to NC 58 bridge

Difficulty A	**Width** 30–50 ft	
Distance 5.8 mi	**Gradient** 1.5 ft/mi	
Scenery A (65%), B (35%)	**Map** page 286	

Gauge USGS *Trent River near Trenton*. Estimated minimum is 80 cfs (3.9 ft). Downed trees are common.

Notes Put in at the Chinquapin Chapel Road bridge or from the roadside about 0.2 miles upstream of the bridge.

The river twists and turns through forests, and a few farms border the river. Cypress and pine trees are numerous.

2 NC 58 bridge to Middle Road (Jones Co. 1300) bridge

Difficulty A	**Width** 30–45 ft	
Distance 5.5 mi	**Gradient** 1.4 ft/mi	
Scenery A	**Map** page 286	

Gauge See Section 1.

Notes Many large trees jut over the river channel. Palmetto plants are dense in areas.

Wild turkey and many deer were sighted on a trip down this section.

3 Middle Road (Jones Co. 1300) bridge to Landfill Road (Jones Co. 1343) access at Trenton

Difficulty	A	**Width**	30–70 ft
Distance	12.6 mi	**Gradient**	0.5 ft/mi
Scenery	A (65%), B (15%), C (20%)	**Map**	page 286

Gauge See Section 1.

Notes A Wildlife boating access is near the end of Landfill Road.

The channel continues its twisting course with banks up to 20 feet. Little development is seen until near Trenton.

The NC 41 bridge (mi 10.5) in Trenton can be used to shorten the trip.

4 Landfill Road (Jones Co. 1343) access at Trenton to Oak Grove Road (Jones Co. 1121) roadside

Difficulty	A	**Width**	65–110 ft
Distance	10.3 mi	**Gradient**	0 ft/mi
Scenery	A (40%), B (60%)	**Map**	page 286

Gauge USGS *Trent River at Pollocksville*. Always above minimum. There is a slight tidal influence near the take-out.

Notes See the previous section about the Landfill Road access.

Access at the Oak Grove Road bridge is difficult. It is easier downstream past the bridge a few hundred yards at the roadside.

The banks are sandy, and the channel is wider than in previous sections. Downed trees are usually not a problem.

Houses on the banks are frequent in areas, and a golf course is passed.

5 Oak Grove Road (Jones Co. 1121) roadside to US 17 access at Pollocksville

Difficulty	A	**Width**	60–90 ft
Distance	6.9 mi	**Gradient**	0 ft/mi
Scenery	A (60%), C (40%)	**Map**	page 286

Gauge USGS *Trent River at Pollocksville*. Always above minimum. There is a tidal influence of about a foot.

Notes See the previous section about Oak Grove Road.

A Wildlife boating access is at the US 17 bridge.

Land on the left bank for the first 4.7 miles is part of the Marine Corps Oak Grove Airfield.

The channel (mi 3.8) to the right is part of an old oxbow. It is a dead-end after a mile and is often visited by fishermen.

Banks vary from 3–15 feet, with many houses built on them in the last 2 miles.

6	US 17 access at Pollocksville bridge to Lawson Creek Park access off US 70 at New Bern		
Difficulty A		**Width** 80–2,000 ft	
Distance 16.4 mi		**Gradient** 0 ft/mi	
Scenery B (75%), C (25%)		**Map** page 287	

Gauge See Section 5. It is wide near the end of the trip, making wind a problem.

Notes See the previous section about the US 17 access.

Lawson Creek Park is downstream left of the US 70 bridge, only 0.6 miles before the mouth of the Trent at the Neuse River. From US 70, take Exit 416 to Pembroke Road (Craven Co.1200) toward downtown New Bern. The entrance to the park is a few hundred yards on the right. Continue over a small creek bridge to the boat ramps on the Trent River.

This is a long section because of a lack of public access. A private access (mi 7.5) is in the town of River Bend off US 17. In the community, off Gatewood Drive, Tar Landing ends in a cul-de-sac, 100 feet from the Trent River. The property is a common area belonging to residents. Ask permission to use it.

The boundary of Croatan National Forest runs near the right bank for most of this section, but all property along the river is private.

There are few long stretches without houses, and the width is 100–200 feet down to Tar Landing (mi 7.5). Here the channel bends right with a large cove to the left.

As the channel widens, jet skis and motorboats are common during warm weather.

Brice Creek (mi 14.7) enters on the right. Move to the left before going under US 70 (mi 16.3) to reach Lawson Creek Park.

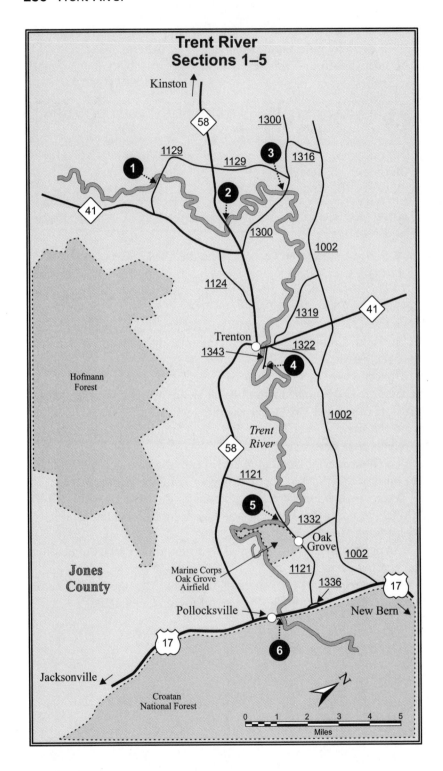

**Trent River
Sections 1–5**

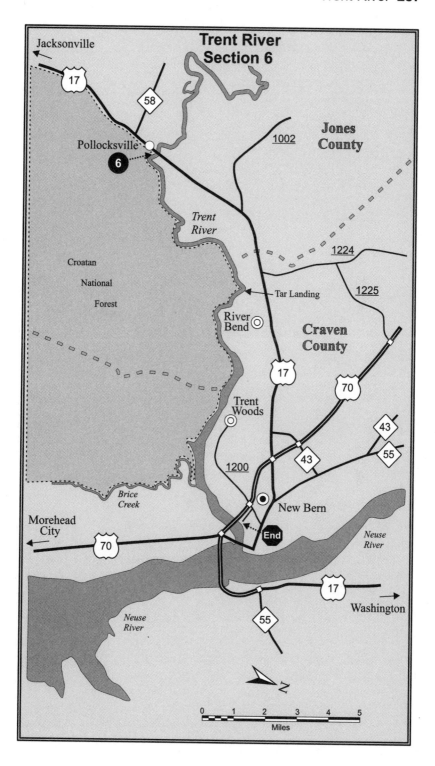

**Trent River
Section 6**

Jacksonville

17

58

Pollocksville

6

Jones
County

1002

Trent
River

1224

Croatan

National

Forest

Tar Landing

1225

River
Bend

Craven
County

17

70

Trent
Woods

43

43

55

1200

Brice
Creek

Morehead
City

New Bern

Neuse
River

70

End

17

Washington

55

Neuse
River

N

0   1   2   3   4   5
Miles

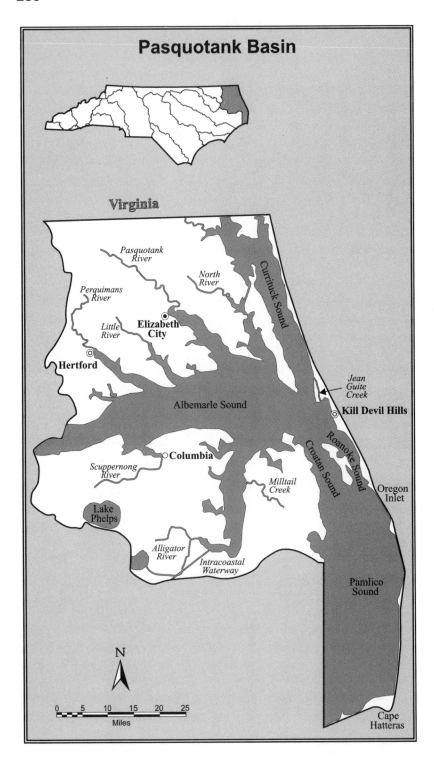

Pasquotank Basin

Virginia

Pasquotank
River

North
River

Perquimans
River

Little
River

Elizabeth
City

Hertford

Currituck Sound

Jean
Guite
Creek

Kill Devil Hills

Albemarle Sound

Roanoke Sound

Columbia

Croatan Sound

Scuppernong
River

Milltail
Creek

Lake
Phelps

Oregon
Inlet

Alligator
River

Intracoastal
Waterway

Pamlico
Sound

N

0   5   10   15   20   25
Miles

Cape
Hatteras

Pasquotank Basin

The Pasquotank Basin is part of the Coastal Plain in the northeast corner of the state. It contains 3,635 square miles of low-lying lands and vast open waters, including Albemarle Sound. Many small watersheds drain into Albemarle, Currituck, Croatan, Roanoke, and Pamlico Sounds. One of these is the Pasquotank River for which the basin is named. A small portion of the basin extends into Virginia.

Major tributaries on the northwestern side of Albemarle Sound are the Pasquotank, Little, and Perquimans Rivers. Major tributaries on the southeastern side are the Alligator and Scuppernong Rivers.

The Alligator River is a blackwater river remote from any urban areas and bordered by wooded swamps and *pocosins*—wet areas with evergreen trees and shrubs growing on peat or sandy soils. The word pocosin comes from the Algonquin Indian word meaning "swamp on a hill."

Parts of the Alligator River headwaters are bordered by Pocosin Lakes National Wildlife Refuge. Where the river becomes miles wide, its eastern shore is bordered by Alligator River National Wildlife Refuge. Endangered red wolves have been reestablished in this refuge.

The Scuppernong River is mainly forested wetlands and farms with widespread use of canals to drain wetlands.

Currituck Sound is a shallow estuary in the northeastern portion of the basin whose circulation is influenced largely by wind movement. A vast marsh area bordering a large portion of the Currituck Sound serves wintering ducks, geese, and swans. The Northwest River is a major tributary, receiving drainage from a number of canals leading out of the Great Dismal Swamp.

The Great Dismal Swamp has 82,000 acres in Virginia and 38,000 acres in North Carolina. The Great Dismal Swamp National Wildlife Refuge protects much of the swamp in both states. North Carolina also protects 17,000 acres in the Dismal Swamp State Natural Area, adjacent to the refuge.

The Pasquotank Basin also includes waters along the Outer Banks south of Currituck Sound, including Roanoke Sound, Croatan Sound, and Pamlico Sound from Oregon Inlet to Hatteras Inlet. Much of the area is adjacent to the Cape Hatteras National Seashore and Pea Island National Wildlife Refuge.

Alligator River

Counties   Tyrrell, Hyde

Topos   Fairfield NW, Fairfield

The Alligator River is the approximate limit of the northern range of American alligators. It begins in swampy land north of Lake Mattamuskeet and is joined by New Lake Fork as it flows generally north. The river crosses the Intracoastal Waterway several times between the waterway's connection of the Pungo and Alligator Rivers.

The Alligator River is joined by the Northwest Fork, draining swampland just east of Phelps Lake, home of Pettigrew State Park. Downstream of the Northwest Fork, the Alligator River widens to become almost 5 miles wide on its 20-mile run to Albemarle Sound.

The Alligator River forms the boundary between Hyde and Tyrrell Counties. The highest elevation on the mainland is west of Alligator Lake, at 18 feet above sea level. Mainland areas at elevations above 10 feet are pocosins created from the accumulation of organic material.

In the 1970s, corporate farms cleared and drained large tracts of pocosins. These areas were mainly organic soils from which large stumps and logs of bald cypress and juniper (Atlantic white cedar) were burned. Because of difficulty in farming and stricter wetland regulations, many acres of this converted land have been donated to the government as wildlife refuges, creating the Alligator River and Pocosin Lakes National Wildlife Refuges (266,000 acres). The refuges are a vital part of maintaining the water quality and wildlife in the area, and they are undertaking large-scale restoration of the drained pocosin wetlands and planting of native wetland vegetation.

The Alligator River and its tributaries are designated as Outstanding Resource Waters.

> ### 1 Northwest Fork at NC 94 access to Kilkenny Landing Road (Hyde Co. 1322) access
>
> | | | | |
> |---|---|---|---|
> | **Difficulty** | A | **Width** | 100–300 ft |
> | **Distance** | 11.0 mi | **Gradient** | 0 ft/mi |
> | **Scenery** | A | **Map** | page 293 |

Gauge None. Always above minimum. There is a small tidal influence from Albemarle Sound. The channel is exposed to wind. Reverse the put-in and take-out if wind is coming from the south.

Notes An Albemarle Region Paddle Trails System access is a few hundred yards north of the NC 94 bridge (downstream left). A dirt road leads to a ramp next to an old wooden loading dock.

Kilkenny Landing Road leads to a dead-end where there is a boat ramp.

This section starts on the Northwest Fork, goes to the confluence with the Alligator River, and continues upstream on the Alligator River. It bypasses the wider, open water of the Alligator River downstream of the confluence.

An alternative or addition to this section is to paddle upstream from the put-in, exploring the upper areas of the Northwest and Southwest Forks, and then return to the starting point.

There are paddle trail mile-markers placed along this section. The markers measure distance from the put-in.

The left bank is mostly marsh and natural pocosin. Pitcher plants and small pond pines are seen on the banks in the first few miles.

At the confluence with the main Alligator River (mi 4.3), turn right to continue to the take-out at Kilkenny Landing.

At the confluence, it is also possible to continue 3.7 miles downstream (straight ahead) on the Alligator River to Gum Neck Creek on the left. The river is 0.5 miles wide here, and a channel leads 0.4 miles up the creek to a Wildlife boating access at the end of Gum Neck Landing (Hyde Co. 1361).

In paddling upstream, there is little current at normal water levels. The view is mainly marsh grass and scattered forest of low trees. Fishermen in motorboats are often seen.

> **2** Kilkenny Landing Road (Hyde Co. 1322) access to NC 94 roadside near Intracoastal Waterway

Difficulty A		**Width** 50–300 ft	
Distance 7.1 mi		**Gradient** 0 ft/mi	
Scenery A		**Map** page 293	

Gauge See Section 1.

Notes See the previous section about the Kilkenny Landing Road access.

To reach the take-out from Fairfield, take NC 94 north for 3.6 miles to the bridge over the Intracoastal Waterway. Continue for 0.5 miles to where the Alligator River goes through a culvert under NC 94. There is little parking space on the road shoulder.

This trip goes upstream, but there is not much current at normal water levels. For this section, left and right are referenced to the paddler's left and right going upstream rather than the usual reference of going downstream.

There are paddle trail mile-markers placed along this section. The markers measure distance from the Section 1 put-in.

The banks are low and covered with marsh grass. There are fewer trees seen here than in Section 1.

Waterfowl and nutria, an animal with the head and coat of a beaver but the tail of a rat, are numerous.

The river joins the Intracoastal Waterway (mi 4.8). Turn right and paddle on the waterway for a few hundred yards. Watch for the wakes from large boats. Turn left where the Alligator River (mi 5.0) leaves the waterway.

The river crosses the waterway (mi 6.0) again, but it is only necessary to paddle diagonally across the waterway to rejoin the river.

Where a small channel (mi 6.9) branches to the left, continue straight to reach the take-out. The small channel leads back to the waterway.

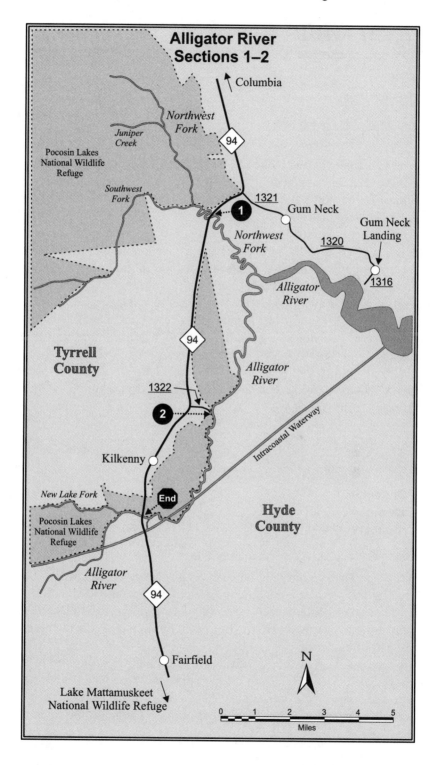

**Alligator River
Sections 1–2**

Columbia

Northwest
Fork

Juniper
Creek

94

Pocosin Lakes
National Wildlife
Refuge

Southwest
Fork

1321

1 Gum Neck

Gum Neck
Landing

Northwest
Fork

1320

1316

Alligator
River

94

**Tyrrell
County**

Alligator
River

1322

2

Intracoastal Waterway

Kilkenny

New Lake Fork

End

Pocosin Lakes
National Wildlife
Refuge

**Hyde
County**

Alligator
River

94

N

Fairfield

Lake Mattamuskeet
National Wildlife Refuge

0   1   2   3   4   5
Miles

Jean Guite Creek

County   Dare

Topo   Kitty Hawk

Jean Guite Creek runs along the Outer Bank's Bodie Island for only 6 miles, making a connection between Currituck Sound near Southern Shores in the north and Kitty Hawk Bay off Albemarle Sound near Kitty Hawk in the south.

The stream is fairly protected from wind by a dune system on the coast. It offers a paddling trip through a maritime deciduous swamp, forest, and marsh. It also offers the chance to explore more open water at the ends of the creek.

The Kitty Hawk Woods Coastal Reserve manages 1,350 acres. South of US 158, most of the land along Jean Guite Creek is within the reserve. It contains a great diversity of wildlife, birds, and rare plants.

Local outfitters refer to a trip on Jean Guite Creek as the Kitty Hawk Woods Maritime Forest tour. The stream is also known as High Bridge Creek.

1	Bob Perry Road (Dare Co. 1210) access to US 158 bridge and return		
Difficulty A		**Width** 30–50 ft	
Distance 4.6 mi		**Gradient** 0 ft/mi	
Scenery C		**Map** page 296	

Gauge None. Always above minimum.

Notes A Dare County public boat ramp is off Bob Perry Road. The creek is 100 yards from the put-in. Turn right to paddle to US 158.

The trip can be extended by turning left, paddling 1.5 miles to the southern mouth at Kitty Hawk Bay, and returning to paddle the northern part of the creek.

The banks are swampy with marsh grass until reaching the Kitty Hawk Road (Dare Co. 1208) bridge (mi 0.7), where banks are a few feet high. The creek runs straight here with many water lilies at the water's edge and pine trees on higher ground. The maritime forest is often dense near the banks.

A private, wooden, covered bridge (mi 1.4) crosses the creek.

Many homes are built along the creek in the half-mile leading to the US 158 bridge (mi 2.3), the return point for this section.

A private access is on the right just before the US 158 bridge at Kitty Hawk Kayaks (252-441-6800). Ask permission to use it.

The creek can be paddled above the US 158 bridge. It broadens rapidly to 1,500 feet and reaches Currituck Sound in 2.5 miles.

Sea kayak on Jean Guite Creek

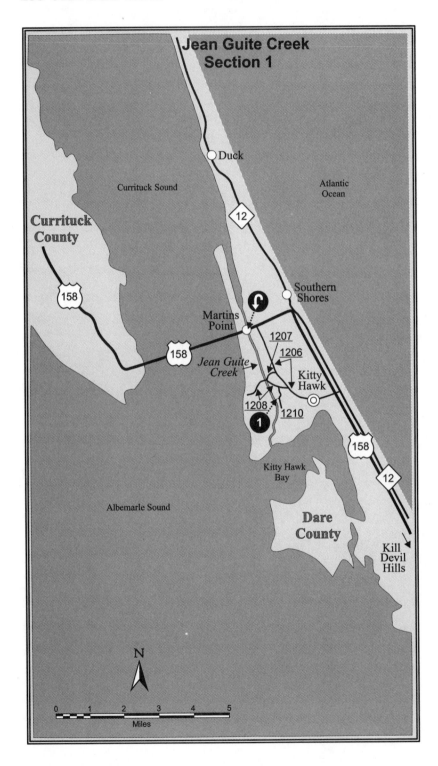

Pasquotank Basin

Little River

Counties   Pasquotank, Perquimans

Topo   Nixonton

The Little River begins at the southern edge of the Great Dismal Swamp near Parkville, 10 miles west of Elizabeth City, and forms the Pasquotank and Perquimans County border.

The river is very narrow until passing US 17. At the confluence with Halls Creek above Nixonton, it begins to broaden rapidly. It reaches more than a mile wide over the next 10 miles where it joins Albemarle Sound.

1 Old US 17 (Pasquotank Co. 1197) access to Halls Creek Road (Pasquotank Co. 1140) access on Halls Creek

Difficulty A		**Width** 25–500 ft	
Distance 4.6 mi		**Gradient** 0 ft/mi	
Scenery A		**Map** page 298	

Gauge None. Always above minimum.

Notes The Old US 17 access has a small gravel parking lot and an old dock.

A Wildlife boating access is on Halls Creek.

The section is short, and there is little current at normal water levels. The put-in and take-out can be reversed, or it can easily be paddled as a round-trip.

At the put-in, there are many trees hanging over the 25-foot wide stream. Sheets of bright green, floating duckweed are common.

Within a mile downstream, the width is up to 50 feet. Several cabins are on the banks.

The stream broadens to 500 feet where Halls Creek (mi 3.8) enters from the left. Paddle up Halls Creek to the ramp near the bridge.

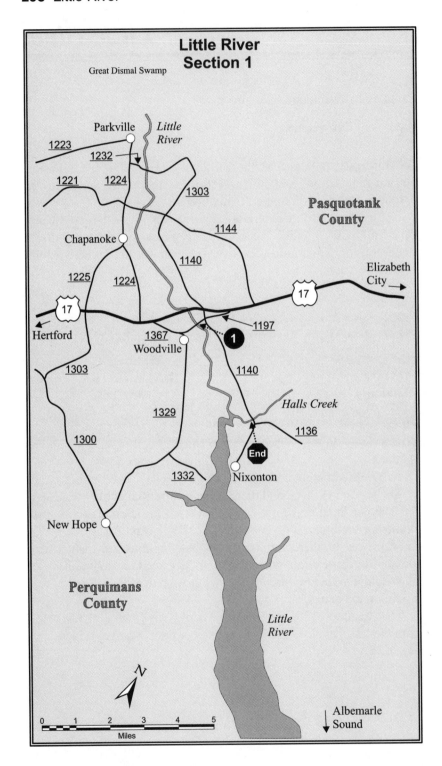

Little River
Section 1

Great Dismal Swamp

Parkville   *Little River*

1223

1232

1221   1224

1303

1144

Pasquotank County

Chapanoke

1140

1225   1224

Elizabeth City

17

17

Hertford

1197

1367
Woodville

1

1140

1303

Halls Creek

1329

1136

1300

End

1332   Nixonton

New Hope

Perquimans County

Little River

N

0 1 2 3 4 5
Miles

Albemarle Sound

Pasquotank Basin

Milltail Creek

County   Dare

Topo   Buffalo City

Milltail Creek is contained within the boundaries of the Alligator River National Wildlife Refuge. It begins in swampy land near the middle of the refuge and flows northwest, broadening into a lake area up to a quarter-mile wide for a few miles in the middle of its run. It turns west and empties into the wide Alligator River, making a total run of only 13 miles.

Milltail Creek has excellent water quality, and it is designated as Outstanding Resource Waters.

The 152,000-acre Alligator River National Wildlife Refuge was created in 1984 to preserve pocosin wetlands and wildlife. The endangered red wolf has been reintroduced here, and the refuge is one of the last strongholds of black bear on the eastern seaboard. Alligator are often seen in Milltail Creek. Many varieties of birds are found on the refuge, including a large number of species that winter here.

In 1885, Buffalo City was built near Milltail Creek to log cedar and cypress. It became Dare County's largest town. Barges landed at the docks to load logs hauled in by railroad. The timber was depleted by 1925. Only ruins of pilings from the old docks and a few collapsed buildings remain.

The sight and sound of jet fighters is not unusual at Milltail Creek. Near the center of the refuge is the Dare County Bombing Range, a 46,000-acre military practice area used by Navy and Air Force pilots.

The refuge is open during daylight hours and has four color-coded paddling trails. Refuge headquarters in Manteo (252-473-1131) can provide additional information and maps. Also see: http://alligatorriver.fws.gov

1 Buffalo City Road (Dare Co. 1103) access to Sawyer Lake to Milltail Creek and return	
Difficulty A	**Width** 10–1,000 ft
Distance 4.5 mi	**Gradient** 0 ft/mi
Scenery A	**Map** page 302

Gauge None. Always above minimum.

Notes The Milltail Creek access is at the end of Buffalo City Road off US 64.

At the put-in, the red trail follows a 20-foot wide canal. The raised wooden boardwalk on the right is the half-mile Sandy Ridge Wildlife Trail.

The red trail joins the green trail (mi 0.4). Turn left and follow the green trail, lined with tall grass, to Sawyer Lake. The lake (mi 1.1) begins to widen. Paddle around the perimeter of the lake. One of the last remaining large stands of Atlantic white cedar in the area is at the northern end of the lake (mi 1.8).

After circling the lake, return down the green trail to where it meets the red trail (mi 3.1) and continue straight on the red trail. Many ferns are on the side, and trees overhang the narrow trail to provide a closed, green canopy.

At a wooden bridge (mi 3.4), it is usually necessary to portage over the bridge because there is not enough clearance to paddle under it. On the other side of the bridge, Sandy Ridge Gut is as narrow as 10 feet.

At Milltail Creek (mi 3.8), it is almost a quarter-mile wide and is more of a lake than a creek. Turn right to return to the put-in.

A channel (mi 4.5) to the right is the red trail. It leads a few hundred feet under the boardwalk bridge and back to the put-in on the left.

The trip can be extended after coming out of Sandy Ridge Gut by going left (upstream) at Milltail Creek instead of right, taking the blue trail. After a half-mile, a large bay is to the left and the main channel is to the right. The creek narrows after a few miles. It is 5.6 miles from Sandy Ridge Gut to Milltail Road. It is possible to take out at Milltail Road, but it is sandy and difficult to travel when wet.

> ② Buffalo City Road (Dare Co. 1103) access to Milltail Creek mouth at Alligator River and return

Difficulty A	**Width**	50–500 ft
Distance 8.4 mi	**Gradient**	0 ft/mi
Scenery A	**Map**	page 302

Gauge None. Always above minimum.

Notes See the previous section about the Buffalo City Road access.

At the put-in, take the channel leading under the boardwalk bridge and into Milltail Creek (mi 0.1) and turn right (downstream) to follow the yellow trail.

The remains of wooden pilings (mi 0.3) on the right are part of the dock used for loading timber when Buffalo City was a logging town.

The creek narrows down to 75 feet. Lily pads, cattails, and tall marsh grass are along the edges. Cypress and pond pine trees are on the low banks.

A decaying hunting cabin (mi 3.6) on the right is the only structure on this section.

At Milltail Creek's 50-foot wide mouth (mi 4.2), the view is across a 5-mile expanse of the Alligator River, part of the Intracoastal Waterway.

Retrace the route to return to the put-in.

Pete Peterson on Milltail Creek, Section 1

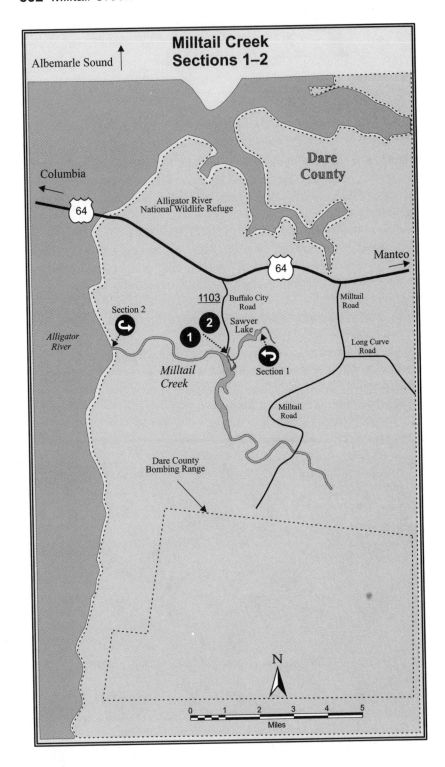

Pasquotank Basin

Perquimans River

County   Perquimans

Topos   Hobbsville, Center Hill, Hertford

The Perquimans River originates in the southern portion of the Great Dismal Swamp. Beginning as a narrow blackwater stream, it widens quickly approaching Hertford and becomes more than a mile wide where it empties into Albemarle Sound.

1 NC 37 bridge near Belvidere to Missing Mill Park access at Hertford off Grubb Street

Difficulty A	**Width** 50–500 ft	
Distance 11.9 mi	**Gradient** 0 ft/mi	
Scenery A (65%), B (35%)	**Map** page 305	

Gauge None. Always above minimum. After the first 3 miles, the river widens enough so that wind can be a problem.

Notes To reach Missing Mill Park from US 17 traveling south, take US 17 Business into Hertford. Turn right at Grubb Street. The park is 0.2 miles ahead. There is no boat ramp, but parking is available 150 feet from a small dock.

At the put-in, the river is small with much duckweed. Lily pads are common, and there are some stately cypress trees. The river widens quickly going downstream. Paddle trail markers are seen at most mile points.

Goodwin Creek (mi 3.0) joins from the right. The first bridge upstream (Perquimans Co. 1111) over Goodwin Creek is listed as an alternative put-in for the paddle trail down to Hertford.

A large island (mi 3.9) is in a wide cove. The shortest way downstream is to the right.

Where the ground is not swampy, breaks in the trees often reveal farmland near the bank.

After going under a railroad bridge (mi 10.7), the high US 17 bridge can be seen in the distance below Hertford.

Missing Mill Park is on the right bank where the river turns to the left.

Duckweed on the Perquimans River

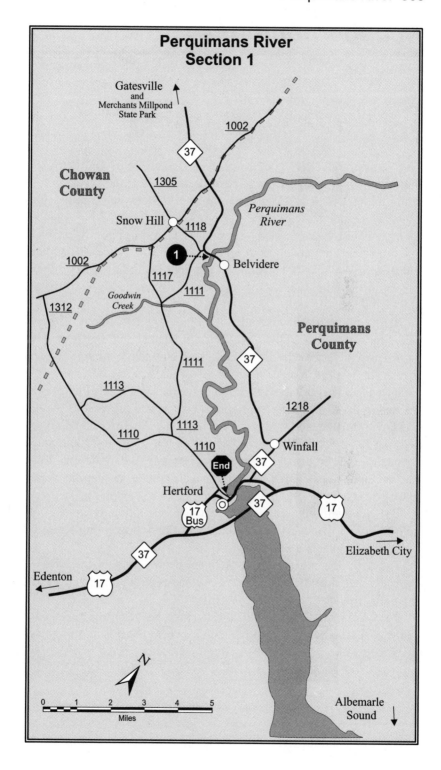

Scuppernong River

Counties   Washington, Tyrrell

Topos   Creswell, Creswell SE, Columbia West

The Scuppernong River begins north of Lake Phelps and Pettigrew State Park. It flows east past Creswell and swings northeast before going under US 64 at Columbia, where it widens and empties into Bull Bay at Albemarle Sound.

Lake Phelps is the second largest of the Carolina Bays. Its origin is open to scientific debate, as is Lake Waccamaw's (page 210). Many Indian artifacts have been found in the area, including thirty dugout canoes in the lake. One canoe has been dated at nearly 4,400 years old.

Before colonists discovered Lake Phelps in 1755, area residents called the swampy area the Great Eastern Dismal and the Great Alligator Dismal. The wilderness was so fearsome that explorers refused to enter its borders.

In the late 1700s, the swampland surrounding Lake Phelps was drained to make productive agricultural fields and prosperous plantations. A 6-mile canal was dug connecting Lake Phelps with the Scuppernong River. The canal served as both a transportation route and a channel for draining the swampland between the river and Lake Phelps. Later an extensive system of canals with locks was developed to irrigate crops.

The Scuppernong grape, a bronze-colored muscadine, takes its name from its discovery on the banks of the Scuppernong River by Sir Walter Raleigh's colony in 1554.

The Scuppernong is typical of rivers beginning near the coast. It starts as a narrow blackwater stream but gains width rapidly in a short run to the sound.

Pocosin Lakes National Wildlife Refuge headquarters and visitor center is on the river bank in Columbia, where there is an interpretative boardwalk.

1 Main Street (Washington Co. 1142) access at Creswell to Cross Landing Road (Tyrrell Co. 1105) bridge

Difficulty A	**Width**	40–150 ft
Distance 4.1 mi	**Gradient**	0 ft/mi
Scenery A	**Map**	page 309

Gauge None. Always above minimum.

Notes A Wildlife boating access is at Spruills Bridge on Main Street (Washington Co. 1142) at Creswell.

This section is short and can be paddled as a round-trip, avoiding the need to set a shuttle.

Many oxbows around islands offer a chance to explore a bit off the straighter channel. Trees overhang the river before it widens, and the banks are low to swampy.

A platform (mi 2.1) attached to the right bank is a public rest stop.

2 Cross Landing Road (Tyrrell Co. 1105) bridge to US 64 access at Columbia

Difficulty A	**Width**	125–800 ft
Distance 8.1 mi	**Gradient**	0 ft/mi
Scenery A	**Map**	page 309

Gauge None. Always above minimum. The river is wide and exposed to wind. Reverse the direction of travel if the wind will be more favorable.

Notes The take-out is at the dock behind Pocosin Lakes National Wildlife Refuge headquarters and visitor center, upstream right of the US 64 bridge.

Another take-out option is to continue 1.6 miles past the US 64 bridge to a Wildlife boating access on the left, at the end of Tyrrell Co. 1228.

Cypress trees with Spanish moss are along the banks. Before the river widens near Columbia, it is good territory to spot wildlife. During weekends with pleasant weather, this is a popular area for fishing boats.

There is little dry ground, but there are three floating platforms in this section. They are attached to the bank and built to serve as public rest stops. The first platform (mi 1.9) in this section is on the right.

A rare piece of dry ground is Dunbars Landing (mi 4.3) on the left. The bank is a few feet high where a canal joins. A platform is downstream right.

In the next mile, the river reaches 300 feet wide and continues to broaden downstream.

On the right are Second Creek (mi 5.5), the last platform (mi 6.6), and Riders Creek (mi 6.8).

Brown water snake and turtle share a log
Scuppernong River, Section 2

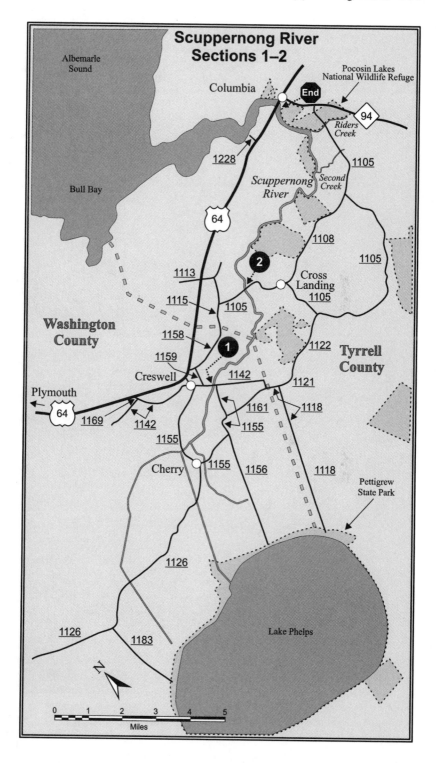

Scuppernong River Sections 1–2

Albemarle Sound

Columbia

End

Pocosin Lakes National Wildlife Refuge

94

Riders Creek

1228

1105

Scuppernong River

Second Creek

Bull Bay

1108

1105

1113

2

Cross Landing
1105

1115

1105

Washington County

1158

1122

Tyrrell County

1159

1

Creswell

1142

1121

Plymouth

64

1169

1142

1161

1118

1155

1155

1156

1118

Cherry

1155

1155

Pettigrew State Park

1126

1126

1183

Lake Phelps

N

0 1 2 3 4 5

Miles

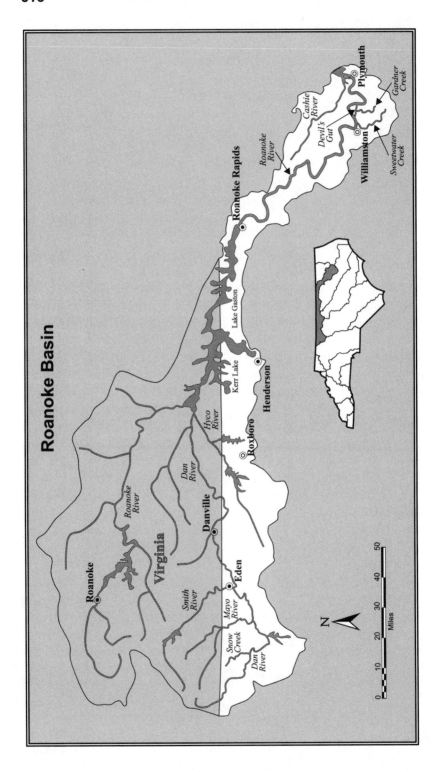

Roanoke Basin

Roanoke Basin

The Roanoke Basin begins in the Blue Ridge Mountains of Virginia and flows to the southeast for 400 miles before emptying into Albemarle Sound in North Carolina. The entire watershed is 9,776 square miles with 3,503 (thirty-six percent) in North Carolina, making it the state's sixth largest basin.

Because the basin gathers water from such a large area of Virginia, the Roanoke River carries more water than any other river in North Carolina. In the lower part of the basin, it has carved a floodplain up to 5 miles wide.

In North Carolina, the basin is composed of two major parts: the Dan River and its tributaries in the northwestern part of the Piedmont, upstream of Kerr Lake; and the Roanoke River as it enters North Carolina in the northeastern part of the Piedmont to Albemarle Sound.

The upper portion of the Dan River is designated as trout waters and flows through Hanging Rock State Park at Danbury. The Dan River and some of its tributaries, such as the Mayo River, contain rare fish and mussel species.

The Roanoke River enters John H. Kerr Reservoir and then flows into Lake Gaston and Roanoke Rapids Lake. After passing through Dominion Generation's hydroelectric plant, the Roanoke River flows freely into the Coastal Plain and on to Albemarle Sound.

The extensive floodplain in the lower reaches of the Roanoke River is considered to be one of the largest intact, and least disturbed, bottomland forest systems on the Atlantic coast.

Many groups have played an important part in protection of over 50,000 acres in the lower Roanoke floodplain. The protected lands include the state-owned Roanoke River Wetlands, the Roanoke River National Wildlife Refuge, and land jointly managed by The Nature Conservancy and Georgia-Pacific Corporation.

The lower Roanoke is important habitat for fish including striped bass, as well as black bear, bobcat, large populations of wild turkey, and many species of waterfowl and birds.

Cashie River

County   Bertie

Topos   Windsor South, Woodard

The Cashie River (pronounced ca-**shy**) begins in the northeastern corner of Bertie (ber-**tee**) County, near the Roanoke River. It winds through the county, running generally southeast, and passes through Windsor on its way to Albemarle Sound at Batchelor Bay, near the mouth of the Roanoke River. The Cashie is said to have a depth of up to 80 feet.

The Cashie Wetlands Walk, a 1,800-foot walkway in Windsor, allows tourists to see and learn more about the value of wetlands.

In the late 1880s, steamboats hauled freight and passengers between Plymouth and Windsor. This type of commercial traffic has disappeared, but a sign of an older style of transportation for crossing rivers is Sans Souci Ferry, downstream of Windsor. It is one of the state's last operational two-car ferries. It is diesel-powered and uses a cable for guidance.

The upper part of the Cashie River is narrow and subject to downed trees. It widens and becomes free of downed trees a few miles before reaching Windsor.

1 Queen Street access off US 17 Bypass at Windsor to Johnson Mill Road (Bertie Co. 1516) access

Difficulty A		**Width** 90–150 ft	
Distance 6.4 mi		**Gradient** 0 ft/mi	
Scenery A (70%), B (30%)		**Map** page 314	

Gauge USGS *Cashie River near Windsor*. Always above minimum. There is a small tidal influence.

Notes The put-in access is a few hundred feet downstream right of the US 17 bridge in Windsor, at the end of Queen Street off US 17 Bypass (Water Street).

A boating access is at the end of Johnson Mill Road. There is a turnaround loop at the ramp.

A channel (mi 0.7) on the left leads to a Wildlife boating access at the end of Elm Street, off US 17/NC 308. It is an alternative put-in.

The channel (mi 1.0) to the left is part of a bend in the river which has been straightened. It rejoins about a quarter-mile downstream.

There are many cypress and tupelo-gum trees along the swampy banks, but there is high ground (mi 2.7) on the right.

In the next 1.5 miles, there are two more loops in the river which have been straightened. Going left takes the shorter route for each loop.

Roquist Creek (mi 4.4) enters on the right.

2 Johnson Mill Road (Bertie Co. 1516) access to Woodard Road (Bertie Co. 1500) access

Difficulty	A	**Width**	100–1,000 ft
Distance	8.2 mi	**Gradient**	0 ft/mi
Scenery	A (50%), B (50%)	**Map**	page 314

Gauge See Section 1. Wind can be a problem because of the width. There is usually little current. Direction of travel can be reversed if the wind is more favorable.

Notes See the previous section about the Johnson Mill Road access.

A Wildlife boating access is at the end of Woodard Road, next to the Sans Souci Ferry station on the southern bank. It is best to park here because there is little parking space on the northern bank, and the ground can be wet when tide and wind raise the water. The free ferry can take two cars per trip. Taking the ferry to run the shuttle saves 9 miles one-way, and provides a unique shuttle experience.

The river continues through swampy land with a few places where high ground borders the river. There are many cypress and tupelo-gum trees, and water lilies are common.

A bay (mi 3.9) on the left has a narrow entrance and can be explored.

The river takes many bends, and an island (mi 6.9) is after a right turn.

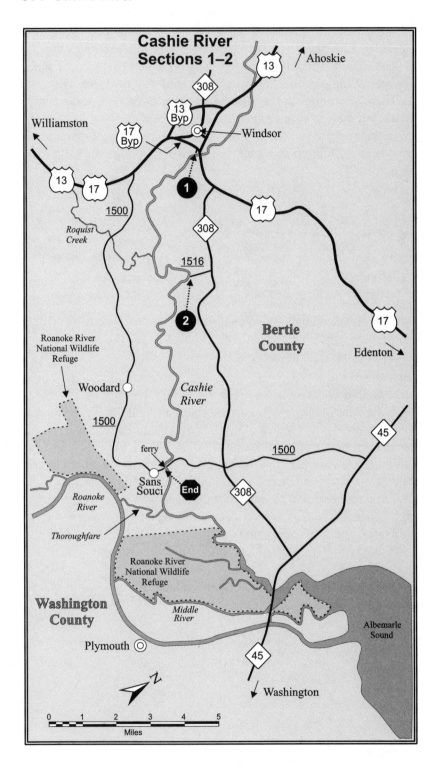

Cashie River
Sections 1–2

Roanoke Basin

Dan River

Counties   Patrick (VA), Stokes, Rockingham, Pittsylvania (VA)

Topos   Meadows of Dan (VA), Claudville, Stuart SE,
Hanging Rock, Danbury, Ayersville, Belews Lake,
Walnut Cove, Ellisboro, Mayodan, Southwest Eden,
Southeast Eden, Northeast Eden, Brosville

The Dan River begins near the Blue Ridge Parkway a few miles above Meadows of Dan, Virginia. It is impounded by Talbott Reservoir and its water used by the Pinnacles Hydroelectric Plant in Kibler Valley to generate electricity for Danville, Virginia, 58 miles east.

The Dan flows into North Carolina and winds its way past Hanging Rock State Park. Below Danbury, it turns northeast and begins its flow toward the Roanoke River. Above Eden, it flows into Virginia and crosses back into North Carolina twice near Danville, before returning to Virginia and meeting John H. Kerr Reservoir (Buggs Island Lake).

The Dan River Trail was formed in the late 1980s. It resulted in the designation of many paddling access areas managed by local government agencies.

The sections below describe 106 miles of paddling on the Dan River from below Pinnacles Hydroelectric Plant to entry into Virginia above Eden.

---

1   Pinnacles Plant access off Kibler Valley Road (VA Patrick Co. 648) to Sawmill Lane (VA Patrick Co. 813) roadside

Difficulty II–III⁻	**Width** 10–50 ft	
Distance 8.3 mi	**Gradient** 32.5 ft/mi	
Scenery A (25%), B (25%), C (50%)	**Map** page 324	

Gauge None. There is sufficient water only when Pinnacles Hydroelectric Plant (276-251-5141) is generating at least 6,000 kilowatts (122 cfs). Avoiding rocks is difficult at this flow. More than 7,500 kilowatts (152 cfs) makes for a clearer run. The maximum generating capacity is 10,500 kilowatts (213 cfs).

The plant releases water when there is a peak power demand in Danville, Virginia. This typically occurs during the week on very hot or cold days. When demand falls, water releases are stopped. Call the plant to find the current status but realize conditions can change quickly. The history of water releases can be seen 29 miles downstream at the USGS gauge *Dan River near Francisco*. Water reaches this gauge about 12 hours after leaving Pinnacles.

Recreational releases are scheduled during July–October for one day of each weekend. The release days alternate between Saturday and Sunday. A recreational release is cancelled if Talbott Reservoir is below 2,520 feet. It is a small reservoir, and dry weather often prevents recreational releases. A race has been held on this section for many years on the last Saturday in July. Water has always been provided for the race event.

Notes Pinnacles Hydroelectric Plant is at the end of Kibler Valley Road. The put-in is inside the plant's fence. Do not drive on the grass, and after unloading boats, park vehicles outside the fence.

At the take-out, there is space for several cars at the side of Sawmill Lane, a few hundred yards from (Virginia) Patrick Co. 773.

The run begins at an elevation of 1,510 feet. Gradient is much greater at the beginning—the first 2 miles drop 58 feet/mile, the next 2 miles at 38 feet/mile, and the last 4 miles only 20 feet/mile. There is no single rapid of great difficulty, but the rapids come quickly in the first part. Because of the speed and narrow channels, strainers are always potential hazards.

Only a few hundred feet from the put-in, a rock splits the channel, and a ledge rapid is just downstream, above the first Kibler Valley Road bridge (mi 0.2).

As the river bends left, rock gardens are in the approach to Basketball Falls (mi 0.4), a ledge of several feet. The most open path at low water is in the center. On the right side, water flows toward the undercut boulder on the bank.

Class I–II rapids continue as the river passes again under Kibler Valley Road (mi 0.6). There are many houses, and people camp near the banks during summer. After passing under Kibler Valley Road (mi 3.3) for the last time, the rapids diminish mainly to Class I with a few Class II rapids.

A field (mi 4.4) on the left is adjacent to the finish line for the races held in July. There are fewer houses downstream, and after passing the (Virginia) Patrick Co. 631 bridge (mi 5.8), there is a small ledge of about 2 feet (mi 7.4).

After the Sawmill Lane bridge (mi 8.2), the take-out is on the right.

2 Sawmill Lane (VA Patrick Co. 813) roadside to Collingstown Road (Stokes Co. 1432) bridge		
Difficulty I–II, and one III	**Width** 30–60 ft	
Distance 14.4 mi	**Gradient** 19.4 ft/mi	
Scenery A (55%), B (45%)	**Map** page 324	

Gauge USGS *Dan River near Francisco.* Minimum is 175 cfs (1.7 ft). The gauge is 21 miles below the put-in. If the water level is falling, a minimum reading at the gauge may be too low at the put-in.

Sufficient water requires rain or Pinnacles Hydroelectric Plant to be generating at least 6,000 kilowatts (122 cfs). Water from the plant takes a few hours to reach the beginning of this section. Since the section is fairly long, releases starting in the afternoon are too late to be useful.

Notes See the previous section about Sawmill Lane.

The take-out is upstream of the Collingstown Road bridge at Jessup Mill. There is little parking space here. Do not block access to the private land.

The rapids in this section are mainly Class I. Often the gradient ahead is obvious but uniform, lacking distinct rapids.

There are several small ledges down to the (Virginia) Patrick Co. 773 bridge (mi 0.5). Rhododendron plants are thick on the banks, and there are clear views of the forested mountains. Downed trees can present a hazard because of the narrow streambed and fast water.

Fall Creek (mi 1.0) enters on the right, where a small waterfall can be seen up the creek.

The (Virginia) Patrick Co. 781 low-water bridge (mi 1.3) requires portage.

Downstream of VA 103 (mi 2.9), a farm's low-water bridge (mi 3.4) must be portaged.

Between (Virginia) Patrick Co. 645 (mi 6.0) and Flippin Road (Stokes Co. 1416) (mi 8.1), the river crosses the Virginia and North Carolina border three times.

Class II rapids are more frequent before a right turn leading to an old bridge (mi 9.5) at Joyce Mill Road (Stokes Co. 1417). Just above the bridge, at the end of the Class II rapids, is Coiled Cobra, a Class III ledge. Scout it because the best route changes depending on water level. The road to the bridge is no longer state-maintained and is on private property. Ask permission to walk into this area.

Jessup Mill Dam (mi 14.2) is 9 feet high. Portage left about 100 feet and lower boats 25 feet down a rocky bank.

3	Collingstown Road (Stokes Co. 1432) bridge to NC 704 Hart access		
Difficulty I–II		**Width** 15–70 ft	
Distance 6.1 mi		**Gradient** 21.3 ft/mi	
Scenery A		**Map** page 324	

Gauge See Section 2. A release from Pinnacles Hydroelectric Plant at Section 1 takes about 12 hours to reach the gauge, upstream left of the take-out.

Notes See the previous section about Collingstown Road.

The NC 704 Hart access is reached from a gravel road meeting NC 704 a few hundred feet from the downstream left side of the bridge. The area is managed by Stokes County.

Few houses or trails to the river are seen on this section. The steep banks, rising over 100 feet above the river, add to the feeling of remoteness in this small gorge.

The section starts with Class I and low Class II rapids. The gradient increases (mi 3.5), and solid Class II rapids become the norm. Following a Class II ledge rapid, two car-size boulders constrict the flow to 15 feet. The gradient of the next 2 miles is 30 feet/mile.

4	NC 704 Hart access to Moore's Springs Campground access off Moore's Springs Road (Stokes Co. 1001)		
Difficulty I, and one II		**Width** 55–70 ft	
Distance 8.5 mi		**Gradient** 11.5 ft/mi	
Scenery A		**Map** page 324	

Gauge USGS *Dan River near Francisco*. Minimum is 125 cfs (1.5 ft).

Notes See the previous section about the NC 704 Hart access.

Moore's Springs Campground is at 2568 Moore's Springs Road. The property is owned by North Carolina State University and is part of the Sertoma 4-H campground and conference center. Camping is open to the public at $10 per site. For registered campers, boat access is allowed via the creek bank, between sites 17–18. Inspect the creek mouth so the take-out will not be missed. For campground information, call 336-593-8290 or see: http://campsertoma.org/

Hanging Rock Outdoor Center is on Moore's Springs Road, a quarter-mile from the Hanging Rock State Park entrance. They rent boats, run shuttles, and have permission to use the Moore's Springs Campground access. Reservations are required (336-593-8283).

As in the previous section, few houses or trails are seen, but the gradient is less. Most of the Class I rapids are widely spaced gravel bars.

Several rock islands (mi 5.4) make a few Class I rapids and a Class II rapid.

Access is difficult at the NC 89 bridge (mi 6.5). Upstream left was the old Whitt's Store access for the Dan River Trail, but it is now private.

Big Creek (mi 6.8) enters from the right.

After Double Creek (mi 7.8) joins from the right, the river makes a left turn (mi 8.3), and Moore's Springs Campground (mi 8.5) is on the right bank, where a small creek (the take-out) enters.

5 Moore's Springs Campground access to Hanging Rock access on Flinchum Road (Stokes Co. 1487)

Difficulty I–II		**Width** 60–80 ft	
Distance 4.3 mi		**Gradient** 6.7 ft/mi	
Scenery A (50%), B (50%)		**Map** page 325	

Gauge See Section 4.

Notes See the previous section about the Moore's Springs Campground access.

The Hanging Rock access, managed by Hanging Rock State Park, is at the end of Flinchum Road.

Dan River Shores (mi 1.9) has many houses on the left bank for the next half-mile. There are steep rock walls on the right and many rhododendrons.

A small part of Hanging Rock State Park land (mi 2.8) extends over the left bank.

6 Hanging Rock access on Flinchum Road (Stokes Co. 1487) to Moratock Park access at Danbury

Difficulty I–II		**Width** 50–90 ft	
Distance 5.1 mi		**Gradient** 4.5 ft/mi	
Scenery A (65%), B (35%)		**Map** page 325	

Gauge See Section 4.

Notes See the previous section about the Hanging Rock access.

To reach Moratock Park from NC 89 in Danbury, take Sheppard Mill Road (Stokes Co. 1674) east a few hundred feet to cross the Dan River. Bear right into Moratock Park to the boat access steps.

In the summer, especially weekends, this section is extremely popular with people floating in inner tubes, and near Moratock Park is especially crowded.

The river passes under NC 89 (mi 0.6) and the one-lane steel bridge (mi 3.0) of Seven Island Road (Stokes Co. 1668).

Just before the Sheppard Mill Road bridge (mi 5.1) is a Class I–II rapid, depending on water level. Moratock Park is on the left bank. The take-out steps are around the bend on the left.

The stonework of Moratock Furnace, built in 1843 for iron making, is still standing in the park.

7 Moratock Park access at Danbury to Power House Road (Stokes Co. 1732) access at Hemlock Golf Course		
Difficulty I–II	**Width** 70–100 ft	
Distance 9.1 mi	**Gradient** 6.6 ft/mi	
Scenery A (80%), B (20%)	**Map** page 325	

Gauge USGS *Dan River near Francisco.* Minimum is 100 cfs (1.4 ft).

Notes See the previous section about the Moratock Park access.

The access at Power House Road is adjacent to Hemlock Golf Course and is managed by Stokes County.

The rapids are mostly Class I down to where Snow Creek (mi 3.8) enters on the left.

Dodgetown Road (Stokes Co. 1695) (mi 4.0) can be used for access. There are several Class II ledges downstream.

A rock face rises over 100 feet on the left where the river takes a right bend (mi 6.1).

A Class II rapid is created by the remains of an old dam (mi 9.0). The access ramp is just downstream right.

8 Power House Road (Stokes Co. 1732) access at Hemlock Golf Course to Pine Hall Road (Stokes Co. 1908) bridge		
Difficulty I–II	**Width** 60–150 ft	
Distance 8.8 mi	**Gradient** 5.9 ft/mi	
Scenery A	**Map** page 325	

Gauge See Section 7.

Notes See the previous section about the Power House Road access.

At the take-out, there is not a clear path from the Pine Hall Road bridge to the river. Some bushwhacking is necessary.

A pedestrian bridge (mi 0.1) spans the river, and Hemlock Golf Course is on the right.

A large island (mi 1.4) extends downriver for 0.3 miles. There are Class II rapids on either side of the island, but the left side is preferred when water is low.

Below the island to the take-out, the river is flatter with only a few Class I rapids. There is little development on the banks but many tires in the river. It appears hundreds of tires were dumped into the river upstream, and they continue to be seen in the next few sections.

After the US 311 (mi 3.8) bridge, Town Fork Creek (mi 6.1) enters on the right, as the river makes a large horseshoe bend.

9	Pine Hall Road (Stokes Co. 1908) bridge to NC 704 access at Madison		
Difficulty I, and one II		**Width** 50–100 ft	
Distance 10.1 mi		**Gradient** 3.3 ft/mi	
Scenery A (60%), B (40%)		**Map** page 325	

Gauge USGS *Dan River near Wentworth.* Estimated minimum is 150 cfs (0.7 ft).

Notes See the previous section about Pine Hall Road.

The NC 704 access at Madison is almost under the NC 704 bridge, but it is reached via East Murphy Street and Water Street. There are Dan River Trail signs on NC 704 in Madison leading to the access. It is managed by the Madison-Mayodan Parks and Recreation Department.

A sand mining company is on the left bank at the put-in.

A few Class I ledges occur until the beginning of backwater (mi 6.0) from the downstream dam.

The dam (mi 7.2) at Pine Hall Brick Company should be portaged on the right. A trail begins 200 feet before the dam and leads to a ramp below the dam. This access is managed by Madison-Mayodan Parks and Recreation Department and can be used to divide this section into 7.2 and 2.9-mile sections. The access is reached from Lindsay Bridge Road (Rockingham Co. 1138), which crosses the river a few hundred feet below the dam.

At low flows, a Class II rapid (mi 8.2) extends for 75 feet and requires maneuvering, but it is only waves at higher flows.

---

10 NC 704 access at Madison to Settle Bridge access off Dan River Road (Rockingham Co. 2149)

Difficulty I	**Width** 50–180 ft
Distance 8.7 mi	**Gradient** 2.3 ft/mi
Scenery A	**Map** page 326

Gauge See Section 9.

Notes See the previous section about the NC 704 access.

The Settle Bridge access is reached from Settle Bridge Road (Rockingham Co. 2145) by taking unpaved Dan River Road to the access parking area.

The Mayo River (mi 0.4) enters on the left.

A long curve leads to the US 220 bridge (mi 1.2), where large rocks under the bridge create a Class I rapid.

A wing dam is similar to a low dam with an open center section. Its purpose is to keep the water level high in mid-river for boats. Old broken wing dams (mi 1.7) from the 1800s form a series of Class I rapids in the center of the river, extending downstream about 100 yards. The remains of timbers with metal spikes are to the sides.

There are a few more Class I rapids before going under the Settle Bridge. The take-out is downstream right. Steps lead to the parking lot, about 60 feet above the river.

---

11 Settle Bridge access to Bethlehem Church Road (Rockingham Co. 2039) access near Eden

Difficulty I	**Width** 75–200 ft
Distance 11.3 mi	**Gradient** 2.6 ft/mi
Scenery A (80%), B (20%)	**Map** page 326

Gauge See Section 9.

Notes See the previous section about the Settle Bridge access.

A Wildlife boating access is off Bethlehem Church Road. Traveling north on NC 14 toward Eden, turn left on NC 87/770 (Harrington Highway) before crossing the river. Go 0.6 miles and turn right on Bethlehem Church Road. Go 0.5 miles to the access on the right.

The rapids in this section are formed by small half-foot ledges and gravel bars.

An island (mi 1.6) runs for a quarter-mile, and there are several small ledges on the right side.

Buffalo Creek enters just above the NC 770 bridge (mi 8.0).

Eden is on the left before the Hamilton Street (Rockingham Co. 2282) bridge (mi 10.0), where an access area is planned to be completed during 2003.

The Smith River (mi 10.8) joins on the left, and the backwater of the dam in the next section is entered before reaching the take-out.

12	Bethlehem Church Road (Rockingham Co. 2039) access to Berry Hill Bridge Road (VA Pittsylvania Co. 880) bridge	
Difficulty I		**Width** 100–200 ft
Distance 11.2 mi		**Gradient** 2.3 ft/mi
Scenery A (65%), B (35%)		**Map** page 326

Gauge USGS *Dan River near Wentworth*. Always above minimum.

The Smith River joins at the end of this section. Its flow fluctuates from power generation upstream. See USGS *Smith River at Eden*.

Notes See the previous section about the Bethlehem Church Road access.

The take-out bridge is on the North Carolina and Virginia border. It is Berry Hill Bridge Road (Rockingham Co.1761) on the right and (Virginia) Pittsylvania Co. 880 on the left. The left bank is covered in kudzu, and the right bank is steeper. Park away from the bridge where the road shoulders are wider.

The section starts in the backwater of the dam downstream. After passing under Mebane Bridge Road (Rockingham Co. 1964) (mi 0.3) and NC 14/87/770 (mi 0.9), Duke Power's dam (mi 2.1) is after a right bend. A portage trail is on the right.

A Class I rapid is under the NC 700 bridge (mi 4.7). There are a few more small ledge rapids before reaching the take-out.

■

It was kind of solemn, drifting down the big, still river, laying on our backs looking up at the stars, and we didn't ever feel like talking loud, and it warn't often that we laughed—only a little kind of a low chuckle.

Mark Twain, *Adventures of Huckleberry Finn* (1884)

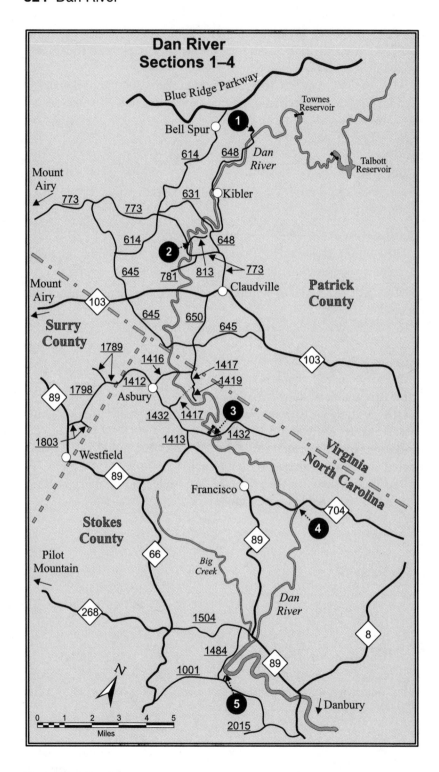

Roanoke Basin

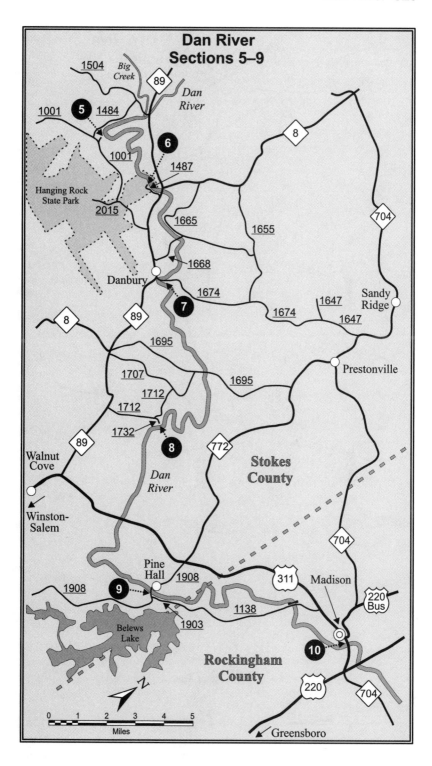

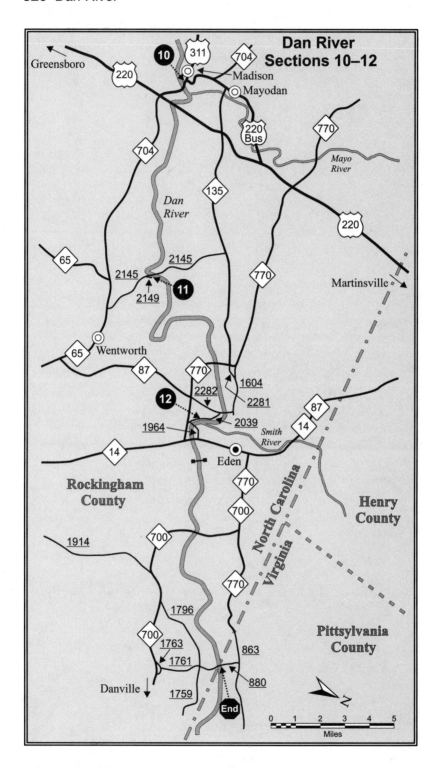

**Dan River
Sections 10–12**

Greensboro

220

10 311

704

Madison

Mayodan

704

220
Bus

770

Mayo
River

135

*Dan
River*

220

65

2145

2145

2149

11

770

Martinsville

65 Wentworth

87

770

1604

2282

2281

12

87

1964

2039

14

*Smith
River*

14

Eden

**Rockingham
County**

770

700

14

1914

700

770

North Carolina

Virginia

**Henry
County**

1796

700

1763

1761

Danville

1759

863

880

End

**Pittsylvania
County**

0 1 2 3 4 5

N

Miles

Roanoke Basin

Gardner Creek

County   Martin

Topo   Jamesville

Gardner Creek is a blackwater stream draining Martin County below Jamesville and emptying into Devil's Gut. The creek is popular with fishermen because it offers easy access to Devil's Gut.

For paddlers, Gardner Creek offers the most direct route to the first two camping platforms built by Roanoke River Partners. The wooden decks (20 by 20 or 28 by 16 feet) are built on creeks running into Devil's Gut. They provide an unusual camping experience in the heart of a cypress and tupelo-gum canopied swamp. There are no roofs over the platforms, but 8-foot posts with eyebolts allow for lashing of tarps or other equipment. No fires are permitted. A portable toilet is provided when picking up a permit.

The fee is $10 per person with a $20 minimum and $50 maximum. Fees are paid and permits picked up at Roberson's Marina (252-792-3583), at the Gardner Creek put-in. For reservations, call 252-794-6501. For more information, see: http://roanokeriverpartners.org/

Two additional platforms have been completed off the lower Roanoke, and more are expected during 2003. A total of ten platforms are planned for rivers and creeks in the lower Roanoke area (Hamilton to the sound) as part of the Roanoke River Canoe Trail. Roanoke River Partners also plans to have campsites in the upper Roanoke. The goal is to have about twenty-five sites from Roanoke Rapids to the sound. See the above Web page for the latest status.

The route described below is from Gardner Creek to Devil's Gut, then east to the Roanoke River and on to Jamesville. An option that eliminates a shuttle is to explore Devil's Gut and return to the put-in on Gardner Creek.

1 US 64 access at Gardner Creek to Stewart Street access at Jamesville via Devil's Gut and Roanoke River	
Difficulty A	**Width** 70–400 ft
Distance 8.0 mi	**Gradient** 0 ft/mi
Scenery A	**Map** page 329

Gauge USGS *Roanoke River at Williamston* and *Roanoke River at Jamesville*. Always above minimum. There is no gauge on Gardner Creek.

Notes Roberson's Marina has a ramp near the US 64 bridge over Gardner Creek. The fee is $3 per boat.

To reach the Jamesville access from US 64, take NC 117 (Andrews Street) into Jamesville. Turn right at Water Street and left at Stewart Street. The ramp is next to the Cypress Grill restaurant.

Gardner Creek's banks are swampy. The channel is wide enough to be free of downed trees. Where it meets Devil's Gut (mi 3.6), a sign marks Devil's Gut, Gardner Creek, and points to the right for the direction to Jamesville.

After turning right and paddling down Devil's Gut, Upper Deadwater Creek (mi 4.2) enters on the left at a back angle. Beaver Lodge platform is 0.4 miles up this creek. To visit the platform, follow the trail markers and bear left where the creek narrows and splits into two channels.

Continuing down Devil's Gut, Lower Deadwater Creek (mi 5.5) enters from the left. Barred Owl Roost platform is 0.7 miles up this creek.

Devil's Gut joins the Roanoke (mi 6.5).

After a right bend (mi 7.4), the high banks of Jamesville can be seen.

■

Thoreau loved a swamp, and so do all lovers of nature, for nowhere else does she so bountifully show her vigorous powers of growth, her varied wealth of botanical wonders. Here the birds resort in flocks when weary of the hot, sandy uplands, for here they find pure water, cool shade, and many a curious glossy berry for their dainty appetites.

—N.H. Bishop, *Voyage of the Paper Canoe* (1878)

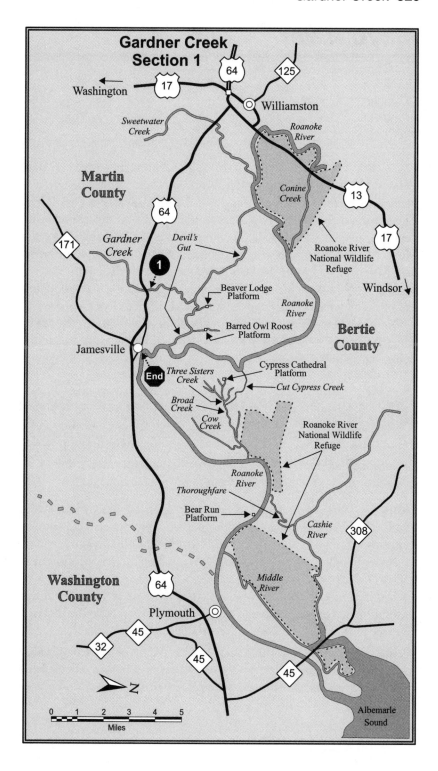

Gardner Creek
Section 1

Washington

Sweetwater
Creek

**Martin
County**

Gardner
Creek

Devil's
Gut

Beaver Lodge
Platform

Barred Owl Roost
Platform

Jamesville

Three Sisters
Creek

Cypress Cathedral
Platform

Cut Cypress Creek

Broad
Creek

Cow
Creek

Roanoke
River

Roanoke
River

Roanoke
River

Conine
Creek

Roanoke River
National Wildlife
Refuge

Windsor

**Bertie
County**

Roanoke River
National Wildlife
Refuge

Thoroughfare

Bear Run
Platform

Cashie
River

**Washington
County**

Middle
River

Plymouth

Albemarle
Sound

Miles

Williamston

Mayo River

Counties   Henry (VA), Rockingham

Topos   Price, Mayodan

The North Mayo River watershed begins below Fairy Stone State Park, northwest of Martinsville, Virginia. The South Mayo River watershed begins northwest of Stuart, Virginia near the Dan River. The North and South Mayo Rivers flow into North Carolina and join near the state border, about 30 miles north of Greensboro. As the Mayo River flows south, it is impounded by two hydroelectric dams near Mayodan and joins the Dan River just east of Madison.

The Rockingham County Watershed Preservation Coalition has established two access areas near Anglin Mill Road (Rockingham Co. 1358), a popular whitewater part of the river. A subgroup, the Mayo River Association, is working toward a goal of making this area into a public park.

 Moores Mill Rd. (VA Henry Co. 629) bridge on North Mayo to Old Anglin Loop Rd. (Rockingham Co. 1385) access

Difficulty I–II	**Width** 25–100 ft
Distance 3.0 mi	**Gradient** 15.3 ft/mi
Scenery A	**Map** page 335

Gauge USGS *North Mayo River near Spencer, VA*. Minimum is 65 cfs (1.6 ft). This gauge is at the put-in. There is also a paddling gauge on a bridge support at the put-in, where minimum is 0 feet.

Near the take-out is USGS *Mayo River near Price*. Minimum is 150 cfs (1.2 ft).

USGS *South Mayo River near Nettleridge, VA* is 15 miles above the confluence of the North and South Mayo Rivers. It can be used for advance notice of water coming down the South Mayo.

Notes There is little parking space at the Moores Mill Road bridge over the North Mayo. Put in on downstream left using the bridge right-of-way rather than entering the private drive.

The Old Anglin Loop Road access is under the Anglin Mill Road (Rockingham Co. 1358) bridge. From the Anglin Mill Road bridge, go 0.8 miles east, and turn right on Old Anglin Loop Road. Go 0.7 miles and where Mayo Beach Road (Rockingham Co. 1359) comes in from the left, bear right on Old Anglin Loop Road. The access is 0.4 miles ahead at the road's end. This last 0.4 miles of Old Anglin Loop Road is known to many locals as part of Mayo Beach Road. The access is managed by the Madison-Mayodan Recreation Department.

Class I rock gardens and a Class II ledge precede Cowpasture Rapid (mi 0.7). At low water, it is usually run near the left bank over a sloping drop of a few feet and around the backside of a 5-foot high boulder.

The Lunchstop Rapid (mi 2.3) ledge can be scouted from sloping rocks on the left bank.

The South Mayo River (mi 2.6) enters on the right. A few hundred yards downstream, many ledges spanning the river can be seen upstream of the bridge at the take-out. There are many different paths and at least three of these ledges offer Class II rapids.

2	Old Anglin Loop Road (Rockingham Co. 1385) access to Mayo Beach Road (Rockingham Co. 1359) access		
Difficulty I–II, and one III		**Width** 90–100 ft	
Distance 1.1 mi		**Gradient** 13.6 ft/mi	
Scenery A		**Map** page 335	

Gauge See Section 1.

Notes See the previous section about the Old Anglin Loop Road access.

The Mayo Beach Road access is at the southern (downstream) end of the road. It is managed by the Madison-Mayodan Recreation Department.

Boiling Hole (mi 0.3), a 3-foot drop close to the left bank, can be scouted from the road before putting in. It is a popular surfing area.

A Class III rapid is at ledges 150 feet below Boiling Hole. At low flows, a traditional route is to start on the left, drop over a couple of small ledges, and turn right to follow a flow of water moving across a ledge and toward the right bank. Near the right bank, a sharp left turn is required to run the flow going downstream. There is a large rock to miss at the bottom. It is also possible to start on the right side of this rapid and work into the same final outflow.

The large sandy beach (mi 0.4) on the left is known as Mayo Beach. It was a take-out many years ago, but it was also a popular party spot. Problems developed, and the area has been posted.

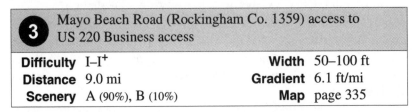

3 Mayo Beach Road (Rockingham Co. 1359) access to US 220 Business access

Difficulty I–I⁺	**Width**	50–100 ft
Distance 9.0 mi	**Gradient**	6.1 ft/mi
Scenery A (90%), B (10%)	**Map**	page 335

Gauge USGS *Mayo River near Price*. Minimum is 175 cfs (1.4 ft).

Notes See the previous section about the Mayo Beach Road access.

The US 220 Business access is upstream left of the bridge.

At low water, there are about 20 Class I–I⁺ rapids scattered down this section. A few hills close to the bank rise over 100 feet and are covered with rhododendron.

The NC 770 bridge (mi 5.6) can be used as a take-out on the left side.

There are few houses until the last mile, where there are several houses and a sand mining operation.

The backwater of the Avalon Dam in the next section starts near the take-out.

4 US 220 Business access to Dan Valley Road (Rockingham Co. 2177) bridge at Madison

Difficulty I–II, and one III	**Width**	60–200 ft
Distance 5.0 mi	**Gradient**	17.0 ft/mi
Scenery B	**Map**	page 335

Gauge USGS *Mayo River near Price*. Estimated minimum is 600 cfs (2.3 ft).

Power is generated at the Avalon and Mayo Dams by taking water from behind the dam and returning it about a half-mile downstream. The river channel between the dam and the water return is called the *bypass reach*. Only 75 cfs is required to be released from the dam into the bypass reach to support aquatic life. Paddling in the bypass reach needs an estimated minimum of 200 cfs. Since the hydroelectric plant can use up to about 400 cfs to generate power, at least 600 cfs must flow upstream of the dam to have sufficient paddling water in the bypass reach when power is being generated.

Flow in the river's bypass reach can change quickly. If maintenance requires stopping or reducing flow into the generators, flow will increase in the bypass reach.

Notes A boating access is at the US 220 Business bridge, upstream left.

The take-out at the Dan Valley Road bridge has steep, brushy banks. A more civilized take-out can be reached by continuing 0.2 miles to the Dan River, then 0.4 miles upstream to the NC 704 access in Madison. See the Dan River, Section 10 (page 322). Check the current on the Dan because this requires paddling upstream.

To reach the NC 704 access from the Dan Valley Road bridge, go south on Dan Valley Road for 0.4 miles. It becomes Water Street in Madison, and the access is 0.2 miles straight ahead.

At a right turn (mi 0.3), the left bank is very steep over the next 1.5 miles. Rocky bluffs rise to 400 feet above the river at Cedder Mountain, left of Avalon Dam (mi 1.2).

Portage the 25-foot Avalon Dam on the left. Use caution on the portage. It is short but over steep rocks. A rope is useful for lowering boats.

The downstream vista of a half-mile shows a dramatic change in the river's character. It is up to 200 feet wide with Class I–II rock gardens and 2-foot ledges before a right turn, where water used in the hydroelectric plant is returned to the river on the right (mi 1.8).

US 220 Business (mi 2.2) is just off the right bank, and the city limits of Mayodan begin near the 15-foot Mayo Dam (mi 2.9).

Portage the Mayo Dam on the left. Use caution because it is over steep rock. There is also a bypass reach of about a half-mile below this dam, and water conditions are similar to those below the previous dam.

Scout the Class III ledge (mi 3.1). It is a 4 or 5-foot drop, but on the right side it decreases to a 3-foot drop followed by a 1-foot drop. A few Class II rapids are downstream of the ledge, and Class I rapids are downstream of the NC 135 bridge (mi 3.7).

■

You done taken a wrong turn somewhere. This-here river don't go nowhere near Aintry.

— James Dickey, *Deliverance* (1970)

Roanoke Basin

Mack Whitaker at Boiling Hole Rapid
Mayo River, Section 2

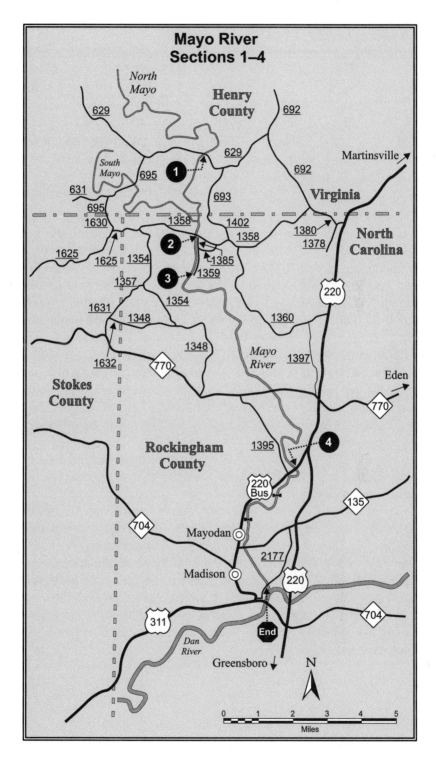

Mayo River
Sections 1–4

North
Mayo

Henry
County

629   692

South
Mayo   629

695   692   Martinsville

631   Virginia

695   693

1630   1358   1402   1380   North
1358   1378   Carolina

1625

1625 1354   1385

1357   1359

1354   220

1631

1348

1348   1360

1632   Mayo
770   River   1397

Stokes   Eden
County   770

Rockingham   1395   4
County

220
Bus   135

704   1395

Mayodan   2177

Madison   220

311   704

Dan
River   End

Greensboro   N

0   1   2   3   4   5
Miles

Roanoke Basin

Roanoke River

Counties   Northampton, Halifax, Bertie, Martin, Washington

Topos   Roanoke Rapids, Weldon, Halifax, Boones Crossroads,
Scotland Neck, Norfleet, Palmyra, Woodville, Hamilton,
Quitsna, Williamston, Windsor South, Jamesville,
Plymouth West, Woodard

The Roanoke River begins in the Blue Ridge Mountains of north-western Virginia. It is known as the Staunton River for the last 85 miles in Virginia. Near the Virginia and North Carolina border, it is impounded in three back-to-back lakes: Kerr Reservoir, Lake Gaston, and Roanoke Rapids Lake. Flow in the river below Roanoke Rapids Lake is regulated by a hydroelectric project. Flow is usually 2,000–14,000 cfs but can go as high as 20,000 cfs depending on power needs.

Upstream of Roanoke Rapids, the Roanoke River drains almost 8,400 square miles. It provides whitewater before flowing over the Fall Line and entering the Coastal Plain below Weldon. Downstream, there is little development and only four bridges as it flows past Halifax, Hamilton, Williamston, Jamesville, and Plymouth before reaching Albemarle Sound.

The Nature Conservancy has designated the lower Roanoke as one of the "Last Great Places," making it one of only two hundred sites so designated in all of the Americas and parts of Asia, and the Pacific.

A paddling trip from Roanoke Rapids to Plymouth covers 124 miles. Because there are large distances between access points, some of the river sections are usually paddled as campers. Between Hamilton and Williamston, camping is allowed on the state-owned Roanoke River Wetlands. Below Williamston, there are platforms located in side creeks and channels, which can be reserved for overnight stays. Plans call for a total of about twenty-five sites from Roanoke Rapids to Albemarle Sound. For additional information, see Gardner Creek (page 327).

1 NC 48 access at Gaston to US 301 access at Weldon	

Difficulty I–II, and one III		**Width** 150–600 ft	
Distance 5.7 mi		**Gradient** 1.8 ft/mi	
Scenery A (65%), C (35%)		**Map** page 344	

Gauge USGS *Roanoke River at Roanoke Rapids.* Always above minimum. At levels above 6,000 cfs (5.0 ft), the usual rapids wash out, but there are waves to surf. Flow is controlled by the hydroelectric project at Roanoke Rapids. Depending upon power needs, flow varies from 2,000–20,000 cfs (3–9 ft). Drought and flood conditions can cause flows outside this range. The projected release schedule is available at: http://dom.com/about/companies/ncpower/flow.jsp

From April 1–June 15, flow is regulated for rockfish (striped bass) coming from the ocean to spawn in fresh water. During this season target flows are 5,300–8,500 cfs but can range from 4,000–13,700 cfs.

A prime paddling attraction of this section is Weldon Falls Rapid, upstream of the take-out. Many paddlers go to the take-out access area just to play in the waves. The rapid is usually a Class III at 2,000–4,000 cfs, but instantaneous water flow does not tell the whole story. As flow increases, the main river channel below Weldon Falls slowly rises, reducing the drop at the rapid. If high flow lasts long enough, the rapid disappears. When the water release is reduced to minimum flow, it may take almost a day before the drop at Weldon Falls is restored.

High electric power demands results in higher water releases. When Weldon Falls Rapid is exposed, a 10,000 cfs release causes powerful waves and holes until the pool below rises and washes out the rapid. Paddlers take advantage of these conditions, but it requires the skills to handle big-water.

As part of relicensing of the dam at Roanoke Rapids, paddlers have requested that Dominion Generation provide the public a means to know the condition of Weldon Falls by either continuing to fund the USGS *Roanoke River at Halifax* gauge or by providing a Web-cam view of the rapid.

At the Halifax gauge, a level of about 18 feet indicates Weldon Falls has its maximum drop, and at 23 feet it is washed out.

Notes A Wildlife boating access is at NC 48.

At Weldon a Wildlife boating access is downstream right of the US 301/158 bridge. Turn into the drive where there is a sign for River Falls Park at Weldon Landing.

At the put-in, a cardboard recycling plant is on the right, and the big smokestacks and buildings of the Champion plant can be seen downstream. The river is wide and flat here. Depending on the wind, there may be an industrial aroma from the plant.

The USGS gauge *Roanoke River at Roanoke Rapids* (mi 1.8) is on the right bank near houses. Downstream, large islands divide the river into channels. Little development is seen from here to the take-out. Although there are cities and industry using the river, there are many mussel shells scattered on the rocks. Eagles, osprey, and heron are sometimes spotted.

After going under I-95 (mi 2.9), the center channel has a Class II rapid called the S's (mi 3.6). At higher water levels (above 5,000 cfs), a whirlpool forms, and slots between large rocks can be paddled. Going down the right channel after I-95 misses the S's rapid and goes by a wastewater treatment plant.

Just beyond the Weldon US 301/158 bridge (mi 5.5), within a few hundred feet of the take-out is Weldon Falls, a river-wide rapid providing a drop of 6–7 feet in stages. The right slot is the most narrow and steepest drop. The break toward the center is wide and offers several options. Paddlers often spend hours surfing this area. It is one of the rare rivers in the eastern part of the state offering a play spot during dry weather.

Striped bass fishing season, March 15–April 30, in the upper Roanoke brings many fishermen to Weldon Falls.

2 US 301 access at Weldon to US 258 access near Scotland Neck

Difficulty A–C		**Width** 125–150 ft	
Distance 28.3 mi		**Gradient** 1.0 ft/mi	
Scenery A (95%), B (5%)		**Map** page 344	

Gauge USGS *Roanoke River at Roanoke Rapids* and *Roanoke River near Scotland Neck*. Always above minimum. Water levels can rise or drop over 20 feet depending on power generation or flood control requirements at Roanoke Rapids.

Notes See the previous section about the US 301 Weldon access.

A Wildlife boating access is at US 258 near Scotland Neck.

There are no bridges or public roads in this section. Because of the distance, it is usually done as a camper. At low water, there are sandbars, but it is best not to camp on them. Water could rise from a dam release. Dry camping is available on the banks, 25–35 feet above the riverbed.

On a trip down this section, several bald eagles were spotted. Eagles are often seen on the Roanoke River.

Few houses are seen except at Halifax (mi 9.3), where there is no public access. A local fishing club owns the only drive coming to the river.

Do not pick up hitchhikers on the river—Caledonia State Prison Farm (mi 16.1) is on the right bank for the next few miles. Few buildings can be seen from the river, but cattle come down the banks. Odom State Prison Farm (mi 18.9) is on the left bank.

3	US 258 access near Scotland Neck to Main Street access at Hamilton		
Difficulty A–C		**Width** 100–175 ft	
Distance 38.1 mi		**Gradient** 0.2 ft/mi	
Scenery A		**Map** page 345	

Gauge USGS *Roanoke River near Scotland Neck* and *Roanoke River at Hamilton*. Always above minimum. Water levels can rise or drop over 20 feet depending on power generation or flood control requirements at Roanoke Rapids.

Notes See the previous section about the US 258 access.

The Wildlife boating access in Hamilton is reached by turning from Front Street (NC 903) onto Main Street. The ramp is at the end of Main Street.

This is another long section requiring camping. It can be combined with the previous section for a more extended trip. At low water, there are sandbars, but it is best not to camp on them. Water could rise from a dam release. The banks are generally 10–25 feet high, with some higher bluffs.

The Boone Tract (mi 0.7) of Roanoke River Wetlands Game Lands is on the left bank and extends down the left bank for about 0.6 miles. Small signs on trees identify this area. Camping is allowed on this land within 100 yards of the river.

The river passes under an old railroad bridge (mi 8.3) with a center swing section, which was turned parallel to the river to allow large boats to pass.

The Urquhart Tract (mi 14.2) of Roanoke River Wetlands Game Lands is on the right bank and extends down the right bank for over 4 miles. It is in a large river loop that is called Buzzard Point on the topo map. There are signs, and camping is allowed within 100 yards of the river.

Parking near the river is difficult at the NC 11/42 bridge (mi 30.3), where there are long guardrails and many no-parking signs.

The Beech House Tract (mi 33.8) of Roanoke River Wetlands Game Lands is on the right bank and extends for 2 miles downstream. There are signs, and camping is allowed within 100 yards of the river.

The left bank becomes part of the Roanoke River National Wildlife Refuge (mi 33.8), where camping is not allowed. Hiking is allowed except during hunting season. The refuge borders much of the left bank in several tracts down to Plymouth.

4	Main Street access at Hamilton to Grabtown Road (Bertie Co. 1100) access		
Difficulty A–C		**Width** 170–200 ft	
Distance 13.5 mi		**Gradient** 0.2 ft/mi	
Scenery A (85%), B (15%)		**Map** page 346	

Gauge USGS *Roanoke River at Hamilton*. Always above minimum. Water levels can rise or drop over 15 feet depending on power generation or flood control requirements at Roanoke Rapids.

Notes See the previous section about the Hamilton access.

A boat ramp is at the end of Grabtown Road.

The banks are generally 10–20 feet high with some higher bluffs.

The only dwellings seen in this section are cabins (mi 1.4), part of Rainbow Hunt Club.

Steps and a trail (mi 4.4) on the right bank lead 0.4 miles to Fort Branch, a well-preserved Confederate star-shaped, earthen fort. It was built on Rainbow Banks, a 70-foot bluff, to protect the upper Roanoke River Valley. The fort's cannons were recovered from the river bottom. Paddlers are welcome to hike to the fort during daylight hours. The museum and bathroom facilities are only open Saturday–Sunday, 1:30–5:30 P.M., April–first weekend in November. For more information, see: http://fortbranchcivilwarsite.com/

Most of the left bank is part of Roanoke River National Wildlife Refuge where camping is not allowed. Hiking is permitted except during hunting season.

After passing power lines (mi 8.3), the Deveraux Tract (mi 9.3) of Roanoke River Wetlands Game Lands is on the right bank and extends down most of the right bank to Williamston. Signs on trees identify this area, and camping is allowed within 100 yards of the river.

5	Grabtown Road (Bertie Co. 1100) access to US 13/17 access at Williamston		
Difficulty A–C		**Width**	150–300 ft
Distance 9.1 mi		**Gradient**	0 ft/mi
Scenery A		**Map**	page 346

Gauge USGS *Roanoke River at Hamilton* and *Roanoke River at Williamston*. Always above minimum. Water levels can rise or drop over 10 feet depending on power generation or flood control requirements at Roanoke Rapids.

Notes See the previous section about the Grabtown Road access.

A Wildlife boating access is upstream right of the US 13/17 bridge. Going north on US 13/17, before going over the bridge, turn left on US 17 Business, go 50 feet and take the first right. The access area is straight ahead.

The Deveraux Tract of the Roanoke River Wetlands Game Lands continues down the right bank to Williamston, and a Roanoke River National Wildlife Refuge tract is on the left bank in the second half of this section. See the previous section for rules governing use of these lands.

Conine Creek (mi 4.9) is on the left, where the river comes within 500 feet of US 13/17. When water is high enough, this creek can be used to travel to the Roanoke, almost 6 miles downstream of Williamston. It is narrow and likely to have downed trees.

Conoho Creek (mi 7.7) enters from the right. Fishing boats are often seen at the mouth.

The banks are generally 5–10 feet high at low water levels.

6	US 13/17 access at Williamston to Stewart Street access at Jamesville		
Difficulty A		**Width** 250–300 ft	
Distance 17.2 mi		**Gradient** 0 ft/mi	
Scenery A (75%), B (25%)		**Map** page 347	

Gauge USGS *Roanoke River at Williamston* and *Roanoke River at Jamesville*. Always above minimum. Water levels can rise or drop over 7 feet depending on power generation or flood control requirements at Roanoke Rapids.

There is a small tidal influence in this section when water is low. Wind can be a problem.

Notes See the previous section about the US 13/17 access.

From US 64 take NC 117 (Andrews Street) into Jamesville. Turn right at Water Street and left at Stewart Street. The ramp is next to the Cypress Grill restaurant.

Sweetwater Creek (mi 2.0) joins from the right, followed by the entrance to Devil's Gut (mi 2.9) on the right. Devil's Gut cuts across a large loop of the Roanoke River and can be paddled instead of the loop, making this section 12.7 instead of 17.2 miles. Devil's Gut is described under Sweetwater Creek (page 348). Subtract 2.1 miles from the mileage given in the Devil's Gut description to correct for distances from the Williamston access.

Conine Creek (mi 5.7) joins on the left, and Spellers Creek (mi 6.9) is on the right.

Remains of narrow gauge railroad tracks, used in past logging operations, can be seen at several places on the banks.

Cut Cypress Creek (mi 11.9) is on the left. It leads to Broad Creek and Three Sisters Creek. It can be used as a route to Cypress Cathedral camping platform. It is 1.7 miles to Broad Creek and an additional 0.8 miles to the platform on Three Sisters Creek. See Gardner Creek (page 327) for platform details and reservations.

The exit of Devil's Gut (mi 15.7) is on the right, and after a right bend, the 40-foot banks and houses of Jamesville can be seen.

7 Stewart Street access at Jamesville to Water Street access at Plymouth

Difficulty	A	**Width**	200–1,000 ft
Distance	12.4 mi	**Gradient**	0 ft/mi
Scenery	A (80%), C (20%)	**Map**	page 347

Gauge USGS *Roanoke River at Jamesville*. Always above minimum. Water levels only vary about 2 feet in this section because low banks below Williamston create a vast flood plain. There is a small tidal influence in this section when water is low. Wind can be a problem, and a northeast wind is a head wind most of the way.

Notes See the previous section about the Jamesville access.

At Plymouth, a boat ramp is just downstream of the police station. From US 64, take Washington Street into the historic district. Turn right at Water Street and go one block. Adams Street is on the right, and the police station is on the left, next to the access parking lot.

For most of this section, little development is seen. Bald eagles and osprey are frequently seen. Motorboats are also common in these fishing waters.

The left side is swampy for the entire trip. The right bank ranges to 35 feet high before becoming swampy (mi 3.7).

Broad Creek (mi 6.2) enters from the left. Cypress Cathedral camping platform is 2.9 miles up this creek and Three Sisters Creek. See Gardner Creek (page 327) for platform details and reservations.

The Thoroughfare (mi 8.1), a link to the Cashie River, joins from the left at a sharp angle. It can be mistaken for a small cove.

Downstream (mi 8.4), the smokestacks of the Weyerhauser plant can be seen far ahead. Sounds from the plant can be heard depending on wind direction.

Bear Run camping platform (mi 8.5) is on the right. See Gardner Creek (page 327) for platform details and reservations.

The Weyerhauser plant (mi 10.3) begins on the right bank and runs for the next mile. A long island also begins here, and taking the left channel blocks the view of the plant. Do not take the left channel just upstream of the island because it is Middle River and does not return to the Roanoke River until miles past Plymouth.

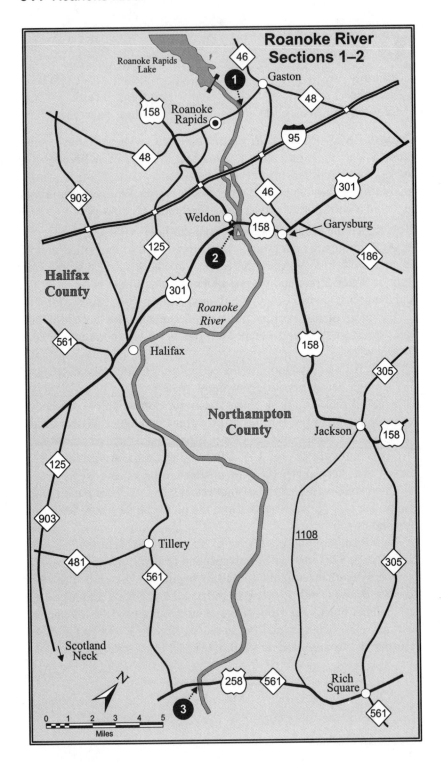

**Roanoke River
Sections 1–2**

Roanoke Rapids
Lake

Gaston

158 Roanoke
Rapids

48

95

903

48

46

301

Weldon

158

Garysburg

186

Halifax
County

125

301

*Roanoke
River*

561

Halifax

158

Northampton
County

305

Jackson

158

125

1108

903

305

Tillery

481

561

Scotland
Neck

N

258   561

Rich
Square

0 1 2 3 4 5
Miles

561

Roanoke Basin

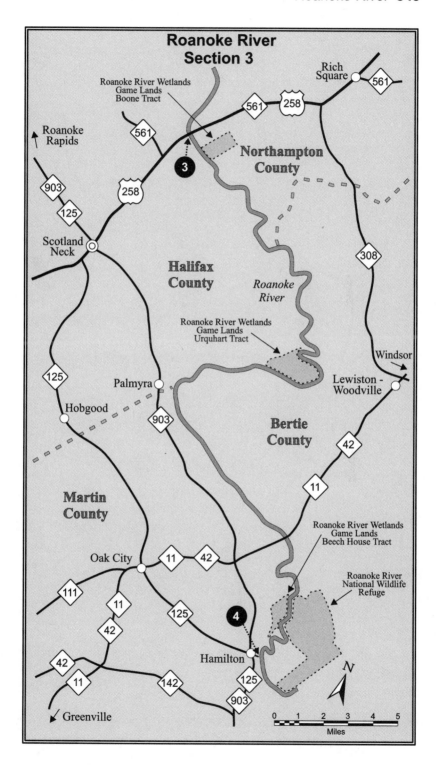

**Roanoke River
Section 3**

Roanoke River Wetlands
Game Lands
Boone Tract

Rich
Square

561

561

258

Roanoke
Rapids

561

3

*Northampton
County*

258

903

125

308

Scotland
Neck

*Halifax
County*

*Roanoke
River*

Roanoke River Wetlands
Game Lands
Urquhart Tract

Windsor

125

Palmyra

Lewiston -
Woodville

Hobgood

903

*Bertie
County*

42

11

*Martin
County*

Roanoke River Wetlands
Game Lands
Beech House Tract

Oak City

11

42

Roanoke River
National Wildlife
Refuge

111

11

125

42

4

42

Hamilton

N

11

142

125

42

903

11

Greenville

0   1   2   3   4   5
Miles

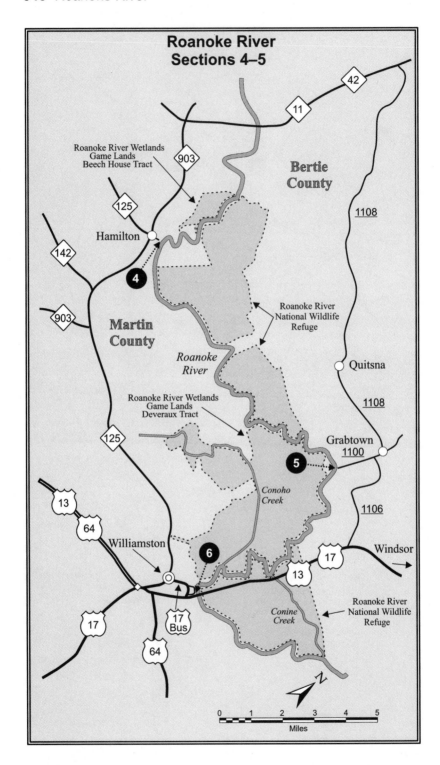

**Roanoke River
Sections 4–5**

Bertie
County

Roanoke River Wetlands
Game Lands
Beech House Tract

Hamilton

Martin
County

Roanoke River
National Wildlife
Refuge

Roanoke
River

Roanoke River Wetlands
Game Lands
Deveraux Tract

Quitsna

Grabtown

Conoho
Creek

Williamston

Windsor

Conine
Creek

Roanoke River
National Wildlife
Refuge

0 1 2 3 4 5
Miles

Roanoke Basin

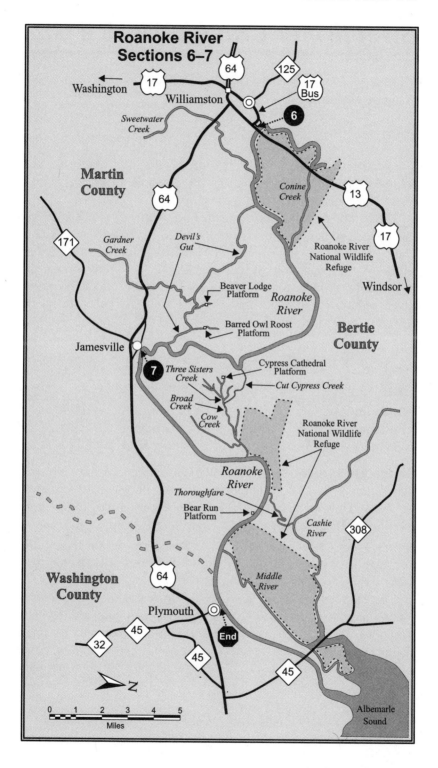

Sweetwater Creek & Devil's Gut

Counties   Martin, Bertie

Topos   Williamston, Jamesville

Sweetwater Creek is a blackwater stream draining Martin County below Williamston and emptying into the Roanoke River. It is a small creek with abundant wildlife.

The section described below starts on Sweetwater Creek at US 64 and takes it to Jamesville via the Roanoke River and Devil's Gut. There are other possible routes after reaching the Roanoke River: return to the put-in on Sweetwater Creek, go upstream on the Roanoke to Williamston, continue to Jamesville on the Roanoke River, or take Devil's Gut to Gardner Creek and go upstream on Gardner Creek to US 64.

 1 US 64 bridge over Sweetwater Creek to Stewart Street access at Jamesville via Devil's Gut and Roanoke River

Difficulty A		**Width**	20–300 ft
Distance 14.8 mi		**Gradient**	0 ft/mi
Scenery A		**Map**	page 350

Gauge USGS *Roanoke River at Williamston* and *Roanoke River at Jamesville*. Always above minimum. There is no gauge on Sweetwater Creek. Downed trees had to be portaged in the last mile before entering the Roanoke River.

Notes From US 64 take NC 117 (Andrews Street) into Jamesville. Turn right at Water Street and left at Stewart Street. The ramp is next to the Cypress Grill restaurant.

There are several places where wrong turns are possible on Sweetwater Creek. It is useful to have a topo map and compass to check directions. A smaller channel (mi 1.7) on the left is actually the main channel. Straight ahead leads about a quarter-mile into a cove. Another dead-end channel (mi 1.9) bears slightly left, but the main channel is to the right.

Banks rise from the swamp (mi 3.0) and reach 4 feet high farther downstream, where the creek is confined to a small channel and current increases.

Sweetwater Creek joins the Roanoke River (mi 4.0). Turn right and paddle downstream.

Paddle into Devil's Gut (mi 5.0) on the right. Devil's Gut varies from 60–200 feet wide. Most of the banks in Devil's Gut are posted by hunting clubs. It is common to see fishermen in motorboats.

A channel on the left allows paddling into Spellers Creek (mi 7.5) when water is high.

Gardner Creek (mi 10.4) enters on the right.

Upper Deadwater Creek (mi 11.0) and Lower Deadwater Creek (mi 12.2) enter on the left. There are platforms up these creeks that can be reserved for camping. See Gardner Creek for details (page 327).

Devil's Gut joins the Roanoke River (mi 13.2). After a right bend (mi 14.1), the high banks of Jamesville can be seen.

Pete Peterson floating the Roanoke River, Section 3

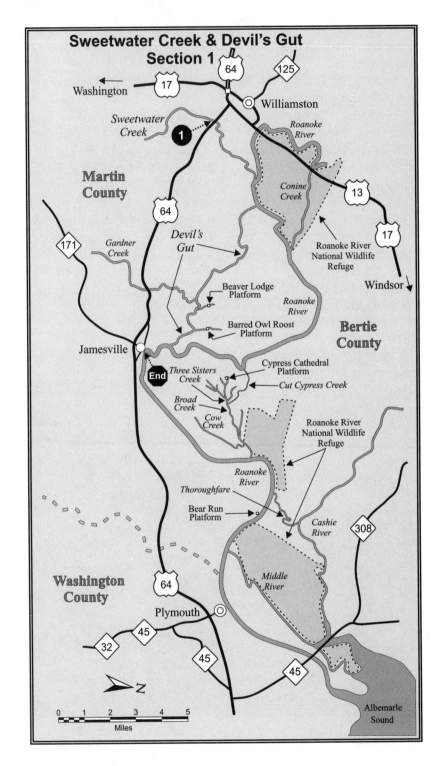

Sweetwater Creek & Devil's Gut
Section 1

Washington

17

64

125

Williamston

Sweetwater Creek

1

Roanoke River

Martin County

Conine Creek

13

64

171

Gardner Creek

Devil's Gut

17

Windsor

Roanoke River National Wildlife Refuge

Beaver Lodge Platform

Roanoke River

Barred Owl Roost Platform

Bertie County

Jamesville

End Three Sisters Creek

Cypress Cathedral Platform

Cut Cypress Creek

Broad Creek

Cow Creek

Roanoke River National Wildlife Refuge

Roanoke River

Thoroughfare

Bear Run Platform

Cashie River

308

Washington County

64

Middle River

Plymouth

45

32

45

45

N

0 1 2 3 4 5
Miles

Albemarle Sound

Roanoke Basin

Tom McCloud at Beaver Lodge camping platform
Upper Deadwater Creek off Devil's Gut, Roanoke River

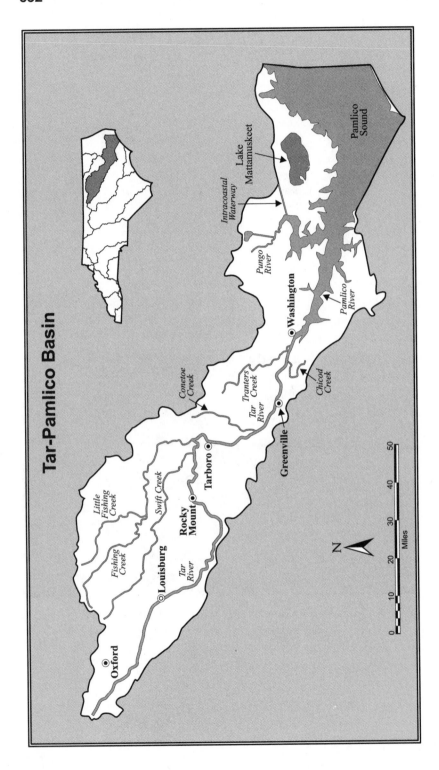

Tar-Pamlico Basin

Tar-Pamlico Basin

The Tar-Pamlico Basin drains 5,440 square miles and is North Carolina's fourth largest river basin. It is one of only four major river basins whose boundaries are located entirely within the state. The Tar River begins in the Piedmont between Oxford and Roxboro and flows southeast.

At Rocky Mount, the Tar River drops over the Fall Line and begins its flow across the flat Coastal Plain, becoming tidal near Greenville. At the city of Washington, it changes names from Tar River to Pamlico River and travels another 37 miles before emptying into Pamlico Sound. Albemarle and Pamlico Sounds form the second largest estuary in the United States.

About eighty percent of the basin is located in the Coastal Plain, which is characterized by blackwater streams, swamplands, and estuaries.

Goose Creek State Park and Medoc Mountain State Park are within the basin as well as three National Wildlife Refuges: Pocosin Lakes, Swan Quarter, and Lake Mattamuskeet (North Carolina's largest natural lake).

Major tributaries include Fishing Creek, Swift Creek, Tranters Creek, and Pungo River.

Swift Creek, Fishing Creek, the upper Tar River, and tributaries support many rare aquatic species. The headwaters of the Tar-Pamlico Basin support populations of mussels that have completely disappeared from other watersheds. Mussels rely on clean, clear water to feed, and they are imperiled in many waters by sedimentation and pollution from forestry, agriculture, industry, and development. The presence of mussels is an indicator of a relatively healthy aquatic system.

A recent step in protecting part of the upper Tar was The Nature Conservancy's purchase of 1,600 forested acres at Shocco Creek, a tributary of Fishing Creek.

Chicod Creek

County   Pitt

Topo   Grimesland

Chicod Creek begins southwest of Washington and flows northwest toward Greenville. It briefly becomes the Beaufort and Pitt County line. Between Simpson and Grimesland, the stream turns east to join the Tar River.

1 NC 33 bridge to Seine Road (Pitt Co. 1566) access on the Tar River	
Difficulty A	**Width** 15–300 ft
Distance 3.0 mi	**Gradient** 0 ft/mi
Scenery A	**Map** page 355

Gauge USGS *Chicod Creek at SR 1760 near Simpson.* Minimum is 100 cfs (8.2 ft). Even at this relatively high flow, there were several downed trees blocking the channel in the first half-mile.

Notes The take-out is on the Tar River at a private access at the end of Seine Road, just upstream left of the Grimestown Road (Pitt Co. 1565) bridge. Pay $3 per boat at the small store near the ramp.

This section is short and easily paddled as a round-trip. By putting in on the Tar River and paddling up the creek, there is the option of returning if there are too many downed trees in the narrow parts.

The creek is narrow at the put-in, but it becomes narrower downstream. It passes through trees only 15 feet apart. Downed trees in the narrow areas are common.

The channel widens (mi 0.7) to 50 feet and continues to widen for the rest of the trip.

Cypress trees with Spanish moss line the banks until the creek joins the Tar River (mi 2.8).

The take-out is 800 feet upstream left of the Grimestown Road bridge.

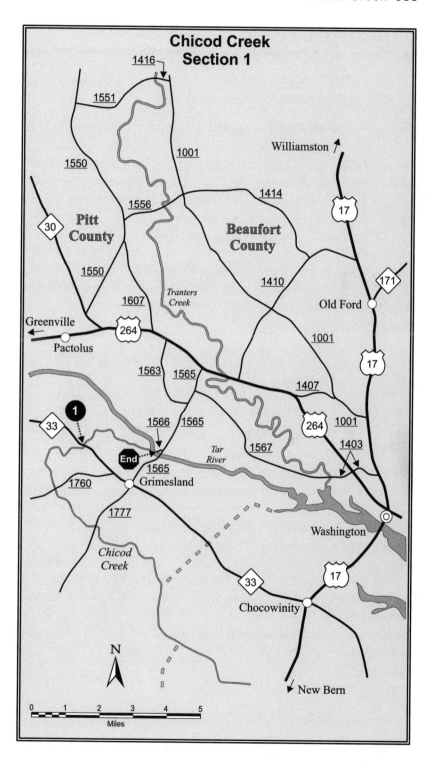

Chicod Creek
Section 1

1416

1551

1001

Williamston

1550

1414

17

1556

Pitt County

30

Beaufort County

1550

1410

171

1607

Tranters Creek

Old Ford

Greenville

264

Pactolus

1001

17

1563   1565

1407

1

1566   1565

264   1001

33

Tar River

1567

1403

End

1565   Grimesland

1760

1777

Washington

Chicod Creek

33

Chocowinity

17

N

New Bern

0   1   2   3   4   5
Miles

Fishing Creek

Counties   Halifax, Nash, Edgecombe

Topos   Essex, Ringwood, Enfield, Whitakers, Draughn, Tarboro

Fishing Creek is the largest tributary of the Tar River. The creek's headwaters begin in Vance County, northeast of Henderson, near Kerr Lake. It flows southeast and joins Shocco Creek near where Warren, Franklin, Nash, and Halifax Counties meet.

Fishing Creek's course becomes more easterly as it picks up Little Fishing Creek before passing 15 miles north of Rocky Mount. It turns south to join the Tar River, 3 miles northeast of Tarboro.

The creek channel constantly twists and turns through farmland and forests. There are no towns of any size near Fishing Creek's banks until it passes near Enfield.

1 Ita Road (Halifax Co. 1327) bridge to NC 48/4 bridge

Difficulty A–I, and one II		**Width** 35–80 ft	
Distance 9.5 mi		**Gradient** 2.0 ft/mi	
Scenery A		**Map** page 360	

Gauge USGS *Fishing Creek near Enfield.* Minimum is 120 cfs (4.3 ft). Many trees were downed during Hurricane Floyd (1999). Cleanup efforts removed trees from Section 3–7, but Sections 1–2 were not done and still contain many blockages.

Notes After passing Ward Road (Halifax Co. 1343) (mi 2.7), Little Fishing Creek (mi 4.3) enters from the left, and the channel widens.

Before reaching Melton Bridge Road (Halifax Co. 1342) (mi 6.5), the run is flatwater. Downstream are several islands and rock gardens, making a few Class I rapids.

Remains of an old dam (mi 8.1) create a Class II rapid with a sloping 2–foot drop on the left.

2 NC 48/4 bridge to US 301 bridge near Enfield

Difficulty A	**Width** 50–125 ft	
Distance 10.4 mi	**Gradient** 1.9 ft/mi	
Scenery A (80%), B (20%)	**Map** page 360	

Gauge See Section 1.

Notes The put-in is in the backwater of the dam in the middle of this section.

Traffic from I-95 (mi 1.2) can be heard long before and after paddling under its bridges.

Bellamy Lake Road (Halifax Co. 1226) (mi 3.9) runs along the left bank and is a popular place for bank fishing. It could be used for boat access.

Portage the 10-foot dam at Bellamy Mill (mi 4.8) on the right. The mill structure is still in good condition. The mill, grounds, picnic tables, and boat ramp are part of a private fishing club.

Wynn Road (Halifax Co. 1222) (mi 5.0) is just below the mill. The first cypress trees seen on Fishing Creek are downstream of the bridge.

The banks vary from a few feet to 20 feet high.

3 US 301 bridge near Enfield to Etheridge Road (Halifax Co. 1109) bridge

Difficulty A	**Width** 20–70 ft	
Distance 9.2 mi	**Gradient** 0.9 ft/mi	
Scenery A	**Map** page 360	

Gauge USGS *Fishing Creek near Enfield.* Estimated minimum is 90 cfs (3.8 ft).

Notes This is a remote stretch with no houses, bridges, or power lines. A few tracts of farmland are near the banks.

Although the section was cleared of downed trees in 2001, erosion of the banks, narrow channels between islands, and a twisting course provide conditions for trees to fall and be prevented from washing downstream.

---

4 Etheridge Road (Halifax Co. 1109) bridge to Draughn Road (Edgecombe Co. 1429) bridge

Difficulty	A	**Width**	40–80 ft
Distance	8.9 mi	**Gradient**	2.2 ft/mi
Scenery	A	**Map**	page 361

Gauge USGS *Fishing Creek near Enfield.* See Section 3.

Notes This is similar to the previous section. It is remote with only a few tracts of logged land. The twisting course continues with views downstream never over 500 feet.

There are many sandbars at low water. The banks run from a few feet up to 30 feet.

Most of the right bank is posted by a hunting club.

---

5 Draughn Road (Edgecombe Co. 1429) bridge to NC 97 bridge

Difficulty	A	**Width**	35–80 ft
Distance	12.9 mi	**Gradient**	0.8 ft/mi
Scenery	A	**Map**	page 361

Gauge See Section 3.

Notes The banks are steep at the NC 97 bridge, but downstream left a narrow cut eases boat access.

The stream continues meandering tightly with eroded banks providing conditions for trees to fall across the creek. Many sandbars are exposed at low water.

In the second half of this section, farmland is near the river, and there are signs of the banks being used for fishing.

---

6 NC 97 bridge to Fishing Creek Road (Edgecombe Co. 1500) bridge

Difficulty	A	**Width**	30–80 ft
Distance	4.5 mi	**Gradient**	2.7 ft/mi
Scenery	A	**Map**	page 361

Gauge See Section 3.

Notes See the previous section about NC 97.

This is a short section. For a longer run, combine it with the next section.

The steeper gradient makes a noticeable current even at low water.

There are many large cypress trees and sandbars.

7 Fishing Creek Road (Edgecombe Co. 1500) bridge to Riverfront Park access at Tarboro on Tar River

Difficulty A	**Width** 30–150 ft
Distance 11.0 mi	**Gradient** 1.3 ft/mi
Scenery A (80%), B (20%)	**Map** page 361

Gauge See Section 3. For the Tar River, see USGS *Tar River at Tarboro*.

Notes See Tar River, Section 15 (page 376) about Riverfront Park.

Fishing Creek is 30–50 feet wide, and the banks are up to 15 feet high where it joins the Tar River (mi 4.0).

See Tar River, Section 15 (page 376) for a description of the remaining part of this trip. Add 0.6 miles to the mileage given in the Tar River description to correct for distances from the Fishing Creek put-in.

■

One of their canoes had just overset and all the baggage wet—the medicine box, among other articles—and several articles lost, a shot pouch and horn with all the implements for one rifle lost and never recovered. I walked down to the point where I waited their return.

On their arrival, found that two other canoes had filled with water and wet their cargoes completely. Whitehouse had been thrown out of one of the canoes as she swung in a rapid current, and the canoe had rubbed him and pressed him to the bottom as she passed over him, and had the water been two inches shallower must inevitably have crushed him to death. Our parched meal, corn, Indian presents, and a great part of our most valuable stores were wet and much damaged on this occasion. To examine, dry, and arrange our stores was the first object. We therefore passed over to the larboard side, opposite to the entrance of the rapid fork, where there was a large gravelly bar that answered our purposes. Wood was also convenient and plenty. Here we fixed our camp and unloaded all our canoes, and opened, and exposed to dry, such articles as had been wet.

—Captain Meriwether Lewis
Journals of Lewis and Clark (6 August 1805)

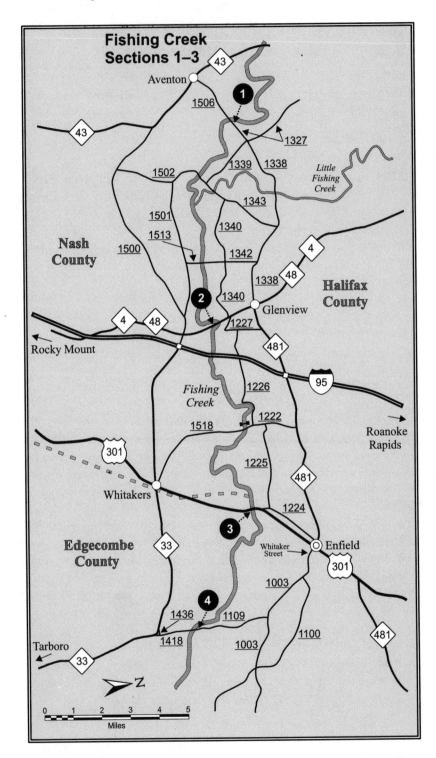

**Fishing Creek
Sections 1–3**

Aventon

43

1506

1

1327

1339 1338

Little
Fishing
Creek

1502

1343

1501

1340

1513

1342

Nash
County

1500

4

1338 48

Halifax
County

2

1340

Glenview

1227

4 48

481

Rocky Mount

95

Fishing
Creek

1226

1518

1222

Roanoke
Rapids

1225

301

481

Whitakers

1224

Edgecombe
County

3

33

Whitaker
Street

Enfield

301

1003

4

1436 1109

1100

481

Tarboro

1418

1003

33

N

0   1   2   3   4   5
Miles

Tar-Pamlico Basin

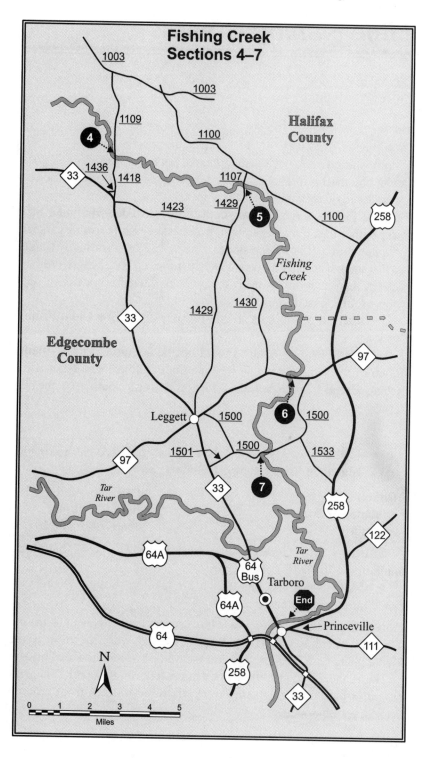

Fishing Creek
Sections 4–7

1003

1003

Halifax
County

1109

4

1436
33

1418

1107

1423

1429

1100

258

Fishing
Creek

1429

1430

97

Edgecombe
County

Leggett

1500

6

1500

97

1501

1500

1533

33

7

258

122

Tar
River

64A

64
Bus

Tar
River

Tarboro

End

64A

Princeville

64

111

N

0 1 2 3 4 5
Miles

258

33

Little Fishing Creek

County   Halifax

Topos   Hollister, Essex

Little Fishing Creek's watershed begins between Warrenton and Littleton, about 10 miles south of the Virginia border. Its major tributaries are Reedy Creek and Bear Swamp.

Little Fishing Creek flows south through Medoc Mountain State Park. Rather than a real mountain, it is eroded granite from an ancient mountain range. It has steep slopes of over 160 feet, unusually rugged for this area. The park is near the Fall Line, an area where the hard rocks of the Piedmont foothills give way to the softer rocks and sediments of the Coastal Plain.

Downstream of the park, Little Fishing Creek flows into Fishing Creek.

This Little Fishing Creek should not be confused with a smaller stream of the same name that is sometimes paddled. The other Little Fishing Creek begins below Oxford and flows south into the Tar River.

1 Medoc State Park Road (Halifax Co. 1322) access to Medoc Mountain Road (Halifax Co. 1002) access

Difficulty A		**Width**	45–60 ft
Distance 2.5 mi		**Gradient**	3.6 ft/mi
Scenery A		**Map**	page 364

Gauge USGS *Little Fishing Creek near White Oak*. Estimated minimum is 70 cfs (3.2 ft).

A paddling gauge is painted on the take-out bridge, where estimated minimum is 4 feet.

Notes The park maintains a canoe access at both the put-in and take-out. There is a small parking area and wooden steps at the Medoc State Park Road bridge and the Medoc Mountain Road bridge.

Hurricane Floyd (1999) downed many trees on the creek. The park has cut a path through them, but newly downed trees from eroding banks are common.

Bear Swamp (mi 0.2) joins on the left, and after a right turn (mi 0.3), the left bank rises 160 feet above the creek. This is the highest ground in Medoc Mountain State Park.

Park hiking trails are often close to the river, and benches are occasionally seen near the banks.

At a left bend (mi 2.0), the right bank rises 40 feet and has exposed rock faces.

From the take-out, it is 11 miles to the confluence with Fishing Creek, Section 1 (page 356). It is likely to contain many downed trees.

Pungo Canal on Pungo River

Pungo River natural channel

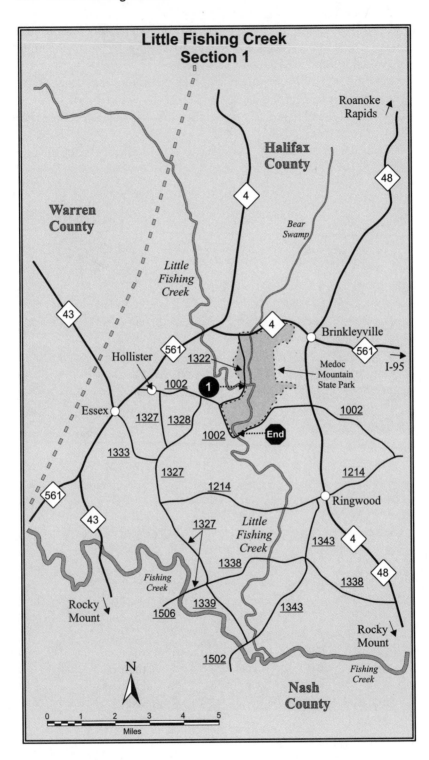

Little Fishing Creek
Section 1

Warren County

Halifax County

Roanoke Rapids

48

4

Bear Swamp

Little Fishing Creek

43

561

Hollister

1322

Brinkleyville

561

I-95

4

Medoc Mountain State Park

1002

Essex

1327

1328

1002

End

1002

1333

1214

1327

1214

Ringwood

1214

4

Little Fishing Creek

1327

1343

48

1338

Fishing Creek

1338

Rocky Mount

1339

1506

1343

Rocky Mount

1502

Fishing Creek

Nash County

N

0   1   2   3   4   5
Miles

Tar-Pamlico Basin

Pungo River

Counties   Beaufort, Hyde

Topos   Pungo Lake, Belhaven

The Pungo River begins in the East Dismal Swamp in Washington County, about 10 miles south of Plymouth. As it flows southeast, it becomes the Beaufort and Hyde County border. Less than 20 miles from the source, the Pungo begins to widen rapidly as it passes under US 264 at Leechville.

Several miles downstream, the Pungo River is connected to the Alligator River by a 21-mile canal, which is part of the Intracoastal Waterway. The Pungo is a over a mile wide here, and the Intracoastal Waterway follows the Pungo as it turns west to pass Belhaven. Below Belhaven, the Pungo turns south to join the Pamlico River close to Pamlico Sound. At its mouth, the Pungo River is over 3 miles wide.

In the 1950s, the Pungo River Canal was dug to improve drainage for farmland in the upper Pungo watershed. The canal runs near the natural river channel.

Pungo Lake is part of the Pungo National Wildlife Refuge and connects to the river by a canal.

1	NC 45 access to Riverside Campground access off Riverside Campground Road (Hyde Co. 1344)		
Difficulty A		**Width**	15–300 ft
Distance 10.5 mi		**Gradient**	0 ft/mi
Scenery A		**Map**	page 367

Gauge None. Always above minimum. Consider reversing the trip if wind is more favorable.

Notes At the NC 45 bridge, there is an old boat ramp on the upstream right.

Riverside Campground and Restaurant is at the end of Riverside Campground Road. There is a $2 charge to use their ramp. Bill Smithwick, the owner, has lived here many years and can answer most any question about the area.

The put-in is on the Pungo River Canal, where it is 60 feet wide and arrow-straight for a mile downstream before it turns. The banks have a narrow, mowed buffer. The canal extends downstream for 6 miles. The natural channel of the Pungo River runs a twisting course to the right of the canal and intersects it several times. The river is more interesting than the canal, but it is narrow and often has downed trees in the upper parts. The description below begins on the canal and takes the river to bypass the last 2.5 miles of the canal. Staying on the canal to its end shortens the trip by 1.1 miles.

The canal (mi 1.0) turns left and before making another left, Indian Run (mi 1.8) joins from the right. The natural river channel crosses Indian Run, but is full of downed trees. Do not mistake Indian Run for the river. It is one of the few ways to go the wrong way when trying to get off the canal to explore the river. A compass and topo maps are useful for exploring.

The river joins the canal (mi 3.7) on the right and can usually be paddled from here on. There are signs of downed trees having been cut to make the river navigable. Alligator weed forms mats on the water. If it is too dense, take the canal.

The river touches the canal (mi 5.5) where Pungo Lake Canal enters the Pungo River Canal on the left.

The river joins the canal (mi 6.2) for a short run but exits again on the right (mi 6.4).

The end of the canal (mi 7.3) joins the river from the left. A few islands are in the remainder of the trip, and the river broadens up to 300 feet wide at the take-out.

■

Nice? It's the only thing, said the Water Rat solemnly, as he leant forward for his stroke. Believe me, my young friend, there is noth-ing—absolutely nothing—half so much worth doing as simply mess-ing about in boats. Simply messing, he went on dreamily: messing about in boats; messing . . .
—Kenneth Grahame, *The Wind in the Willows* (1908)

Tar-Pamlico Basin

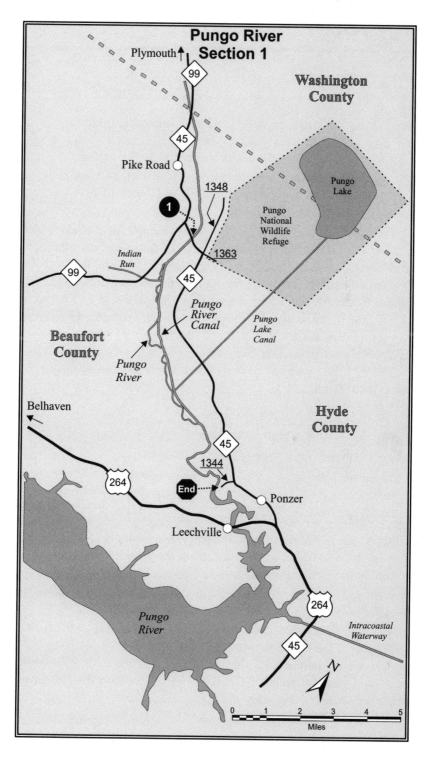

**Pungo River
Section 1**

Plymouth↑

99

Washington
County

45

Pike Road

1348

1

Pungo
Lake

Pungo
National
Wildlife
Refuge

Indian
Run

1363

99

45

*Pungo
River
Canal*

*Pungo
Lake
Canal*

**Beaufort
County**

*Pungo
River*

**Hyde
County**

Belhaven

45

1344

264

End

Ponzer

Leechville

264

*Pungo
River*

*Intracoastal
Waterway*

45

N

0   1   2   3   4   5
Miles

Tar River

Counties Granville, Franklin, Vance, Nash, Edgecombe, Pitt

Topos   Berea, Stem, Wilton, Kittrell, Ingleside, Louisburg,
          Justice, Bunn East, Spring Hope, Bailey,
          Winstead Crossroads, Nashville, Rocky Mount,
          Hartsease, Tarboro, Speed, Old Sparta, Falkland,
          Greenville NW, Greenville SW, Greenville SE

Most historians believe the Tar River was named for its heavily forested land of pines, an important source of tar to early settlers. The
river begins in Piedmont farmlands between Oxford and Roxboro and
flows southeasterly. It passes through Louisburg and crosses the Fall
Line at Rocky Mount, where it enters the Coastal Plain.

The Tar River passes Tarboro and becomes tidal near Greenville.
At the city of Washington, the Tar River changes its name to Pamlico
River and flows to Pamlico Sound.

The paddling sections described from near Oxford to Greenville
comprise 165 miles.

1 Gooch's Mill Road (Granville Co. 1150) bridge to US 15 bridge near Oxford			
Difficulty I–II		**Width** 20–120 ft	
Distance 8.6 mi		**Gradient** 7.8 ft/mi	
Scenery A (45%), B (55%)		**Map** page 379	

Gauge USGS *Tar River near Tar River.* Minimum is 250 cfs (3.1 ft).
The gauge is 14 miles downstream from the put-in. If the water level
is falling, more flow is needed.

Notes The first half of this section is flatwater with one dam. The
gradient of the second half is 14 feet/mile.

After the Enon Road (Granville Co. 1139) bridge (mi 1.6), the
backwater of the dam downstream is entered.

The 4-foot dam (mi 3.2) has a strong hydraulic with rebar in the
outflow. Upstream right of the dam, water flows to the right over
small boulders in a two-stage drop. Portage the dam on the left.

Downstream from the dam, banks on the left rise to 50 feet with many mountain laurel bushes. The first rapids are just before the Old Route 75 (Granville Co. 1004) bridge (mi 4.6).

Below Old Route 75, there are several sets of Class I–II rapids, and a Class II is at the approach to both the Belltown Road (Granville Co. 1133) bridge (mi 6.8) and the I-85 bridge (mi 7.0).

Many river birches grow on low islands, constricting the route to small channels.

A stretch of Class II rapids is found near an old 4-foot dam (mi 7.5). The dam extends from the left side but is broken away on the right.

Near islands (mi 8.1), the main channel is on the right and only 20 feet wide. The river drops 2 feet over a 25-foot run.

2 US 15 bridge near Oxford to NC 96 bridge

Difficulty A, and one I		**Width** 40–80 ft	
Distance 5.7 mi		**Gradient** 3.5 ft/mi	
Scenery A		**Map** page 379	

Gauge USGS *Tar River near Tar River.* Minimum is 130 cfs (2.8 ft). Downed trees will require portage.

Notes The gradient of this section is much less than the sections above and below. It is almost all flatwater, and tree blockages have been in this section for many years. One large blockage was 8 feet high.

The only rapid is 500 feet upstream of the take-out.

A low concrete dam is at the gauge, upstream right of the take-out. The dam has a break through the center and does not present an obstacle.

3 NC 96 bridge to Green Hill Road (Franklin Co. 1203) bridge

Difficulty I–II⁺		**Width** 25–80 ft	
Distance 6.3 mi		**Gradient** 10.3 ft/mi	
Scenery A		**Map** page 379	

Gauge USGS *Tar River near Tar River.* Minimum is 130 cfs (2.8 ft). Approaching 700 cfs (4.5 ft), it becomes a Class III run. At much higher flow, the rapids tend to wash out, except for a few areas where there are powerful waves and currents.

Notes Much of the scenery is of forested hills rising up to 150 feet above the river. There are few signs of development.

Be careful of downed trees, especially in the narrow channels between islands.

There are a few Class I–II rapids before passing Cannadys Mill Road (Granville Co. 1622) bridge (mi 1.8).

Small rapids and ledges continue, and islands often divide the river. One of the better rapids (mi 2.9) is in a left channel, where it is rather constricted. A large rock at the bottom of the chute must be avoided. Part of an old mill wall can be seen on the left bank.

At the last significant rapid (mi 3.7), where there is an old school bus on the bank, the river necks down to 25 feet with a big rock in the middle of the run. This rapid develops large waves at high flows.

4	Green Hill Road (Franklin Co. 1203) bridge to Sims Bridge Road (Franklin Co. 1003) bridge		
Difficulty A		**Width** 45–75 ft	
Distance 11.2 mi		**Gradient** 1.6 ft/mi	
Scenery A		**Map** page 379	

Gauge USGS *Tar River near Tar River.* Minimum is 80 cfs (2.6 ft). There are usually many downed trees in this section. At 80 cfs, six blockages were found. Higher flows would reduce the problems.

Notes Steep terrain up to 150 feet above the river continues, but this section has no rapids.

Just before the US 1 bridge (mi 4.1), water is added from Tabbs Creek on the left. After the highway bridge, a railroad bridge is 75 feet above the river.

Near the end of the trip, several large rocks (mi 9.9) extend from the right bank to the middle of the river and rise up to 4 feet high. These are unusual for their size, and little other rock is seen in the riverbed.

5	Sims Bridge Road (Franklin Co. 1003) bridge to River Bend Park access at Louisburg		
Difficulty A, and one I⁺		**Width** 60–80 ft	
Distance 7.4 mi		**Gradient** 2.2 ft/mi	
Scenery A (75%), B (25%)		**Map** page 380	

Gauge USGS *Tar River at Louisburg.* Estimated minimum is 75 cfs (5.1 ft).

Notes To reach Louisburg's River Bend Park, go north on South Main Street (Old US 401), cross the Tar River, take the first left at Johnston Street, and turn left on South Church Street. The park is one block ahead.

Downed trees requiring portage are common, but there are usually fewer than in the previous section.

A power substation (mi 7.0) is on the left bank, and a water intake tower is on the right. A low concrete dam runs across the river. At a flow of 500 cfs (7.7 ft), the dam is 8 inches below the surface and creates a wave. At low flows, it might have to be portaged.

River Bend Park is after a sharp left bend, where an old stone dam makes a 2-foot drop. The dam is broken on the right side, creating a Class 1$^+$ rapid.

6	River Bend Park access at Louisburg to Ferrells Bridge Road (Franklin Co. 1001) bridge		
Difficulty A–I		**Width** 35–100 ft	
Distance 11.5 mi		**Gradient** 1.4 ft/mi	
Scenery A (85%), C (15%)		**Map** page 380	

Gauge See Section 5.

Notes See the previous section about the River Bend Park access.

Downed trees are common. On a trip at minimum water, two large blockages were found about halfway down.

At low flows, there are three Class I rapids.

In the first half-mile, the river passes the Main Street and US 401 bridges, leaving behind the development at Louisburg.

Downstream, there are cypress trees, sandbars, and even views of 50-foot rock banks with mountain laurel.

7	Ferrells Bridge Road (Franklin Co. 1001) bridge to Quiet Waters Road (Nash Co. 1344) end		
Difficulty A–I$^+$		**Width** 80–100 ft	
Distance 10.9 mi		**Gradient** 0.7 ft/mi	
Scenery A (80%), B (20%)		**Map** page 380	

Gauge See Section 5.

Notes Quiet Waters Road ends near the river, where a barricade prevents driving over the old bridge. Downstream right, a trail goes downhill and about 150 feet over flat, brushy ground to the bank.

Cypress trees, some large with dense stands of knees, are along the banks. There are a few small rapids. Hills near the banks are up to 80 feet.

The left side of a large island (mi 4.0) ends in a Class I and Class I⁺ rapid, and the Baptist Church Road (Franklin Co. 1609) bridge (mi 4.2) can be seen downstream.

Sledge Road (Franklin Co. 1611) bridge (mi 6.7) can be used to shorten the trip. It is about where the dam's backwater begins.

The take-out at the old bridge is a few hundred feet upstream of Webb Milldam.

8	Quiet Waters Road (Nash Co. 1344) end to NC 581 bridge		
Difficulty A, and one I		**Width** 80–100 ft	
Distance 7.0 mi		**Gradient** 3.9 ft/mi	
Scenery A (70%), B (30%)		**Map** page 381	

Gauge See Section 5.

Notes See the previous section about Quiet Waters Road.

Put in near the old bridge at the end of Quiet Waters Road. The 8–10 foot Webb Milldam is only a few hundred feet downstream. Stay back from the dam because water flows over it. Portage on the right bank along the short trail. To avoid the portage, put in at the end of the trail leading from the road, through the woods, to below the dam.

The US 64A bridge (mi 0.7) can be also be used as a put-in. Access at the US 64 bridge (mi 0.9) is difficult.

Rocky banks (mi 3.0) with mountain laurel are on the right, where hills rise to 100 feet.

At the Nash Co. 1145 bridge (mi 4.5), rocks from an old dam form the only rapid to reach Class I on this section.

9	NC 581 bridge to Tar River Church Road (Nash Co. 1981) bridge		
Difficulty A		**Width** 85–200 ft	
Distance 10.2 mi		**Gradient** 0.7 ft/mi	
Scenery A		**Map** page 381	

Gauge See Section 5.

Notes The Old Bailey Highway (Nash Co. 1001) bridge (mi 6.4) can be used to shorten the trip.

At normal water level for the Tar River Reservoir, its backwater is entered above the I-95 bridge (mi 9.8). Motorboats often come upriver into this deep water.

10	Tar River Church Road (Nash Co. 1981) bridge to Braswell Road (Nash Co. 1746) access		
Difficulty A		**Width** 100–800 ft	
Distance 7.6 mi		**Gradient** 0 ft/mi	
Scenery B (75%), C (25%)		**Map** page 381	

Gauge None. Always above minimum.

Notes A Tar Reservoir access area is at the take-out. There is parking and a trail but no boat ramp.

This section is entirely on the Tar River Reservoir, a water supply for Rocky Mount. It would be a difficult paddle in high wind. On warm weekends, many motorboats and jet skis are here.

There are three bridges before the dam: NC 58 (mi 1.9), Nash Co. 1603 (mi 3.6), and Bend In The River Road (Nash Co. 1745) (mi 6.3). A boat ramp at Bend In The River Road allows for a shortened trip and easier take-out.

At the dam, take out on the right side, up a grassy hill to the access area. Stay back from the dam because water flows over it.

11	Braswell Road (Nash Co. 1746) access to Sunset Park access at Rocky Mount		
Difficulty I		**Width** 80–110 ft	
Distance 7.3 mi		**Gradient** 3.0 ft/mi	
Scenery A (25%), B (55%), C (20%)		**Map** page 381	

Gauge USGS *Tar River below reservoir near Rocky Mount*. Minimum is 90 cfs (4.0 ft).

Notes See the previous section about the Braswell Road access.

To reach Sunset Park from US 64, take the Sunset Avenue and US 64 Business exit. Follow Sunset Avenue and US 64 Business to the bridge over the Tar. Take the first left after crossing the bridge into Sunset Park. The boat ramp is 100 yards ahead on the left.

A 10-foot milldam (mi 1.3) should be portaged on the right side. There is a narrow slot cut in the dam center producing a drop of 3–4 feet which is tempting to run, but there is a rock in the chute below.

South Halifax Road (Nash Co. 1544) (mi 1.8) can be used as a put-in to avoid the upstream dam portage.

There are a few Class I rapids before reaching the US 301 bridge (mi 4.8) and backwater from the dam in the next section.

A boating access (mi 5.2), managed by Rocky Mount, is on the right bank. Travelling north on Nashville Road (Nash Co. 1714) toward the bridge, turn left on Azalea Street before crossing the bridge, then right on Griffin Street. There are steps leading to the river.

Signs of the city are frequent as the river flows under the Bethlehem Road/Nashville Road bridge (mi 5.4) and US 64 Business (mi 7.2). Sunset Park is 100 yards downstream of US 64 Business.

12	Sunset Park access at Rocky Mount to Springfield Road (Edgecombe Co. 1250) bridge		
Difficulty I–II, III		**Width**	50–500 ft
Distance 4.9 mi		**Gradient**	6.3 ft/mi
Scenery B		**Map**	page 382

Gauge USGS *Tar River at NC 97 at Rocky Mount*. Minimum is 75 cfs (3.3 ft) except for Class III rapids just below the dam. They have sufficient water only when water is flowing over the dam.

Notes See the previous section about the Sunset Park access.

The NC 43/48 Business bridges (mi 1.0) are only 300 feet upstream of the dam at Rocky Mount Mills, recognized as the second cotton mill in the state. A historic marker notes it was built in 1818, burned by the Federals in 1863, and soon rebuilt. It is now an active hydroelectric plant and runs whenever there is sufficient flow in the river.

The dam spans 500 feet, and rock formations below it are impressive. This is the Fall Line, which provided a catalyst for early development in the area.

Several islands below the dam create multiple channels. The area of rapids extends for about 1,000 feet downstream of the dam. There is usually not enough flow to paddle most of the rapids. A gate in the center of the dam provides a minimum flow to support aquatic life. The mill takes in water to generate electric power and releases it back into the river downstream of the rapids. When flow is greater than can be used by the mill, water begins to flow over the dam, and the rapids can be paddled. As flow increases, the rapids will become Class III and higher. Scout carefully and watch for strainers.

At high flows, portage on the left bank, where Battle Park runs along the left bank for almost a mile. There are trails, decks overlooking the river, and a boat ramp well below the rapids.

Above the dam, stay clear of the water intake to the right. When there is no water flowing over the dam, it is possible to paddle to the right of the dam's center, portage down a sloping rock face, and put in. Short portages through the rapids are likely to be required.

At the end of the islands (mi 1.4), water used in the plant is returned in a channel to the right of the last island.

The Battle Park boat ramp (mi 1.8) is reached from Battle Park Road off Benvenue Road. Use this put-in to avoid the dam portage and rapids. Downstream of the ramp, the US 301 Business bridge (mi 1.9) and NC 97 bridge (mi 2.2) can be seen.

Close to the US 64 bridge (mi 2.9), the river narrows to 50 feet with boulders, making a Class I rapid at low flows. The topo map notes this area as Little Falls. At high flows, there would be turbulent water, but there is little gradient here.

13 Springfield Road (Edgecombe Co. 1250) bridge to Dunbar Road (Edgecombe Co. 1252) bridge

Difficulty A–I		**Width** 60–90 ft	
Distance 12.2 mi		**Gradient** 1.5 ft/mi	
Scenery A (85%), B (15%)		**Map** page 382	

Gauge USGS *Tar River at NC 97 at Rocky Mount.* Minimum is 75 cfs (3.3 ft).

Notes Banks up to 50 feet high and overhanging trees provide shade for summer paddling.

Sounds of traffic can be heard because NC 97 runs close to the river until reaching Leggett Road (Edgecombe Co. 1243) bridge (mi 3.1). Put in here to shorten the trip and lessen the sounds of civilization.

There are a few low Class I rapids and some impressive rows of cypress knees at the water's edge.

14 Dunbar Road (Edgecombe Co. 1252) bridge to NC 33 access

Difficulty A		**Width** 40–100 ft	
Distance 12.5 mi		**Gradient** 1.1 ft/mi	
Scenery A		**Map** page 382	

Gauge See Section 13.

Notes A Wildlife boating access is at NC 33.

There are no bridges, little development, and numerous sandbars as the river goes through many bends. The banks range up to 50 feet. High flows have eroded the soil, making the banks steep and with little vegetation.

15 NC 33 access to Riverfront Park access at Tarboro		
Difficulty A	**Width**	55–150 ft
Distance 10.4 mi	**Gradient**	1.1 ft/mi
Scenery A (75%), B (25%)	**Map**	page 382

Gauge USGS *Tar River at Tarboro*. Always above minimum.

Notes A Wildlife boating access is at NC 33.

To reach Riverfront Park, take US 64 Exit 486 to Princeville. Take US 64 Business and NC 33 West across the Tar River, where the road is called Main Street in Tarboro. Take the second right, Granville Street. A few blocks ahead, Granville becomes Panola Street. Turn right on River Road into the Riverfront Park east entrance. The park has a boat ramp.

The put-in and take-out are only 2.5 miles apart by road. The river takes a giant loop outside Tarboro, and the short distance makes for an easy biking or hiking shuttle.

Fishing Creek (mi 3.4), the Tar's largest tributary, joins from the left. At low flows, a large sandbar is off the Tar's right bank.

The river passes under an old railroad swing bridge (mi 5.6).

Little development is seen on this section until passing near Shiloh Mills (mi 7.9), where US 258 stays close to the river until the take-out.

16 Riverfront Park access at Tarboro to NC 42 access		
Difficulty A	**Width**	100–150 ft
Distance 7.8 mi	**Gradient**	0.3 ft/mi
Scenery A (75%), B (25%)	**Map**	page 382

Gauge USGS *Tar River at Tarboro*. Always above minimum.

Notes See the previous section about the Riverfront Park access.

A Wildlife boating access is at NC 42.

In the first mile, the river passes US 64 Business, US 64 Bypass, and a wastewater treatment plant, and leaves Tarboro and Princeville behind. Downstream, there is little development.

The riverbanks have cypress trees, and the course is straighter than in previous sections, offering views of the river up to a mile ahead.

17 NC 42 access to NC 222 access		
Difficulty A	**Width** 125–150 ft	
Distance 8.3 mi	**Gradient** 0.6 ft/mi	
Scenery A	**Map** page 383	

Gauge USGS *Tar River at Tarboro*. Always above minimum.

Notes The put-in and take-out are Wildlife boating access areas.

Cypress trees continue down the banks, and sandbars are exposed at low flows.

Upstream of power lines, where NC 33 (mi 2.8) comes close on the left, people use warm weather and shallow water to swim, fish, and set up lawn chairs on a low sandbar.

The NC 222 bridge can be seen for more than a mile before reaching it.

18 NC 222 access to Port Terminal Road (Pitt Co. 1533) access at Greenville		
Difficulty A	**Width** 100–300 ft	
Distance 14.9 mi	**Gradient** 0.5 ft/mi	
Scenery A (60%), B (25%), C (15%)	**Map** page 383	

Gauge USGS *Tar River at Greenville*. Always above minimum. The lower part of this section is tidal with variations at the gauge of about a foot. Wind can make for difficult paddling.

Notes The put-in and take-out are Wildlife boating access areas.

There are many sandbars at low flows. After passing under three road bridges—US 264 (mi 5.8), NC 11/US 13 (mi 9.8), and Greene Street (mi 10.7)—the trip can be shortened by taking out at Greenville's Town Commons Park boat ramp (mi 11.0) on river right, off First Street.

Motorboat and ski traffic increases, and many houses are upstream of the US 264A bridge (mi 13.4).

The take-out is in what appears to be another channel (mi 14.7) joining from the right, at a back angle. The boat ramp is a few hundred yards up this cove.

Tar River, Section 1

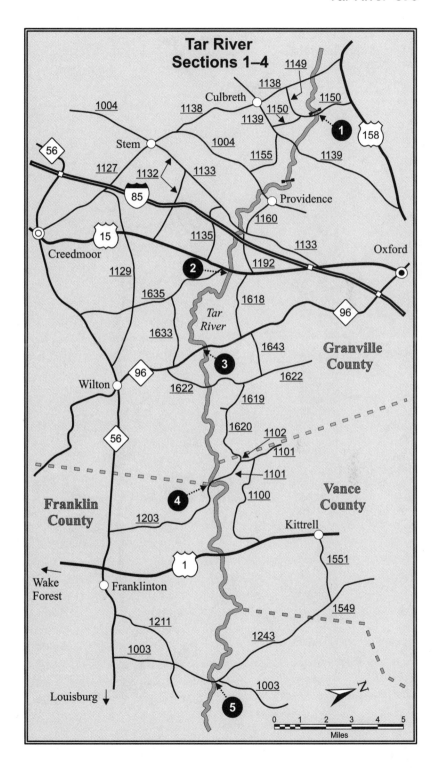

**Tar River
Sections 1–4**

1004
1138
Culbreth
1149
1138
1150
1150
158
1139
1004
1155
1139
Stem
56
1127
1132
1133
85
Providence
1160
15
1135
1133
Oxford
Creedmoor
1129
1192
2
1635
1618
*Tar
River*
1633
**Granville
County**
1643
96
3
1622
Wilton
96
1622
1619
56
1620
1102
1101
1101
1100
**Vance
County**
4
Kittrell
**Franklin
County**
1203
1551
1
Wake
Forest
Franklinton
1549
1211
1243
1003
Louisburg
1003
5

0 1 2 3 4 5
Miles

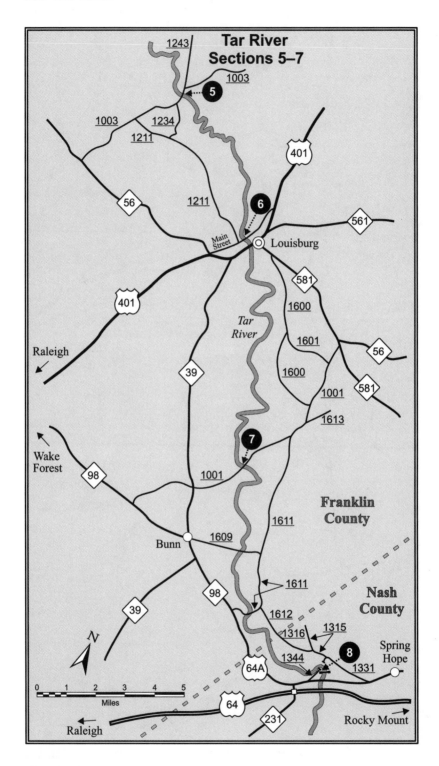

Tar River
Sections 5–7

Tar-Pamlico Basin

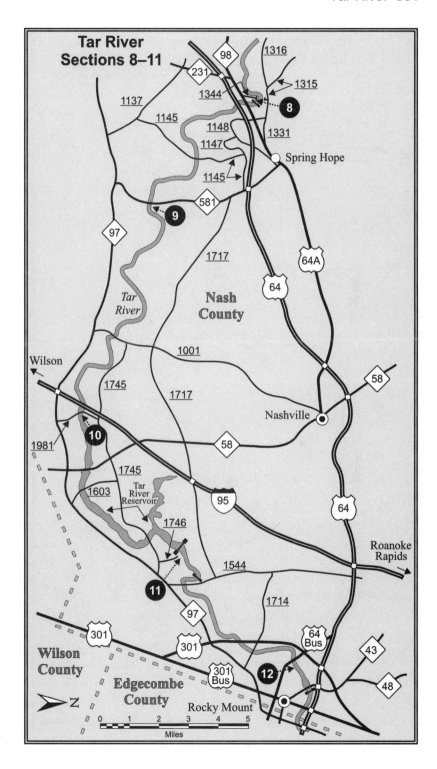

**Tar River
Sections 8–11**

Spring Hope

*Tar
River*

**Nash
County**

Wilson

Nashville

Roanoke
Rapids

*Tar
River
Reservoir*

**Wilson
County**

**Edgecombe
County**

Rocky Mount

N

0 1 2 3 4 5
Miles

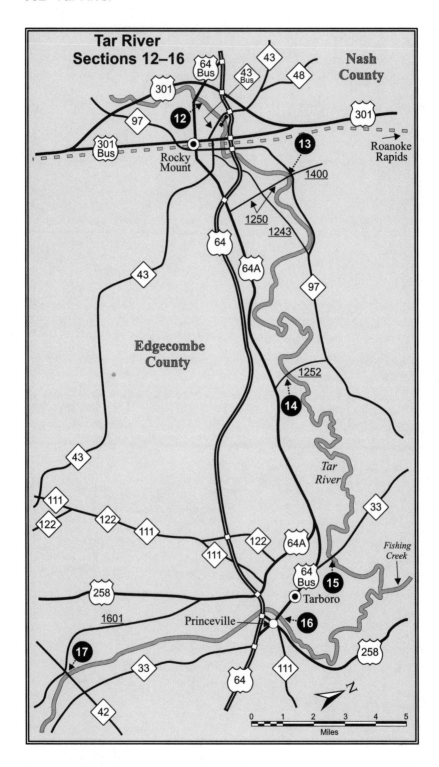

Tar-Pamlico Basin

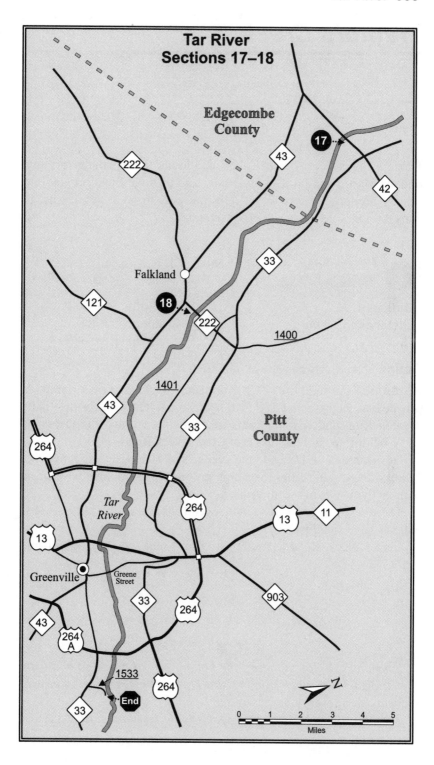

**Tar River
Sections 17–18**

Edgecombe
County

Falkland

Pitt
County

Tar
River

Greenville

Greene
Street

End

N

0   1   2   3   4   5
Miles

Tranters Creek

Counties   Beaufort, Pitt

Topos   Grimesland, Washington

Tranters Creek begins near Robersonville and flows south, forming first the Martin and Pitt County border and then the Beaufort and Pitt County border. Tranters Creek does not pass through any towns. It joins the Tar River, just east of Washington.

1 US 264 bridge to Clarks Neck Road (Beaufort Co. 1403) access near Washington		
Difficulty A	**Width** 50–300 ft	
Distance 10.9 mi	**Gradient** 0 ft/mi	
Scenery B (35%), C (65%)	**Map** page 385	

Gauge None. Always above minimum.

Notes The put-in at the US 264 bridge is brushy and over riprap. A private boat ramp, about 100 feet downstream left of the bridge, is in Tranters Run subdivision. Permission is required to use this access.

A Wildlife boating access is at Clarks Neck Road.

Downstream of US 264, the creek is a blackwater stream with cypress trees, water lilies, and high ground. Many homes have been built on the banks in recent years.

There are many bends and several oxbows (mi 3.0). A few oxbows have small islands.

Clarks Neck Road (Pitt Co. 1567) is just off the right bank (mi 9.7).

■

Sometimes, if you stand on the bottom rail of a bridge and lean over to watch the river slipping slowly away beneath you, you will suddenly know everything there is to be known.

—inspired by A. A. Milne, *Pooh's Little Instruction Book* (1995)

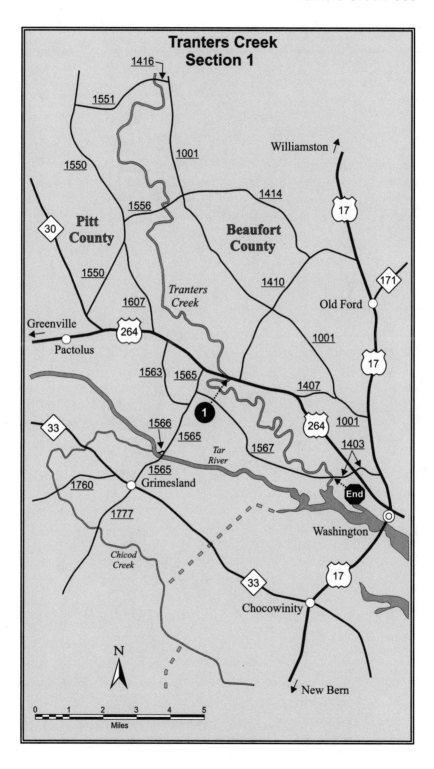

Tranters Creek
Section 1

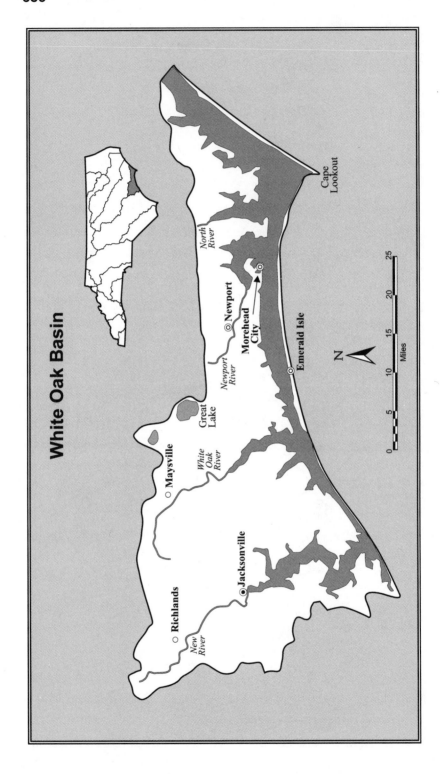

White Oak Basin

Cape Lookout

North River

Newport

Morehead City

Newport River

Emerald Isle

Great Lake

Maysville

White Oak River

Jacksonville

Richlands

New River

N

Miles

0 5 10 15 20 25

White Oak Basin

The White Oak Basin is named for the White Oak River, but the basin actually includes four separate rivers and their tributaries: New River, Newport River, North River, and White Oak River.

The basin encompasses 1,264 square miles. In addition to the freshwater streams and rivers, it contains extensive estuaries in Bogue and Core Sounds and 91 miles of Atlantic Ocean coastline.

The New River is a coastal blackwater river with a watershed entirely within Onslow County. At Jacksonville, the river widens into a broad, slow-moving, tidal bay. It flows into the Atlantic Ocean through a narrow opening called New River Inlet. Jacksonville and the Marine Corps at Camp Lejeune occupy the majority of land in the watershed below the US 17 bridge.

The Newport River watershed begins in Croatan National Forest in Carteret County. It flows through Newport and becomes a few miles wide before passing Morehead City. It enters the eastern end of Bogue Sound, close to Beaufort Inlet and Fort Macon State Park.

The headwaters of the North River originate in Carteret County and flow for only a few miles before becoming a wide bay leading into Back Sound near Harkers Island. Jarrett and Nelson Bays are also included in this basin.

The White Oak River headwaters begin in Hofmann Forest (part of North Carolina State University) in Jones and Onslow Counties. After flowing past Maysville, most of the tributaries from the east drain from Croatan National Forest. It becomes a wide estuary and flows into the Atlantic Ocean at Bogue Inlet, passing Hammocks Beach State Park on Bear Island.

■

In all things of nature there is something of the marvelous.
—Aristotle (384–322 B.C.)

New River

County   Onslow

Topos   Richlands, Catherine Lake, Jacksonville North

When the New River is mentioned, many think of the mountain river above Boone, flowing toward Virginia. The New River of the Coastal Plain starts in the northwest corner of Onslow County. It flows through Richlands and on to Jacksonville, where it becomes a slow-moving, tidal bay, reaching several miles wide. About 20 miles below Jacksonville, the New River meets the Atlantic Ocean through a narrow opening called New River Inlet.

The New River was the site of the one of the most notorious hog farm spills. In 1995 a waste lagoon was breached, sending 25 million gallons of waste into the river.

More recently the news has been better. The New River has a Riverkeeper®, and there have been programs to clear a path through downed trees and control aquatic weeds.

1	NC 24 bridge west of Richlands to NC 24/US 258 bridge south of Richlands		
Difficulty A		**Width** 10–30 ft	
Distance 6.0 mi		**Gradient** 4.6 ft/mi	
Scenery A		**Map** page 391	

Gauge USGS *New River near Gum Branch*. Estimated minimum is 90 cfs (3.7 ft).

Notes The New River Pentecostal Free Will Baptist Church at the NC 24/US 258 bridge has allowed paddlers to use the church parking lot to access the river.

The river is a small creek at the put-in. It is 10–15 feet wide with sandy banks up 10 feet.

In the first mile, several riffles are created by small ledges of a few inches.

Banks Bridge Road (Onslow Co. 1231) (mi 3.0) and Turtle Shell Road (Onslow Co. 1225) (mi 4.4) can be used for river access.

The banks in the first half of the trip are covered in bushes. More trees appear in the second half, and the banks are lower.

Just upstream of the take-out, the river goes under NC 24/US 258 through a 75-foot long culvert, divided into three channels, each about 8 feet wide. Ensure it is clear of debris before paddling through.

2	NC 24/US 258 bridge south of Richlands to Rhodestown Road (Onslow Co. 1316) bridge		
Difficulty A, and one I		**Width** 35–40 ft	
Distance 5.7 mi		**Gradient** 1.2 ft/mi	
Scenery A (65%), B (35%)		**Map** page 391	

Gauge USGS *New River near Gum Branch*. Estimated minimum is 50 cfs (3.1 ft).

Notes See the previous section about NC 24/US 258.

About 100 feet below the bridge, a Class I rapid is at a small ledge. Rocks on the right bank have rough edges, and there is an eddy to the right.

The stream picks up more water from two tributaries on the left: Squires Run (mi 1.0) and Cowhorn Swamp (mi 1.2).

Limestone, eroded into coral-like rock, shows on the bank in several areas. There are also places where the streambed is rock rather than sand.

The banks rise in this section, and on the right (mi 3.0) they are more than 40 feet above the river.

The gauge is downstream right of Northwest Bridge Road (Onslow Co. 1314) (mi 4.1).

3	Rhodestown Road (Onslow Co. 1316) bridge to US 17 access at Jacksonville		
Difficulty A		**Width** 35–400 ft	
Distance 10.5 mi		**Gradient** 0.5 ft/mi	
Scenery A (60%), B (40%)		**Map** page 391	

Gauge USGS *New River near Gum Branch*. Always above minimum. Tides ranging up to 1.5 feet affect this section. Wind can be a problem as the river widens toward the take-out.

Notes A Wildlife boating access is downstream left of the US 17 bridge. Take Riverview Street to the signs for New River Waterfront Park.

The river begins a straight section (mi 2.3) for over a mile where it was channeled to increase flow. Downstream, the character of the river changes to swamp with occasional small bluffs.

Palmetto and reeds are dense in places, and there are some cypress trees.

An unusual house (mi 7.4) is at a bluff on the right bank in a left turn. The three-story house is only a few feet back from the water, and the bottom floor is only about 6 feet above river level. Much glass faces the river, and the roof has a large array of solar cells.

Jacksonville can be seen where the river widens (mi 9.8). Bear to the right side and then to the left going under the US 17 bridge.

Elmer Eddy on the New River, Section 1

White Oak Basin

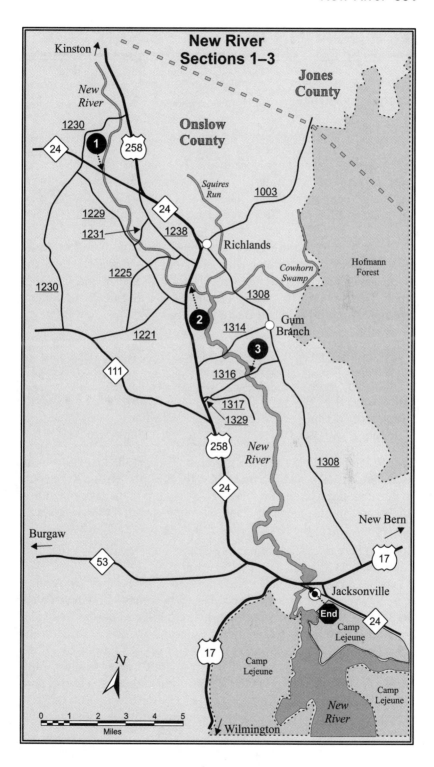

White Oak Basin

Newport River

County   Carteret

Topo   Newport

The Newport River begins near the Pocosin Wilderness area of Croatan National Forest as two blackwater streams: the Northwest Prong and Southwest Prong. The prongs join west of the town of Newport, and the river flows southeast, passing just south of Newport.

About 3 miles northwest of Morehead City, the Newport River becomes a bay up to 2 miles wide. This bay has a water path to the Neuse River through Harlowe Creek, Harlowe Canal, and Clubfoot Creek. The Newport River flows to the eastern end of Bogue Sound, between Morehead City and Beaufort.

---

1 Old Highway 70 (Carteret Co. 1247) access near Newport to Oyster Point access off Mill Creek Road (Carteret Co. 1154)

Difficulty A	**Width** 45–5,000 ft
Distance 8.1 mi	**Gradient** 0 ft/mi
Scenery A (75%), B (25%)	**Map** page 394

Gauge None. Always above minimum. Tides at the take-out run 3–4 feet. For the take-out, use tide tables for Newport River. At the put-in, tide is delayed about 3 hours. Avoid arriving at the take-out at low tide because it becomes very shallow. Wind can affect the last part of this section where the river is wide.

Notes There is a Wildlife boating access on Old Highway 70. This road is called Chatham Street in Newport.

The take-out is a Croatan National Forest access area. To reach it from Newport, take Orange Street east. It becomes Mill Creek Road. Go 3.5 miles beyond Newport and pass a millpond on the left. Continue for 2.6 miles and turn right at the narrow gravel road on the right. This road is Forest Service 181, but it is not sign-posted. (If the turn is missed, 100 feet beyond the turn is a Carteret County solid-waste unit behind fencing on the left.) Continue down the gravel road for 1.1 miles to an access area known as Oyster Point. Walk down to the sand beach and observe the take-out because it is not so obvious from the wide bay when paddling in.

The put-in is on a small channel off the river. Paddle to the left of the ramp to reach the Newport River (mi 0.1) and turn right.

A small island (mi 0.3) divides the river at a railroad bridge.

The river is about 50 feet wide with low banks covered with cypress, tupelo-gum, and pond pines. The plants are typical of a river estuary. In the first half of the section, there are occasional 10-foot banks on the right with houses.

Near the end, the vista ahead changes to a wide bay. Stay to the left and paddle to Oyster Point.

Oyster Point take-out
Newport River

White Oak Basin

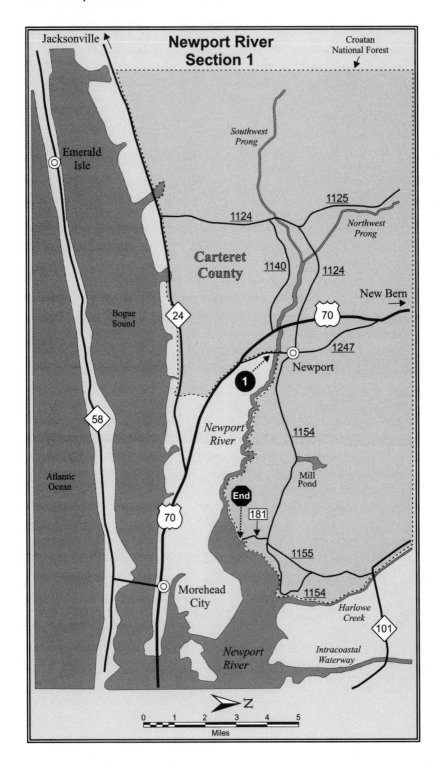

Newport River
Section 1

White Oak Basin

White Oak River

Counties   Onslow, Jones, Carteret

Topos   Jacksonville NE, Maysville, Stella

The headwaters of the White Oak River originate in Hofmann Forest as a narrow, swampy, blackwater stream. After passing US 17 between Belgrade and Maysville, it flows thorough lakes created by quarry operations. Croatan National Forest borders the east bank of the river, but most of the riverfront is privately held.

As the river widens and deepens, it becomes tidal freshwater. Below Stella, the White Oak becomes more than a mile wide before reaching Swansboro and Bogue Sound/Inlet.

① Gibson Bridge Road (Onslow Co. 1332) bridge to US 17 campground access near Maysville			
Difficulty A		**Width** 15–35 ft	
Distance 4.2 mi		**Gradient** 2.4 ft/mi	
Scenery A		**Map** page 399	

Gauge A paddling gauge is on a cypress tree, 50 feet downstream of the US 17 bridge. Estimated minimum is 1.0 feet.

Notes The White Oak River Campground (910-743-3051) owns the land on all sides of the bridge at US 17. The fee is $2 per person to put in or take out. Pay at the campground office. They also rent boats and run shuttles. See: http://whiteoakrivercampground.com/

Beavers have been active in this section, but local paddlers have made efforts to keep a path clear. Downed trees sometimes require portaging, depending on water level.

There are large cypress trees along the banks just downstream from the put-in. The banks are generally low but rise to 15 feet (mi 0.6) on the right, where there are a few houses.

A 25-foot bank (mi 3.3) on the left is only 0.3 miles from US 17.

②	US 17 campground access near Maysville to Croatan National Forest Haywood Landing access		
Difficulty A–I		**Width** 15–120 ft	
Distance 10.0 mi		**Gradient** 0.7 ft/mi	
Scenery A (80%), B (20%)		**Map** page 399	

Gauge See Section 1 for gauge location. Minimum is 0.5 feet. At levels below 0.5 feet, the first mile before reaching the lakes has several places requiring walking a short distance.

An alternative put-in is at the quarry lakes, where downstream the river is always above minimum.

At Haywood Landing, the tides range about a foot.

Notes See the previous section about the US 17 campground access.

To put in at the quarry lakes, from NC 58 go south on US 17. Before crossing the bridge, turn left at the first break in the guardrails where a sign says "Lake Fishing." Follow the signs 0.6 miles to the shelter and pay $2 per boat. The first two lakes are not connected to the river. Go 0.3 miles to the ramp on the lakes leading to the river. This begins at mile 0.8 in the description below. The river enters the lake 100 feet to the right of the ramp.

Haywood Landing is a Wildlife boating access. From Maysville take NC 58 south for 7.4 miles. Turn right and follow the signs to Haywood Landing.

The river is narrow at the US 17 put-in. A small ledge (mi 0.6) creates a Class I rapid under an old steel bridge. When the water level has been low, there is a 1-foot ledge where the river meets the first quarry lake (mi 0.8). As the lake rises, the ledge becomes covered.

For the next mile, there is a series of quarry lakes. The route to follow is not obvious because the lakes have irregular shapes, and there is no discernible current. The most direct path is to bear right through each lake and look for a 30–50 foot wide neck connecting to the next lake. In one small lake, the neck will be seen to the left. If it is missed, continuing to bear right will add less than a half-mile.

After a bridge (mi 1.8) used by the quarry, the last lake ends, and the river channel (mi 2.0) returns. The banks are swampy to several feet high with occasional banks to 15 feet. Many cypress trees and other hardwoods overhang the river.

The Croatan National Forest's outside borders extend from the left bank all the way east to the Neuse River, but not all the land within the borders belongs to the forest. Black Swamp Creek (mi 4.1) enters from the left. The next 0.7 miles on the left bank are forest property.

In the first few hundred yards, land rises over 5 feet and is suitable for camping. A narrow, rough road, Dixon Field Road (Forest Route 3057), leads into this area.

Below power lines (mi 5.9), the river widens, fishermen are often seen in motorboats, and side channels or coves are off the main river.

A rare straight stretch (mi 8.5) begins, giving a half-mile view downstream to where Holston Creek (mi 9.0) joins on the left. Forest property begins below the creek and extends 6.5 miles down the left bank.

Haywood Landing is National Forest property, but camping is not allowed in the area cleared for boating access and parking. There are possible camping areas on the left bank past the boat ramp. High ground extends for 0.2 miles downstream.

3 Croatan National Forest Haywood Landing access to Wetherington Landing Road (Carteret Co. 1101) access		
Difficulty A	**Width**	90–200 ft
Distance 7.7 mi	**Gradient**	0 ft/mi
Scenery A	**Map**	page 399

Gauge None. Always above minimum. Tides at the take-out run about 1.5–2 feet and are delayed about 3–4 hours from tides at Bogue Inlet. Wind is a greater problem than tide.

Notes See the previous section about the Haywood Landing access.

There are two private take-outs on the left at the Wetherington Landing Road bridge in Stella. A private boat ramp is downstream left of the bridge, where the fee is $3 per boat. Boon Docks has a store and dock on the upstream left. Request permission to use their dock. They rent canoes/kayaks, run shuttles, and offer tent camping. Call 252-393-8680 or see: http://theboondocks.net/

The road on the right (west) side of the bridge is called Stella Road (Onslow Co. 1442).

There is little high ground near the river as the White Oak flows through marshes. Cattails and saw grass are abundant. Saltwater reaches into this section and produces changes in the vegetation. The sides of the river are a thicket of many plants, including the carnivorous pitcher plant. It is also an good area for spotting birds, snakes, turtles, and alligators.

There are many places where straight ditches connect to the river. These were cut to drain the land and make it suitable for growing pine trees. The practice was widespread throughout coastal areas of North Carolina, but draining of wetlands is now restricted.

Dry ground on the left has a picnic table and small dock (mi 3.0). It is a Croatan National Forest primitive campsite at the end of Long Point Road.

Hunters Creek (mi 5.5) joins on the left and is a popular side trip. The land on the left bank from Haywood Landing to Hunters Creek is Croatan National Forest property.

Below the take-out bridge at Stella, the river broadens to over a mile wide on its 9-mile run to Swansboro. Wind and tide can make paddling difficult.

Elmer Eddy on the White Oak River, Section 1

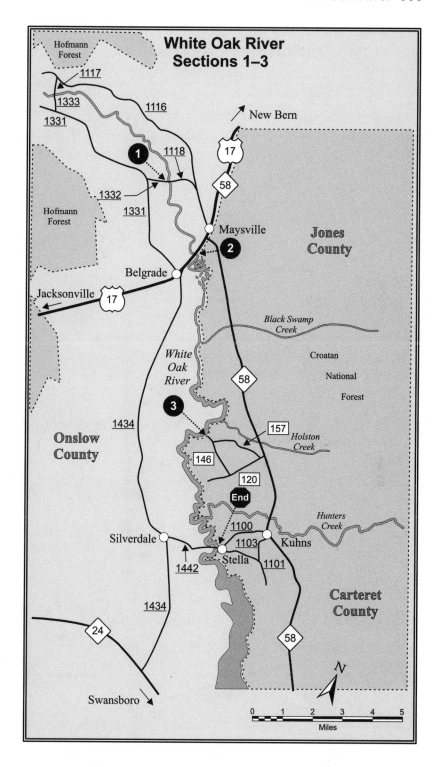

White Oak River
Sections 1–3

Hofmann Forest

1117

1333

1116

1331

1118

1

New Bern

17

58

1332

1331

Hofmann Forest

Maysville

2

Jones County

Belgrade

Jacksonville

17

Black Swamp Creek

White Oak River

58

Croatan

National

Forest

3

157

Holston Creek

1434

Onslow County

146

120

End

Hunters Creek

1100

1103

Kuhns

Silverdale

Stella

1101

1442

Carteret County

1434

24

58

N

Swansboro

0   1   2   3   4   5
Miles

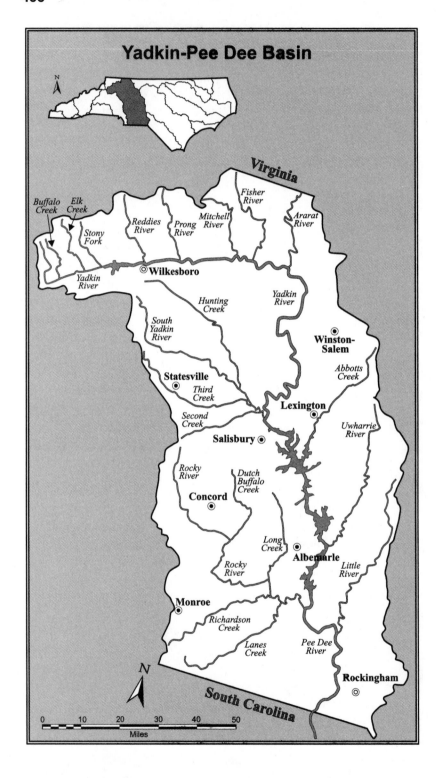

Yadkin-Pee Dee Basin

Virginia

Buffalo Creek

Elk Creek

Fisher River

Ararat River

Reddies River

Prong River

Mitchell River

Stony Fork

Yadkin River

◎ Wilkesboro

Hunting Creek

Yadkin River

South Yadkin River

Winston-Salem

Statesville

Third Creek

Abbotts Creek

Second Creek

Lexington

Salisbury ◎

Uwharrie River

Rocky River

Dutch Buffalo Creek

Concord

Long Creek

Albemarle

Little River

Monroe

Rocky River

Richardson Creek

Lanes Creek

Pee Dee River

Rockingham ◎

South Carolina

0 10 20 30 40 50
Miles

Yadkin-Pee Dee Basin

The Yadkin-Pee Dee Basin covers 7,213 square miles, includes all or part of twenty-four counties, and is the second largest basin in the state. It is located primarily within the Piedmont, but it also drains the Mountain and Coastal Plain regions.

The basin originates on the eastern slopes of the Blue Ridge Mountains, marked by the Eastern Continental Divide, in Caldwell, Wilkes, and Surry Counties. A small portion of the headwaters is in Virginia.

The Yadkin River flows southeast from the foothills then turns northeast for about 100 miles. In this northeast run, the Yadkin is impounded by W. Kerr Scott Reservoir. Many of the tributaries flowing south from the mountains and foothills are cold water trout streams, and some are designated Outstanding Resource Waters. To the west of Winston-Salem, the Yadkin River turns to flow southeast again.

From the confluence with the South Yadkin River near Salisbury, the next 84 miles of the Yadkin and Pee Dee Rivers are interrupted by six dams to form a chain of lakes: High Rock Lake, Tuckertown Reservoir, Baden Lake, Falls Lake, Lake Tillery, and Blewett Falls Lake.

Above Lake Tillery, the Uwharrie River joins the Yadkin River, and the Yadkin River becomes the Pee Dee River.

Near Blewett Falls Lake, the Pee Dee River enters the Coastal Plain. From the dam, it flows 15 miles before entering South Carolina, on its way to the Atlantic Ocean.

The Yadkin-Pee Dee Basin includes Uwharrie National Forest, Pee Dee National Wildlife Refuge, Morrow Mountain State Park, Pilot Mountain State Park, and Stone Mountain State Park.

■

Nature does nothing uselessly.
—Aristotle (384–322 B.C.)

Ararat River

County   Surry

Topos   Mount Airy South, Siloam

The Ararat River begins just above the North Carolina border in Patrick County, Virginia. It flows through Mount Airy and comes within 3 miles of the majestic pinnacle of Pilot Mountain on its way to join the Yadkin River.

---

 1 Hamburg Street (Surry Co. 1759) bridge at Mount Airy to side of Radar Road (Surry Co. 2026) near Ararat

Difficulty I–I⁺	**Width**	20–100 ft
Distance 12.4 mi	**Gradient**	9.1 ft/mi
Scenery A (70%), B (15%), C (15%)	**Map**	page 404

Gauge USGS *Ararat River at Ararat*. Estimated minimum is 200 cfs (1.1 ft).

Notes Old Buck Shoals Road (Surry Co. 1772) ends near the river (mi 3.9) and was used in past years as a put-in. It is now gated and posted. Use Hamburg Street as a put-in.

Radar Road runs along the right bank near the end of this section. About 0.2 miles upstream of the Ararat Road (Surry Co. 2019) bridge, there is room to park on the shoulder.

The first few miles have several Class I rapids as the rivers flows through heavily developed areas of Mount Airy. After passing the US 52 Business (mi 0.6) and US 52 (mi 1.8) bridges, development lessens.

The outflow from a wastewater treatment plant (mi 1.9) sometimes has a reddish tint from dyes. Lovills Creek (mi 2.2) enters from the right, adding water and helping to dilute the dyes.

Downstream of power lines near a quarry operation (mi 3.9), a 1-foot drop and other smaller ledges in the next few hundred yards create rapids up to Class I⁺.

The banks often reach over 100 feet high and are covered in rhododendron. It is remote and scenic, but trash in the river often mars the view.

After passing the Sheep Farm Road (Surry Co. 2119) bridge (mi 7.4) and I-74 bridge (mi 7.7), railroad tracks follow the left bank for the remainder of the section.

There are more ledges in the 1-foot range and rock gardens before reaching the take-out.

2	Side of Radar Road (Surry Co. 2026) near Ararat to Quaker Church Road (Surry Co. 2080) bridge		
Difficulty I–II		**Width**	40–100 ft
Distance 12.2 mi		**Gradient**	8.8 ft/mi
Scenery A		**Map**	page 404

Gauge See Section 1.

Notes See the previous section about Radar Road.

The gauge is on the right bank, just upstream of the Ararat Road (Surry Co. 2019) bridge (mi 0.2).

Many Class I rapids and a Class II rapid, formed by two closely spaced ledges, are before reaching the NC 268 bridge (mi 3.5).

A few hundred yards above the Pilot Power Dam Road (Surry Co. 2044) bridge (mi 3.8) is the best rapid on this section. It is the remains of an old dam. At low water, the right side cannot be run, but left of center is a 3-foot sloping drop requiring maneuvering in the outflow.

Pilot Power Dam Road can be used for access to shorten this section.

As the river swings east (mi 5.3), it gives a brief view of Pilot Mountain, 3 miles away.

Rock formations are on the banks, along with ferns, rhododendron, and mountain laurel. There are many small Class I rapids and one Class II.

Beyond the take-out, the river flows 1.9 miles before reaching the Yadkin, but there is no access at the confluence. See the Yadkin River, Section 11 (page 439).

■

The stewardship of environment is a domain on the near side of metaphysics where all reflective persons can surely find common ground. . . . An enduring environmental ethic will aim to preserve not only the health and freedom of our species, but access to the world in which the human spirit was born.

—Edward O. Wilson, *The Diversity of Life* (1992)

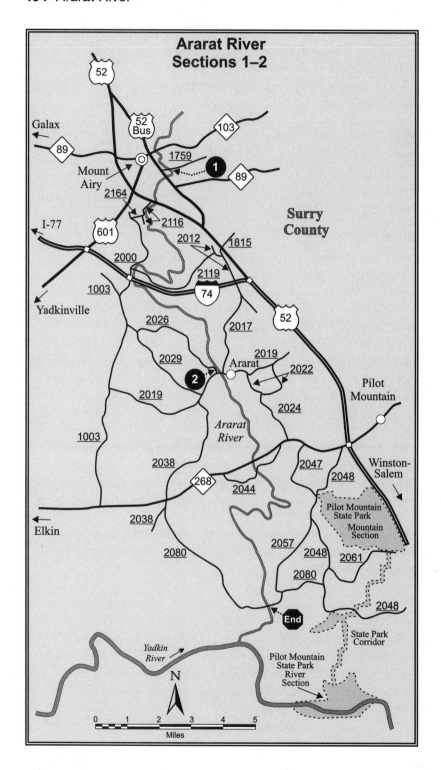

Ararat River
Sections 1–2

Galax

Mount
Airy

I-77

Yadkinville

Surry
County

Ararat

Pilot
Mountain

Ararat
River

Winston-
Salem

Elkin

Pilot Mountain
State Park
Mountain
Section

Pilot Mountain
State Park
River
Section

State Park
Corridor

Yadkin
River

End

N

0 1 2 3 4 5
Miles

Yadkin-Pee Dee Basin

Buffalo Creek

County   Caldwell

Topo   Buffalo Cove

Buffalo Creek begins at an elevation above 3,600 feet near Blowing Rock, on the eastern slopes of the Blue Ridge Mountains. Its small watershed is just east of the Yadkin River headwaters. It flows south and passes by the small town of Buffalo Cove and joins the Yadkin River at the Yadkin River, Section 1 put-in (page 434).

1	Stone Mountain Road (Caldwell Co. 1503) bridge near Buffalo Cove to NC 268 bridge over the Yadkin River

Difficulty	II–III	**Width**	25–70 ft
Distance	6.7 mi	**Gradient**	34.6 ft/mi
Scenery	B (70%), C (30%)	**Map**	page 407

Gauge None. Elk Creek is only 7 miles east of Buffalo Creek. The USGS *Elk Creek at Elkville* gauge is usually a good indicator of water conditions. Estimated minimum is 140 cfs (1.4 ft).

Notes A creek (mi 0.4) adds water, and Buffalo Cove Road (Caldwell Co. 1504) follows the river off the left bank.

There are only Class I rapids down to the portage at the first low-water bridge (mi 1.7).

At a right turn (mi 2.0), the road leaves the valley and starts up the mountain. A Class II rapid marks the entrance to the gorge, where the gradient ramps up to 55 feet/mile. Be alert for downed trees because of fast water through narrow passages.

Boulders are in the riverbed, and a small waterfall (mi 2.3) drops in on the right as Class II rapids continue.

An 8-foot dam (mi 2.6) extends from left bank, but it is broken away on the right side. Scout the rapid just below the dam because rebar has been reported in some of the chutes.

At low water, a rapid (mi 2.8) on the left requires quick maneuvering to pass through slots only a few feet wide. It can be scouted from the right bank.

The creek emerges (mi 3.4) from the rugged gorge, and the road on the left comes back into view.

A low-water bridge (mi 3.9) must be portaged.

The creek passes under the Buffalo Cove Road bridge (mi 4.5).

In a wide turn to the right and back to the left, there are ledges (mi 5.0) with Class II rapids.

Downstream of the Class II rapids, backwater of the dam begins. Approach the 10-foot dam (mi 5.5) with caution, especially when there is good flow, and portage to the left.

Just below the dam is the Riverside Drive (Caldwell Co. 1505) low-water bridge (mi 5.6). At other than minimum water level, it must be portaged because there is not enough clearance.

The terrain downstream near the river changes to farmland.

Pete Peterson below the broken dam
Buffalo Creek

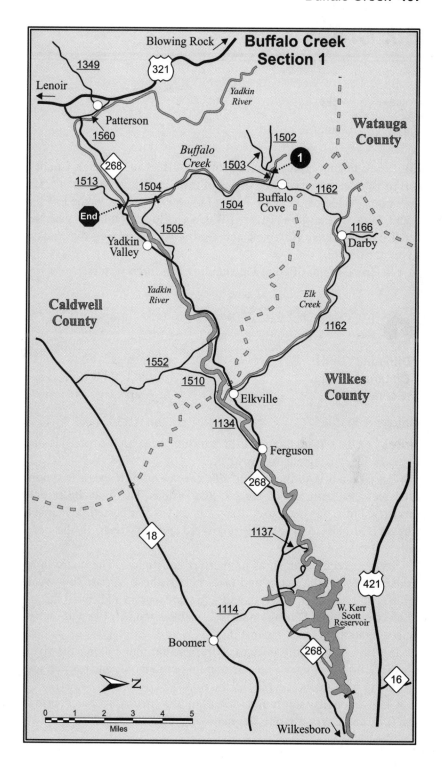

Elk Creek

County   Wilkes

Topo   Grandin

Elk Creek begins at an elevation of 3,200 feet in Watauga County, east of Boone, on the eastern slopes of the Blue Ridge Mountains. On the opposite side of the Blue Ridge Parkway is the watershed of the South Fork of the New River. Elk Creek flows southeast past the small communities of Triplett and Darby, before joining the Yadkin River at Elkville.

Elk Creek is classified as Outstanding Resource Waters.

---

① Elk Creek/Darby Road (Wilkes Co. 1162) bridge to side of Elk Creek/Darby Road near NC 268 bridge

Difficulty II–III		**Width** 25–80 ft	
Distance 8.5 mi		**Gradient** 23.8 ft/mi	
Scenery B (75%), C (25%)		**Map** page 410	

Gauge USGS *Elk Creek at Elkville.* Minimum is 130 cfs (1.3 ft).

Notes At the put-in, there is little parking space on the roadside and barbed wire fencing near the bridge.

The take-out is to the side of Elk Creek/Darby Road, a few hundred feet upstream left of the NC 268 bridge. This may be private property, but it has been used for years and is not posted. When setting shuttle here, scout the biggest rapid, just upstream of the take-out.

Bridges seem almost as numerous as rapids. There are nine bridges between the put-in and take-out. Of these, six are low-water bridges and must be portaged, and a few present an additional hazard of electric fencing. During one trip, a paddler found a live wire when he accidentally brushed against it.

In spite of the many bridges, wire, and farmland along the river, the creek offers a view of the surrounding mountains, clear water, and an ending with the best rapids of the run.

Class I rapids are found down to the first low-water bridge (mi 0.7), and Class II rapids begin downstream.

A low-water bridge (mi 2.1) is followed by another (mi 2.3). Watch for wire strung across the river near the bridges.

After a high bridge (mi 2.5), there are Class II rapids and much rhododendron along the bank.

Two low-water bridges are between the Wilkes Co. 1175 bridge (mi 4.7) and Wilkes Co. 1163 bridge (mi 7.2).

The next low-water bridge (mi 7.7) is the last, and the gradient picks up. A series of ledges (mi 8.1) drops 5 feet over 50 feet.

Cabins and the USGS gauge (mi 8.3) are on the left, and the NC 268 bridge can be seen. A horizon line marks the final ledge. Scout it. At minimum water, a route is to the right of center, angling right, taking three drops totaling about 8 feet over a 45 feet run.

About a half-mile downstream of the NC 268 bridge, Elk Creek joins the Yadkin River, Section 2 (page 434).

Len Felton running ledges near the Elk Creek take-out

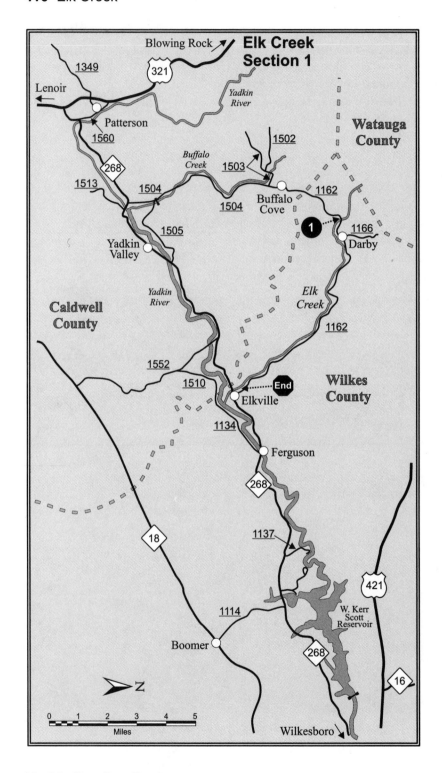

Yadkin-Pee Dee Basin

Fisher River

Counties   Surry, Yadkin

Topos   Dobson, Copeland

The Fisher River watershed begins at an elevation above 2,500 feet on the eastern slopes of the Blue Ridge Mountains, near where the Blue Ridge Parkway enters Virginia. It flows southeast, takes a more southerly course near Dobson, and joins the Yadkin River, 10 miles east of Elkin.

1   Old NC 601 (Surry Co. 2258) bridge to NC 268 bridge

Difficulty	I–II	**Width**	40–90 ft
Distance	9.4 mi	**Gradient**	9.5 ft/mi
Scenery	A	**Map**	page 413

Gauge USGS *Fisher River near Copeland.* Minimum is 110 cfs (2.4 ft).

Notes The section has over forty small rapids, mostly Class I, but a few are Class II in the second half of the trip. There are few houses, and steep banks are covered with rhododendron.

The rapids are mainly formed by ledges dropping up to a foot. Often the gradient is noticeable and fairly uniform. There are many bends and few places giving a view far downstream.

Surry Co. 1100 (mi 3.9) and Hamlin Ford Road (Surry Co. 2222) (mi 7.9) bridges are passed before reaching the take-out.

The USGS gauge (mi 9.3) is on the left just before going around a bend where the NC 268 bridge comes into view.

2	NC 268 bridge to Jenkinstown Road (Surry Co. 2233) bridge		
Difficulty I–II		**Width** 45–50 ft	
Distance 4.7 mi		**Gradient** 10.6 ft/mi	
Scenery A		**Map** page 413	

Gauge See Section 1.

Notes This section is often combined with the following one to make a longer trip.

Class I rapids continue with a few rapids near the end reaching Class II.

Rockford Road (Surry Co. 2221) (mi 0.5) is also a possible access point.

There are steep, rhododendron-covered banks and rock outcroppings on this clear-water stream. The view has been marred by tires dumped into the stream, and tires have washed into the next section.

3	Jenkinstown Road (Surry Co. 2233) bridge to Rockford Road (Surry Co. 2221) access on the Yadkin River		
Difficulty I–II		**Width** 50–300 ft	
Distance 6.6 mi		**Gradient** 6.2 ft/mi	
Scenery A (50%), B (50%)		**Map** page 413	

Gauge See Section 1.

Notes See the Yadkin River, Section 10 (page 438) about the Rockford Road access.

A large rock island (mi 0.8) is 2 feet above water at minimum water level. The only passage is to the left, a Class II, where it narrows to 3–4 feet and drops a few feet. The bottom of the drop has rocks that must be avoided.

The Fisher River joins the Yadkin River (mi 3.3). For the remainder of this trip, see the Yadkin River, Section 10 (page 438).

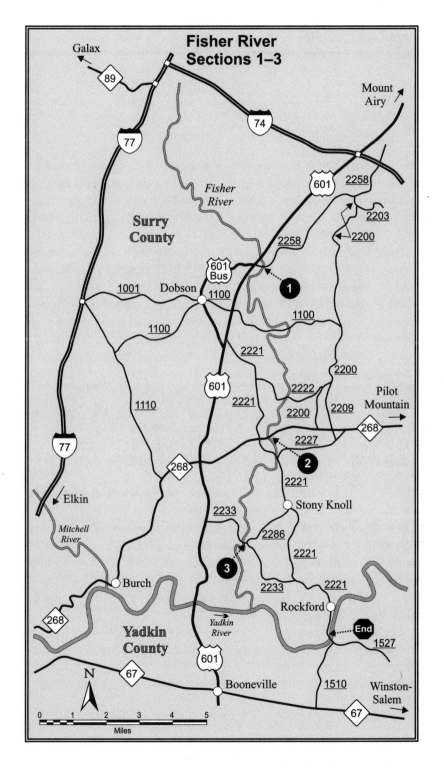

Fisher River
Sections 1–3

Galax

89

77

74

Mount
Airy

*Fisher
River*

601

2258

Surry
County

2258

2203

2200

601
Bus

Dobson

1001

1100

1100

1

1100

1100

1100

2221

2200

2222

601

2221

2200

2209

Pilot
Mountain

1110

268

2227

2

2221

268

2221

Elkin

*Mitchell
River*

2233

Stony Knoll

2286

2221

3

Burch

2233

2221

268

Rockford

*Yadkin
River*

End

Yadkin
County

601

1527

N

67

Booneville

1510

Winston-
Salem

0   1   2   3   4   5
Miles

67

Yadkin-Pee Dee Basin

Mitchell River

County   Surry

Topos   Bottom, Elkin North

The Mitchell River watershed begins at an elevation above 3,000 feet on the eastern slopes of the Blue Ridge Mountains, in Alleghany County, northeast of Stone Mountain State Park. It flows southeast without passing through any towns and joins the Yadkin River, 5 miles northeast of Elkin.

The Mitchell River, upstream of the South Fork, is classified as Outstanding Resource Waters. The South Fork brings in much sediment. Efforts are underway to restore the South Fork.

The Piedmont Land Conservancy is working with public agencies, private organizations, and landowners to secure permanent protection along the Mitchell River. Several tracts have already been conserved.

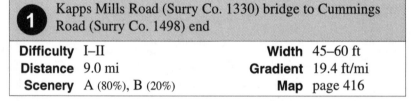

1 Kapps Mills Road (Surry Co. 1330) bridge to Cummings Road (Surry Co. 1498) end

Difficulty I–II	**Width** 45–60 ft
Distance 9.0 mi	**Gradient** 19.4 ft/mi
Scenery A (80%), B (20%)	**Map** page 416

Gauge USGS *Mitchell River at State Road*. Minimum is 175 cfs (2.4 ft).

Notes Cummings Road is upstream right of the Poplar Springs Road (Surry Co. 1001) bridge. It ends at the USGS gauge, 300 feet upstream. The bank is steep, but it is an easier access point than using the bridge.

At the put-in, an 8-foot milldam can be seen a few hundred feet upstream.

The relatively steep gradient yields about fifty small rapids. They are Class I with six reaching Class II, and the ledges are all less than 2 feet.

The banks are often steep, rising a few hundred feet and densely forested.

The Zephyr Mountain Park Road (Surry Co. 1315) bridge (mi 2.3) can be used for access on the left side. There is fencing on the right.

A private trail can often be seen on the left bank, and a shelter (mi 5.9) is near the trail's end.

The South Fork (mi 6.6) enters from the right. Its sediment load is usually noticeable.

---

2 Cummings Road (Surry Co. 1498) end to NC 268 bridge

Difficulty I–II	**Width**	40–65 ft
Distance 4.7 mi	**Gradient**	15.7 ft/mi
Scenery A (40%), B (60%)	**Map**	page 416

Gauge USGS *Mitchell River at State Road*. Minimum is 130 cfs (2.2 ft).

Notes See the previous section about Cummings Road.

The rapids are Class I–I$^+$ with a Class II at the beginning and end of this section. More houses are seen than in the previous section, and the banks are not as steep.

A Class II is between the gauge and the Poplar Springs Road (Surry Co. 1001) bridge. The I-77 bridges (mi 0.1) cross just ahead.

Within sight of the take-out bridge, a ledge (mi 4.6) drops 2.5 feet and kicks up waves on the right side.

Only 0.2 miles beyond the take-out at NC 268, the Mitchell joins the Yadkin River, Section 9 (page 438). Continuing on to the Yadkin take-out adds 4.7 miles to the trip.

■

Life is either a daring adventure or nothing. Security does not exist in nature, nor do the children of men as a whole experience it. Avoiding danger is no safer in the long run than exposure.
— Helen Keller, *The Open Door* (1957)

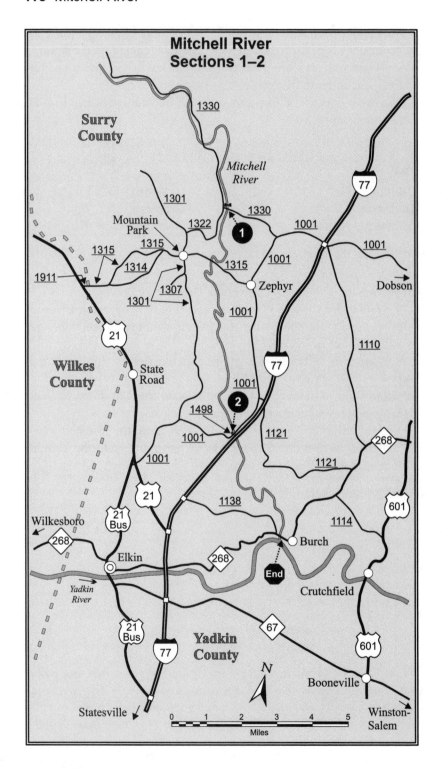

**Mitchell River
Sections 1–2**

Yadkin-Pee Dee Basin

Rocky River

Counties   Cabarrus, Stanly, Union, Anson, Montgomery, Richmond

Topos   Stanfield, Midland, Oakboro, Aquadale,
Mount Gilead West, Ansonville, Mangum

The Rocky River begins north of Charlotte near Mooresville. It flows southeast before swinging toward the east to join the Pee Dee River below Lake Tillery. It drains a watershed of about 1,500 square miles.

Reed Gold Mine, location of the first authenticated discovery of gold in the United States, is on Little Meadow Creek, a tributary 5 miles north of the Section 1 put-in. In 1799, a 17-pound nugget was found in the creek. The mine has been preserved as a state historic site and is open to the public.

1 Garmon Mill Road (Cabarrus Co. 1114) bridge to Love Mill Road (Union Co. 1001) bridge

Difficulty	I–II	**Width**	70–200 ft
Distance	8.5 mi	**Gradient**	7.4 ft/mi
Scenery	A (25%), B (75%)	**Map**	page 421

Gauge USGS *Rocky River near Stanfield* is within this section. Estimated minimum is 350 cfs (2.2 ft). A paddling gauge is on the NC 205 bridge, where minimum is 2.2 feet.

USGS *Rocky River above Irish Buffalo Creek near Rocky River* is 14 miles above the put-in and can be used to estimate Section 1–2 conditions in the next 12–24 hours.

Notes Love Mill Road bridge has no-parking signs on all sides. Unload and park about 100 yards away from the bridge.

Houses and farms border this section, and banks near the river rise 100 feet in places. The rock formations display a uniform gray color.

It is flatwater until Goose Creek (mi 3.4) joins on the right. Past the creek, there are a dozen Class I rock gardens and small ledges under a foot, before reaching Renee Ford Road (Stanly Co. 1140) (mi 5.9).

Several Class I⁺ and II rapids are downstream. A river-wide ledge (mi 7.3) drops 2 feet, where the river is 200 feet wide. The water spreads out, making this ledge difficult to find a clean route through at low water.

2 Love Mill Road (Union Co. 1001) bridge to NC 205 bridge	
Difficulty I–I⁺	**Width** 100–175 ft
Distance 7.3 mi	**Gradient** 9.9 ft/mi
Scenery A (45%), B (55%)	**Map** page 421

Gauge See Section 1.

Notes See the previous section about Love Mill Road.

At NC 205 request permission to access the river from the home-owners on upstream left of the bridge. Part of the old roadbed is next to their driveway. They have been friendly to paddlers who ask permission and respect their property rights.

There are a few dozen rapids, with some up to Class I⁺. As water rises there will be Class II rapids. Rocks are up to 3 feet above water at low flows.

A diagonal ledge (mi 0.1) is one of many ledges in this section.

A steep 75-foot bank (mi 0.3) has much exposed rock.

NC 200 (mi 3.2) can be used for access, but the banks have dense brush and parking space is limited.

3 NC 205 bridge to NC 138 bridge over Long Creek	
Difficulty I–II	**Width** 75–110 ft
Distance 7.6 mi	**Gradient** 7.6 ft/mi
Scenery A (50%), B (50%)	**Map** page 421

Gauge USGS *Rocky River near Stanfield.* Estimated minimum is 200 cfs (1.9 ft). A paddling gauge is on the NC 205 bridge, where minimum is 1.4 feet.

Notes See the previous section about NC 205.

The take-out at the NC 138 bridge over Long Creek requires paddling 0.3 miles upstream from the confluence with the Rocky River. Inspect the flow in Long Creek to make sure it is not too fast to paddle against.

There are a few dozen rapids, with some up to Class II.

After a sharp, left bend (mi 1.7), a long sandbar is on the left. Locals are often here on weekends during warm weather.

Islands and ledges are found before reaching NC 742 (mi 2.9). Access is possible on the left, but there are many no-parking signs and a steep bank.

Hills-Ford Road (Stanly Co. 1970) low-water bridge (mi 5.0) has about 6 feet of clearance at minimum paddling level. Parking is prohibited near the bridge.

From the low-water bridge, there are Class I rapids down to Long Creek (mi 7.3) on the left. Turn into Long Creek to reach the take-out.

4	NC 138 bridge over Long Creek to Gaddy's Ferry Road (Anson Co. 1609) bridge		
Difficulty I–II		**Width**	70–100 ft
Distance 6.3 mi		**Gradient**	6.5 ft/mi
Scenery A		**Map**	page 421

Gauge USGS *Rocky River near Norwood.* Minimum is 250 cfs (1.0 ft). A paddling gauge is on the NC 205 bridge, where minimum is 1.2 feet.

Notes See the previous section about NC 138 over Long Creek.

Long Creek joins the Rocky (mi 0.3) where a steep, rocky bluff rises 100 feet on the left.

The river bends to the right (mi 2.1), starting the steepest gradient of this section at 30 feet/mile over 0.7 miles. The left bank is steep and rocky. Class II rapids begin, and at low water the best one (mi 2.6) must be run on the left through a narrow slot, requiring turning right and back to the left at the bottom. At higher water, the right side has a more straight-through route.

Richardson Creek (mi 4.6) joins from the right, and a few Class I rapids are found before reaching the take-out.

5	Gaddy's Ferry Road (Anson Co. 1609) bridge to US 52 bridge		
Difficulty I		**Width**	60–120 ft
Distance 9.8 mi		**Gradient**	2.3 ft/mi
Scenery A		**Map**	page 422

Gauge USGS *Rocky River near Norwood.* Estimated minimum is 175 cfs (0.8 ft).

Notes This section has about ten Class I rapids at low water. As water rises, they are likely to wash out.

After a half-mile long island (mi 1.5), Lanes Creek (mi 2.3) enters from the right, and the USGS *Rocky River near Norwood* gauge (mi 2.4) is on the left bank.

Plank Road (Anson Co. 1621) (mi 4.0) can be used for access.

6 US 52 bridge to NC 109 bridge access on Pee Dee River			
Difficulty A–I		**Width**	75–500 ft
Distance 10.8 mi		**Gradient**	1.5 ft/mi
Scenery A		**Map**	page 422

Gauge USGS *Rocky River near Norwood*. Always above minimum. Water in the Pee Dee River is controlled by Progress Energy's Lake Tillery plant, 5 miles above the confluence with the Rocky. When the plant is not generating, there is little water in the river, and many rocks are exposed. At maximum power, 18,000 cfs is released. Depending on power needs, releases may start and stop several times within an hour. Be prepared for changing conditions on the Pee Dee River.

Notes A Wildlife boating access is downstream right of the NC 109 bridge. It is reached from Anson Co. 1671, 0.3 miles south of the bridge.

Dense stands of bamboo grow to 40 feet high on Buzzard Island (mi 3.8).

The Rocky River joins the Pee Dee River (mi 4.3). The confluence area is known locally as The Forks.

Leak Island (mi 5.6) offers a chance to paddle to the left in a relatively narrow channel. A bridge (mi 6.5) connects the left bank to the island. The side channel joins the main Pee Dee River at the island's end (mi 7.0).

The Pee Dee National Wildlife Refuge includes almost 9,000 acres and borders much of the river in this section. Camping is not allowed.

The few Class I rapids in the Pee Dee River are mostly covered when Progress Energy is releasing water at its Tillery plant.

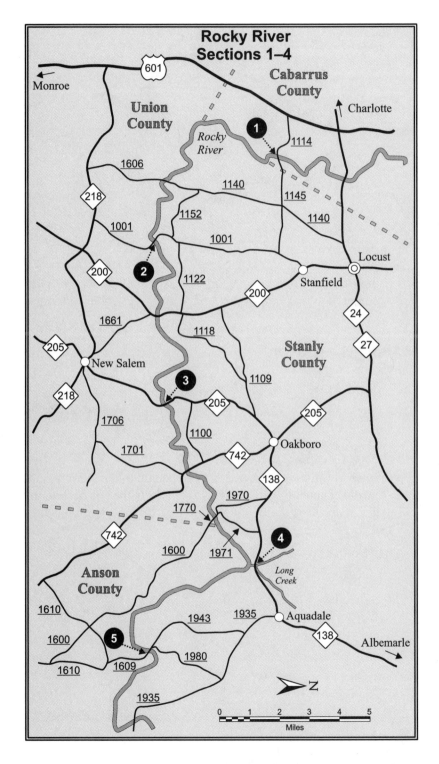

Rocky River
Sections 1–4

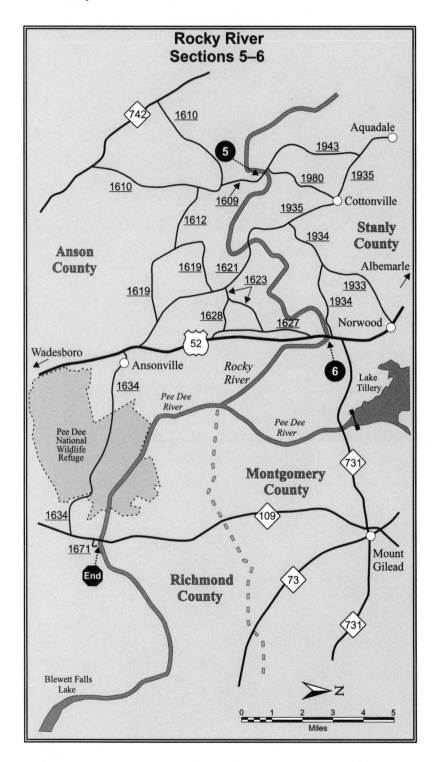

Yadkin-Pee Dee Basin

South Yadkin River

Counties   Iredell, Davie, Rowan

Topos   Harmony, Statesville East, Cool Springs, Calahaln,
            Cooleemee, Churchland, Salisbury

The South Yadkin River gathers water from the southern part of the
Brushy Mountains above Taylorsville. It flows generally southeast
through rolling farmland and joins its bigger sibling, the Yadkin
River, north of Salisbury.

One of the few towns the South Yadkin flows through is Cooleemee, where there is a dam. Public access to the river will be provided by a park being developed near the dam.

There are many downed trees in the river, especially above Section 1.

1	Church Lake Road (Iredell Co. 2156) bridge to Old Mocksville Road (Iredell Co. 2158) bridge		
Difficulty A		**Width** 35–55 ft	
Distance 4.0 mi		**Gradient** 3.0 ft/mi	
Scenery B		**Map** page 427	

Gauge USGS *South Yadkin River near Mocksville*. A minimum of
175 cfs (2.1 ft) is recommended to reduce portages around downed
trees.

Notes At the put-in bridge, access and parking are difficult. A few
hundred feet upstream left of the bridge, a farm road leads to the
riverbank. Ask permission to use the farm road. Keep the gate closed
and the area clean.

Many trees are down before reaching Rocky Creek (mi 0.6). At
low flows, some of these trees will have to be portaged.

Sand mining and a few large farms are seen in this section. One
farm is near the Chief Thomas Road (Iredell Co. 2152) bridge
(mi 1.8). Banks occasionally rise up to 60 feet.

2 Old Mocksville Road (Iredell Co. 2158) bridge to Garden Valley Road (Iredell Co. 2145) bridge

Difficulty A		**Width** 45–60 ft	
Distance 6.7 mi		**Gradient** 2.5 ft/mi	
Scenery A (70%), B (30%)		**Map** page 427	

Gauge See Section 1.

Notes Many downed trees are in the river, but most can be easily paddled around.

Where the river starts to run near I-40 (mi 5.0), mountain laurel grows on steep, rocky banks.

After going under I-40 (mi 6.6), the take-out bridge can be seen downstream.

3 Garden Valley Road (Iredell Co. 2145) bridge to Ratledge Road (Davie Co. 1142) bridge

Difficulty A–I		**Width** 45–60 ft	
Distance 8.9 mi		**Gradient** 2.6 ft/mi	
Scenery A		**Map** page 427	

Gauge See Section 1.

Notes Downed trees continue, and at low flows, portages will be required.

Downstream from US 64 (mi 0.5), steep, rocky banks (mi 1.6) have mountain laurel and rhododendron.

There are a few riffles around rocks, but the first Class I rapid (mi 5.9) is at a small ledge.

Downstream right of Foster Road (Rowan Co. 1972) bridge (mi 6.6) is the USGS gauge. Structures housing gauge equipment are usually cinder block or metal, but this one fits with the surroundings because it is built of native stone.

A small ledge (mi 7.9) makes the second and last Class I rapid of this section.

4 Ratledge Road (Davie Co. 1142) bridge to Junction Road (Davie Co. 1139) access

Difficulty	A	**Width**	45–80 ft
Distance	4.9 mi	**Gradient**	2.0 ft/mi
Scenery	A	**Map**	page 427

Gauge USGS *South Yadkin River near Mocksville*. Estimated minimum is 70 cfs (1.6 ft).

Notes A Wildlife boating access is off Junction Road. Junction Road is Davie Co. 1142, but it was numbered 1116. Road signs may still have the old number. A Wildlife boating access sign is near a gravel road, 100 feet west of a railroad crossing. Take this road 0.2 miles to the ramp.

Motorboats come into the latter part of this section because the dam at Cooleemee backs up water, and a boat ramp is at the take-out.

Hunting Creek (mi 2.8) and Bear Creek (mi 3.8) enter on the left.

A high railroad bridge is 100 feet downstream of the take-out.

5 Junction Road (Davie Co. 1139) access to US 601 access

Difficulty	A, and one II	**Width**	50–300 ft
Distance	6.5 mi	**Gradient**	4.0 ft/mi
Scenery	A (70%), B (30%)	**Map**	page 427

Gauge USGS *South Yadkin River near Mocksville*. Always above minimum.

Hunting Creek joins the South Yadkin in the previous section. The USGS *Hunting Creek near Harmony* gauge is 24 miles upstream of the confluence. Add this flow to the Mocksville gauge to estimate the total South Yadkin flow.

Notes See the previous section about the Junction Road access.

A Yadkin River Trails access is at US 601.

It is deep water down to the 12-foot Cooleemee Dam (mi 1.6). A sign on the left bank warns of the dam and says to portage 250 yards ahead to the left. The right side is a better portage route. Stay back from the dam when water is flowing over it. The dam was originally for a cotton mill. It is now being used for hydroelectric power.

The power company diverts water through its sluice and into turbines. Unless there is fairly high flow in the river, little water is left in the main river channel for 800 feet below the dam. There has been controversy over this, and the matter has been taken to the courts.

Near the dam, 80 acres covering both sides of the river are being developed into a public park known as Riverpark at Cooleemee Falls —The Bullhole. Plans include a pedestrian walkway over the river, parking, boat access, shelters, and shops. Initial phases are planned for completion during 2003. The portage route around the dam will be on the right.

One of the oldest American Indian archaeological sites in North Carolina has been found near the proposed park. Rock flakes and stone tools are about 10,000 years old.

About 1900, when the mill village was being constructed, a man made a valiant but futile attempt to save his favorite bull when it lost its footing in rising water. The bull drowned in a whirlpool, and the area became known as The Bullhole. It is below the dam on the right and is a popular fishing and swimming hole.

Below the dam and to the left, a Class II rapid can be run when there is sufficient water.

Metal debris from an old steel bridge (mi 1.8) is in the river where the park plans to build a new pedestrian bridge. Water from the sluice on the left returns, creating a Class I rapid at low water levels.

It is flatwater from the NC 801 bridge (mi 2.2) to the take-out.

6 US 601 access to Hannah Ferry Road (Rowan Co. 1926) Pump Station access		
Difficulty A	**Width**	50–120 ft
Distance 5.4 mi	**Gradient**	0 ft/mi
Scenery A	**Map**	page 427

Gauge USGS *South Yadkin River near Mocksville.* Always above minimum. This section is in the backwater of High Rock Lake.

Notes Yadkin River Trails access areas are at both the put-in and take-out.

Second Creek (mi 2.0) enters on the right. Downstream, rocky banks rise 60 feet. A 300-acre tract here is Catawba College's South Yadkin Wildlife Refuge. It was acquired with the cooperation of many, including the Land Trust for Central North Carolina. Mountain laurel on the rocky banks was in full bloom during a May trip down this section.

The Pump Station access is only 0.1 miles before reaching the confluence with the Yadkin River.

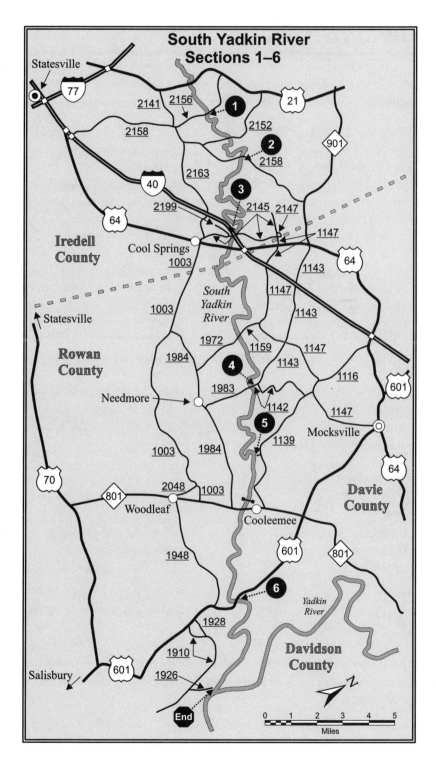

Uwharrie River

Counties   Randolph, Montgomery

Topos   Farmer, Eleazer, Handy, Badin, Lovejoy

The Uwharrie River begins in northwest Randolph County below High Point. It flows south and passes 10 miles west of Asheboro. Several miles southwest of Asheboro, the river enters Uwharrie National Forest boundaries.

The Uwharrie River meets the Yadkin River below Falls Lake, in the backwater of Lake Tillery. The confluence forms the Pee Dee River, which flows through South Carolina to the Atlantic Ocean.

The Uwharrie National Forest area is located where there were many prehistoric and historic settlements, and it has one of the greatest concentrations of archeological sites in the Southeast.

The Uwharrie Mountains, rising about 1,000 feet above sea level, are remnants of ancient mountains believed to have been 20,000 feet high.

In the early 1800s, gold was found in the Uwharries, with a later boom during the depression of the 1930s. Many old mining sites are near the Uwharrie River. Part-time prospectors still pan in the streams and find traces of gold.

1   NC 49 bridge to High Pine Church Road (Randolph Co. 1143) bridge

Difficulty	I, and one II	**Width**	35–90 ft
Distance	10.1 mi	**Gradient**	3.1 ft/mi
Scenery	A	**Map**	page 432

Gauge A paddling gauge is on the NC 109 bridge. Minimum is 0.6 feet. An abandoned USGS gauge is downstream right of the NC 109 bridge, where the minimum is 1.6 feet.

USGS gauges *Abbotts Creek at Lexington* and *Little River near Star* are on nearby watersheds and can be used as rough indicators of adequate water in the Uwharrie River. Look for flows above 50 cfs on these gauges.

Notes This is a small stream with high banks, often rising over 50 feet. Most of the Class I rapids are found before reaching the Waynick Meadow Road (Randolph Co. 1174) bridge (mi 4.4). Downstream of this bridge, a golf course occupies the left bank for 1.5 miles.

The two-story Lassiter Mill building (mi 9.9) is on the left bank at a 6-foot dam. Portage either left or right. The left side of the dam, just right of the sluice intakes, can be used to lift over to rocks below when water is near minimum paddling level. Do not approach the dam at higher water.

Below the dam, small islands and rocks form a Class II rapid with a 6-foot wide slot. The take-out bridge is downstream where the river turns left.

---

2 High Pine Church Road (Randolph Co. 1143) bridge to Low Water Bridge Road (Montgomery Co. 1301) bridge

Difficulty I	**Width**	35–75 ft
Distance 7.4 mi	**Gradient**	3.0 ft/mi
Scenery A	**Map**	page 432

Gauge See Section 1.

Notes A dozen Class I rapids are in this section. The banks near the river often rise over 75 feet, blocking long-range views of the surrounding mountains.

At Burney Mill Road bridge (Randolph Co. 1105) (mi 4.1), the river enters Uwharrie National Forest boundaries, but most of the property bordering the river is private. Look for signs on trees to identify forest property. In this section, national forest property is on the right bank from mile 5.5–6.3 and mile 6.6–6.8.

Below Burney Mill Road bridge (mi 4.1), a Class I ledge is formed by a 6-inch concrete ledge across the river.

Crow Creek (mi 6.8) is on the right. Gold was produced at the Russell Mine, located on national forest property about a mile upstream on Big Creek, a tributary of Crow Creek.

The low-water bridge at the take-out cannot be paddled under. Be prepared to get to the bank quickly when the water is up.

3	Low Water Bridge Road (Montgomery Co. 1301) bridge to NC 109 bridge

Difficulty I–I⁺	**Width** 60–90 ft
Distance 6.9 mi	**Gradient** 5.5 ft/mi
Scenery A	**Map** page 432

Gauge See Section 1.

Notes National forest property is on the left bank from mile 0.5–0.6, mile 3.1–3.8, and on the right bank from mile 5.5 to the take-out.

The first rapid below the low-water bridge needs more water to paddle than other rapids need because it is in a wide area. The river narrows a bit downstream.

About fifteen rapids are along this section, with deep flatwater stretches between the rapids. A couple of the rapids are Class I⁺.

A convenient lunch stop is where a large rock outcropping (mi 2.9) extends 40 feet from the right into the river. The rocks are 4 feet above water at low flows.

Some of the private land on the right bank has been logged.

4	NC 109 bridge to Forest Route 555 end

Difficulty I, and one II	**Width** 80–90 ft
Distance 4.7 mi	**Gradient** 4.0 ft/mi
Scenery A	**Map** page 432

Gauge See Section 1.

Notes To reach the take-out, from NC 109 traveling south from Eldorado, turn right on Reservation Road (Montgomery Co. 1153). Go 0.5 miles and turn right on Moccasin Creek Road (Forest Route 576). After 0.2 miles, turn left on Cotton Place Road (Forest Route 555) and go 2.7 miles to where the road is rough. The beach on the left is the take-out.

National forest property is on the right bank from mile 1.5–3.0 and on the left bank from mile 4.0 to the take-out.

An abandoned USGS gauge is downstream right of the put-in. A few hundred feet downstream, a low concrete dam (less than 2 feet) is broken away on the left side.

A possible take-out (mi 1.7) is on the right where Cotton Place Road (Forest Route 555) comes close to the river.

Go left at a large island (mi 4.4) because downed trees clog the right side. After the island's end (mi 4.5), there is a good view of Shingle Trap Mountain rising 650 feet above the river.

There are several Class I rapids in this section, but the rapid near the take-out is a Class II at low water.

From the take-out, it is 2.7 miles to the confluence with the Yadkin River. At Morrow Mountain State Park, a boat ramp is on the west bank, 0.3 miles directly across the Pee Dee River from the Uwharrie River's mouth. The driving distance between the take-out for this section and the boat ramp is 26 miles one-way.

Rocky bluff on the South Yadkin River, Section 1

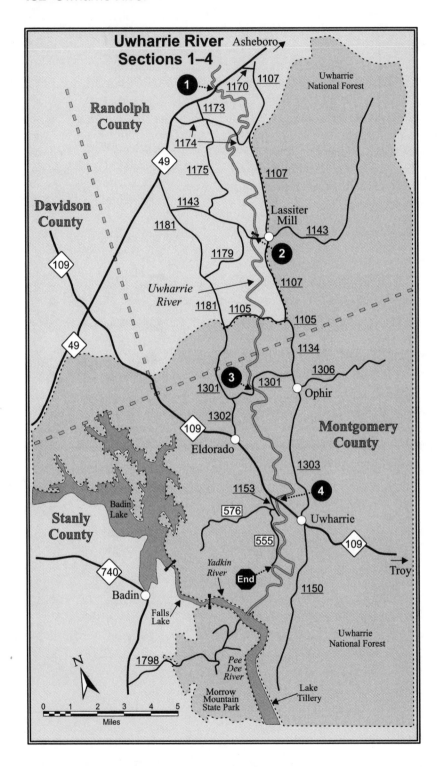

Yadkin-Pee Dee Basin

Yadkin River

Counties Caldwell, Wilkes, Yadkin, Surry, Forsyth, Davie, Davidson, Rowan

Topos Buffalo Cove, Grandin, Boomer, Purlear, Wilkesboro, Roaring River, Ronda, Elkin South, Elkin North, Copeland, Siloam, Pinnacle, Vienna, Clemmons, Farmington, Advance, Welcome, Churchland, Salisbury

The Yadkin River begins at an elevation above 3,600 feet near Blowing Rock, on the eastern slopes of the Blue Ridge Mountains. It flows southeast toward Lenoir, but near Patterson and Happy Valley it turns northeast, flowing through Ferguson and into W. Kerr Scott Reservoir.

Leaving the reservoir, the Yadkin runs between North Wilkesboro and Wilkesboro. South of Pilot Mountain, it passes through a small section of Pilot Mountain State Park and makes another direction change, swinging south and passing just to the west of Winston-Salem.

After passing Tanglewood Park and Boone's Cave State Park, the Yadkin joins the South Yadkin River near Salisbury. Downstream, the Yadkin River is impounded by four large dams to become High Rock Lake, Tuckertown Reservoir, Badin Lake, and Falls Lake. These dams supply hydroelectric power to the Aluminum Company of America (Alcoa).

Below Falls Lake, the Yadkin River joins the Uwharrie River and becomes the Pee Dee River. It is impounded by large dams at Lake Tillery and Blewett Falls Lake, before flowing to South Carolina.

The Yadkin River Trail runs for 126 miles from the outflow of W. Scott Kerr Reservoir to York Hill access near the beginning of High Rock Lake. The trail goes another 35 miles across reservoirs to the beginning of the Pee Dee River. It is the longest river trail with developed access sites in North Carolina's trail system. It was developed in 1985 with the cooperation of many agencies. The coordination was done by the North Carolina Division of Parks and Recreation.

The Yadkin River sections described total 141 paddling miles from near Patterson to High Rock Lake.

1 NC 268 bridge near Patterson School to Grandin Road (Caldwell Co. 1552) bridge

Difficulty I⁺		**Width** 25–65 ft	
Distance 6.6 mi		**Gradient** 9.8 ft/mi	
Scenery B (70%), C (30%)		**Map** page 445	

Gauge USGS *Yadkin River at Patterson*. Minimum is 50 cfs (1.4 ft).

Notes NC 268 crosses the Yadkin several times within a few miles. The put-in for this section is at the bridge where Buffalo Creek joins the Yadkin River.

The river is narrow. Rapids are all Class I, but occasional downed trees and limbs require maneuvering and good boat control.

The course winds through farmland. NC 268 is never far away and crosses the river (mi 2.7). Many houses are nearby, but there are some attractive natural areas with rock formations, rhododendron, and hemlock trees.

2 Grandin Road (Caldwell Co. 1552) bridge to NC 268 bridge at Ferguson

Difficulty I	**Width** 50–60 ft	
Distance 5.8 mi	**Gradient** 6.4 ft/mi	
Scenery B	**Map** page 445	

Gauge See Section 1.

Notes Farmland borders the first part of this section. The view is marred by pockets of trash and rusting vehicles embedded in and on the banks.

Elk Creek (mi 2.8) enters on the left.

3 NC 268 bridge at Ferguson to Warrior Creek Park campground at W. Kerr Scott Reservoir

Difficulty A–I	**Width** 60–125 ft	
Distance 5.8 mi	**Gradient** 4.7 ft/mi	
Scenery A	**Map** page 445	

Gauge See Section 1.

Notes Warrior Creek Park is one of the campgrounds within W. Kerr Scott Reservoir. The entrance is off NC 268, and the park is open April–October 15. Camping area C borders a cove just off the river channel and offers easy access to the water. Use of the area is only for registered campers. Campsites 11–15 are closest to the water, and the camping fee is $12. For additional information, call the reservoir (336-921-3390) or see: http://www.reserveusa.com/nrrs/nc/wari/

If not camping, continue to the next section take-out.

Fewer houses and farms are seen than in the previous sections. Rhododendron bushes and hemlock trees are along some of the high banks.

A few Class I rapids are encountered until Stony Fork (mi 2.2) enters from the left.

Just past Stony Fork, there is a view downstream of Little Mountain rising about 700 feet above the river. This is about the point reservoir waters extend to, at the normal pool level.

NC 268 (mi 3.1) is on the right bank for about a quarter-mile.

4	Warrior Creek Park campground to Keowee Park boat access at W. Kerr Scott Reservoir		
Difficulty A		**Width** 90–3,000 ft	
Distance 3.4 mi		**Gradient** 0 ft/mi	
Scenery A (60%), B (40%)		**Map** page 445	

Gauge USGS *Yadkin River at Patterson*. Always above minimum. This section is within the reservoir.

Notes See the previous section about Warrior Creek Park.

Keowee Park uses the same entrance off NC 268 as Warrior Creek Park. There is a fee of $2 per vehicle, and the park is open all year.

This section is lake paddling. Many coves connect to the main channel.

Where the lake becomes a half-mile wide (mi 2.5), continue south, staying near the right bank.

Channel markers run to the left toward the dam. For paddlers on extended trips down the Yadkin, it is 4.2 miles to the dam. The portage around the dam requires gaining and losing 100 feet in elevation and walking at least a half-mile to the Tailwater access.

A picnic shelter is high on a peninsula (mi 3.1). The channel to the right is a cove leading into a swimming area. Take the left channel around the peninsula and stay near the right bank to reach the boat ramp.

---

5 W. Kerr Scott Reservoir Tailwater access below the dam to Smoot Park access in North Wilkesboro

Difficulty I–I⁺		**Width** 65–120 ft	
Distance 6.7 mi		**Gradient** 3.4 ft/mi	
Scenery B (30%), C (70%)		**Map** page 446	

Gauge USGS *Yadkin River at Wilkesboro*. Always above minimum.

Notes The Tailwater access is off Old NC 268 (Wilkes Co. 1176). It is marked by a Yadkin River Trail sign.

A sign on NC 268 in North Wilkesboro points to Smoot Park. Take Vance Street and turn left on Chestnut Street.

Browns Ford Road (Wilkes Co. 1143) bridge (mi 0.2) is downstream of the put-in.

In the next 2 miles, a couple of the five Class I rapids in this section occur. The area becomes more developed, and there are factories near Wilkesboro.

A Class I⁺ rapid is at the US 421 bridge (mi 3.1), and a few Class I rapids are before reaching Curtis Bridge Road (Wilkes Co. 1185) (mi 3.4).

The Reddies River enters from the left, upstream of the NC 16/268 bridge (mi 5.4).

Memorial Park access (mi 5.7) on the left is off Wilkesboro Avenue. Smoot Park has parking closer to the river and is only a mile away.

Blairs Island (mi 6.0) splits the river. A small rapid is in the left channel.

---

6 Smoot Park access in North Wilkesboro to Roaring River Road (Wilkes Co. 2327) bridge

Difficulty I–I⁺		**Width** 60–100 ft	
Distance 8.9 mi		**Gradient** 3.3 ft/mi	
Scenery A (55%), B (45%)		**Map** page 446	

Gauge See Section 5.

Notes See the previous section about Smoot Park.

Roaring River Road does not have a Yadkin River Trail access. The bank at the bridge is rather steep. For an easier take-out, paddle to the next section take-out.

A Class I⁺ rapid is under the NC 115/US 421 Business bridge (mi 0.1). It is the first of about six rapids in this section.

After passing an island (mi 3.7) over a half-mile long, another island is in sight. Past a "Danger Sand-Pit" sign, machinery is on the right bank near the head of the island (mi 4.5), where sand and rock are piled on a gravel bar.

Roaring River (mi 8.7) enters from the left, near the take-out.

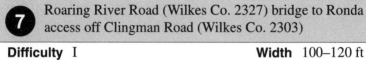

7	Roaring River Road (Wilkes Co. 2327) bridge to Ronda access off Clingman Road (Wilkes Co. 2303)		
Difficulty I		**Width** 100–120 ft	
Distance 6.8 mi		**Gradient** 3.1 ft/mi	
Scenery A (70%), B (30%)		**Map** page 446	

Gauge USGS *Yadkin River at Elkin*. Always above minimum.

Notes See the previous section about Roaring River Road.

The Ronda access is part of Ronda Memorial Park, managed by the town of Ronda. It has a shelter and picnic tables.

This section runs through farmland. Gravel bars create some Class I rapids.

Rocky banks (mi 3.3) rise more than 75 feet on the left, and high, rocky banks (mi 4.6) on the right are covered with rhododendron.

8	Ronda access off Clingman Road (Wilkes Co. 2303) to Crater Park access in Elkin near US 21 Business bridge		
Difficulty I		**Width** 100–200 ft	
Distance 6.9 mi		**Gradient** 2.8 ft/mi	
Scenery A (30%), B (70%)		**Map** page 446	

Gauge See Section 7.

Notes See the previous section about the Ronda access.

To reach Crater Park access, traveling north on US 21 Business (North Bridge Street), turn left on Elm Street before crossing the river and turn right on South Bridge Street. Cross the river and turn right on Commerce Street into the park. The boat ramp is 100 feet upstream left of the US 21 Business bridge.

Crater Park is managed by the Elkin Recreation and Parks Department. Paddlers on extended trips are allowed to camp in the park. Permission must be obtained in advance (336-835-9814).

A railroad is near the left bank for much of this section. There are a few Class I rapids and much pastureland.

A sand-pumping operation (mi 1.6) on the left works the river for about a half-mile.

Near the take-out, the Elkin River (mi 6.6) enters from the left, near South Bridge Street (mi 6.8).

9 Crater Park access in Elkin near US 21 Business bridge to Yadkin Shores access at US 601		
Difficulty I	**Width** 100–150 ft	
Distance 10.6 mi	**Gradient** 3.2 ft/mi	
Scenery A (60%), B (40%)	**Map** page 447	

Gauge See Section 7.

Notes See the previous section about the Crater Park access.

The Yadkin Shores access is managed by the Yadkin County Recreation Department. Paddlers on extended trips are allowed to camp at the access. Permission should be obtained in advance from Mr. Henry Shore (336-367-7272), landowner and caretaker.

After I-77 (mi 1.7), there are about six Class I rapids scattered down this section.

A railroad runs near the left bank, and a few factories are seen along the left.

The Mitchell River (mi 6.1) joins from the left.

10 Yadkin Shores access at US 601 to Burgess/Rockford access at Rockford Road (Surry Co. 2221)		
Difficulty I	**Width** 125–300 ft	
Distance 5.1 mi	**Gradient** 3.5 ft/mi	
Scenery A (60%), B (40%)	**Map** page 447	

Gauge See Section 7.

Notes See the previous section about the Yadkin Shores access.

Rockford access parking is upstream left of Rockford Road. Steps to the river are on the downstream left. The access is managed by the Surry County Recreation Department.

A railroad runs along the left bank, and the Fisher River (mi 1.9) enters from the left.

Several rapids run over shoals, some as long as 100 yards.

The low bridge at the Rockford access can present a great hazard. At very low water, there is clearance on the left side to duck and float under the bridge to reach the access steps. If there is any doubt about sufficient clearance, paddling ability, or blockages, take out 100 yards above the bridge on the left and portage.

11 Rockford Road (Surry Co. 2221) access to Shoals access at Shoals Road (Yadkin Co. 1546) end

Difficulty	I–I⁺	**Width**	100–500 ft
Distance	11.8 mi	**Gradient**	4.3 ft/mi
Scenery	A (50%), B (50%)	**Map**	page 447

Gauge See Section 7.

Notes See the previous section about the Burgess/Rockford access.

To reach the Shoals access, bear left at the end of Shoals Road. A dirt road leads to the riverbank, where there is a small parking area and steps to the river. This is within the River Section of Pilot Mountain State Park. The more well-known Mountain Section, 5 miles north, contains Pilot Mountain itself. The two sections of the park are linked by a narrow corridor.

The railroad tracks from previous sections continue along the left bank.

Most of the small rapids in this section are found before reaching Siloam Road (Yadkin Co. 1003) (mi 7.7). Access here is difficult because of fences and long guardrails.

The Ararat River (mi 8.5) enters on the left.

The take-out steps are on the right bank, about 0.3 miles upstream of several islands.

12 Shoals access at Shoals Road (Yadkin Co. 1546) end to Donnaha access at NC 67

Difficulty	I–II	**Width**	90–500 ft
Distance	6.8 mi	**Gradient**	4.1 ft/mi
Scenery	A (70%), B (30%)	**Map**	page 448

Gauge USGS *Yadkin River at Enon*. Always above minimum.

Notes See the previous section about the Shoals access.

The Donnaha access is entered from Donnaha Park Road (Yadkin Co. 1607). It is managed by Yadkin County Recreation Department. Paddlers on extended trips are allowed to camp at the access.

In the first 2.4 miles of this section, islands and property on both banks belong to the River Section of Pilot Mountain State Park.

Islands (mi 0.3) and shoals mark the start of Class I–II rapids in the first mile. The park map notes these as Bean Shoals.

Near the left side of the river, a mile-long island (mi 0.9) begins. Pilot Mountain State Park provides two primitive campsites on this island. The sites are adjacent and have a picnic table and fire-ring.

Sites are free and available on a first-come basis. Take the left side of the river if a visit to these sites is planned.

The rocky right bank rises 100 feet and has thick stands of rhododendron.

Railroad tracks, which have followed the left bank for many sections, finally swing away from the river near the take-out.

13	Donnaha access at NC 67 to Old US 421 Park access at Yadkinville Road (Forsyth Co. 1525)		
Difficulty I, and one II		**Width** 100–160 ft	
Distance 6.8 mi		**Gradient** 5.1 ft/mi	
Scenery A		**Map** page 448	

Gauge See Section 12.

Notes See the previous section about the Donnaha access.

The Old US 421 Park access is managed by the Forsyth County Parks and Recreation Department.

The river passes through farmland, and there are a few Class I rapids.

Several large islands (mi 3.1) extend downstream for a half-mile.

A 7-foot high dam for Winston-Salem water supply is expected to be completed during 2003. The backwater (mi 5.0) will be entered, and at the dam (mi 5.8), a portage trail will be on the right. A primitive paddle-in campsite is planned.

A diagonal ledge (mi 6.7), forming a Class II rapid at low water, is near the take-out.

14	Old US 421 Park access at Yadkinville Road (Forsyth Co. 1525) to Pate access at Huntsville Road (Yadkin Co. 1001)		
Difficulty I		**Width** 100–175 ft	
Distance 5.4 mi		**Gradient** 1.9 ft/mi	
Scenery A		**Map** page 448	

Gauge See Section 12.

Notes See the previous section about the Old US 421 Park access.

The Bob Pate Memorial access is at Huntsville Road (Yadkin Co. 1001). Huntsville Road becomes Shallowford Road (Forsyth Co. 1001) on the east side of the river. The access is managed by the Yadkin County Recreation Department. Paddlers on extended trips are allowed to camp at the access.

This section begins as fairly deep and flat for a mile, followed by a few rapids in the next 2 miles.

After the US 421 (mi 4.5) bridge, Deep Creek (mi 5.3) enters from the right, near the take-out.

15 Pate access at Huntsville Road (Yadkin Co. 1001) to Tanglewood access at US 158 bridge

Difficulty I–I+	**Width** 120–175 ft
Distance 10.8 mi	**Gradient** 1.9 ft/mi
Scenery A (60%), B (40%)	**Map** page 448

Gauge See Section 12.

Notes See the previous section about the Bob Pate Memorial access.

The Tanglewood access, managed by Forsyth County, is down-stream left of the US 158 bridge. Do not go into Tanglewood Park to reach the Yadkin River Trail access. Tanglewood Park offers camping, but the sites are about a mile from the river.

About eight rapids are found in this section. The first consists of rocks (mi 0.6) stacked in a diagonal formation, thought to be remains of Indian fish traps.

In the middle of this section, cattle frequently enter the river from farms on the right bank.

I-40 (mi 10.6) is just before reaching the take-out at US 158. Steps are on the left, and a trail leads up the bank to the parking lot.

16 Tanglewood access at US 158 bridge to US 64 access

Difficulty I–I+	**Width** 100–200 ft
Distance 16.7 mi	**Gradient** 2.0 ft/mi
Scenery A (50%), B (50%)	**Map** page 449

Gauge USGS *Yadkin River at Yadkin College*. Always above minimum.

Notes See the previous section about the Tanglewood access.

The US 64 access parking is on the downstream left side of the bridge. A sign says vehicles are not allowed beyond the parking lot. It is about 100 yards from the parking lot to the river. The access is managed by Davidson County Recreation Department.

The backwater of historic Idols Dam is reached within the first mile of paddling. A railroad bridge (mi 3.6) crosses just above the 10-foot dam. Portage to the right along the marked trail.

Idols was the oldest commercial hydroelectric plant in North Carolina. It began in 1898 and operated until 1998, when a fire destroyed the generating capacity. Winston-Salem now owns the property and operates a pump station, using the dam reservoir to supply most of Forsyth County's water. There is no public river access here.

Muddy Creek (mi 7.6) joins from the left. Farther down on the left bank is the Eureka gristmill building (mi 8.2), built in the 1840s. The remains of the milldam create a Class I$^+$ rapid.

At a small island (mi 10.9), rocks from an old dam create a Class I$^+$ rapid.

17 US 64 access to Concord Church access off NC 801

Difficulty I, and one II		**Width** 100–200 ft	
Distance 9.3 mi		**Gradient** 1.3 ft/mi	
Scenery A (80%), B (20%)		**Map** page 449	

Gauge See Section 16.

Notes See the previous section about the US 64 access.

To reach the Concord Church access from the intersection of US 64 and NC 801, take NC 801 south 3.8 miles. Turn left at the Wildlife boating access sign.

A pile of rocks (mi 1.0), running diagonally, creates a Class II rapid at low water. On the left side, there is a chute with a rock in the outflow that could broach a boat. The rocks here are from an old dam or an Indian fish trap.

Land on the right bank (mi 2.5) is part of a conservation easement donated by the Hairston family to the Land Trust for Central North Carolina. It protects the 1,900-acre Cooleemee Plantation and more than 2 miles of river frontage.

The river goes through several large horseshoe bends. Often the banks rise to 100 feet, showing rock and rhododendron.

18 Concord Church access off NC 801 to Pump Station access off Hannah Ferry Road (Rowan Co. 1926)

Difficulty A	**Width**	150–200 ft
Distance 8.3 mi	**Gradient**	0.6 ft/mi
Scenery A (70%), B 30%)	**Map**	page 449

Gauge See Section 16.

Notes See the previous section about the Concord Church access.

The Pump Station access, managed by Rowan County, is on the South Yadkin River a few hundred yards upstream from the confluence with the Yadkin River. It is at the end of Hannah Ferry Road, next to the pump station.

This section is all flatwater as it passes through both farmland and areas of steep banks. At normal levels, the High Rock Reservoir backwater (mi 2.9) reaches into this section.

Boone's Cave State Park (mi 3.4) is on the left. There is a twisting wooden walkway leading up the steep bank to a park shelter, 100 feet above the river. Boat access would be a difficult carry. Daniel Boone's family homestead, built in 1750, stood on a high hill overlooking the river. Visitors can see the reconstructed home and explore the cave believed to have been his hideout on the Yadkin River.

A concrete structure (mi 8.1), part of a water intake on the right, is just before where the South Yadkin River joins from the right. Turn into the South Yadkin (mi 8.2) and go upstream a few hundred yards. The ramp is adjacent to the pump station.

19 Pump Station access off Hannah Ferry Road (Rowan Co. 1926) to York Hill access near US 29/70

Difficulty A	**Width**	250–400 ft
Distance 4.8 mi	**Gradient**	0 ft/mi
Scenery B	**Map**	page 449

Gauge See Section 16.

Notes See the previous section about the Pump Station access.

York Hill access is upstream left of the US 29/70 bridge. Take Old Salisbury Road (Davidson Co. 1138) 0.1 miles and turn left into the access area. It is managed by Yadkin Incorporated, a subsidiary of Alcoa.

At normal lake level, this section is flatwater because High Rock Reservoir backs up water above the put-in.

The South Yadkin River joins the Yadkin River (mi 0.1). Motorboats are common, and depending on lake levels, there are mud flats in the channel.

For paddlers continuing beyond this section, it is 35 miles to the confluence with the Uwharrie River, where the Pee Dee River begins. There are four dams requiring portages of up to a half-mile. From the Pee Dee River to the South Carolina border is 57 miles, with two dams to portage.

∎

We were now on the solitude of the river. There is hardly a spot anywhere more secluded than mid-stream. Most of the dwellings are built on the hills half a mile or more from the river bottoms. This was the season of the year, too, when crops on the low lands required little attention; so we traveled the entire day meeting but three people on the river. If you want a peaceful spot far from the noises of humankind, embark at any point along the upper Yadkin. Of course there is the occasional music of the water rushing over shoals or hidden boulders, sometimes the cry of water fowl and other birds, but the rest is silence. Shut in by the velvety fringe of willows, which presented a beautiful border of foliage lace work, a more peaceful picture is hard to find. In the mellow light of the setting sun, fancy can easily transform the Yadkin into a winding ribbon of gold with emerald borders. To drift smoothly, silently along is a wonderful relaxation which we enjoyed to the full. We had left behind our watches, bunches of keys, and other reminders of duties and appointments. We were in a new world, all our own.

In this contented mood we rowed or drifted all afternoon. As shadows lengthened over the waters, we espied on an anchored ferry flat two boys shooting with sling shots at bull bats or night hawks. They stared at us dumbly as if we were creatures from a new world and informed us in monosyllables that we were at the Yadkin College ferry. The small town is a mile or more from the river and was once the site of a prosperous college, which has been moved in recent years, however, leaving a large vacant brick building on the brow of a high hill as a silent testimony of departed prestige.

—Reverend Douglas Rights
A Voyage Down the Yadkin-Great Peedee River (1928)

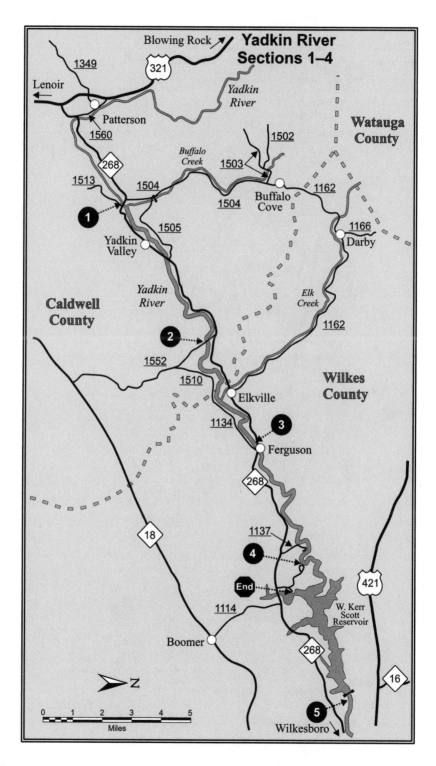

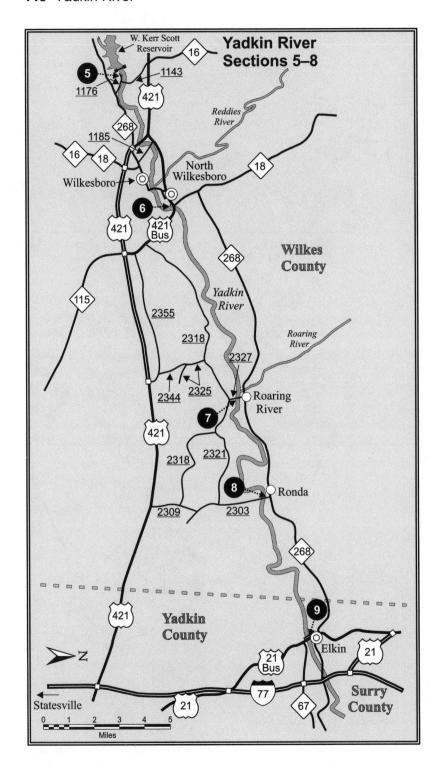

Yadkin-Pee Dee Basin

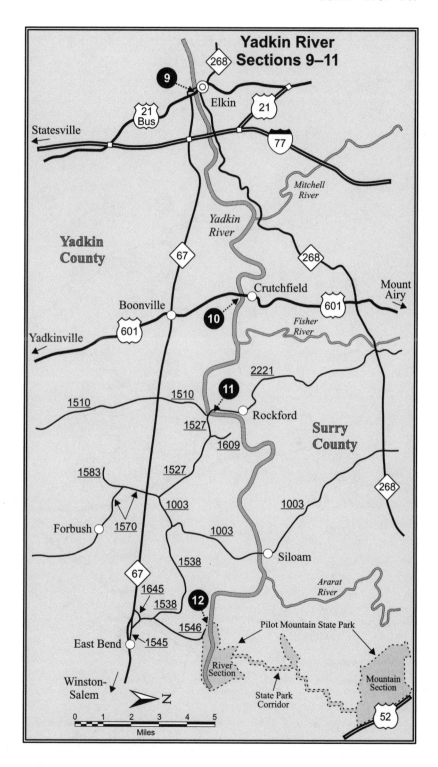

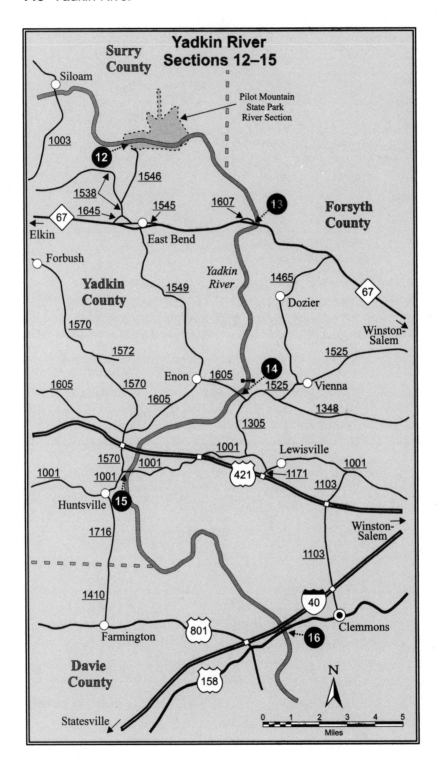

Yadkin-Pee Dee Basin

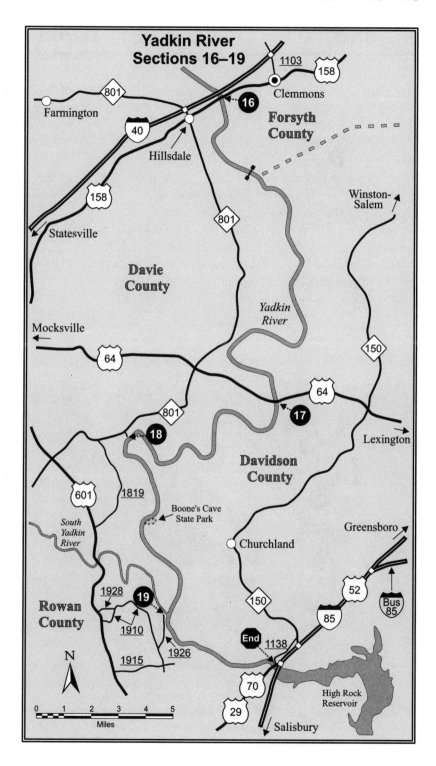

Yadkin River
Sections 16–19

Appendix A - State Water Trails

The North Carolina Trails Program is part of the Division of Parks and Recreation. The program originated in 1973 with the North Carolina Trails System Act. It is dedicated to helping citizens, organizations and agencies plan, develop and manage all types of trails ranging from greenways and trails for hiking, biking, horseback riding to river trails and off-highway vehicle trails. Additional information about the trails program is available at:
http://ils.unc.edu/parkproject/trails/home.html

There are many paddle trails in the Coastal Plain, and information is available at: http://www.ncsu.edu/paddletrails/

North Carolina Paddle Trails Association is assisting in the development of water trails. See: http://ncpaddletrails.org/

Jean Guite Creek

Appendix B - USGS Gauges

The following gauges are referenced in the detailed river descriptions. The list provides the USGS gauge name, gauge location, and drainage area of the watershed above the gauge in square miles.

Cape Fear Basin

Black River *near Tomahawk, NC*
NC 411 bridge, 30 ft upstream left (676 square mi)

Buffalo Creek *near McLeansville, NC*
Guilford Co. 2819 bridge, upstream left (89 square mi)

Cape Fear River *at Lillington, NC*
US 401 bridge, 60 ft downstream right (3,464 square mi)

Cape Fear River *at Fayetteville, NC*
NC 24 bridge, 700 ft upstream (4,395 square mi)

Cape Fear River *at Wilm O Huske Lock near Tarheel, NC*
William O. Huske Lock, 100 ft upstream right (4,852 square mi)

Cape Fear River *at Lock #1 near Kelly, NC*
NC 11 bridge, 2 mi upstream right, at lock (676 square mi)

Deep River *at Ramseur, NC*
Main Street bridge in Ramseur, 0.2 mi downstream right (349 square mi)

Deep River *at Moncure, NC*
US 1 bridge, 1.2 mi upstream right (1,434 square mi)

Haw River *at Haw River, NC*
NC 49 bridge, 800 ft downstream left (606 square mi)

Haw River *near Bynum, NC*
US 15/501 bridge, 1.1 mi downstream right (1,275 square mi)

Haw River *below B. Everett Jordan Dam near Moncure, NC*
B. Everett Jordan Dam, 300 ft. downstream right (1,689 square mi)

Little River *at Manchester, NC*
NC 24/87 bridge (127 square mi)

Northeast Cape Fear River *near Chinquapin, NC*
NC 41 bridge, 540 ft downstream right (599 square mi)

Northeast Cape Fear River *near Burgaw, NC*
NC 53 bridge, left (920 square mi)

Reedy Fork *near Gibsonville, NC*
Guilford Co. 2719 bridge, 0.2 mi downstream right (131 square mi)

Rockfish Creek *at Raeford, NC*
US 401 bridge, upstream side (93 square mi)

Rocky River *at SR 1300 near Crutchfield Crossroads, NC*
Chatham Co. 1300 culvert, downstream right (7.4 square mi)

Tick Creek *near Mount Vernon Springs, NC*
US 421 bridge (15.5 square mi)

Chowan Basin

Ahoskie Creek *at Ahoskie, NC*
  NC 11 bridge, 10 ft downstream right (63 square mi)
Blackwater River *near Franklin, VA*
  Virginia Southampton Co. 619 bridge, downstream (617 square mi)
Meherrin River *at Emporia, VA*
  US 301 bridge, downstream left (747 square mi)
Nottoway River *near Sebrell, VA*
  Virginia Southampton Co. 653 bridge, upstream (1,421 square mi)
Potecasi Creek *near Union, NC*
  NC 11 bridge, downstream right (225 square mi)

Lumber Basin

Big Swamp *near Tarheel, NC*
  Robeson Co. 1004 bridge, downstream left (229 square mi)
Drowning Creek *near Hoffman, NC*
  US 1 bridge, 10 ft downstream right (183 square mi)
Lumber River *near Maxton, NC*
  NC 71 bridge, downstream near right center (365 square mi)
Lumber River *at Lumberton, NC*
  Fifth Street bridge (708 square mi)
Lumber River *at Boardman, NC*
  US 74 bridge, 150 ft downstream right (1,228 square mi)
Waccamaw River *at Freeland, NC*
  NC 130 bridge, 150 ft downstream left (680 square mi)
Waccamaw River *near Longs, SC*
  SC 9 bridge, downstream right (1,110 square mi)

Neuse Basin

Contentnea Creek *near Lucama, NC*
  NC 581 bridge, 250 ft upstream right (161 square mi)
Contentnea Creek *at Hookerton, NC*
  NC 123 bridge, left (733 square mi)
Crabtree Creek *at Ebenezer Church Rd. near Raleigh, NC*
  Wake Co. 1649 bridge, downstream left (76 square mi)
Crabtree Creek *at Highway 70 at Raleigh, NC*
  US 70 bridge, upstream left (98 square mi)
Crabtree Creek *at US 1 at Raleigh, NC*
  US 1 bridge, downstream (121 square mi)
Eno River *at Hillsborough, NC*
  NC 86 bridge (66 square mi)
Eno River *near Durham, NC*
  US 501 bridge, 275 ft downstream right (141 square mi)
Flat River *at Bahama, NC*
  Durham Co. 1616 bridge, 1.2 mi upstream right (149 square mi)
Little River *at SR 1461 near Orange Factory, NC*
  Durham Co. 1461 bridge, downstream right (78 square mi)

Neuse Basin (continued)

Little River near Princeton, NC
Johnston Co. 2320 bridge, 600 ft downstream left (232 square mi)

Neuse River near Falls, NC
Falls Lake Dam, 300 ft downstream right (771 square mi)

Neuse River near Clayton, NC
NC 42 bridge, downstream left (1,150 square mi)

Neuse River at Smithfield, NC
US 70 bridge, 10 ft downstream left (1,206 square mi)

Neuse River near Goldsboro, NC
Wayne Co. 1915 (NC 581) bridge, downstream left (2,399 square mi)

Neuse River at Kinston, NC
NC 11, 600 ft downstream left (2,692 square mi)

Neuse River at Fort Barnwell, NC
Craven Co. 1470 bridge, 0.2 mi upstream left (3,900 square mi)

Trent River near Trenton, NC
Jones Co. 1129 bridge, 50 ft downstream left (168 square mi)

Trent River at Pollocksville, NC
US 17 bridge, 0.5 mi downstream (370 square mi)

Roanoke Basin

Cashie River near Windsor, NC
Bertie Co. 1257 bridge, downstream (108 square mi)

Dan River near Francisco, NC
NC 704 bridge, 200 ft upstream left (129 square mi)

Dan River near Wentworth, NC
Rockingham Co. 2145 bridge, 600 ft downstream right (1,053 square mi)

South Mayo River near Nettleridge, VA
Virginia Patrick Co. 700 bridge (85 square mi)

North Mayo River near Spencer, VA
Virginia Henry Co. 629 bridge (108 square mi)

Mayo River near Price, NC
Rockingham Co. 1358 bridge, 350 ft downstream right (242 square mi)

Roanoke River at Roanoke Rapids, NC
NC 48 bridge, 1.2 mi downstream right (8,384 square mi)

Roanoke River at Halifax, NC
Halifax, 0.5 mi east, off private road (8,450 square mi)

Roanoke River near Scotland Neck, NC
US 258 bridge, 50 ft upstream right (8,671 square mi)

Roanoke River at Hamilton, NC
Main Street Wildlife ramp, downstream right (8,890 square mi)

Roanoke River at Williamston, NC
US 17, 175 ft upstream right (9,070 square mi)

Roanoke River at Jamesville, NC
Water Street ramp, 50 ft downstream right (9,250 square mi)

Smith River at Eden, NC
NC 14/87 bridge, 0.2 mi downstream (538 square mi)

Tar-Pamlico Basin

Chicod Creek *near Simpson, NC*
Pitt Co. 1760 bridge, downstream left (45 square mi)

Fishing Creek *near Enfield, NC*
US 301 bridge, 15 ft downstream right (526 square mi)

Little Fishing Creek *near White Oak, NC*
Halifax Co. 1338 bridge, 8 ft downstream right (177 square mi)

Tar River *near Tar River, NC*
NC 96 bridge, 90 ft upstream right (167 square mi)

Tar River *at Louisburg, NC*
US 401 bridge, 0.1 mi downstream left (427 square mi)

Tar River *below Reservoir near Rocky Mount, NC*
Nash Co. 1544 bridge, downstream center (777 square mi)

Tar River *at NC 97 at Rocky Mount, NC*
NC 97 bridge, 20 ft downstream left (925 square mi)

Tar River *at Tarboro, NC*
US 64 bridge, downstream right (2,183 square mi)

Tar River *at Greenville, NC*
NC 11 bridge, 200 ft downstream right (2,620 square mi)

White Oak Basin

New River *near Gum Branch, NC*
Onslow Co. 1314 bridge, 5 ft downstream right (94 square mi)

Yadkin-Pee Dee Basin

Abbotts Creek *at Lexington, NC*
Davidson Co. 1243 bridge, 150 ft upstream right (174 square mi)

Ararat River *at Ararat, NC*
Surry Co. 2019 bridge, 265 ft upstream right (231 square mi)

Elk Creek *at Elkville, NC*
NC 268 bridge, 700 ft upstream left (48 square mi)

Fisher River *near Copeland, NC*
NC 268 bridge, 500 ft upstream left (128 square mi)

Hunting Creek *near Harmony, NC*
Iredell Co. 2115 bridge, 50 ft downstream right (155 square mi)

Little River *near Star, NC*
Montgomery Co. 1340, downstream left (106 square mi)

Mitchell River *at State Road, NC*
Surry Co. 1001 bridge, 280 ft upstream right (179 square mi)

Rocky River *above Irish Buffalo Creek near Rocky River, NC*
0.5 mi upstream of confluence with Irish Buffalo Creek (278 square mi)

Rocky River *near Stanfield, NC*
Union Co. 1606 bridge (628 square mi)

Rocky River *near Norwood, NC*
Stanly Co. 1935 bridge, 1.5 mi upstream left (1,372 square mi)

South Yadkin River *near Mocksville, NC*
Rowan Co. 1972 bridge, 90 ft downstream right (306 square mi)

Yadkin-Pee Dee Basin (continued)

Yadkin River at Patterson, NC
  NC 268 bridge, 200 ft upstream left (29 square mi)
Yadkin River at Wilkesboro, NC
  NC 18 bridge, 150 ft upstream right (504 square mi)
Yadkin River at Elkin, NC
  US 21 bridge, downstream right (869 square mi)
Yadkin River at Enon, NC
  Forsyth Co. 1525 bridge, 50 ft upstream left (1,694 square mi)
Yadkin River at Yadkin College, NC
  US 64 bridge, downstream right (2,280 square mi)

Mike Britt paddling through a Class II rapid
Rocky River (Yadkin-Pee Dee Basin), Section 4

Appendix C - Books and Maps

Paddling Guidebooks

Altman F. *The Dan River Book*. Semora, NC: Star Square Press, 1996. 304 pp. — Paddling trips on the entire Dan River with anecdotes and history.

Benner B., and D. Benner. *Canoeing and Kayaking Guide to the Carolinas*. 8th ed. Birmingham, AL: Menasha Ridge Press, 2002. 256 pp. — Previously titled *Carolina Whitewater*. Concentrates on whitewater of the North Carolina Mountains region but also covers other rivers.

Benner B., and T. McCloud. *A Paddler's Guide to Eastern North Carolina*. Birmingham, AL: Menasha Ridge Press, 1987. 257 pp. — Rivers of North Carolina's Piedmont and Coastal Plain.

Corbett R. *Virginia Whitewater*. Rockville, MD: Seneca Press, 2000. 600 pp. — Coverage of 200 Virginia rivers and creeks in all basins, including much historical information.

Grove E. *Classic Virginia Rivers*. Arlington, VA: Eddy Out Press, 1994. 352 pp. — A paddler's guide to premier whitewater and scenic float trips in Virginia.

Malec P. *Guide to Sea Kayaking in North Carolina*. Guilford, CT: Globe Pequot Press, 2001. 208 pp. — Paddling the coast and barrier islands from Currituck to Cape Fear.

Watkins B. *Blackwater Paradise*. Wilmington, NC: Cape Fear River Watch, 1996. 46 pp. — Guide with anecdotes to the Northeast Cape Fear River and its tributaries.

White E. *Exploring Flatwater*. Virginia Beach, VA: Flatwater, Inc., 1997. 144 pp. — Small streams and swamps in the coastal area of eastern Virginia and northeastern North Carolina.

Paddling Safety

Bechdel L., and S. Ray. *River Rescue*. 3rd ed. Boston, MA: Appalachian Mountain Club. 1997. 336 pp. — Rescue techniques and accident prevention.

Walbridge C., and A. Sundmacher. *Whitewater Rescue Manual*. Camden, ME: Ragged Mountain Press, 1995. 198 pp. — River rescue techniques and practical solutions.

Paddling Technique

Bennett J. *The Essential Whitewater Kayaker*. Camden, ME: Ragged Mountain Press, 1999. 180 pp. — Equipment. skills, safety and rescue, advanced kayaking, squirt boating, whitewater racing, surf kayaking, and overnight trips.

Dutky P. *The Bombproof Roll and Beyond*. Birmingham, AL: Menasha Ridge Press, 1993. 192 pp. — Kayak Eskimo rolling techniques and an introduction to playboating.

Jackson E. *Whitewater Paddling*. Mechanicsburg, PA: Stackpole Books, 1999. 96 pp. — Expert instruction in beginning and advanced whitewater kayak strokes.

Jacobson C. *Canoeing and Camping*. Guilford, CT: Globe Pequot Press, 2000. 192 pp. — Instruction and techniques for overnight canoe camping trips.

Mason B. *Song of the Paddle*. Toronto, Ontario: Key Porter Books, 1997. 208 pp. — Lists, hints, and strategies covering day trips to wilderness trips. Also includes section on canoe safety and the basic paddling strokes.

Mason B., and P. Mason. *Path of the Paddle*. 2nd ed. Toronto, Ontario: Firefly Books Ltd., 1999. 200 pp. — An illustrated guide to the art of canoeing.

Nealy W. *Kayak*. Birmingham, AL: Menasha Ridge Press, 1986. 184 pp. — An animated manual of intermediate and advanced whitewater kayaking techniques in the classic William Nealy style.

Ray S. *The Canoe Handbook*. Harrisburg, PA: Stackpole Books. 1992. 210 pp. — Canoe paddling techniques with emphasis on whitewater. Also includes safety and equipment selection.

Seidman D. *The Essential Sea Kayaker*. 2nd ed. Camden, ME: Ragged Mountain Press/McGraw Hill, 2000. 160 pp. — Sea kayak boat and gear selection, paddling techniques, and safety.

North Carolina

Selected books on history, geology, and environment of eastern North Carolina rivers.

Beyer F. *North Carolina: The Years Before Man*. Durham, NC: Carolina Academic Press, 1991. 244 pp. — A geologic history of the formation of North Carolina's Mountains, Piedmont, and Coastal Plain.

Frankenberg, D. *Exploring North Carolina's Natural Areas*. Chapel Hill, NC: The University of North Carolina Press, 2000. 412 pp. — Thirty-eight tours of natural areas by car and foot. Emphasis on understanding and appreciating North Carolina's natural heritage.

Frankenberg, D. *The Nature of North Carolina's Southern Coast*. Chapel Hill, NC: The University of North Carolina Press, 1997. 249 pp. — A field guide to the ecosystem of the coast from Ocracoke Inlet to the South Carolina border.

Hairr J. *From Mermaid's Point to Raccoon Falls*. Erwin, NC: Averasboro Press, 1996. 123 pp. — A history of the upper Cape Fear River from its source to Fayetteville.

Hairr J. *Stories from Deep River*. Erwin, NC: Averasboro Press, 1999. 125 pp. — A collection of articles on the history of the Deep River.

Map Books

DeLorme. *North Carolina Atlas & Gazetteer*. 4th ed. Yarmouth, ME: DeLorme, 2000. 88 pp. — Topographical maps of the state at scale of 1 inch = 2.4 miles (1:150,000).

Puetz C. *North Carolina County Maps*. Lyndon Station, WI: Thomas Publications, Ltd., 1989. 156 pp. — Maps of all counties of North Carolina.

Puetz C. *South Carolina County Maps*. Lyndon Station, WI: Thomas Publications, Ltd., 1989. 128 pp. — Maps of all counties of South Carolina.

Other Map Sources

A North Carolina State Transportation Map is available free from North Carolina Travel and Tourism, 301 North Wilmington Street, Raleigh, NC 27626 (877-308-4968).

Paper copies of topo maps at 1:24,000 scale can be purchased at many outfitters or ordered directly from the USGS. See http://www.usgs.gov/ and click on *Topographic Maps*.

Many companies sell topo maps on CD-ROM or DVD with software to view, print, and manipulate the maps. Examples of products are Topo USA® by DeLorme, Terrain Navigator by Maptech, and Topo! by National Geographic.

The North Carolina Geological Survey sells CD-ROMs containing digitized topo maps. Each CD contains thirty-two or sixty-four topo maps (scale of 1:24,000). The complete set covering North Carolina and some of the bordering states is on twenty-eight CDs. The price is about $8 per CD, available from the North Carolina Geological Survey. Call 919-715-9718 or see: http://www.geology.enr.state.nc.us/maps/drg.html/

Sites on the Internet offer free viewing of topo maps and aerial photography. A USGS page has several links. See: http://mapping.usgs.gov/partners/viewonline.html/

From this page, click on *Microsoft TerraServer*. It offers the ability to view an area and switch between topo and aerial photo views. The aerial photos are often more recent than topo maps and can show features not seen on the topos.

Between a rock and a hard place
Rocky River (Cape Fear Basin), Section 4

Appendix D - Organizations

The following groups, organizations, and agencies focus on water quality management, river preservation and access, environmental education, advocacy, recreation, or research.

Paddling Clubs

Some of the paddling clubs listed are traditional clubs with officers, dues, newsletters, meetings, and scheduled trips. Others are less formal Internet-based groups offering paddling information or paddling trips.

Black River Paddler, http://groups.yahoo.com/group/blackriverpaddler/ — Internet community for paddling information on the Black River and its tributaries.

Cape Fear Paddlers Association, 6748 Market Street, Wilmington, NC 28405, http://capefearpaddlers.org/ — Monthly meetings in the Wilmington area, Trips in the lower Cape Fear River Basin.

Carolina Canoe Club, PO Box 12932, Raleigh, NC 27605, http://carolinacanoeclub.com/ — Large club with quarterly meetings at various locations. Offers trips and classes.

Carolina Paddlers Assembly, http://groups.yahoo.com/group/carolinapaddlersassembly/ — Internet community for paddlers.

Crystal Coast Outing Club, PO Box 5165, Emerald Isle, NC 28594, http://ccckc.org/ — Monthly meetings in the Emerald Isle/Morehead City area. Trips in the White Oak Basin.

Lumber River Canoe Club, PO Box 7493, Lumberton, NC 28358, http://groups.yahoo.com/group/lumberrivercanoeclub/ — Monthly meetings in Lumberton. Trips on the Lumber River and other streams.

Mecklenburg Regional Paddlers, http://groups.yahoo.com/group/mrpaddlers/ — Charlotte-based Internet community for paddlers.

Outer Banks Paddlers Club, 432 W Sothel Street, Kill Devil Hills, NC 27948-6824, http://outerbankspaddlersclub.org/ — Monthly meetings at the Outer Banks. Trips in the Pasquotank Basin.

Tarheel Paddlers Association, http://groups.yahoo.com/group/tarheelpaddlersassociation/ — Monthly meetings in Greensboro. Trips to various locations.

Triad River Runners, PO Box 24094, Winston Salem, NC 27114-4094, http://trronline.org/ — Monthly meetings in Winston-Salem. Offers trips and classes.

National River Conservation Organizations

American Canoe Association, 7432 Alban Station Blvd., Suite B-226, Springfield, VA 22150, http://acanet.org/ — Promoting canoeing, kayaking, and rafting as wholesome lifetime recreational activities. The largest nonprofit paddle sports organization with 50,000 members.

American Whitewater, 1430 Fenwick Lane, Silver Spring, MD 20910, http://americanwhitewater.org/ — Conserving and restoring America's whitewater resources and enhancing opportunities to enjoy them safely.

American Rivers, 1025 Vermont Avenue, NW, Suite 720, Washington, DC 20005, http://amrivers.org/ — Protecting and restoring rivers nationwide.

Center for Watershed Protection, 8391 Main Street, Ellicott City, MD 21043-4605, http://www.cwp.org/ — Providing technical tools for protecting streams, lakes and rivers.

River Network, 520 SW 6th Avenue #1130, Portland, OR 97204, http://rivernetwork.org/ — Supporting grassroots river and watershed conservation groups.

Government Agencies and Programs

Environmental Protection Agency, 1200 Pennsylvania Avenue, NW, Washington, DC 20460, http://epa.gov

Fish and Wildlife Service, http://southeast.fws.gov/maps/nc.html

Natural Resources Conservation Service, 14th and Independence Avenue, Washington, DC 20250, http://www.nrcs.usda.gov/

North Carolina Division of Parks and Recreation, NC Department of Environment and Natural Resources, 1615 Mail Service Center, Raleigh, NC 27699-1615, http://ils.unc.edu/parkproject/ncparks.html

North Carolina National Estuarine Research Reserve, 5600 Marvin K. Moss Lane, Wilmington, NC 28409-1611, http://ncnerr.org/ — Acquires largely undisturbed natural coastal areas and preserves them for future research, education, and non-disruptive public recreation and use.

North Carolina Soil and Water Conservation Commission, 1614 Mail Service Center, Raleigh, NC 27699-1614, http://www.enr.state.nc.us/dswc/

North Carolina Wildlife Resources Commission, 1712 Mail Service Center, Raleigh, NC 27699-1712, http://www.wildlife.state.nc.us/

Stream Watch, Division of Water Resources, 1611 Mail Service Center, Raleigh, NC 27699-1611, http://www.dwr.ehnr.state.nc.us/wrps/swhome.htm/ — A program for citizens and groups promoting the well-being of a waterway.

Statewide Groups

Clean Water For North Carolina, 29 1/2 Page Avenue, Asheville, NC 28801, http://www.cwfnc.org/ — Working for clean, safe communities and workplaces.

Clean Water Management Trust Fund, http://cwmtf.net/ — Allocating grants to local governments, state agencies and conservation non-profits to help finance projects that specifically address water pollution problems.

Conservation Council of North Carolina, PO Box 12671, Raleigh, NC 27605, http://www.serve.com/ccnc/ — Protecting, preserving, and enhancing North Carolina's natural environment.

Conservation Trust for North Carolina, PO Box 33333, Raleigh, NC 27636, http://ctnc.org/ — Supporting land trusts in North Carolina.

Nature Conservancy, North Carolina Field Office, 4011 University Drive, Suite 201, Durham, NC 27707, http://nature.org/northcarolina/ — Protecting critical natural lands in North Carolina.

North Carolina Big Sweep, PO Box 126, Zebulon, NC 27597, http://ncbigsweep.org/ — Ridding waters of litter by promoting environmental education and an annual waterway cleanup.

North Carolina Coastal Federation, 3609 Hwy. 24, Newport, NC 28570, http://nccoast.org/ — Protecting and restoring the state's coastal environment, culture and economy through citizen involvement in the management of coastal resources.

North Carolina Environmental Defense Fund, 2500 Blue Ridge Road, Suite 330, Raleigh, NC 27607-6454, http://edf.org/ — Working for clean air and water, healthy and nourishing food, and a flourishing ecosystem.

North Carolina Paddle Trails Association, PO Box 1434, Washington, NC 27889, http://ncpaddletrails.org/ — Promoting and enabling paddle trails in North Carolina.

North Carolina Watershed Coalition, PO Box 122, Franklin, NC 28744, http://ncwatershedcoalition.org/ — Restoring and protecting North Carolina's water.

North Carolina Wildlife Federation, PO Box 10626, Raleigh, NC 27605-0626, http://ncwf.org/ — Advocating for all North Carolina wildlife and its habitat.

Sierra Club, North Carolina Chapter, 1024 Washington St., Raleigh, NC 27605, http://sierraclub-nc.org/ — Protecting and restoring the quality of the natural and human environment.

Southern Environmental Law Center, North Carolina Office, 137 E. Franklin St., Suite 404, Chapel Hill, NC 27514-3628, http://southernenvironment.org/ — Protecting the natural resources of the southeastern United States.

Trout Unlimited, North Carolina Council, 438 Armfield St., Statesville, NC 28677-5702, http://tu.org/ — Restoring streams and improving habitat for cold water fisheries.

Multi-Basin Groups

The following organizations focus on river monitoring, protection, or land conservation in more than one river basin.

Albemarle Environmental Association, PO Box 1706, Elizabeth City, NC 27906, http://members.inteliport.net/~aea/ — Focusing on conservation of the Albemarle Sound watershed through environmental education.

Carolinas Land Conservation Network, c/o UNC Charlotte Urban Institute, 9201 University City Blvd., Charlotte, NC 28223-0001 — Assisting land conservation efforts in central North Carolina.

North Carolina Coastal Land Trust, 3806-B Park Avenue, Wilmington, NC 28403, 910-790-4524, http://coastallandtrust.org/ — Conserving land in the Coastal Plain region.

Partnership for the Sounds, PO Box 340, Washington, NC 27889, http://albemarle-nc.com/pfs/ — Promoting ecotourism in the Albemarle-Pamlico region.

Piedmont Land Conservancy, PO Box 4025, Greensboro, NC 27404, http://piedmontland.org/ — Conserving land in Alamance, Caswell, Forsyth, Guilford, Randolph, Rockingham, Stokes, Surry, and Yadkin Counties.

Triangle Greenways Council, PO Box 14671, Research Triangle Park, NC 27709-4671, http://trianglegreenways.com/ — Promoting greenways in Wake, Durham, Orange, Johnston, Chatham, and Lee Counties.

Triangle Land Conservancy, 1100A Wake Forest Road, Raleigh, NC 27604, http://tlc-nc.org/ — Conserving land in Chatham, Durham, Johnston, Lee, Orange and Wake Counties.

Cape Fear River Basin Groups

Cape Fear River Assembly, 508 Person St., PO Drawer 1089, Fayetteville, NC 28302, (910) 223-4920, http://www.cfra-nc.org/ — Protecting and improving the water quality of the Cape Fear River Basin.

Cape Fear River Watch, 617 Surry St., Wilmington, NC 28401, 910-762-5606, http://capefearriverwatch.wilmington.org/ — Protecting and improving the water quality of the lower Cape Fear River Basin.

Lower Cape Fear River Program, UNC at Wilmington, 7205 Wrightsville Ave., Wilmington, NC 28403, http://www.uncwil.edu/cmsr/aquaticecology/lcfrp/ — Improving water quality and providing an environmental assessment program for lower Cape Fear River and estuary.

Deep River Coalition, PO Box 4196, Sanford, NC 27331, http://www.deeprivernc.org/ — Advancing public understanding and appreciation of the Deep River's unique natural environment, and actively working to protect it.

Friends of Sampson County Waterways, 2503 W. Main St., Clinton, NC 28328, http://clubs.yahoo.com/clubs/sampsoncountywaterways/ — Preserving the waterways of Sampson County.

Haw River Assembly, PO Box 187, Bynum, NC 27228, http://hawriver.org/ — Restoring and protecting the beauty and health of the Haw River and Jordan Lake.

Middle Cape Fear River Basin Association, http://www.cfra-nc.org/mcfrba.htm/ — Protecting and enhancing water quality in the middle Cape Fear River Basin.

New Hope Creek Corridor Advisory Committee, PO Box 90328, Durham, NC 27709-0328

Sandhills Area Land Trust, PO. Box 1032, Southern Pines, NC 28388, http://here-ye.com/here-ye/Salt/ — Conserving land in the Sandhills region plus the middle Cape Fear River region. Includes Moore, Hoke, Cumberland, Scotland and parts of Richmond, Lee, and Harnett Counties.

Upper Cape Fear River Basin Association, http://www.cfra-nc.org/ucfrba.htm/ — Protecting and enhancing water quality in the upper Cape Fear River Basin.

Lumber River Basin Groups

Lumber River Conservancy, Dickson McLean Jr, PO Box 1087, Lumberton, NC 28359, 910-738-5257 — Conserving land along the Lumber River and tributaries in Hoke, Scotland, Robeson, and Columbus Counties.

Neuse River Basin Groups

Ellerbe Creek Watershed Association, http://ellerbecreek.org/ — Restoring Ellerbe Creek in Durham.

Eno River Association, 4419 Guess Road, Durham, NC 27712, http://enoriver.org/ — Protecting the Eno River from threats of development and pollution.

Neuse Riverkeeper, http://neuseriverkeeper.com/ — Neuse River history and news from the Neuse Riverkeeper.

Neuse River Foundation, PO Box 15451, New Bern, NC 28561, http://neuseriver.org/ — Restoring and protecting the Neuse River and its tributaries.

The Umstead Coalition, PO Box 10654, Raleigh, NC 27605, http://umsteadcoalition.org/ — Appreciating, using, and preserving William B. Umstead State Park and the Richland Creek natural area.

Roanoke River Basin Groups

Dan River Basin Association, PO Box 103, Wentworth, NC 27375, http://danriver.org/ — Preserving the natural and cultural resources of the Dan River Basin by promoting stewardship, recreation, and education.

Roanoke River Basin Association, PO Box 27, Gasburg, VA 23857-0027, http://rrba.org/ — Developing, preserving, and enhancing resources of the Roanoke River Basin.

Roanoke River Partners, PO Box 488, 102 N. York St., Windsor, NC 27983, http://roanokeriverpartners.org/ — Developing projects for economic opportunities that steward and sustain the environment.

Rockingham County Watershed Preservation Coalition, PO Box 337, Colfax NC 27235, http://geocities.com/Yosemite/Rapids/4604/ — Protecting river, watershed and groundwater resources in Rockingham Co.

Tar-Pamlico River Basin Groups

Pamlico-Tar River Foundation, PO Box 1854, Washington, NC 27889, http://www.ptrf.org/ — Protecting, preserving, and promoting the environmental quality of the Tar-Pamlico River and its watershed.

White Oak River Basin Groups

New River Foundation, 179 Woodbrook Drive, Midway Park, NC 28544, 910-353-3352, e-mail: newriver@onslowonline.net — Restoring and protecting the New River and its tributaries in Onslow County.

Izaak Walton League, White Oak River Chapter, 126 Sutton Drive, Cape Carteret, NC 28584, http://iwla.org/ — Protecting soil, air, woods, waters, and wildlife.

Yadkin-Pee Dee River Basin Groups

Yadkin-Pee Dee Lakes Project, PO Box 338, Badin, NC 28809, http://lakesproject.org/ — Promoting and supporting efforts to balance economic development and environmental management in the Uwharrie Lakes Region.

Yadkin River Commission, PO Box 2511, Winston-Salem, NC 27102, http://www.co.forsyth.nc.us/ccpb/YRC_page.htm — Taking a cooperative regional approach to Yadkin Valley issues.

Land Trust for Central North Carolina, PO Box 4284, Salisbury, NC 28145, http://landtrustcnc.org/ — Conserving land in Anson, Cabarrus, Davidson, Davie, Stanly, Iredell, Montgomery, Randolph, Richmond, Rowan Counties.

Yadkin River Trail Association, 280 South Liberty Street, Winston-Salem, NC 27101, http://geocities.com/p_grizz/yadkinrivertrail.html — Planning, developing, and protecting the Yadkin River Trail.

Boats are not necessary to enjoy the river
Haw River, Section 8

Looking across Alligator River
At the mouth of Milltail Creek, Section 2

Index - Basins and Rivers